Blow-Up
and
Other
Exaggerations

DAVID HEMMINGS

ROBSON BOOKS

First published in Great Britain in 2004 by Robson Books,
The Chrysalis Building, Bramley Road, London, W10 6SP

An imprint of Chrysalis Books Group plc

British Library Cataloguing in Publication Data
A catalogue record for this title is available from the British Library.

ISBN 1 86105 789 X

Typeset by SX Composing DTP, Rayleigh, Essex
Printed by Clays Ltd, Bungay, Suffolk NR35 1ED

To Lucy

Last Orders, 2001

Contents

The Charge of the Light Brigade, 1968

Editor's Note

It has been a joy to work on David Hemmings' extraordinarily full and diverse account of his life and experiences. He and I sat together for many months, trying to separate fact from fantasy. We couldn't always see the joins, but he seldom failed to find the humour in the myriad bizarre circumstances in which he found himself throughout a long and astonishingly full career.

The book was almost finished before he died so suddenly while filming in Romania last year, and I am deeply grateful to all those who have helped me to complete the task in the way he would have wanted.

Peter Burden,
Spring 2004

'Have We Been Introduced? Ascot', 1993

Preface

When I was cast in the part of Polonius a dozen years ago at the Community School in Ketchum, Idaho, I realised that I'd reached an age when autobiographical review is at least permissible, if not always desirable. I am conscious, too, that although I've always admired the old Chancellor's wise counsel to his son, Laertes, 'Give every man thine ear, but few thy voice', I've never found it easy to follow. In fact, it's often been said, sometimes appreciatively, sometimes not, that Hemmings gives great ramble, and I freely admit that I've always loved giving it; for that, I crave your indulgence.

If you're clever and determined enough, you may find a way of side-stepping an unsuitable future. But life has taught me there's absolutely no escaping history, especially your own. You can deny, you can revise, you can hope it's all forgotten, but you always know it's lurking there, like a hunk of hard rock buried beneath the earth of time, just waiting for someone to dig it up. It seems to me, if there are skeletons in your armoire, the best strategy is to visit them regularly and remain on speaking terms. Then, with luck, when you let them out for an occasional daylight sortie, there's a fair chance they'll climb back in when you ask, before too much damage has been done.

I thank, therefore, ex-wives, ex-partners and co-vivants for all their willing contribution to what follows.

Battersea Power Station, 1996

1

London, 1966

Late April and the first day's filming with Michelangelo Antonioni on his new movie was scheduled to take place alongside a chain of soot-stained railway arches that still march across Queenstown Road in Battersea.

I was nervous as hell, but disguising it. Luckily, I knew most of the crew. I was on good terms with the props man and knew his wicked sense of humour.

In those days, when the money involved in making a picture was a lot less than it is now, it wasn't an uncommon opening ritual to test the mettle of a director by winding him up a little. In this case, we thought it would be a good wheeze to blow up a beautiful Mulliner Park Ward convertible Rolls-Royce.

In one of the earliest shots, my character, Thomas – a photographer – drives the Rolls away from a dosshouse where he's spent the night, snapping the run-down inmates. Thinking fast and with most of the crew ready to help, we suspended a pair of large steel plates under the engine and loaded them with nuts and bolts and any other oily metal objects we could find that looked like bits of engine. We also wired in under the bonnet a small, harmless bomb that would explode with a loud bang and a dense cloud of smoke.

We were all set for the first shot and the cameras were rolling. I drove the car round the corner into view and Props gave me the nod. I pulled a lever that had been rigged up for me under the dashboard and, instantly, a muffled explosion echoed off the walls of the drab brick buildings, immediately followed by a metallic clatter of detritus tumbling onto tarmac and a plume of blue-grey smoke spewing from under the bonnet of the vehicle. I snapped off the motor and came to a screeching halt.

An ominous silence followed the bang and the last rattle of metal. In the mirror I saw what looked like an entire engine scattered along the street behind me. It was so convincing, I almost believed the car *had* blown up.

Pierre Rouve, the producer, stood rigid at the roadside, as if paralysed by cardiac arrest. He had bought the car for the production from Jimmy Savile and I guess he was planning to keep it for himself afterwards. Now it looked a write-off.

The Maestro himself barely winced. With a few tidy strides, he walked up to the sick-looking Roller, beckoning a spark to open the bonnet. He peered inside. Everyone on the set was laughing.

Antonioni slowly straightened his back and looked up at me where I still sat, pale and shamefaced, in the driver's seat. There was a shrewd, angry glint in his eye.

'*Che cazzo fai?*' he rasped icily. '*Stronzo!* You have to learn now, David, this is not a picnic. We are here to work!'

He knew perfectly well we'd been trying wind him up, but now, a little late and with a nasty hollowness in my gut, I realised he was far too intense about his work to be ragged. I soon learned that he was a very serious man indeed, entirely his own master, accountable to no one. And one of the greatest directors I ever worked for.

At that stage, the picture had no name. Indeed, it was some weeks before it acquired one, but there is for me a pleasing irony in the fact that I started my first day's shooting on this picture, which in many ways changed my life, with my own, somewhat artless version of *Blow-Up*.

Certainly for me, there has been no escaping *Blow-Up*. And that's OK. Much talked about, much vaunted, the definitive film of London in the 'swinging sixties'. There's no question that it has found a certain resonance with several generations and still stands as a cult strip of celluloid that is forever a part of sixties folklore.

But why? It is not, in my view, such a great movie; perhaps not even a good one. It's confusing and offers no solutions to the problems it creates. But it's certainly beautiful. Antonioni's eye is percipient and imaginative. For me, he is the best translator to the screen of his own brand of mystique (as in *L'Avventura, La Notte* and *L'Eclisse*), and he brought to us in *Blow-Up* a slight story – framed with apparent simplicity – a loosely drawn hero and an elegance infected with an enigmatic air. I don't know that anyone can truly define *Blow-Up*; not Antonioni himself, nor Carlo Di Palma, his director of photography, nor even the elegant Piers Haggard, who spent a lot of time patiently scratching his head as the official interpreter of the script.

It's been called a masterpiece; it's been the backbone of more seminars and film courses at universities around the world than you can shake a propeller at, as well as required study for photographers. If my mailbag is to be trusted, the guy sitting on the steps of the church when you emerge on your wedding day will probably tell you it was *Blow-Up* that inspired him to become a snapper. God bless.

It's also been called 'A joke', 'A story without a mystery or a mystery without a story . . .', 'A film can that should have been canned . . . there's nothing within', although, while on the subject of Cannes, it also won the Palme d'Or at the 1966 Film Festival – leaving not a few puzzled folk along the Croisette – and was nominated for two Oscars.

The original script was no more than a 24-page drama, bound in a soft red cover, known at first simply as 'the Antonioni Picture'. Essentially, it was an idea born of the director's sympathy for the story, and his urge to make a film in Britain, perhaps because he was impressed by the (largely exaggerated) reputation of the liberated English female. Without a doubt, he recognised the cultural revolution and rejection of the old order that was taking place here, more than anywhere else in Europe – after all, Paris didn't riot until two years later. Even *Time* magazine in 1966 declared on its front cover that London was the most happening place in the world – unquestionably a Mecca for a *Maestro dell Cinema*, and a man in his fifties with lead in his pencil.

Ken Russell has said that he would never have had the opportunities he had until the arrival of this iconoclastic decade, when Huw Weldon, the head of the BBC, encouraged him to make pictures like *Women in Love*, not even a remote possibility a few years before. But frankly, I never really found Britain at the time quite as swinging as it was cracked up to be. For a lot of people, the sixties didn't really happen until the following decade, after the Isle of Wight Rock Festival had spawned Glastonbury and an era in which Bowie and Pink Floyd straddled the world and the taste was for rock gently stirred with a dash of hash.

Nevertheless, the sixties had arrived, albeit suddenly, stealthily, as if by some trick of media magic. Who could have predicted this legendary decade? Popular musical taste in the late forties and the fifties had for the most part slumbered safely under the influence of undemanding melodies delivered by a coterie of American crooners like Pat Boone and Dean Martin, and watered-down English mimics – Frankie Vaughan, Max Bygraves, for heaven's sake – singing songs that didn't remotely pretend to have anything to say to England's future flower children, still watching *Andy Pandy* or reading Dan Dare and Dennis the Menace.

But by the late fifties, Elvis had built Graceland in Memphis and over here London was poised on the brink of a massive, media-driven musical explosion. At the epicentre, in the Soho coffee bars, the Macabre – a sleazy hovel in matt black with coffin tables and ghouls for waiters – and the 2 'I's in Old Compton Street, new ideas in music and fashion were being nurtured, ideas designed to shock the older generation out of its post-war apathy and convince the new young spenders that they deserved a culture all of their own.

From this cauldron of mild revolt emerged a new and unlikely type of music mogul in the form of Larry Parnes, who created more British pop stars than you could waggle a pelvis at. He and his imitators gave their protégés new names and identities in a bizarre nonsense of word association. Their images, unsophisticated as they seem in retrospect, were meant to match their names – Billy Fury and Marty Wilde for youthful defiance; Cliff, for Beachy Head, perhaps, solid and permanent; Tommy Steele for enduring strength; Adam Faith ('What do you want if you don't want money?' – trust me, I'm a financial adviser); Vince Eager and Dickie Pride for God knows what; Eden Kane, an Old Testament amalgam (whose brother appeared a decade and a whole new mood later as Peter Sarstedt – 'Where did *he* go to, my lovely?'); and my own supposed lookalike, Terry Dean, named after moody American actor James, dangerous and inscrutable behind a haze of cigarette smoke.

So, for half a dozen years, Alma Cogan, Lonnie Donegan, the crooners and skiffle were usurped in England by these ersatz Elvises, until, in 1963, the Beatles and the Stones burst onto the scene and music across the world was changed for all time, pumped out by an entirely new breed of broadcasters.

I'd grown up with Radio Luxembourg (and Horace Bachelor) on a home-made crystal radio set or a cumbersome Bakelite valve wireless, listening to Petula Clark's latest hits, but, like everyone my age, I was beguiled by the pirates the moment they appeared. Brazenly seditious and reflecting irreversible changes of taste in an emerging teenage culture, Radio Caroline and Radio London hijacked Luxembourg's monopoly of the airwaves, transmitting from rusting hulks wallowing in the North Sea or redundant Second World War marine forts on offshore sandbanks. These stations were the brainchildren of wacky entrepreneurs, Ronan O'Rahilly, Ian Ross and Jocelyn Stevens among them. Under their flags and in studios the size of a broom cupboard, Tony Blackburn, Simon Dee and almost every major DJ of the seventies started their careers. Some ended there too. Few will ever know what became of the Emperor Roscoe or the Marshall Mike Lennox, although, as it happens, the Marshall did resurface in my life many years later, at Oranmore Castle in Ireland, and was just as funny.

But back then the kids were listening in their millions, the BBC Light Programme was kicked into touch, the sixties were up and running and with them emerged a horde of style-setting retailers who influenced almost everything we bought – miniskirts, tights (and the tragic demise of the suspender belt), a new take on make-up, hairstyle and art, patchouli oil and health food, along with Crayola-coloured Sobranies and, in the end, films like *Blow-Up*.

Ken Tynan and Bernard Levin, the principal bears in the critics' pit at the time, were unanimous in their complete denial of any merit in the picture, but while I have my own reservations about the intrinsic worth of *Blow-Up*, there is no escaping the truth that this strongly iconic film was probably *the* critical event of my professional life. It was, however, by no means the first.

Although I was a mere 25 when it happened, I'd been performing in public, one way or another, since I was six. When 'the Antonioni Picture' first impinged on my consciousness, I was an experienced actor, earning a good living by acting standards – which meant keeping your head just above water, and smiling when they could see your lips.

My agent, Beryl Seton, had rung me with an air of surly excitement to tell me I'd been offered the part of Sam Bennett, effectively the young Dylan Thomas, in *Adventures in the Skin Trade* at the Hampstead Theatre Club. The Club in 1966 was relatively new, looking more like a library than a palladium, but it was surprisingly well designed, for both audiences and performers. As a result of inspired, user-friendly planning, it was doing splendidly, at least compared to most other small theatres, which tended to struggle for survival. The Club was well thought of and attracted some of the finest writers and directors around. For those who had not yet been offered much exposure, it was an excellent stepping stone.

It's worth remembering that this was the age of N. F. Simpson and the *Resounding Tinkle*. Here you have a man, holed up in the basement of an extravagant apartment block, teaching a hundred 'I Speak Your Weight' machines to sing the 'Hallelujah Chorus'!

Much of this experimental drama was utter bollocks, of course, but it had the air of being very exciting and significant. It didn't matter if you didn't understand it; all you had to do was talk plausibly about it, because if you hadn't seen it, you were absolutely no one at cocktail parties for the next few months. In defence of experimental theatre – or any other experimental art form, for that matter – experiments, by definition, tend to fail, but without them, nothing would ever change, develop or move on.

Critics in chunky knitwear of leftish hues came along to Hampstead with leaky pens to scribble enthusiastically about most productions, making the place at once trendy and chic. The house style seemed to be faded sweaters darned with mismatched wool, and the *Guardian* tucked under one arm.

The artistic director at that time, Jimmy Roose-Evans, was, by contrast, very clean-cut and fresh of face, aglow with burning ambition and a charm which oozed from him like mustard gas. He had tightly curled hair and wore cravats tucked neatly into suede-trimmed cardigans, with pale ecru trousers pressed into razor-edge creases and sandy desert boots. He was a forceful, elegant man, erudite and woolly at the same time – a sort of early Gyles Brandreth. But he was also just a soupçon mad – an enthusiast with more energy than was entirely healthy. He had masterminded the funding and the building of the Hampstead Theatre Club; he was the prime mover and shaker there and directed most of the plays that were performed in its early years. He wanted the Club to be populist, but not so populist that everyone could understand all the plays he put on.

Jimmy was widely thought of as the George Devine of north London. (George Devine, director of the Royal Court Theatre in Sloane Square, was at the time unnecessarily derisory about the Hampstead Theatre Club, with much talk of visas and passports to reach the place.) But the Club was a rather snug establishment – still is, I assume – and besides introducing new writers, actors and directors, James was quite prepared to put on golden oldies by Coward and Agatha Christie to keep the less adventurous punters paying the bills.

*

When *Adventures in the Skin Trade,* opened on Monday 6 March 1966, it wasn't as radical as it might have been. It used some of Dylan Thomas's best poetry, which was delivered directly to the audience in monologues, by me mostly. I can still recite it, and do so frequently to anyone who'll listen.

Curiously, Dylan Thomas himself didn't have much of a Welsh accent. He sounded closer to John Gielgud than a miner from the valleys. I found that I sympathised strongly with him: he was a serious drunk; he was hopeless at maintaining relations with Caitlin, his wife; he lived by the sea and wrote unfailingly poetic crappolata with a great sense of music to it. After a childhood centred almost entirely around music, I recognised quite naturally the rhythmic beauty of his words. *Under Milk Wood* is, above all, about sound and cadence. Analysis of the sense of it, if required, is best left to a professor of poetry. 'Velvet snouting dingles'? I'd rather just listen to Richard Burton reading it and let the words wash over me – in my view as good as hearing a piece of Brahms.

I wish I'd met Dylan before he drank himself to death in 1954. I did meet Caitlin, though. There was no doubt that she was bitter and very angry at having been put through such indignities during her husband's lifetime, struggling in poverty while he soaked up the booze. She resented that very much. But at heart, I think, she was a much gayer person than she was ever allowed to be, although those who knew her only at the fag end of their life together might disagree.

There's no question, however, that Dylan was, fundamentally, an extreme rotter. He exploited anyone he could get his hands on who had expressed interest in his poetry. He was far more concerned about where the next drink was coming from than whence the next poem would spring. Slumped against the bar of the Salisbury, in St Martin's Lane, he might write five lines of poetry, read them in return for a pint or two, then forgetfully leave the scrap of manuscript lying around after he'd gone, rather as Picasso might have done in Villauris. I wish I'd been there to hear him.

In any event, *Adventures in the Skin Trade* was my new gig. If the job hadn't come up, I'd probably have gone back to playing Billy McGee in *Dixon of Dock Green.* I'd been turning up regularly in television shows like *Dixon, Billy Bunter* and *Home Tonight* since I was about fourteen, as well as in a string of teen movies. This production was due to run for just four weeks, which was standard for the Club.

Although the play was based on works by Dylan Thomas, it was adapted for the stage by Andrew Sinclair, a man of great singularity who was to have a profound influence on my future. He was also one of the most eccentric people I've ever met.

Andrew was an Old Etonian, a dour academic who gave the impression of being in a permanent state of mental trauma, as if the world might collapse under the weight of his thoughts. He was a highly regarded historian who'd published much fine work, but he dressed like an extra in a spaghetti western with that sort of studied rumpledness which only a top wardrobe designer could have concocted. His suits, when he wore them, looked like rejects from the Fifty Shilling Tailor, and his shirts had wide, unbuttoned collars, loosely held together by drab ties in vast Windsor knots.

His extraordinary, triangular brow, furrowed like an ill-ploughed field, seemed to stretch several feet up to a great pink dome, topped by a few dark strands of hair, cascading wildly in a forlorn attempt to hide the baldness. Below, a glorious hooter swept in a great Gothic curve from brow to lower lip. From the depths beneath when he spoke, there emerged a grumbling murmur, like a volcano with a sore throat, while a floppy lower lip burbled in harmony, as if plucked from the point of his chin.

It was an amazing visage, but believe me, I couldn't have written the last couple of paragraphs if I hadn't adored him. He was an utterly unique man in whose Hindenburg head lay seams of knowledge I could only dream of. His adaptation of Dylan Thomas is a stunning work. Not only because it translates Thomas so well to the stage, but also because it does this with such elegance, and a patina of nonsense the poet himself would have recognised and admired.

But I'm sorry, I'm rambling. What I'm trying to say is that I was a working actor, appearing in Hampstead, when Michelangelo Antonioni walked into my life. He had come to the Club, as Andrew's guest, with his muse and lover, the beautiful Monica Vitti, hanging off his arm.

Originally it was the idea of Antonioni's producer, Carlo Ponti, that he should make a film that reflected the new breed of unorthodox and independent fashion photographers like David Bailey, Terry O'Neill and Terry Donovan. However, nothing had come of it until Ponti heard that Antonioni was adapting a Julio Cortázar story about a photographer and planning to shoot it in Milan, at which point he suggested that the Maestro should set it in London.

Antonioni had come to London over the winter specifically to see if the media portrayals of the city were real. He wanted to go to parties, to sit in Soho trattorias and the new clubs, to see the boutiques and listen to the music, to absorb the flavour and the mood of the place. He gave parties in his suite at the Savoy to meet people he'd been told were the movers behind the phenomenon of London. 'I *hate* parties,' he said at the time. 'I only go for the film.' It was rumoured that he'd talked to Bailey; he'd met Terence Stamp when Terence and Monica Vitti were making *Modesty Blaise*; he'd already cast the part of the photographer.

It was our third night and the play was well run in. Antonioni settled down to watch.

Inevitably, there was a great buzz behind the scenes. Italian directors of his eminence didn't walk into the theatre every day, and everyone knew he was in London to make a movie. But we got on with it, gave the performance, and afterwards Andrew brought them both backstage. Frankly, I didn't take a lot of notice of the director, as my attention was much more acutely engaged by Miss Vitti, at whom I gazed, I admit, with undisguised lust. She possessed a perfect symmetry of luscious long brown legs, challenging blue eyes and flawless features framed with blonde hair that gave her the look of a Grace Kelly with a hint of olive oil.

To say that my first meeting with the great director himself was a disappointment would be understating it. As far as I could tell, he didn't react at all to what I'd just done. He took my hand perfunctorily with a doleful shake of his head, as if he'd just slept through the play, showing, as far as I could see, absolutely no interest in my performance, and that was that.

The following morning, Carlo Ponti called me from Bridge Films' office in Haymarket. 'The Maestro would like to see you.'

I was flabbergasted. Sitting in my small flat in Croydon, I couldn't believe he even remembered who I was after his obvious lack of curiosity the evening before.

I tried not to stammer. 'When?'

'Now.'

I caught my breath. 'Where? At your office?'

'He's staying at the Savoy. He'd like to see you there.'

*

The first thing that struck me as I walked into his room, one of the finest the Savoy Hotel had to offer, was a strong smell of garlic. The Maestro must have been indulging in some exotic snack, although there was no sign of it. He was sitting at a coffee table under a bay window, elegantly draped in one of those chic tweed jackets that Italians have always made so well, aping an English look while injecting a stylishness that we never seem to achieve. I coveted it at once.

I sat down at the coffee table opposite him, looking rather drab in comparison, I thought.

After a perfunctory greeting, he studied me and waggled his head from side to side in a gesture of profound negativity. I had been in the room less than five minutes and I was already convinced the interview wasn't going well. After a few moments he confirmed this with another prolonged bout of head shaking, as if rejecting an unacceptable truffle.

In a thick Italian accent, he said, 'You looka too younga.'

I wasn't going to give in that easily. 'Oh no,' I answered emphatically. 'I can look older. I've done it before. You can trust me on this. I *am* an actor.'

He smiled indulgently; he was a much older hand at this game than me. His halting English gave him the excuse to insert death-defying chasms of silent suspense. He shook his head again. 'How do you look blond?'

'Much older,' I replied instantly.

His mouth drooped with what I took to be scepticism and he looked at me a little longer, making no move to produce the 24-page script everyone was talking about.

That's it, I said to myself. Please piss off. Leave the stage now, while you're behind.

Frankly, I thought all the head wagging was bloody rude. Nevertheless, he did thank me for coming.

I left the Savoy in the certain knowledge that my encounter with the Maestro had been a total failure and I'd blown a big chance. I took the train back to Elmhurst Court in Croydon in a state of deep depression.

Here was a director I admired hugely, who was in London to make a picture, who had asked to see me, only then to convey his clear lack of interest by his persistent head shaking.

I wallowed for a while in the sympathy offered by Jane Merrow, an actress I'd first met on the set of *The System*, who had been living with me for the past three years, and Jasper, our very special Border collie, who that evening accompanied me to the pub, as usual, to quell my disappointment with a few pints and a game of darts.

When Carlo Ponti called me early next morning to tell me that Antonioni wanted me to do a screen test, I was totally baffled.

I put the phone down and stared at Jane. 'I don't know what the hell's going on here. They want me to do a test – but he *hated* me yesterday, I know he did. Everything about him said he thought I was wrong for the part.'

But, whatever I thought, it seemed at least I still had a chance, and I wasn't going to kick it in the teeth. The next day I set off on the train and allowed my natural cockiness to quash my serious doubts about the exercise.

The test was being done in a large photographic studio in Pottery Lane, off Holland Park Avenue, which was where the movie was ultimately to be made, and belonged to a successful fashion snapper called John Cowan.

The cameraman, Carlo Di Palma was already set up there, with the Maestro sitting directly under the camera.

He asked me what I wanted to do.

I guessed he must have liked what I'd done in *Skin Trade,* so I decided to spout 'In My Craft or Sullen Art' – a Thomas poem I loved and thought I could deliver well.

Evidently, though, Antonioni didn't agree. He just sat there, gloomily shaking his head again.

I was boiling with resentment. Why did the bastard ask me here? Could you please just not waggle that chin again!

But I kept the thought to myself, took a long breath and persevered. 'Let me give you something else,' I offered as nonchalantly as I could.

I wandered around the set improvising furiously; then I came up with a piece from Ted Willis's *A Woman in a Dressing Gown,* in which I'd been performing at the New Theatre, Bromley the day Jack Kennedy was assassinated in Dallas.

The director sat unmoving beneath the camera and watched. Every time I looked at him, his head was still shaking. No, no, it said. Wrong.

More unpleasant thoughts crossed my mind. Well, fuck you! I've given you my best shot. I can't do any more.

Carlo Di Palma started to thank me.

'Yeah, yeah, I know,' I said, without much grace. 'Thanks, anyway.'

I just wanted to get to the nearest pub as soon as possible. I walked out aching with a massive depression and a badly bruised ego.

Nothing could have prepared me, two days later, for the call I got at Elmhurst Court from Carlo Ponti's assistant.

'You've got the role. Can you come to Bridge Films this afternoon?' He went on about wardrobe and scripts while I tried to grasp what he was saying.

When he'd finished and I'd put the phone down, I still couldn't believe it. Shivering with excitement, I shouted to Jane. 'He's given me the bloody part!'

She clattered out of the kitchen, eyes wide with amazement. 'What? That's fantastic!'

'Yeah, I suppose so,' I said uncertainly. 'But I just don't understand it. Everything in his body language said he thought I was crap. Now he's given me the bloody part,' I repeated.

When the call had come, I'd been on the point of taking Jasper for his daily route march through the concrete boulevards of Croydon, but even his obvious dismay at being told it was all off didn't stop me from dropping everything to get straight up to Bridge Films' offices in the West End.

I had a costume fitting that same afternoon, where they threw a pair of white jeans and a green corduroy jacket at me. And for the first time, I was allowed to see the script and was given a copy to take away.

As soon as I was out of the building, I dived into the nearest pub, probably didn't even notice its name, ordered what I've always called a PoG – a pint of Guinness – which I didn't remember drinking, opened the script and buried myself in it. I read it three times from cover to cover before I rang Jane and told her.

'What's it like?' she asked eagerly.

'God knows,' I said, shaking my head rather like the Maestro. 'I don't understand what the hell it's all about.'

All I cared about then was that I had secured one of the most coveted film roles in Britain at the time. What made it perhaps more surprising for me was the industry whisper that Terence Stamp had already been signed for the role – a fait accompli.

Subsequently I learned that after Stamp had met Antonioni on the set of *Modesty Blaise*, the director had talked to him at some length about the picture he was proposing to make, and even asked him for a list of his presumably 'swinging' friends. He offered Stamp's then lover, Jean Shrimpton, a role, but didn't show him the script or tell him much more. Terence was determined to work with the Maestro and, despite the vagueness and secrecy surrounding the project, put off a lot of other work to keep himself free for it when it eventually happened. He went and saw Antonioni in Rome a few times, but was so in awe of the great director that he didn't follow his instincts and others' advice to extract a contract or some kind of written commitment from him. Negotiations with MGM got under way and Stamp settled in to the task of learning how to behave like a photographer.

Nevertheless, once Antonioni was in London making the final preparations for the movie, for some reason it seemed he changed his mind and no longer saw Terence in the role. Someone phoned Stamp to tell him that I'd got the part.

He'd never heard of me. 'Who's he when he's at home?' he is said to have asked bitterly.

Although he'd never had a contract, he still managed to get MGM to pay him some money to compensate him for all the other jobs he'd blanked in order to work with the Maestro.

Astonishing as it may seem, I've never met Terence, although I fear he's never forgiven me for doing him out of Thomas in *Blow-Up*. But then, he did me out of Captain Troy in *Far from the Madding Crowd*, so I guess we're quits.

Three or four PoGs later and no less confused, I left the pub in the Haymarket and walked up to Piccadilly to catch the tube home.

I'd stopped in the infamous loo there to release some of the stout when I heard myself being accosted by a vaguely familiar voice. I looked up and standing at the next urinal to me was the actor Peter Bowles.

He was full of beans and, like me, some liquor. 'I've just been to see Michelangelo Antonioni, and I may be getting a part in his film,' he said gleefully.

'Well,' I said, with forgivable hubris in the circumstances, 'I've just been to see Michelangelo Antonioni and I've got the lead part in his film.'

Peter was fulsome and generous in his congratulations. We leaped around, shaking hands and hugging each other – the last time we have allowed ourselves to become excited in a public lavatory together in the course of a great friendship that has lasted over several films, one or two bizarre scams and 35 years.

I'd already been told that we would start shooting in a week, but those intervening seven days were among the most angst-ridden of my life. Apart from all the usual strain of meeting dozens of new people involved in a production, at the front of my mind was the fiercely nagging doubt as to whether I could deliver the nebulous character. There seemed, on paper, so little to him; and anyway, the director himself in our acquaintance thus far had demonstrated no faith whatsoever in my abilities – apart, of course, from giving me the role.

However, while I longed to get started on the first day's shooting, the week passed in a haze of frantic preparation. The last couple of days were the worst.

I've always been fond of butterflies, but not in my stomach. Dentists evoked them in me as a child; Antonioni was doing it to me now.

In fact, just being an actor can do it.

You dream constantly that you're late for a performance no one has told you about. You haven't learned the lines for *Richard II*, the curtain goes up in four minutes and no one can find a script. Or you know the words and the play, but you've arrived at the wrong theatre. If there are dreams that are shared, for actors these certainly are they.

But once you've got a particular role, once you're on the path to a job, that's exciting. You read and re-read the script and then one morning, you can't get your cornflakes down and you realise that you start tomorrow. Frantically you look at the call sheet, a document normally delivered with intense panic in the middle of the night, which is supposed to tell everyone what everyone else thinks might happen the following day. Having read this piece of approximate guesswork, you thumb through the script yet again, look at the call sheet again, check that your alarm is working, set it carefully for three hours before you really need to get up, check the fridge, deny yourself alcohol, mix a stiff Horlicks and go to bed at three in the afternoon, then wake up at four-thirty, your alarm having gone off just as you set it to. You'd forgotten about the little a.m.-p.m. switch.

You can't sleep now, so you read the script again, read the call sheet twice more, set the alarm again, make more Horlicks and go back to bed. You bang your head on the pillow to coincide with wake-up time, change your pyjamas for a less sweaty pair, rehearse your lines with the ceiling, bang your head on your knees to concur with your wake-up time again, plunge your head into the pillow and listen to the clock until it's time to get up.

You watch intently for a car/driver to take you to the set, check your watch, check the clock, check the pillow, check your knees. All synchronised. The driver's late. Who do you call? You get the taxi's number, but where's the location? You consult the call sheet and look at the script. In blind panic now, you rush to the fridge, pull out an enormous bottle of Smirnoff and notice the calendar behind the magnet. Sunday the 12th: no shooting; no lines; no car. You drink the Smirnoff. Goodbye butterflies. Until tomorrow.

So it was then, as it always has been and will be, I suppose, as long as I keep acting. The fear never leaves you at the start, not until the first scene is done and the character you've been trying to shape in your mind through the long sleepless nights is finally committed to the sharp-edged actuality of celluloid.

2

Blow-Up

On the first day of shooting I arrived on the set of *Blow-Up* still convinced that Antonioni had no faith in what I had to offer. I tried to overcome my paranoia by constantly reminding myself that he had chosen me. Thus cloaked in a confidence which I certainly didn't feel, I walked up to him and held out my hand.

He took it, but to my horror and utter amazement, he was still shaking his head, even with a broad smile of welcome on his normally severe countenance. *'Bene. Grazie mille.'*

In those few seconds, with a tremendous surge of relief, I realised that all the head shaking that I'd miserably taken as an expression of serious doubts about my suitability for the role meant absolutely nothing. I'm sure if I'd been seeing him objectively from the start, I'd have known much sooner that he was suffering from Tourette's syndrome or something similar – a complaint that manifests itself in a constant, involuntary movement of the head from side to side, in Michelangelo's case suggesting serious personal criticism of whomever he happened to be addressing. Now I knew what I was dealing with, I soon discovered that the tic could become more pronounced as the day wore on, and by the end of the production, if his head was still shaking, I didn't notice. Once the mystery was solved, I was prepared to love him; and I never told him about the week of hell he'd put me through as a result of his affliction.

I was relieved, too, when I realised that Antonioni did not expect his cast to offer him their own views on the script, because it had become increasingly clear to me in the week leading up to the shoot that, with this particular picture, I was going to have to rely very heavily on the director to interpret the story. It had been written by Antonioni himself with Tonino Guerra, adapted from the original short story by Julio Cortázar called, I believe, 'A Girl, a Photographer and a Beautiful April

Morning', a rather slight and, frankly, somewhat clumsy little tale, at least in translation.

Superficially there seemed little to it – the story of a young photographer, obviously successful, who has become detached by his profession from reality. Happening on a pair of lovers meeting in a deserted park, he snaps them. The girl chases after him, desperate to have the film, but he refuses her and takes it home. As he develops the shots, and progressively blows them up, it appears that a murder may have taken place; what looks like a body is lying beneath some bushes nearby. It is never made clear whether this is reality or illusion – a dichotomy which is the central enigma of a flimsy plot.

Naturally, though, I understood that in a film by Antonioni plot is only a minor element.

One of the biggest hurdles in the early stages of a new movie is the continuing flurry of first-day nerves, which torment nearly all actors (except, perhaps, Oliver Reed, who, as I knew from my experience with him on *The System*, often didn't even know that we'd started shooting). There is something eerie and unreal about a movie set – not surprisingly, given that the creation of false reality is its *raison d'être* – and however familiar the experience, a new set is always a little daunting.

You know where you are; you know the jargon and terms of reference; you know, more or less, what will be expected of you, but you're still very glad to see any old acquaintances.

I'd been in thirty to forty films and television dramas by the time I made *Blow-Up* and I'd got to know a lot of the regular crews working around London, particularly the special effects men. I got on well with them, I guess, because I'd always enjoyed 'magic', practical jokes and the business of creating illusion.

Most of the interior sequences of the film were shot in and around John Cowan's Pottery Lane studio, near Notting Hill, which was then a cosy, familiar place, a village with a pleasing, rackety grace to it. The scenes in the park were all shot over a series of consecutive days in Maryon Park, Woolwich, an extraordinary and underused oasis of *rus in urbe*, just beyond Charlton Athletic's football ground.

When finally we got under way, the director was as laid-back as anyone on the set, relaxed in his chair, smoking a cigar that looked like a withered branch of a diseased elm. I've seldom seen such a repulsive object, gnarled, crooked and smelling like a funeral pyre on the banks of the Ganges.

I sat opposite him while the crew busied themselves with the first set-up, in which I was to follow a line of homeless down-and-outs as they were let out onto the streets for the day. They would return again at night. I carry a brown paper bag, inside which is not a packet of sandwiches but a camera. I turn a corner and reach my half-hidden Rolls-Royce.

Once the crew had cleaned up the Rolls-Royce after our futile attempt to prank the Maestro, we were plunged straight into *Blow-Up* like travellers in space. We had really no idea where we were going, and how it was going to make any sense, but from the start, without a moment's uncertainty, Antonioni conducted the whole movie with the ruthless authority of a Thomas Beecham. He had the backing of a gang of key operators he'd brought from Italy. They'd worked with him many times and had learned his moods and whims.

Carlo Di Palma was his lighting cameraman, a man with whom he never seemed to stop arguing. Carlo was in his early thirties, slim and shorter than the Maestro. He had an expressive, small, round face with black hair and brown eyes that seemed as bright as the lights he used. His jeans were tight, his heels enhanced. He was feisty, hot and, in an Italian way, good-looking, which gave him the confidence to deal on equal terms with his quieter, cooler boss. He also had a hard eye for Monica Vitti, as well as for Jane Birkin and all the other models on the set.

The chief grip was a deep Neapolitan called Lello, a person of warm chubbiness whose second name we never discovered. Strangely, considering the place of his birth, he often acted as the unit's peace-maker, always ready to referee between his squabbling countrymen, at least when he wasn't taking part himself, which happened occasionally.

If in the end Antonioni and Carlo were unable to reach a solution to their differences, Lello would shrug his shoulders and walk away. 'I ama just poppinga down to the pubba' – an expression he'd learned very quickly when he came to England – 'until they make uppa their mind just where they want theesa light.'

While the director and cameraman carried on arguing, I sat quietly on the sidelines, trying to grasp what these Latin *locos* were yelling about. I'd already decided that I could work much better with the great Italian genius if I could speak his language and I still have a picture of myself on the set on the first day, reading *How to Speak Italian*. I hadn't learned enough then to appreciate their foul vernacular, but I made inroads, and as a result Italian is now my second language and Rome is my favourite city.

There was also a sense that Di Palma was pretender to the Maestro's throne, Carlo's Iago to Antonioni's Othello, which may have added to the palpable tension between them. He certainly had no qualms about challenging his boss. Antonioni, being the Maestro, never let him have his way completely but, in the end result, it was clear that their explosive rapport produced astonishing images. In achieving this, though, there were these moments of quite alarming aggression, which never perhaps reached their natural conclusion, inasmuch as the two men never hit each other, but a great deal of shouting, arm waving and surrogate kicking went on – fireplaces, ladders, tables, anything. Kick, kick, kick.

This all seemed to be a quite normal part of their creative cinema, as if they had to get all the passion out of their systems to achieve the best results. If any of us looked shocked or surprised by the apparent vehemence, they would shrug it off, as if to say, 'This is how we make films in Italy.'

It's also true to say that on an Italian film set in those days, there was always more talking, because they weren't recording sound. It's well documented, for instance, that when Fellini was making films, he would tell his actors simply to recite numbers while giving them whatever expression he demanded. The real dialogue would be dubbed on afterwards in several languages. Strange as it may seem, it worked in the case of *Blow-Up*, delivering a distinctive and eerie lack of ambient sound in the outdoor shots.

Antonioni was used to the technique and, although we spoke our lines as on the script, we were still going to overdub, allowing the constant chatter all the time we were shooting.

In one of the best-known scenes in *Blow-Up* – the purple-paper romp with Jane Birkin and Gillian Hills – we were urged on with a non-stop barrage of shouting as the cameras rolled.

'Getta her knickers off, now!'

'I can'ta see her tits! She's got to move over there.'

'Pulla down more paper.'

Watching that particular sequence, where we're tugging down rolls of backing paper and I am scrabbling among it with two enthusiastic wannabe models, apparently getting my end away, you might have thought what a wonderfully erotic experience I was having. Sadly, it didn't quite develop into that, even after we'd stopped shooting. Jane Birkin was undeniably one of the most luscious women with whom it has ever been my good fortune to cavort, but she didn't have the camera experience of Veroushka, with whom I engage in the famous 'Coitus with Camera' scene, or the other girls who worked in the modelling sequences. As a result, the whole romping scene, as it was shot, felt somehow unsatisfactory. The girls seemed to have enjoyed it and threw themselves at me with flattering enthusiasm, and I guess I threw myself back, but I always felt there was something missing. There was, though, a magic moment after the camera had been switched off when we just lay about laughing, hysterical and exhausted, as though it had all been for real.

One result of the scene was that the film became the first in which the international distributors had actually seen three triangular inches of pubic hair on the screen and they were expected to distribute the film as a major company. They declined to do so. As a result, it was only released in a very few cinemas under MGM's art movie label, Première, until everyone was talking about it and projectionists started cutting out the few critical frames so that they could take them home and have a closer look.

Although up until then I'd been asked to do many strange things in my professional life, I'd certainly never shot any scenes quite as bizarre as this, which went on for quite so long under camera. I snipped off a couple of pieces of the purple paper as a memento. It's odd, but they were both triangular, too.

The rich creative relationship between Antonioni and his cameraman was observed with insouciance by the Anglo-Saxon crew, who didn't give a toss and anyway didn't understand what the Italians were arguing about. Meanwhile, between these voluble foreigners and the natives stood Piers Haggard, now a deservedly well-known director in his own right, then script editor and interpreter – a vital role in a transnational production like this. Piers was a good friend and comfort to us all, doing his best to explain the 24-page script to us.

Once shooting was well under way and despite the chronic uncertainty and frustration of working with a solipsistic genius, I loved every moment of my time on *Blow-Up*. I never could make much sense of the script, but Antonioni became a good friend. This was a hell of a relief, after all my early doubts, and a warning about the director's autocratic manner from Richard Harris. He told me while he and the Maestro were making the extraordinary *Il Deserto Rosso* in Sardinia, he'd fallen out of his tree and landed a fist on the Italian's finely chiselled jaw – whacked Michelangelo in the upper molars and felled him. Richard was not specific about the grounds of the dispute, but I'm certain he would have found it almost impossible to submit to Antonioni's rigidly dictatorial approach to film-making. Whatever it was about, he was summarily thrown off the picture and for the unshot portions of the film his character appears only as a false headpiece, viewed from the rear. I don't often offer advice to young actors who ask for it, but rule one of my *Guide to Acting in the Movies* might well be not to punch the director in the mouth. This leads to discomfort on both sides and, bruised or not, the director always wins.

I was an energetic 25-year-old – probably more so than most – and I was fascinated by the way Antonioni, at 54, could operate around the clock and still sustain the momentum he needed to get him through the production. It seemed that, however late he'd gone to bed the night before, he appeared on the set each morning as bright-eyed as a bantam cock, and just as well groomed. Close-shaven, with lean, dark eyebrows, he'd be wearing one of his chic tweed jackets, a checked shirt, perfectly pressed trousers and snappy little hand-stitched loafers.

For a man of his age, he was impressively eager for new experiences. I think perhaps he was a little in thrall to the idea of 'swinging London' and even once shooting had started, he spent a great deal of time hanging around in search of oscillation, often with photographers and models. Perhaps he considered it all research, but in his quest he raved ceaselessly, night after night in clubs and discothèques, in the company of the new goddesses of the fashion world, with his fierce eyes shining intensely in his dark, grave face as he drank grappa till his ears bubbled and tried to extract every last ounce from the swinging city – a man from Rome, a modern Bellini, determined to leave his mark in the middle of this liberated new world.

I never quite discovered how he dealt with his male appetites, assuming he still had any. Although Monica Vitti arrived on the set from time to time, it seemed that Antonioni had abandoned her. I noticed, though, that she had an eye for an indifferent Carlo Ponti; and I had an eye for Monica Vitti, I have to admit. I nursed a faint hope that she might be, as they say in Italian, up for grabs, though I never took the risk of sneaking in under Carlo's nose.

Whatever the Maestro did for female companionship, he must have done very late, because I never saw. After a few nights on the prowl with him, I realised that he seldom went home before the Piccadilly sparrows had broken wind. He must have got very tired and I wondered vaguely how he dealt with it until I discovered he slept only when he was filming.

He would arrive on the set first thing, along with the bleary-eyed crew, and work furiously to set up a shot. It seemed that the longer it took the crew to complete his instructions, the better it suited him. Several times I would then find him later in some small room at the back of the studio where he'd crept, slouched in a chair with his head on his chest, sound asleep.

On other days he would come to the set and just stare silently at it for a long time. He would place objects entirely arbitrarily, then take his actors and position them at random, until he decided that they looked right. Then he might announce that what he needed to perfect the scene was some smoked glass. After a brief confrontation with his harassed producer, people would be dispatched to find it. Without a qualm or an apology, Antonioni would vanish again for an hour or two's kip.

I didn't mind at all. I always had things to do and I liked sitting in pubs. There's no question that making 'the Antonioni Picture' in sixteen weeks was a very different experience from knocking out a British B-movie in a fortnight. Frankly, in some ways it felt much the same as a B-movie: there were the same tricks, the same gags, and there was no sense at all that we were doing anything particularly significant here. However, unlike any B-movie I'd ever made, I've always treasured the experience of working for a director with Antonioni's astonishing gifts.

To a journeyman actor like me, unburdened by philosophical pretensions, he could be totally enigmatic. On the set he would say, 'Do this,' or 'Do that,' unequivocally, with no invitation to debate.

'OK, David, you lean forward, you pick up the glass, you bring it here. You go to drink it, you decide not to, you put it down again – Tac! You walk across the room, you look at the painting, the painting is circular and you move your finger round and round in circular movements, like this.'

I did exactly as I was told. The scene is in the film, and I've never heard a satisfactory explanation for this direction. Or, for that matter, why

Thomas stares at Sarah Miles making love to her husband. The Maestro told me to do it and so I did. Of course, I didn't mind. Strange as Sarah could be, I'd always rather fancied her and admired her in *The Servant*.

Having submitted in this very un-English way to his total control of the movie, I enjoyed it. I understood clearly now that he didn't consider it his job to enlighten or educate his actors; to him we were like the colours on an artist's palette. When people have been kind enough (and I mean that) to tell me I was good in *Blow-Up*, I've often felt that I'd done no more than a dab of yellow paint in Van Gogh's *Sunflowers*.

One didn't question Antonioni. I took the view that my job was to turn up on time and do as I was told. In any event, I've never seen much point in trying to be too clever about a role. Anthony Hopkins says he never reads the whole script. Michael Caine says he never reads more than his own part because whatever happens beyond his role he shouldn't know anyway.

I don't think I'd go that far. I read Antonioni's script many times, trying to extract some clarity from it, admittedly without much success. In any case, he was so aggressively obtuse and wrapped up in his own vision that I felt I couldn't contribute anything that he would consider useful.

Nevertheless, I found that the longer we worked together, the greater was my appreciation for his extraordinary eye. He had such a feeling for his subject that the script became almost secondary to his personal vision. Actors weren't important. They were there merely as one element of the pictures that would tell the story he carried in his head.

He never explained the significance of the propeller that Thomas buys in the antiques shop, although David Bailey told me later that he had done exactly that – but how the hell did Michelangelo know?

Nor did he choose to reveal the purpose of the rock'n'roll scene in the Ricky Tick Club in Windsor, where the Yardbirds (lead guitarists, J. Page and J. Beck) played and Janet Street-Porter grooved lankily; even less the man who picks up and discards a broken guitar neck afterwards.

Antonioni didn't recognise the concept of compromise. He was feverishly attentive to detail. A massive Alitalia sign in the Elephant and Castle was painted black and whole streets in Brixton were sprayed red.

When he told Di Palma, 'I want every tree in the park painted green,' Carlo understood.

But the British set designer, Michael Balfour, gazed at him with puzzled horror. 'They *are* green.'

'The trunks are brown. I want them green, too,' the Maestro ordered lightly, as if it were a perfectly reasonable request, 'to match this fence. And I want all the paths sprayed black.'

Some deferential gofer on the crew was dispatched to find the paint; the rest of us sat in the White Horse on a corner near an entrance to Maryon Park, while the crew improved upon nature by spraying all the vegetation in the park a vernal green. It was soon made clear that cutting corners to save money had no place in Antonioni's film-making.

We waited around, unaccustomed to the luxury of such long breaks in filming, especially after the Michael Winner pictures we were used to making, where time between shots was kept to the minimum to meet budgets of astonishing meagreness. I was used to a British film tradition where you were told, 'Hit your marks!' and that was it. With the Italians it was, 'No, we are not ready yet. Go back and wait.'

This was long before the now standard-issue American Winnebago motor-homes had appeared on movie sets, and our only option was to go off to the pub, which conveniently became the headquarters, make-up studio and recreation room for much of the shoot.

However, I found my relationship with Antonioni was different from that of the rest of the cast. I wanted to hang around on the sidelines, letting him know I was ready as soon as he wanted me. I wasn't there out of a simple eagerness to please; I was fascinated by the entire process of film-making and I'd never seen it done the way he did it. I loved to watch him working, as did Piers Haggard, who never left the set either. We would sit together, chatting while we watched what the Maestro was doing, wondering why he had placed the camera where he had or had lit the shot in a certain way.

Sometimes, I would summon up the confidence to ask him, 'Michelangelo, why are you doing it like that?'

He would usually brush the question aside. 'Don't ask me for a reason. There are no reasons. There is only the camera.'

It was nothing like any actor-director relationship I'd known – more like a painter-student relationship. I thought he was magnificent, but while I'd have jumped through hoops to work with him again, I never fully understood what he was doing at the time. I accepted that I was simply the clay in the potter's hands. I was certainly no Al Pacino to his Martin Scorsese. Antonioni just didn't work like that; he was God on a film set. Only Carlo Di Palma or Lello dared to question his orders.

However, on occasions, when he seemed less than usually absorbed in his own creativity, I did try to ask him about his methods.

'OK,' he said with obvious impatience. 'When I put the camera here' – he jerked it above his shoulder – 'it means one thing.'

I nodded, feeling foolish.

He went on, 'When I put the camera here' – he held it below his knees – 'it means another thing.'

I didn't learn a lot from this. However, another time he tried to explain something of his technique for creating tension in a movie.

'A man walks up to a door, in a long empty hotel corridor, where he stops and visibly thinks about opening it. If you show just the moment while he's thinking about opening the door – that's boring. If you have him wait and wait before he thinks about opening the door – that's not necessarily boring. But if you have him wait and wait and wait and wait before he even thinks about it – that is *very* boring. *However*, if you have him wait, wait, wait, wait *until you have overcome the audience's boredom threshold*, and he waits and waits a little longer, the audience starts to think, "Ahhh, there is something else going on here. There is danger." That is the way I work,' the Maestro declared, flattering me with his confidence. 'I like to keep my audience in suspense for as long as it is possible. *I* am the man of suspense. Hitchcock, eata your heart out. I can do it better, with no props, nothing. Just with a man, standing alone in a corridor, waiting to turn the handle of a door.' He shrugged in mild awe at his own genius.

Not surprisingly, given the Maestro's distaste for hurrying things, it was a few weeks into shooting before the film acquired its name. He canvassed our views about the title – at least, he wandered across the set towards me at the end of a day's filming. 'Whata do you think about *The Blow-Up*?'

Although unconvinced and still uncertain what the movie was trying to say, I obeyed my aversion to confrontation and told him I liked it, knowing that, anyway, he'd have taken very little notice of my opinion. In fact, I left *Blow-Up* thinking I'd put very little into the film, or even the part I'd played, and all the creativity had come from Antonioni. But I didn't have time to let it worry me then, as I became more involved in the major upheavals that were taking place in my career, and in my love life.

Before we'd started making *Blow-Up*, I moved out of the flat in Croydon I'd been sharing with Jane Merrow, to be nearer my work. In fact, I was still appearing in *Skin Trade* at the Club when its writer, Andrew Sinclair, offered to rent me his house in the then bohemian district of Limehouse, in the old docklands of east London.

It was a wonderful house, one of a terrace of early 18th-century lightermen's cottages, wavy-ridged and clapboarded. Andrew had also managed to buy the first floor of the adjoining house and make a massive living room with wonderful and almost unique views of the river and the busy flow of shipping that still used it.

Once there, on my own and fired up by the buzz of working with the Maestro, I was in no frame of mind to fend off the temptations of amorous adventure offered by this new freedom, and when I bumped into Linda Estall Cole in Tramp, Blazes or Samantha's – I just don't remember which – I was more than ripe for it.

By then she was known, in her acting persona, as Linda Cole, but I'd known her at a distance for years. In my early teens, one of my favourite hunting grounds for close-up views of blood-stirring women had been the Hook Heath Tennis Club, where my friend Peter Goodchild was something of a star. This was in an era when local tennis clubs often provided the only mutual territory for teenage boys and girls to meet and mix. I look back with no shame on my flagrant exploitation of the venue, or, for that matter, on its siting in suburban Woking. As a child of the A3 corridor of south-west London, I was in my natural habitat and proud of it.

In my world, then, the Hook Heath Tennis Club was the pinnacle of social aspiration, and as far as I know, I'm still on the waiting list for membership. Linda was the star, and I went to watch her and worship the court she played on. I was besotted; she was utterly out of reach. Her family lived in a big house in a smart part of Woking, with a large beautiful garden and a billiard room.

I may have thought I looked the business in my white shorts and Fred Perry shirt, with a little superficial skill in racket twirling, but my already abysmal tennis was severely compromised by my underhand service. I was no match for the spotty charms of the well-groomed boys from public schools, who fell all over her with their blazers and the gall to wear ties around their waists as belts. By comparison, in these genteel surroundings, I was a scruffy oik, with the appeal of a mongrel puppy that people might like to take home but knew would pee on the carpets. To Linda, I wasn't worth a second glance.

Nevertheless, I was encouraged by an absurd optimism which has seldom deserted me throughout a life that has for the most part run its course like a roller-coaster with a death wish, and I set about concocting ways of seeing more of her. I sent her anonymous telegrams and left unattributed messages making appointments at coffee bars, where I would lurk in a corner to watch her arrive. As she waited in vain for her date to show up, I would gaze in silent, innocent admiration.

I didn't see her after that for several years, until I bumped into her in a restaurant on the King's Road, when I at least re-established contact and got her number into the filing system. It was about the time *Skin Trade* started that I next saw her in one of London's sweaty, onion-flavoured discothèques.

Still conscious of my unrequited love for her a dozen years before, I couldn't ignore the chance to make up for it and it was undoubtedly her total indifference in my vulnerable early teens that urged me to impress more than I would normally have thought necessary.

While I'd been filming *Blow-Up* I'd managed, with small financial inducements, to gain the confidence of the chauffeur who drove the Rolls-Royce to the set every day and I'd been making regular arrangements with him to borrow the car. A Rolls was something of a rarity then, even in a 1966 Mayfair crowd, and not something your average oik turned up in.

When Linda reappeared on my radar, I was determined to use it to take her out, to expunge my childhood humiliations.

With the hood down and the Spirit of Ecstasy gleaming on the bonnet, I drove down to her family's house in Woking and swept up the grandiose driveway, not to be put down by her notorious old snob of a father. I collected Linda and drove her to the Swan at Thames Ditton – a handsome, if somewhat flashy gin-and-Jag establishment that was very picturesque on a sunny Sunday morning. With the top still down, I swept up to the car park, just in front of the river and in full view of the pub. Linda looked stunning, as if she'd been specially designed to sit in the passenger seat of a convertible Roller; I perhaps less so. But we waited in the car for a few moments, looking at the river and watching the ducks before we got out. I flicked a switch and the hood swung silently up and over to enclose the car. I took Linda's hand and walked her up a short flight of stone steps to the front door. As it happened, the landlord was standing on the top step with a group of friends.

He looked at to me with a knowing grin. 'Ah, you mechanics have all the luck, don't you?'

He wasn't that far off the mark.

Nevertheless, despite this public put-down, over lunch Linda and I managed to concoct a relationship. And then suddenly – inevitably, it seemed – there she was in Limehouse, standing naked in front of the double windows, watching the ships pass slowly up the river. In my eyes, she was still the Hook Heath tennis player I'd lusted after with teenage passion and I could hardly believe my good fortune in landing such a spectacular catch.

For the next few weeks, we lay in bed together to the sound of foghorns. She slept with me and shared *Blow-Up* with me, as well as life in Limehouse, where we would lie gazing at the shipping, with *Lloyd's Register* at hand to identify the history of each vessel that passed.

We spent a lot of warm, friendly hours playing 'arrers' in the pub just across Narrow Street, a real old East End boozer with a carpet of sawdust that resounded every evening to the racket of an untuned Joanna and a raucous knees-up. We'd go to Chinatown, where the New Friends and the Old Friends restaurants were the best Chinese restaurants in London, and just a short walk from our front door the air was full of the aroma of Peking Duck or Egg Fu Yung. If we wanted a change, there was Dan Farson's Waterman's Arms, the Bunch of Grapes just down the road and the Prospect of Whitby less than a mile away. It said a lot about Linda that she had allowed herself to be so drastically uprooted from her upper-middle-class background and transplanted in the heart of the East End, and she was taking it all in her lovely long stride. Conscious of the gulf that had existed between us when I'd first seen her radiant presence on the tennis courts, I couldn't stop myself trying to impress her all the time. She didn't mind – I think she found it flattering – but I suffered painful retribution for this urge late one night, walking by the Serpentine in Hyde Park with her and my friend John Daly. It was hot and I boasted that I needed to cool down. Not wishing to excite the assorted low-lifes I was convinced always lurk in the bushes of the park, I kept my shirt and jeans on, took a few paces back and, with a short run, I took a long, shallow dive into what turned out to be four inches of water lapping over concrete. The front of my chest and stomach were scraped to hell and blood soaked my dripping shirt. I was in agony, but all I could think of was that I didn't have a clean shirt and, with my propensity for making my life as complicated as possible, I was still seeing Jane Merrow and had promised to pick her up first thing next morning to go to the country. God knows what bullshit I'd told Linda. In any event, she wasn't impressed.

After a while, the strain of making a movie like *Blow-Up* did tell on our brief liaison. Towards the end of the production, she came along to the filming of the party scene, which was shot in a beautiful flat in Cheyne Walk, overlooking the houseboats on a part of the river known as Turner's Reach. The flat belonged to the flamboyant antiques dealer Christopher Gibbs – now adviser in all ancient things to Mick Jagger. By any standards, it was a strange sequence, shot over five days and peopled by students and assorted groovers being very well paid to be there.

My character, Thomas, arrives at the party in a disturbed state because he's just blown up the shot which reveals what might be a corpse lying in the bushes near the lovers he'd snapped in the park.

The scene didn't turn out to be as simple as I'd expected.

I say to Veroushka, 'I thought you were in Rome.'

She replies, obviously stoned, 'I am in Rome.'

Then there is a brief exchange between me and Peter Bowles, in which I tell him about my suspicions of murder in the park.

To give as much verisimilitude as possible to this party scene, Antonioni had adopted the risky strategy of instructing that all the extras be given massive joints made with the best Lebanese hash. The air was thick with ganja smoke and the bit players were all lolling around, giggling inanely and doing nothing to help the concentration of the speaking parts.

I'm always a little uptight when I'm filming – on tenterhooks and easily irritated. Linda could see I was getting worked up over the whole scene and took it upon herself to protect my interests. It didn't go down well, with me or anyone else on the set. She responded by becoming rather more vociferous, nudging over the embarrassment threshold, until Vincent Fleming, my trusty stand-in, escorted her to the door and she went home to Surrey. I didn't see her again for more than half a dozen years.

I was saddened, though not greatly put out, by her departure. It seemed to fit in with the way other changes in my life were taking place. But I was grateful to her. For the brief time – not much more than a month – that we'd spent together in Andrew's house, I was very comfortable and relaxed with her. I still can't go to Limehouse without thinking of Hook Heath Tennis Club and Linda, and short, pleated white skirts. Sad to say, though, I still can't get a ball over the net with any kind of panache.

Whether or not it was making *Blow-Up* or the interlude with Linda Cole that sealed the demise of my previous relationship with Jane Merrow, I don't know. Probably that had run its natural course. It has often seemed to me that love affairs are destined to stay fresh and sweet only for as long as they are meant to last and no longer. Like fine clarets, once they have turned sour, there's not a lot you can do to revive them.

I didn't have the heart to tell Jane exactly what I was feeling; or possibly it was a case of sheer moral cowardice. Either way, when Linda had gone and I'd finished working on *Blow-Up*, I moved back into Elmhurst Court for the couple of months before I was due to depart for the States, where Hollywood was beckoning like a siren with extra-large breasts.

I told Jane the film was over and I was back, and she seemed to accept that. She knew I'd rented Limehouse from Andrew Sinclair. She had probably already sussed that it was over between us but, as usual, I found it hard to make a clean break. I tried to leave her with the impression that we'd get together again when I came back.

It was a long time later that I recognised Jane deserved better. There was no doubt that I'd been very happy with her. She had been a great companion and support right up until filming *Blow-Up* had started. And then she'd never once been on the set. I knew I didn't deserve her support now and I suppose the truth is that I thought I was on a roll. I didn't quite know what was going to happen to me in the States and, rather selfishly, I was keeping all my options open.

Even before Antonioni picked me for the part in his film, I had the feeling that my career, a long time in the making, was about ready to wind itself up a few more notches. I guess that being picked by a director of Antonioni's standing did a lot to help, but by the time I'd finished filming with him, I had deals with two major Hollywood studios.

Beryl Seton, my agent, called me to her office in Charing Cross Road to tell me the outcome of the negotiations she'd been conducting on my behalf. She kept a large blackboard in her office – assuming a low level of mathematical education in her clients, I suppose – and used it to help her explain even quite simple contracts. When I arrived that day, she wrote all the figures on the board in chalk, to show me exactly what my earnings would be over the next few years.

I had earned a modest £2,000 for *Blow-Up*, but when I had signed to play in it, my contract was not with Carlo Ponti's Bridge Films, but with the distributors, MGM, and, as was the practice at that time, I was contracted to do a further six pictures for them (one a year for the next six years), which meant that if the first film was a hit, the company had a proven artist at a very reasonable rate for their next few pictures. This kind of deal was a hangover from the old studio system; nobody signs long-term contracts like that any more. (Two years later, I was in a position to help things along a little when, in *The Best House in London*, I played two leading roles, and argued that I'd therefore fulfilled two of my commitments. I also argued that I should be paid twice, which, after a big show of pain on the studio's part, I was.) If I had completed the five films (which I didn't after the *Best House* fiasco), I would have earned £25–35,000.

I could remember, at a time when I was uncertain about my final choice of career (as, indeed, I still am), my father telling me, 'Your aim in life should be to become a thousand-a-year man.'

I was glad that I had at least fulfilled that ambition for him.

At about the same time I'd been chosen for *Blow-Up*, Warner Brothers were casting for their much-talked-about production of Lerner and Loewe's stage musical *Camelot*. They had an Anglophile casting director, who may have been helped by Mary Selway in England, and I was among an overwhelmingly British group of actors. So, while I was working for Antonioni, negotiations were also under way for me to play the part of Mordred in *Camelot*. This was also a multi-picture deal, although at the time the chances of actually seeing it through to the end seemed pretty remote to me.

Glossing over a few easily quelled misgivings, I was looking forward to heading for the States a couple of months after finishing my part in *Blow-Up*. Antonioni had stayed on in London for a while to do his edit. I went to see him once in the cutting room. He was hunched over a very new kind of editing device, a flat-bed KEM, which he'd had specially brought over from Italy.

He was as unforthcoming as ever about what he thought of the picture at that stage. He still didn't like to be asked questions any more than he had on set. I left the edit suite with absolutely no idea of the prospects for *Blow-Up*. I could only hope it hadn't all been a waste of time. Antonioni and I didn't talk about it again for a few months, until we watched it together for the first time that December in LA, when it was screened at the Directors' Guild of America.

'America' is a word which, to the uninitiated European, evokes images created from a sackful of fantasies that lurk in the brain, implanted by cinema or television, depending on your age. For me, it was the movies, and the principal setting for my fantasies was the Wild West.

However, on my first ever trip across the Atlantic, my first true image of America wasn't of the Wild West but of the inescapably stirring, iconic skyline of Manhattan Island, which never fails to impress and never disappoints the newcomer. I knew I was very lucky to be seeing it from the back of a limousine, which had picked me up from Kennedy airport. Still trying to take in the random geometry and sheer scale of the mighty city, I found myself gliding over the Queensboro Bridge into New York in the back of this ridiculous vehicle, driven by a short, stout chauffeur (known in America as a 'shuvver') of Italian origin and with surprisingly little display of deference.

I didn't give a damn about the lack of deference. I still just found it almost impossible to believe that at the age of 26, a native of Worplesdon, Surrey, and a former choirboy like me was being welcomed to the world's most exciting city as a guest of one of Hollywood's premier studios. I still wasn't sure how I'd pulled it off, but I wasn't going to let that – or anything else – stop me extracting every drop of pleasure or experience this adventure had to offer. I sighed happily and leaned back into a seat of over-squashy, maroon plush moquette and reflected on the bizarre series of chances – missed and taken – that had finally brought me here.

3

An A3 Boy, 1941–1953

In 1939, a year or so before I was conceived, my mother had been hurriedly evacuated from Tolworth, near Surbiton in Surrey, to the more bucolic and assumedly less perilous milieu of my grandmother's house at 16 Gravetts Lane, Worplesdon. It was an insignificant distance and, had I been party to this decision, I think I'd have expressed grave doubts as to whether Hitler had any particular interest in Tolworth. There were certainly never any reports of bombing there, or in Surbiton come to that. Bizarrely, by contrast, Gravetts Lane sometimes gave a good impression of being a prime target for doodlebugs and incendiaries, as if the Luftwaffe had received intelligence that the blacksmith at the end of the lane was forging something a great deal more deadly than horseshoes. Although I spent a lot of time in my early walking years hanging around his smithy, the most offensive object I ever saw him make was a fire poker.

I was born in Guildford in 1941 and spent my earliest years in Gravetts Lane, where my mother had moved as much to be near my grandmother, Lucy Wharf, and her family as to avoid the bombs in Tolworth. My father had enlisted dutifully and, despite his comparatively advanced age (in his late thirties), gone off to join the RAF as ground crew in East Anglia. As a result of his pre-war occupation as a musician, he was detailed to lead a small RAF dance band, which occasionally, with much excitement, we heard playing on the wireless in *Workers' Playtime* or a morale-boosting programme called *Ack Ack Beer Beer* (short, apparently, for 'anti-aircraft barrage balloons'). Other than that, he figured only sporadically during my first four years.

Gravetts Lane, however, still exists in my memory as a hazily romantic realm of adventure and discovery, although there's not much obvious romance about the place now. As I emerged from my first few years of busy growth, the world seemed a tremendously dark place, as if I'd been always hiding and had somehow made a swift, uneventful journey from my mother's womb to the cupboard under the stairs.

At the merest hint of danger from the air, I would be pulled hurriedly into this dark place, optimistically considered 'safe', where I found myself floundering in undergarments and skirts. This was my grand-mother's idea of extra protection from the Führer's bombs – if not from suffocation. An overpowering smell of mothballs permeated the small cupboard and even now the slightest whiff of naphthalene in a suddenly opened wardrobe gives me a terrible urge to clamber inside.

Historically, we were bombed quite heavily in Worplesdon, but the great urgency to lock ourselves in a cupboard to keep out of harm's way has always seemed thoroughly futile to me. I can't imagine a direct hit on a rural semi-detached cottage leaving only the staircase standing, reaching up like a short stairway to heaven, while beneath it, alive and well, smothered in cami-knickers and mothballs, lay three generations of Wharfs. But survive we did and, as the months trundled by, I became used to the doodlebugs and the incendiaries, like fireworks, spluttering and crackling in the fields along the lane.

As the scope of my toddling increased, I was warned never to go near the bottom of the garden, or take a step beyond the rickety wrought-iron archway that served to hold up a bank of copious roses that separated the more formal flower garden from the vegetable patch beyond.

Wartime, of course, took its toll on both the vegetables and the flower garden, although in the early spring and summer there were always daffodils to pick for the house, daisies on the lawn to make chains, and lupins at the back of the herbaceous borders. There were snap-dragons, too, which I loved to squeeze, to see their mouths yawn and gape back at me.

But beyond the flowerbeds and borders was this forbidden garden where there was a good stock of vegetables for the table throughout the war years. It was tilled by my family and, in communal spirit, the Mackies from next door. Dorothy Mackie was a bright Scot, always known as Dorothymac, like an early harbinger of e-mail.

'Go next door and see Dorothymac,' my mother might urge when she felt like a break or needed an errand run, and off I would trot. I liked Daaarmak, as I used to call her. Her husband, Mac, was a giant of a man with a bushy black moustache and swashbuckling hair. I liked him, too, although some of the family considered him a thoroughly rude man, due, in part, to his habit of wandering around outside in his vest. He'd been awarded a medal in France for what he described as an 'act of utter bleeding stupidity'. This had left him with a gammy leg, which leaked, apparently, since it was forever bandaged roughly over his trousers and was always moist after an hour or so. He never went back to the war and never put on his uniform again. It was thanks to him, though, that I finally found myself in the forbidden garden.

On a mission to check cabbages, he accidentally led me there. He didn't know it was out of bounds to me, but I certainly did and, nappyless by this time, I strutted behind him, a willing soldier marching into the unknown, looking forward to a confrontation with whatever horrors lurked among the weeds and stinging nettles at the far end.

My heart was racing. Why had I been banned from such a wonderful place? Mac trundled forward and gave a cursory glance at the cabbages. 'They look fine,' he said.

They always looked fine and would be as mushy as porridge by the time they reached the plate. My mother never, even later in life, accepted the 'al dente' concept. 'Uncooked' would be her verdict on any vegetable that, once boiled, could not be squashed by a fork into something close to soup.

Beyond the nettles, on tiptoes, I could see a large expanse of unkempt meadowland. It was radiant with wild flowers, deep-yellow buttercups and dandelions, purple thistles and white cow-parsley, while the air was heavy with the scent of wild herbs that my grandmother, in her long cotton skirt, would pick for the kitchen. There were mushrooms, too, under a cluster of ancient oaks in the middle of the field, which she gathered in the early autumn sunshine. Creatures of all kinds and temperament seemed to inhabit the meadow: friendly rabbits and hares, less friendly foxes (often seen in the back garden in late winter) and a couple of charming, almost toothless donkeys that would hang their heads over the nettles to beg for sugar. Although severe rationing made it difficult for me to satisfy their craving, as often as I could I sneaked out through the forbidden archway to them with a lump or two, doing nothing to help their tooth decay in the process.

There was a rough copse on the far side of the meadow, filled with nests, where, a few years later, I would wander for hours, often until dusk, when crepuscular shadows drove me out in panic to race across the field pursued by my own heartbeat to the lights of the cottage.

*

The blacksmith's forge was a mere hundred fantasy-filled yards from my grandmother's tiny cottage. To reach it I had to pass by a long blackthorn hedge that protected the large cornfields beyond, where old and soon-to-be-obsolete Suffolk Punches ambled among the fresh sheaves at harvest time. It was a big hedge, which a small boy could only peek through, not over, and wonderful in September for picking blackberries. Those berries that weren't put straight into my mouth ended up in Nana's jam, stored in earthenware jars in the pantry, later to be smeared thickly on home-made bread with butter shaped by ribbed wooden paddles.

For an independent and inquisitive little boy, the forge was a sufficiently challenging distance from home to become a favourite destination. It was a low, black wooden structure which leaned to one side, as if from fatigue. It had a stable door and a roof of well-worn red and brown tiles, with a good few missing and moss creeping over the rest. Inside, the beams and walls, like the outside, were a heavy creosote black and the whole place reeked of tar.

That smell of creosote has always stayed with me, in the way strong scents of childhood do. Thirty years later, when my then wife, Prue, was pregnant, she developed an almost insatiable appetite for tar and I was regularly dispatched to find a local road-up team and gather some.

'Could I have some tar in this tin, please?'

'What'ya want it for?'

'My wife. She likes eating it.'

'Oh yeah? Bun in the oven?'

Apparently I wasn't the only man ever to have been sent on this eccentric quest, and the pungent smell of tar has always dragged me straight back to the Gravetts Lane forge.

Then, to me, it was a frightening place in some ways, but always exciting. An enormous anvil stood stout and solid in the middle of a rough stone floor which was littered with old horseshoes, bits of wrought iron, strange shapers and metal bars of various lengths and profiles. I was transfixed by the roar of the blazing kiln and the vicious clang of a 4lb hammer on red-hot iron, scattering sparks into a fiery halo around the smith's bulky forearms.

His dark, gypsy face and scrubby black beard reminded me of a pirate's. It was the kind of face that we see no more, a real rawhide, working face, on which every sweat-ridden moment was etched in furrows around the eyes and mouth. He always wore a long leather apron, gleaming with use, and a flat cap, threadbare and grimy.

The forge has long gone, of course. I used to have a small square black-and-white photograph of it in an unglazed frame, but by the time I'd reached sixty that had also disappeared, either with removal men or through my own carelessness. I'm sorry to say the blacksmith's name has gone, too, but I do remember he was always friendly to me. He would keep an eye on me and send me home when he thought it was time.

In any case, my mother always knew where to find me. I'd be hanging over the bottom of the stable door, where I would gaze happily for hours, chatting idly and prodding him with questions. He always answered, though he seldom took his eyes off his work, other than for an occasional pull on an earthenware bottle which dangled on a piece of cord nearby.

Sometimes he did stop and sit for a moment, when he would open a big old biscuit tin with a picture of some stately palace on the top and faded, dented portraits of deceased members of the royal family on the sides. He would take out a cheese sandwich and wrap his face around it while the bread turned black in his hands. I was strictly not allowed to eat bread with dirty hands, much though I would have liked to. When I told the smith, he was disparaging. 'You got to eat a peck of dirt afore you die.'

I think he was right. It's certainly true that in an average lifetime you'll probably have to eat a great deal of shit – particularly if you decide to become an actor – so you may as well get used to it early and build up antibodies. Now I think of him fondly as a revered caricature, like an N. C. Wyeth illustration for *Treasure Island*, Blind Pew tapping down the lane to the Admiral Benbow. I guess he represented perma-nence and security in my tiny life. Certainly, when sirens wailed, this favourite shelter seemed to get more use than the cupboard under the stairs in the cottage.

I still loved the meadow, though, and once, when my forays into the forbidden lands were accepted, I found the field looking as beautiful as ever but with something strange about it. At first glance, it looked as if there were blue, man-sized lumps dotted about the grass.

I was accustomed to seeing the odd walker in the field, and certainly painters, since my mother's father had been head attendant at Brookwood Mental Hospital and he used to bring some of the patients over to paint in the meadow as therapy. He had died a couple of years before the war, but the tradition had been kept up. They produced beautiful miniature watercolours. When my mother showed me her collection of them after I'd developed an interest in painting, I thought it very strange that they were *all* so small.

'It's quite usual,' she said. 'It's something in the normal mind that sees things bigger than they really are. They always paint things as tiny as they look in the distance. Their paintings are like stamps.' And they were truly minuscule, but so incredibly crafted that they were best looked at through a magnifying glass. I would spend hours bending over them and, although I don't believe I could ever have painted anything so small, they did a great deal to fire up my own enthusiasm for painting early in life.

Whether my mother's clinical diagnosis as to their cause was sound or not I have no idea, but she could be very emphatic about that sort of thing.

However, the blue bumps in the field this time weren't painters.

Mac called out to them from behind me. *'Buon giorno!'* He put a hand on my shoulder and looked down to reassure me. 'Itie POWs. They're picking up stones. It gives them something to do.'

They got to their feet and ambled over to us. Mac pulled some lunch from a paper bag – sandwiches and a large bottle of home-brewed beer. He also produced a packet of tobacco and some papers. It was all very friendly as they jabbered away in an unintelligible language – a precursor to my weeks spent on a film set with Antonioni two decades later.

At the time, though, I was deeply puzzled. I was sure that people became prisoners because they were crooks, Italian or otherwise, and it followed that they should have been chained to each other and regularly flogged, not having a high old time of it, with beer, fags and dinner with the enemy. That didn't seem any kind of a punishment to a three-year-old, and I could only stand there, eyes wide with excitement at the sight of these new inhabitants at the end of the garden. I had no idea, of course, that this was to be the first of many connections with Italians, leading to a love of their culture, their language, their art, their wines and food that has never waned.

The war ended and my father arrived to drive us from our pointless evacuation in Gravetts Lane to live, once again, in Alpine Avenue, Tolworth, a deeply grey place of dwellings just a cut above a council house. Ours was a small detached villa on an 'estate' in which all the gates were the same, all the front doors the same but for colour, and each slender front garden distinguishable only by the horticultural skills of whoever tended it. My mother was very fond of roses, which piled our fence. She pruned them to within an inch of their lives, so they grew better and stronger, to the great envy of the daisies plopping over the other fences in the street. She looked after her garden with a firm purpose, a handful of green fingers and a fag – a Players' Weight – drooping from her lips and colouring the underside of her nose a nicotine gold.

As I mentioned earlier, my father had been a pianist in a dance band before the war. (When I was a youngster, everything seemed to have happened 'before the war', as if time had stopped and the war had cancelled all future prospects.) After he came home from his duties with the RAF, when I was about four, he was in uniform, I think to make clear to everyone that he'd done his bit before quitting.

He was short, grinning and bitter. He knew he couldn't go back to dance bands – the economy wasn't up to creating a demand for them – but somehow he had to provide for his family, which he earnestly set about doing. He reluctantly took a job selling carbon paper and ribbons for Caribonum – Carbons and Ribbons Bonum – whose little badge he wore every day on a lapel of his suit.

His principal source of refuge from life's drudgery was playing the piano, usually a Victorian upright at his parents' house (we didn't have one at home). Every weekend we would drive to Woking in his old Riley, which smelt of fresh leather and the old blankets my mother put in the back to keep me warm. It was registered ALB 196, a number plate I shall always remember. To my bitter disappointment, my father later changed it for a Vauxhall Victor, of which he was very proud. But I had learned to pretend to drive on the Riley, grabbing at the gear stick and generally interfering in a life-threatening way, and I'd become very fond of it.

Within the narrow horizon of my child's mind, driving in the old Riley to Redstacks, my father's parents' house in Goldsworth Road, Woking, was the major event of the week. It was only eighteen miles, though it will give you some idea of my parents' anal nature that they treated it as a major trek.

My grandmother, Nancy Hemmings, who ran Redstacks, seemed more fond of her lodgers than of her family. She had started taking them in during the war, whether for reasons fiscal or public-spirited, I don't know, but the habit had stuck. She ruled the roost at the local branch of the WRVS (Women's Royal Voluntary Service), which gave her first choice of lodgers, and I think she enjoyed a little vicarious status by picking the most cultivated of them. Sam Hinchcliffe was an artist, while Leslie Brickman was a fabric designer working at Courtaulds, known to the neighbours as 'Fancy-Pants', on account of his somewhat exotic air and his habit of sunbathing in the garden wearing only a pair of very small and decorative swimming trunks.

Nancy was a heavy woman, grey and bespectacled, and always something of an enigma to me. She was not an obviously warm person and the closest she came to kindness was tolerance. She was barely even tolerant of Auntie Bec, a live-in relation of ninety and obscure dynastic connection. Auntie Bec was a Cook and, I discovered eventually, my grandmother's aunt, but I'd always been told there was some kind of tension between the Cook family and the Hemmingses. Certainly, when it came to Arthur Cook, Bec's son, a vitriolic loathing was quite undisguised.

But whatever my grandmother's perceived shortcomings, we seldom missed a Sunday ride to Woking because my father loved to play the piano there for hours, his fingers racing up and down the keys with tuneful grace while he lost himself in a world of his own improvisation.

My grandfather, Percy Hemmings, unlike my father in almost every way, was a master carpenter of great talent. He was also quite a boozer, but he knew how to deal with it. And I loved him a lot. He liked to tell me that life was a pleasure to be endured but not revered, though he might have been referring to my grandmother. He made wonderful furniture and drank Guinness by the bucketful. He was an expert on the precise depth of head a good pint of stout should carry, and drank each one in a single heave, letting it gurgle down his throat like a storm down a drainpipe. He often bemoaned the Guinness produced in England, claiming that the true stuff was made only with water from the River Liffy in Dublin. Perversely, at the same time, he always said he couldn't abide the Irish.

While my father was playing the piano on a Sunday morning, Grandfather would be making furniture in his work-shed at the end of a long garden. I liked to go out and see him, passing a line of apple trees from which I would scrump a few ripe young Cox's on the way. His balding head with its halo of drifting white hair was a source of wonder to me, and I loved the smell of wood shavings and the way he gently pushed a chisel across the surface of a block of mahogany, his hands flowing over the wood like a snake charmer's. He loved showing me how he worked and the intricacies of the dovetail joint or the mortise and tenon. I still don't understand them, but I enjoyed him hugely, so I pretended to listen and learn.

In the course of my life I have been asked, like most husbands, to build a shelf or two. Mine invariably seem to threaten the lives of children, collapsing on their beds in the early hours, and it's clear to me that skills in carpentry are not inherited. I fully appreciate now that my grandfather was a truly gifted man who loved his work and considered it an art. The Department of Agriculture and Fisheries at Pirbright still pull out drawers in their offices that flawlessly return and fit in perfect harmony with the other thousand that 'Pop' made. And children at schools all over the country still sit at desks individually hand-crafted by him.

But after a morning's work in his old shed in Woking, once finished and satisfied with what he'd done, Pop would pull a black bottle from a pile of sawdust and suck a long draft from its neck. Methodically, he would stow his tools in their individual places, each hugged by nails or hooks set in the long planks of the back wall, and sigh heavily, replacing his porter in its cache.

'Don't you go telling Grandma about the stout,' he would warn sternly.

Reaching out to give a final stroke to whatever wood he'd been working on, he heaved himself off his stool and set off for the pub, the Goldsworth Arms.

If it was early, and it often was, I would be pulled unwillingly to the Baptist Chapel by Auntie Bec. As soon as the service was over, though, I'd run along to join my grandad, and my father, who'd already be in the pub too. He wouldn't come to chapel; I didn't know why then, but much later, my mother told me about his younger brother, Leslie.

When they were boys, my father took Leslie to Sunday school in Woking each week, but one day my father played truant, leaving his brother at the school while he went over the road to sit in a small café. When Leslie came out of church, he knew where my father was. While he was trotting across the road to meet him, he was run down by a car and instantly killed.

The guilt my father felt for the part he played in this disaster never left him and must have contributed to the bitterness which afflicted him for as long as I knew him. This was reflected in an unforgiving hardness in the way he dealt with me. Of course, it's only at a distance of many years that one finally comes to recognise the full extent of one's parents' shortcomings, especially when there's no comparative measure available. That my father physically chastised me as much as he did was, for me, the norm, although I learned later in life that my mother's family had seriously considered calling in the NSPCC.

He had another fearsome habit of coming into my bedroom in the dark, often when I was already asleep, and uttering a terrifying growl or ghoulish howl. It seemed to be his idea of a joke to frighten the daylights out of his small son, just so he could tell me that everything was all right really. It's alarming to conjecture whether or not he knew just how intensely he scared me, but I suspect he did. I can only hope it never occurred to him how afflicted I would become as a result of the experience. Ever since, and to this day, I can hardly sleep, and never without a visible light in the room.

But in the Goldsworth Arms, he could forget all his woes and relive his pre-Caribonum, pre-war career as a dance-band musician and play the piano, with me beside him, singing.

My dad loved playing. I believe it was his only true joy and, although he never showed it, I'm sure he felt very proud that I was standing there beside him and knew every song by heart. I could sing anything he played. I was only six when we first did it, but I could hit an E above top C with a clarity and pitch that must have been pretty devastating, and I suppose you could call the Goldsworth Arms the seedbed of my theatrical career.

I was skinny and slight in every way, shy and barely educated, but the undemanding audience in the pub thought I could sing. Sometimes I would sing night after night, only just peeking over the piano keys, but I loved every moment of it. The splatter of applause, the bellows of encouragement, the smell of beer, the lurch of the drunks were, for me, my first taste of the stage and the warm approbation of an audience. Although a few years later, after a great deal of formal training, I had the opportunity to sing in highly professional circumstances, I believe now that I never sang better than I did with my father in the pub. It was partly, I think, because I wanted to please him, and I'm sure I did, but in all his life he never told me so.

If that sounds a tad self-pitying, I am conscious that I gained other advantages by performing in the Goldsworth Arms: I also learned to play darts and snooker, and it was at the Arms that I discovered the true value of English pubs and the people who inhabit them. I learned, too, to like these people for themselves and whatever they had to offer, whether or not they were inarticulate or lurching drunk. I still play darts and snooker today, and not infrequently with those whose ability to walk has been temporarily impaired by alcohol.

Another benefit I had from our trips to Redslacks was the presence there of Granny's much-favoured lodger Sam Hinchcliffe. He was the art teacher at Woking Grammar School and evidently deeply committed to this calling. Once he'd recognised that I had at least an interest in painting pictures, he set about doing all he could to develop it. He taught me most of the basics that I have applied ever since in a long secondary career as a painter. He encouraged me by telling me stories as he drew them on great big sheets. He impressed on me the importance of observation and draughtsmanship, and that I should sometimes forget the rules and let my emotions express themselves directly through painting. It seems to me that without the serendipity of his presence in my grandmother's house, I would surely have missed out on the huge pleasure I've derived from my painting, as an end in itself and as an antidote to the crushing frustrations and sometimes rank boredom that surround the making of movies.

I was also, to some extent, spurred on by my admiration for my mother's own considerable skill as an artist. Totally untrained, she was quite an accomplished watercolourist; she worked in oils, too, but her true medium, extraordinarily, was icing sugar. People came from far and wide to have her decorate their cakes and she could produce a cluster of tiny, delicately petalled sugar roses on demand. She also won many prizes for some of the most spectacular works of icing art I've ever seen.

I suppose I was about five when I started my formal education, such as it was. First days at school are hideous and I remember well setting off in a *Just William* sort of outfit – grey flannel shorts and a cap – for the walk from Alpine Avenue, down Knollmead, across the Hogsmill River and then the long, slight climb of half a mile or so through sparse woodland, up to Malden Manor Primary. Perhaps the first walk to school is the longest that any of us ever take. Aged five, are we ready for it?

It must depend to some degree on what skills we already possess. I could read, which would surely have helped a bit. I was a talker, although I'm uncertain if that was good or bad.

I told my mother before I left that my tummy felt funny.

'There's butterflies in it,' she said.

That puzzled me. An appreciation of butterflies, which has stayed with me for life, was established even then, but not pinned or in my stomach. I also hated underpants and I wasn't affectionate towards socks. Or feet. Or toenails. Or teeth. Teeth very especially, since I had worn plates to shift my gross molars about, and had a dentist who might just as well have lived in with us, given the amount of time I spent in his suspiciously frightening chair. Not to mention the bus fares.

At first, school was a source of unbelievable fear to me, the same fear that I would feel regularly throughout my professional life, until I discovered I could get out of being teased or bullied by using my ability to tell a story or two. And so the seeds of a career that had been sown in the bar of the Goldsworth Arms continued to thrive. I soon learned that, as in the pub, there was both kudos and personal satisfaction to be gained from entertaining others. I was often called on to tell tales I made up about a physically flawed creature called Ally Alligator. And I was beginning to hone my verse-writing skills, targeting them, for optimum audience response, at our kind-hearted teacher, Mrs Selly:

Old Ma Selly, with a bamboo belly,
and her tits tied up with string,
lying on the grass with a trumpet up her arse,
playing 'God Save the King'.

(It was still five years before our current queen succeeded to the throne.)

As far as I can remember, I was never chastised for this gross slur on a dedicated teacher, but the headmaster, Mr Vine, did once find it necessary to deliver six short, hard whacks on my hand with his cane for lurking in the girls' lavatories. However, my fascination with this female territory, and whatever mysterious things went on within, was in no way diminished, which may come as some comfort to educationalists of a PC persuasion.

The daily walk to school could also provide its challenges. A boy called Victor Choules was with me one day. We had something in common, in that both our mothers worked as dinner ladies at the school. In a spirit of boastfulness, he told me that he had a half a crown, which he showed me. Not to be outdone, I told him I had two. I took one from my pocket, the only one I had, and, in an elaborate display of ineptness, tried to convince him that I had two.

Victor didn't find my antics amusing. He quickly became truculent and abusive, until he was so angry he started to walk away, before turning abruptly and punching me in the eye. He ran off, jeering, while I, humiliated and in pain, decided to bunk off school and go home. I spent the rest of the day planning my revenge. Before Victor was due to walk back from school, I climbed a big elm tree whose branches dangled over the path at Hogsmill Bridge and lay in wait, clutching a house brick in my small, sweaty hand. The plan worked like a dream. He had no inkling that I was stretched along a branch, concealed among its foliage, in a perfect position to drop the brick on his head as he passed. I waited with the concentration of a Lancaster bomber pilot and released it straight on to his crown. He crumpled as if struck by a sledgehammer and fell unconscious on the bridge.

Like all good stories of wicked deeds, the wrongdoer suffered in the end. Victor was found and taken to our house, the nearest that he knew, and once he was fully revived my mother insisted on him having my whole collection of Marvel comics to make up for the pain and indignity he'd suffered. I couldn't bring myself to speak to him for at least a week.

I never did have many friends in Tolworth – my father strongly discouraged them – but in Woking, next door to Redstacks, lived a couple called Goodchild, with an only son, Peter, who was a year younger than me. Peter became a very good friend and we would spend hours together, roaming the railway lines, where I did a *little* train-spotting, patrolling the Basingstoke Canal and wandering through the huge Slococks nurseries, from which my grandfather Percy's fruit trees were said to have arrived clandestinely.

With some insistent urging from me, Peter was game for the kind of bad behaviour I frequently proposed. He was doubtful, though, when I suggested a little minor shoplifting or insisted that we break into a small secondary modern school just beyond the fence at the end of the garden. Once inside, we didn't take anything, but he was shocked when I drew a very large penis and testicles on the blackboard for the edification of the children next morning. I had undoubtedly become interested in girls and the tantalising gifts they offered much sooner than he. Peter wouldn't come in with me when we found a frankly pretty tame and rudimentary strip show at a fair in Byfleet, and not just because it was a quid a go (an enormous amount of money). But although I was just thirteen, and obviously so, I was determined to get in; and I did, while Peter waited patiently outside, and I was able, of course, to exaggerate freely in my account of what was on offer within the walls of damp, murky canvas.

We were both enthusiastic shots, using my air rifle, although Peter didn't always approve of my choice of targets. On one occasion, when I'd been allowed to have him to stay at home in Alpine Avenue, I had an idea to shoot all the pegs off the washing line next door. We did brilliantly, until the whole thing collapsed, and the neighbours came round and ranted at my parents, leading to an interminable fuss and discussion before the inevitable physical chastisement.

After I'd been singing at the Goldsworth Arms for a year or so, my first truly public performance took place in Cliftonville, near Margate. This was, and may still be, a frankly unexciting resort where my father took us to stay for the occasional Christmas or summer holiday. I enjoyed it much more when I revisited it just about half a century later, in order to make *Last Orders*. At the first hint of salt spray and a howling onshore gale, I found I loved to stand in the blustering, trouser-soaking rain while Bob Hoskins, Tom Courtenay and Ray Winstone were cowering inside the nearest boozer.

When I went there as a child, I would sing with my father, as usual, anywhere he could find a piano that was reasonably in tune – at the hotel in the evenings, in a pub at lunchtime. The spectacle of a small, innocent boy singing lustily alongside his father was enough to appeal to holidaymakers with low expectations and we soon built up a reputation in the town. I was just as interested in the ice-cream and sweet stalls that lined the promenade, but when my father spotted a poster proclaiming that a sea-front dance hall was holding a talent competition, he entered us, more for fun than anything else, on a wet afternoon. I was to deliver Norman Wisdom's 'Don't Laugh at Me ('Cos I'm a Fool)'. I'd sung it dozens of times and knew it well. In those low-tech times, the competition was judged by the compère holding up a handkerchief behind each contestant while the audience showed their comparative appreciation with the volume of their applause. Amazingly, we scored a resounding victory and I was given a small tin globe as a prize (this was firmly placed on the mantelpiece at home, never to be spun except in geographical emergencies – like, where on earth's Malta?). My father, proud as Pickwick, decided that, rather than throw away a talent which he guessed I was mis-using by singing in the smoky pubs of Woking, my voice should be properly trained and looked after. And soon after our success in Cliftonville I was packed off for twice-weekly lessons with a singing teacher in Twickenham.

Lisette Brooks had a reputation for training young voices to glory. When I started with her she was in her late fifties, an ardent, fiery creature with alarming pink hair. She insisted that I learn the piano as well as singing – an unattractive prospect for a young lad of spirit, I felt, but there was no resisting my father's edict. She would crouch beside me at the keyboard with a piercing stare as I did scale after scale for what seemed like an eternity. In fact, I was to be with her for almost four years, at the end of which I was still singing early scales and the traditional airs of a boy soprano, though now with considerably more panache and professionalism. Sadly, however, I didn't persevere with the piano, which I've regretted more as I've grown older.

I'd spent a dutiful year or so at her side, making the tedious bus journey to her place after a long school day twice a week without fail, when she decided I should be entered, tentatively, for some of the local music festivals – Heston and Isleworth, Richmond and Twickenham – way down the pecking order of such musical events. If we had any luck there, she said, we might venture further afield and attempt the larger and more prestigious affairs held in Kingston and Wimbledon.

These festivals were great institutions, wonderfully encouraging outlets for young children and a fine entry platform for the performing arts. At the same time, children sometimes came under tremendous pressure. At festival after festival, we saw the same faces, the same pushy, competitive and desperately aggressive mothers who, when their offspring triumphed, would swagger with the kind of misplaced pride that Ethel Merman had for Baby June in *Gypsy*.

I was lucky to avoid that sort of thing. My parents didn't expect me to win; I think they were simply happy to see me utilising a gift. Their attitude was so downbeat that my father insisted on playing the piano for me at every event, despite the disastrous consequences this sometimes led to. Although within the context of his usual playing, he was a good pianist, he wasn't in any sense classically trained. He'd learned how to play from a set of famous tutorial books put out by pianist Billy Mayerl. His method relied heavily on a solid bass hand and plenty of syncopation, an area of music not well thought of by the adjudicators at traditional music festivals.

My father would painstakingly learn the piece from the sheet music, then get to know it well enough to play it by memory, with the music on the piano as a rough guide. While this approach might have been fine for tunes from *Show Boat*, it could make a terrible hash of the Bach-Gounod *Ave Maria*.

Nevertheless, the judges seldom seemed to mind, and we began to win consistently, going home with medals, cups and encyclopaedias galore. From time to time, an adjudicator would refer to my father's piano technique with the strong implication that, 'This child has a wonderful voice and a great talent – pity about the pianist.'

As the competitions grew harder and it became acknowledged that I was, for the moment, *the* young soloist to beat, pressure was brought to bear on my father to relinquish the accompanist's seat to Lisette Brooks. This came to a head when a judge in Wimbledon told us bluntly and publicly that I needed a 'proper pianist'. My father was from then on relegated to watching with the audience and swiftly lost interest in my singing, and indeed my subsequent career.

But then, I wasn't too happy about this more formal approach, although my relentless, precocious rise continued, making me a sort of young Tiger Woods of the singing circuit.

My father took to staying at home. My mother still came and watched, but, win or not, we always came back to a sour, uninterested household, and that was how it would remain for the rest of my father's life.

Lisette Brooks, on the other hand, continued to work on my voice with great vigour, refining it and finding greater depth. She wanted me to develop a rounder tone, a larger range, more 'quality'.

While my musical career progressed, my academic education had taken a serious turn for the worse. I spent so much of my time travelling to Twickenham or festivals that there was little left for book learning. This became even more acute when Lisette suggested I should audition for the Hampton Court Palace Chapel Royal choir. Along with Westminster and St Paul's, it was one of the most highly regarded sacred choirs in the country and the choir master, Mr Reynolds, was looked upon as the very best.

The gateway to Hampton Court is awesome even to a casual tourist, but to the small boys of the choir the portals are truly formidable. Stories of Anne Boleyn's ghost wandering the stairways at night, carrying her head under her arm, were in constant circulation and it was an unhappy chorister who found himself late after practice on a winter's evening walking the long, dim cloisters towards the infamous Anne Boleyn's Gateway.

I didn't want to join the choir at all, but I was given no choice, and this was made harder by the fact that, unlike the other boys, who led a relatively sane life, I was always having to rush off to music festivals, to carve a name for myself and gain experience. But having passed Reynolds's severe audition, the kudos of being in the Chapel Royal choir was too great to overlook. It was a considerable concession and, I suppose, a measure of Reynolds's view of my voice that I didn't have to attend the choir school proper for the traditional six months before being received into the choir. I was allowed to take my place in the stalls immediately and had to pick up the finer points of ecclesiastical life as I went along. This wasn't made any easier, though, by the boys, all of whom resented this upstart from Tolworth and used every chance to show it.

Choirboys, as a species, must rank among the most vicious and least God-fearing of any company of individuals you're likely to find outside a football ground. The Chapel Royal boys wasted no time in showing what they thought of me. Hymn books were stolen, crib sheets went missing, orders for the wrong Sunday would be placed in my locker, and there'd never be time to look for the right one during the mad panic to clamber into cassock and surplice and to attach a fiddly starched collar.

But I wouldn't be cowed and was determined to survive. Gradually, at Reynolds's behest, I moved along the choir stall towards the soloist's spot, and it seemed that whenever a special solo was to be delivered at a particular ceremony, I was chosen. I was small, disgustingly cherubic and had a voice that was remarkable for my size.

I don't say this boastfully, because I know my voice itself wasn't top flight in the traditional sense. It was thinner than most, but high, with a fine range. It also lacked the round quality that is naturally expected from a boy soprano. I couldn't deliver those oval plummy 'O's, which don't convince me, even today, though it was certainly considered the right way for young trebles to sing then, particularly within a choir. But the pub singing with my father had given my voice an extra quality which was far more helpful in making it work for an audience: I could *act* a song.

I'd realised very early in my singing career that the words of a song were all-important in the telling of the story. And to sing a good standard torch song, which, after all, had been my foundation, you have to *sell* it. I could sell a song, sell 'Panis Angelicus' or 'Where e'er You Walk', as if I were leaning against a piano in a seedy bar, weaving a story. I think it was this that added an element of risk to my voice that wasn't part of the standard choirboy training. It brought a maturity to a young face and body that must have been unusual and a little unnerving, as this small, plaintive creature reached an audience with fine music in a way that they could feel, beyond normal technical judgements.

It was while I was singing at the International Eisteddfod in Llangollen, North Wales, in the summer of 1953 that Lisette Brooks came to the conclusion that I was getting more attention than was good for a boy of my age and it was perhaps time to test me by throwing me in among the professionals of the real musical world.

My father was against the idea from the start, but I'd already realised that his attitude to my singing – and me – had been utterly soured by resentment at being left out of the picture. My mother, however, stood by me and supported my every move with love, attention and sensible strictness. She had the advantage, I feel, of being slightly, if pleasantly, mad, which helped her bridge the gap between these hard divided loyalties with never a cross murmur.

4

The Turn of the Screw, 1953

Towards the end of 1953, Lisette Brooks heard that Benjamin Britten had put out a call across the music world to find a boy treble to play the part of Miles in his new opera, *The Turn of the Screw*. The English Opera Group, who were to perform the work, had been holding auditions up and down the country, and Lisette suggested that I should go to one at the Scala Theatre in London. Unenthusiastic about the idea, I perfunctorily passed on the message to my parents and did nothing to goad them into action. When Lisette phoned them a week later to see what had happened, my mother had to confess that she knew nothing about it. Lisette urged my mother to ring the English Opera Group right away, because the final audition was on Saturday. Without much commitment, my mother made the call.

'Sorry,' a woman at the EOG told her, 'the list is closed.'

'Oh, well, it doesn't really matter,' my mother replied.

'What singing has your boy done anyway?' she was asked kindly, to soften the disappointment.

My mother outlined my experience to date.

'Just a minute please.' A few moments later the woman was back on the line, asking if I could come to the audition on Saturday and what I could sing.

My mother quickly blurted out that I knew 'Where e'er You Walk'.

'And we'll want him to recite something, too.'

'I think he knows "O, to be in England".'

'That will do nicely.'

As Mum put the phone down, I had to correct her, thinking that this audition was going wrong already. 'There's no such poem as "O, to be in England". It's called "Home Thoughts from Abroad", and I don't know it properly.'

*

My memory of the audition is of a vast stage in the middle of which stood a small boy, very conscious that in the audience sat Benjamin Britten, arguably the finest living British composer. Beside him, as always, was Peter Pears. With them was perched the eccentric, vibrant and scatty Imogen Holst, daughter of Gustav, composer of the *Planets Suite*, huddled in conversation with Myfanwy Piper, librettist and wife of the painter John Piper, whose work adorns our great cathedrals. Myfanwy and Imogen had an alarming, witch-like presence and would have looked quite at home in the Scottish play, crouched over a cauldron, casting spells with eye of newt and adder's fork. Also visible to the small boy on the stage when the house lights came up was the producer, Basil Coleman, sitting aloof in a tweed jacket, tie and cords, a symphony in autumn colours, curly-haired and tall, protruding above the seats as if he were standing.

I couldn't see any of this to start with, of course – just the vast spotlight directed full on me and the great wall of darkness beyond. It was my first taste of stage lighting, since music festivals and Sunday services tended to be well lit all round. But I came to know these people so well, I could imagine them, watching each nervous applicant step out for their appraisal.

However, I was, strangely, not the slightest bit nervous, such is the pluck of the young, even when I looked down and discovered with a shock that my shoelaces had untied themselves. Taking great care not to trip over them, I made my way confidently to the centre of the stage. In an unprecedented gesture, Lisette Brooks had offered to accompany me, then relinquished that responsibility at the last moment to the pianist provided. She sat in the wings chewing her nails, while my mother looked the other way with the inevitable Players' Weight dangling untouched from her lips, spreading smoke across her upper lip – a familiar and much-loved visage.

I sang 'Where e'er You Walk' and recited Robert Browning's poem. Then it was over. From the auditorium there came a brief 'Thank you', but the words carried such unmistakable overtones of congratulation that I knew I'd done well. I'd found that I could tell my mark at a festival, almost to a percentage point, by the tone of those words from an adjudicator. Children in particular can judge tones to a whisker. Their security level or even their survival in a family structure depends on it. It's a shame we most of us lose a skill that should be nurtured for life – the art of listening.

*

Several days later, to Lisette's astonished rapture, we were called to be told that I was being offered the part of Miles. I'm sure now that it was the ability to sell a song, which I had used to such great effect in the Goldsworth Arms, in the Chapel Royal and in not a few competitions since, that had persuaded Benjamin Britten I might be right for Miles in his new opera. However, this would be confirmed only after I had met the composer himself and had a session with him.

Today the suggestion that I should have a 'session' with Benjamin Britten would be a questionable way of putting it, and eyebrows would be raised. But then, without any cynical overtones, it was a source of pure delight to me. My schooling was, for all practical purposes, to be abandoned for the foreseeable future. I was to sing professionally with the English Opera Group, no less, and move to Aldeburgh to live with the great man himself while he wrote the final opera around the voices he had cast.

My father listened moodily to all the excitement surrounding the arrangements. He uttered only one observation: 'He's a homo.'

From this distance, it's not easy to imagine what a sudden induction like this into the rarefied world of opera might mean to a twelve-year-old from Tolworth. To me it didn't only mean a move away from home, into what my father averred was a distinctly sinister environment; it also meant that I was now surrounded constantly by adults, not by my contemporaries, children to play with who might have become friends for life. I didn't even have any friends back in Tolworth to whom I could write about the curiosities of my new life. It was one of the many strange aspects of my father that he never let me have friends of my own. Our neighbours were almost always 'not good enough' and not allowed in the house.

To a maturity that was already some way beyond my years was added the discovery of a world that neither my parents nor friends like Peter Goodchild in Woking could even contemplate. Because of the demanding nature of the role, the pressure of rehearsals and the delicately balanced finances of the English Opera Group, I was considered to be one of the players. I was thus encouraged to demonstrate a responsibility far beyond my experience; to behave like an adult and expect to be treated like one.

*

I had my session with Britten, as agreed – a full day in his flat near Regent's Park. He crouched over the piano and played the outline of what was to be Miles's aria, 'Malo'. It occurs in a lesson with the Governess, a scene which has sinister undertones and was to be the centrepiece of the Miles section of the opera. It would also be reprised to great effect in the final moments of the story.

I sang tentatively, reading the pencilled notes from the score in front of him (rather badly, for I was never a good sight reader), and began gradually to learn its tricky phrasing. Britten would change the odd note, rubbing out a previous thought, and we would sing on, interrupted only by tea and crumpets in the mid-afternoon. Peter Pears was there too – looking on, I suppose, in consternation, though he was polite, generous and funny. Their relationship appeared quite natural to me and the atmosphere cosy and elegant in a cluttered way, with books and sheet music carelessly strewn about on every available surface. After the session, my part in the opera was confirmed without it ever needing to be said.

My mother had virtually to abandon me for the time being, leaving me with her normal peck on the cheek at St Pancras to make the journey alone to Saxmundham. Ben, as I was to call Britten always, met me at the station in a big old convertible Alvis which smelt of leather, like my father's Riley. We set off along the country lanes to the coast with the top off and the exhaust purring gently. We didn't talk about opera or singing, but about tea and trains and fishing and East Anglia. Ben loved to laugh and joke and talk, like Nigel Molesworth, of 'chizzes' and 'whizzes' – 'A chiz is a swiz or swindle, as any fule kno.'

With my parents' approval, Ben had adopted the role of my guardian, there to protect me and – as he assured them – keep me out of harm's way. This, to silence all rumours to the contrary, he did with a gentle affection that I'll never forget.

He drove me to Cragge Cottage, on the sea at Aldeburgh. It was a small blue-and-white cottage at the end of a terrace that faced directly out over the North Sea, just along from the wobbly Moot Hall, which stood alone and dark brown in the middle of its own curtilage. The long pebbled strand in front of both the hall and the house was littered with fishing boats and fishermen, mending their nets with long 'perrocks', kind of net-needles that were shuttled between gnarled fingers with a deftness that was guaranteed to deliver arthritis upon them in old age. I would sit on the side of a boat, watching and trying to help when they let me.

I look back on my months with Ben at Aldeburgh with great affection. I still love the place, the uncompromising broad, lofty skies and grey, blustery coast. Most days I would walk up to Marks Tey, captivated by the way the sun lit the Moot Hall in the evenings and the early mornings. The village itself didn't then sparkle with the trappings of tourism. It was a working place, hard on its men and women, with the sea unwilling to yield up its bounty without a fight; the lifeboat resting on its chocks and sliders up on the beach would willingly attest to that.

This was truly the country of *Peter Grimes*, an opera which had been extremely successful for Britten and captured the flavour of the Suffolk psyche to perfection. I had heard a recording of the opera – in fact, all of Britten's works – as part of Lisette Brooks's insistent preparation. I had read the libretto too, a stark and worrying work about the isolation and damnation of a lonely spirit and the foibles of prejudice.

Misunderstood, Peter Grimes was left to perish by his own hand at the whim of merciless waves while the village folk, in a sudden fit of repentance, clambered across the headland, torches flickering in the night, calling for him across the sound of the oncoming storm.

'Peter Grimes!' they call. 'Peter Grimes!' A melancholy air whisked away on the wind, so beautifully described in Britten's urgent and poignant score. Listening to this powerful opera affected me in many ways, perhaps most because even then I felt I understood it. *Peter Grimes* delivers you, after all, the four 'Sea Interludes', extraordinary pieces of evocative music that sound as if they themselves had come humming on the wind, straight off the Suffolk sea, thrashing this minute, calm and sublime the next. The libretto and the music moved me considerably and, short though the opera is, I often come back to it and I never hear of Suffolk without the tale crossing my mind.

I loved the cottage too, confined as it was, with the Alvis parked on the street outside because there wasn't a garage. It was much like the atmosphere of the Regent's Park flat: cosier, perhaps, with more rural furnishings, but still with the clutter and the casual air of the creative soul who needs everything close to hand, in case inspiration should suddenly strike or, worse, fail. If there are two things that evoke memories of the place itself, they are the metronome and the baton, both conspicuous on the piano and both much cherished. I never saw the metronome operate, for some reason, but the baton was always in use, until its end was broken off on the edge of a music stand while we rehearsed in the beautifully gilded, tiny Grand Opera House in Schwetzingen. Ben later gave it to me and it has had pride of place in my collection of musical instruments, where it sulks, no doubt, through lack of a sure hand to guide it through the air.

The cottage became the central rehearsal room for some weeks. I had live-in quarters in a blue-chintz bedroom at the end of the first-floor landing with a chess set underneath the window and a set of Molesworth books by the Malvern water on the bedside table. Others of the cast were in hotels or staying in rented cottages nearby.

Once during my months at Cragge Cottage my parents came to see me. I was very conscious of my father's antagonism towards Ben, and I could only hope, desperately, that it would not surface too obviously. I wanted Dad to see what a kind and funny man Ben was. The four of us went for a walk together along the pebble strand, and at one point, showing me something – I can't remember what – Ben emphasised his remark with a gentle pat on my head.

My father's outrage was palpable. I turned to see him tight-lipped and shaking his head in bitter disapproval. Ben saw it too, and for a moment his own eyes flared with affront at the suggestion that he should in any way take advantage of his position. After that I was in no doubt that Ben thought very little of my father – although, of course, he never told me so – and I couldn't blame him.

Aldeburgh then was already famous for its festival, the product of Britten's own efforts. It's much busier now than in earlier years, but there is still something timeless about it, the Jubilee and Moot Halls and the Suffolk wind, ever prompting one to bring a spare sweater.

If I was frightened when the winds were howling off the North Sea and it was easy to imagine Norse demons prowling across the churning grey waters, I would patter along to Ben's room and creep into his bed for security. I slept with him often, to be sure, when the dark got the better of my sense of reason. It never occurred to me that there was anything untoward about this. Britten had quickly become an important and considerate father figure, making up, perhaps, for the lack of warmth in my own father; certainly he was more interested in my singing and, for that matter, my general well-being.

There was no question of anything that these days would be called 'inappropriate', but I have to say that it's a measure of the cynical, prurient world in which we live now that everyone would assume the worst of him. And I say this after I learned in later life that Ben, who was without question a homosexual, was for a while infatuated with me. Since then there have been many suggestions that our relationship *was* untoward, that Peter Pears was furiously jealous (he was, but I didn't know that until almost forty years later) and that Ben had cast me more for passion and personal favour than for talent. That may have been true, but if so, he was never to show it in any physical way, although there are those who have tried to imply otherwise over the years.

Frankly, I'd been mildly assaulted several times before then, as choirboys will be, and I was very clear about the difference between those odious moments and my closeness to Ben. The seamy man on the 137 trolley bus to Hampton Court Palace, pressing my palm into his groin until a damp stain appeared on his thigh, was a very far cry indeed from anything I remotely encountered at Aldeburgh. (My mother dispatched Mr Bullion, as his name turned out to be, into the hands of the police in a most dashing display of bravado.)

Britten himself stood tall, with a mass of curly, close-cut hair and an anxious frown, from which would sometimes appear a cheeky grin, sometimes a sharp burst of temper, always regretted. While he worked, in a corner sat Imogen Holst, who had been at the audition at the Scala. Her job was quite unfathomable to me. With a blank piece of music manuscript paper in front of her and her grey hair constantly dangling over her eyes like a curtain of whitened string-candy, she would feverishly jot down notes and bar-lines with symbols above or across them, in some indecipherable code, so that the paper would become a mess of pencil marks that looked fit only for chucking in the bin.

Britten would play a note or a chord, or a cadenza, trickily, with sudden flights of musical fantasy, gently returning to his melodic theme almost as if by chance. Then he might stride off again up the keyboard to a complicated aside, muttering in other instruments by way of personal notation, from, say, a bassoon or a cello to a gong. He would do all this to a shaking of his head, a quick retreat, a jump to another thought, a quick pencil mark, then he'd be off again, like a grasshopper traversing a meadow in short, sharp hops before returning to the theme once more, coming home.

Imogen, astonishingly, managed to record all these sorties into the musical unknown on her paper. As fast as he could play, she would write. Looking back, it was an extraordinary achievement on her part, without the luxury of a tape recorder to play back. She could hear a note and, from all 88 on the keyboard, she'd identified it and written it down – not just single notes, but whole chords, and the speed at which they were played, the key in which a sudden flight might be written and so on.

The other singers gradually became part of these piano sessions. They would turn up early in the morning for a breakfast of croissants with an endless supply of fresh coffee, then settle around the piano for long and tiring repetitions of the more tricky passages. After a late lunch, a few might stay on for an afternoon rethink of various passages. Then there might be a day or two off, while Ben worked alone. He was intent on writing the opera specifically for the voices he had, so as not to put pressure on them to bend to awkward or impossible tasks.

At times like these, I was left pretty much on my own. I was supposed to have normal school lessons, according to laws relating to the employment of minors, but they never happened. The company manager, Basil Coleman, had said he would undertake the tutorial duties himself, which was always an unlikely proposition, but he had convinced my father that he would for the four hours a day that the rules demanded. I'd be surprised if I did four hours of official schoolwork during the whole of the time I was rehearsing *The Turn of the Screw*.

The following year, when I was singing in Britten's *Let's Make an Opera*, things were different as there were so many minors on board. Then, as we toured, we would be carted off to a local grammar school, where we were neither taught nor tolerated, though it was enough to satisfy anyone in the Department of Education who might have been watching.

Now I had time to wander, which may seem strange and a little frightening for a twelve-year-old, but I didn't mind a bit. I made friends with the fishermen, who sometimes took me out on calm days or let me sit around with them, or I simply wandered around the countryside nearby.

In some ways my gentle and carefree relationship with the English Opera Group was surprising, because most of the men with whom I found myself were distinctly camp, if not actively gay. In any event, as the opera progressed I became captivated by the delights on offer from the wardrobe mistress, who stroked my shoulders and hair with a wonderful sensuousness. She laid me to rest more than once among the clothing in the costume department and gave me my first experiences of the joys of bodily contact. I was growing up fast.

In general, my abiding impression of the treatment I received in Aldeburgh is overwhelmingly one of kindness from all the adults. Once John Piper, who was designing the set for the opera, came up on the train to Saxmundham. He was very kind and offered to do a drawing for me. He only had a new, expensive Pentel, a piece of chalk and a small pad. He drew a church – part of his design for *The Turn of the Screw* – which I still have.

From time to time my mother would come to visit for a day or two, not getting in the way, but trying to help. Sometimes she would make tea for the odd rehearsal, more so when we moved on to more formal rehearsals at Marks Tey scout hall, a few miles away. Together, then, we got to know better the rest of the cast, all of whom were very protective of us both.

My younger sister in *The Turn of the Screw*, Flora, was played by Olive Dyer, a stage veteran in her late thirties, pretty, vivacious, and about four foot two. Perfect for short roles, so to speak, but I wondered what else she might have played had she been a foot or so taller. By contrast, she was married to Bill, who was a giant, well over six foot and broad too. Even then I wondered about their bedroom configurations, for he could easily have snapped her in two with one bite.

Which, of course, reminds me of Noël Coward's comment at the Coronation that same year, when the Queen of Tonga – all nineteen stone of her – rode gloriously in an open carriage with her tiny finance minister.

'Oh, look!' Coward said with glee as he peered at them both from his balcony overlooking the Mall. 'She's brought her lunch!'

Bill and Olive were terribly in love. They doted on each other and my mother adored them.

Joan Cross, who played the frightened Housekeeper of Bly, was very aloof and quite forbidding. An old hand at this sort of thing, she worked when required but didn't like hanging about. She held considerable sway over the group management, who were manifestly terrified of her. She was very professional, stern and strong, and reminded me of my Auntie Bec, whose aprons I used to untie from the back. Thus I didn't hold Joan in a great deal of awe, though I certainly wouldn't have tied her shoelaces together.

Jennifer Vyvyan was the Governess, perhaps the finest soprano of the time, whose stark aquiline features were a direct contradiction of her charming gentleness. Though I had little to do with her, other than our brief appearances on stage together, her performance in *The Turn of the Screw* was to have a profound effect on my childhood and my attitude to the theatre.

Arda Mandikian was a Greek of Armenian origin, mad, hot-blooded and very eccentric – perfect, you might say, for the role of Miss Jessel, the ghost of governess past. Miss Jessel had died in questionable circumstances after unspeakable steamy wrongdoings with Peter Quint, the ghost of butler past – played, with splendour and a severe threat to the sanity of the innocent new governess, by Peter Pears.

Thus we were assembled, rehearsed and polished until Britten was sure that we were ready to perform. And of all the wonderful cities in the world, the opera was to hold its première in Venice.

5

Venice and a Little
Learning, 1954–1958

It's hard to describe the impression Venice made on a twelve-year-old boy who had never ventured further from home than Margate. I knew no other foreign cities with which to compare it, so I could have believed that all 'abroad' was like Venice. In fact, I didn't. As usual, flexing my incorrigible inquisitiveness, I had pumped everyone for information about the place before we'd left England and was well aware of its unique aquatic thoroughfares and absence of cars.

I set off chaperoned by my mother, who knew no more than me what to expect. I was prepared to be impressed by the place and, inevitably, I was. The English Opera Group were greeted and treated with considerable respect. The Venetians were not so arrogant as not to be pleased, even a little flattered, that a composer of Britten's eminence should have chosen to première his new opera at their city's Biennale that November. As part of the group and, after all, one of only six performers, I was given enough attention to turn the head of any young boy.

Curiously, though, I didn't feel at the time that this was anything special – again, I suppose, because I'd had nothing similar to compare it with. I certainly wasn't treated with the awe that a pre-pubescent Charlotte Church might experience now, with hustling hordes around her, all trying to grab a handful of the potential future earnings of her precocious singing talent.

Our first night at the Gran Teatro La Fenice was, I suppose, an extraordinary experience for a twelve-year-old. At the end of *The Turn of the Screw* Jennifer Vyvyan, the Governess, has reprised the aria that I've just sung – 'Malo, I would rather be, Malo in an apple tree, Malo, than a naughty boy.' Then, when I'm dying in her arms, she sings it again, but instead of being a rather plaintiff, treble voice, it's a full soprano. 'Malo, what have we done between us?' fades away, followed by four chords. As a coda it's an absolute knockout, and I can't remember it that first time without a lump in my throat. The curtain came down and there was not a sound from the audience. I looked up at Jenny, not knowing quite what to expect, and then it started, a few isolated claps that were slowly joined and speeded up, until the entire place erupted.

I was just a tiny boy and the emotion I felt gave me the most astonishing rush, as it built up to a massive standing ovation. We took a dozen curtain calls and, like any performer, I've never completely lost my taste for it.

After the performance, the Mayor of Venice (in the absence of a Doge, no doubt) threw a reception for us, where I was plied with orange juice and presented with a Märklin train set. All of us, especially me, were so high on adrenalin from the reaction to our performance that none of us could go to bed, and we decided to walk down to the Grand Canal, by the Doge's Palace.

While the festival was going on, the Piazza San Marco had a stage in the middle with seating all around it, but at two in the morning, when we walked into it, there was not a soul to be seen. My mother had gone to bed, and the adults in the cast were looking after me. I had no intention of missing out on whatever was happening and I certainly wasn't going to bed, although I'd been asked to several times.

We sat on the seats in the deserted square, listening to the peace of the night and the water lapping at the side of the canal. Arda Mandikian suddenly jumped up on to the small stage. She was the most extraordinary, fiery woman who, from her passion and demeanour, could have come from another planet. Now she stood in the middle of the stage, threw her head back and, in her rich chocolate voice, began to sing folk songs from Greece.

The acoustics in the square when it was empty were powerful and Arda's voice echoed off the tall, dark, elegant faces of the colonnaded buildings all around. I could hardly believe what I was hearing. I was with adults; I had shared the supreme experience of singing with them that night and from the first moment of Arda's extraordinary impromptu performance, in a subtle way, I aged several years. As her voice rang out around the *piazza*, one by one the shutters on the buildings began to open, and under the cloisters, people emerged from the side streets until, in the end, perhaps a thousand of them were gathered, utterly silent, not moving, or applauding, because they knew that she was singing not for them, but for herself.

She sung for over an hour, in Greek – which none of us, or the Venetians, could understand – but her voice was so sublime as it echoed around the ancient square, it was impossible not to be strongly moved by it.

When she finished, it was clear that she'd had no idea so many had been listening. She looked around, touched her fingers to her lips and everyone waved back. It was an absolutely unforgettable night.

It never occurred to me then that my mother must have been utterly out of her depth on a trip like this with the English Opera Group in Venice, although I'm sure she must have had some strategy for dealing with it and, anyway, would not have let her discomfort show.

When we weren't performing, I was allowed to wander round the narrow streets and alleyways, as enchanted as anyone by the fairy-tale notion of people getting around in gondolas instead of cars. Even then it occurred to me that Venice's charms lay as much in the complete lack of Fiat Cinquecentos clogging up the streets, and the para-phernalia that motor traffic demands, as in the greasy-looking and slightly whiffy waterways.

In narrow, flaky-walled canyons I found glass-blowers buried in hot little rooms, and I stood and watched fascinated as the resulting artefacts (some of them spectacularly foul) began to take shape. There was an aura of the magician or creator about the glass-blowers, turning small lumps of glass into various species of Baroque Bambi and chubby dolphin.

Most of the cast, the twelve-piece orchestra and the production team did their best to put me at my ease and teach me the ways of the performing world, an education that inevitably advanced my outlook on life. There were, in any event, some scenes that would have raised the brow of the most cynical adult.

As well as Jennifer Vyvyan looking after me with such gentleness, there was the lovely harpist, Edith Simon, who, incongruously even to my young eye, liked to relax after a performance with a pipe full of sticky black shag.

By the time my mother and I arrived back in England, I was feeling I'd aged a lot more than the few months I'd been away. My experience on stage had confirmed to both of us that I had a promising future in performance, for the time being in singing. To my disappointment, my father feigned little interest in what I'd been doing. I was puzzled and hurt by his attitude, although it didn't then occur to me to blame him. I thought it must be my fault – that I simply wasn't coming up to his high standards. I spent many years after that trying to prove to him that I was making a good job of what I was doing, although I'm sure he was never convinced.

Back in Tolworth, I was also greeted by my first experience of press coverage – albeit only in the *Children's Newspaper* and the *Surrey Advertiser* – and thus my first exposure to the difference between actuality and what the papers say. I learned, for instance, that I spent most of my free time at home mending bicycles and tending five white mice in the garden shed, which was news to me.

It was decided, despite my father's previous misgivings about the composer's sexual proclivities, that I should carry on working with Britten. With the English Opera Group I sang in several more of his works: *Ceremony of Carols*, *Saint Nicholas* and *Let's Make an Opera (The Little Sweep)*. In the last of these I was understudied by Michael Crawford, and, looking back, I could never have guessed then that he would go on to play roles as diverse as Frank Spencer in *Some Mothers Do 'Ave 'Em* and the Phantom in *Phantom of the Opera* – about as unimaginable then as me playing Thomas in *Blow-Up*, I suppose.

I haven't seen Michael for years, but we were good friends then, and worked together again on the television series of *Billy Bunter*. It was also he who encouraged me, aged thirteen, in my pursuit of a dark-haired beauty called Marilyn, who was a couple of years older than me. We fell in love on the steps of our rehearsal studio for *Let's Make an Opera* and she took me on to the next stage of my sex education. She lived somewhere in the north-west London wastes of Willesden, which necessitated long journeys on the Bakerloo Line and hours of talking on the phone as I tried to work through my fevered obsession with her.

At the same time, I had my first real taste of straight acting when, as a result of being seen in *The Turn of the Screw*, I was given small parts in several films – *The Rainbow Jacket*, by Basil Dearden, about racing; Otto Preminger's *Saint Joan*, the first time I worked with John Gielgud; *The Heart Within*, a real tear-jerker about a black man on the run; and I was chosen to play a leading juvenile in a six-part children's matinée film, *Five Clues to Fortune*, or *The Treasure of Woburn Abbey*. This gave me the opportunity to get to know the technicians behind the making of films and I soon established a strong rapport with them. It seemed to me that they went out of their way to be kind to me, letting me sit in the pub in Woburn village with them at lunchtime, learning three-card brag and the mechanics of film-making. Ever since then, I've always had an affinity with the technicians behind the scenes in movies. This experience undoubtedly sowed the seeds of my subsequent move from the front to the back of the camera. Thus I had a better rapport with the crew than with the other child actors. I got on very well with Joe Mendoza, the director. I must have been strangely old for my age, but I'd been working with adults for a lot of my life and, as a result of my father's strictures, I had no contemporary school friends and none of the normal bits of childhood baggage that most people carry.

Five Clues to Fortune was made with the backing of the Children's Film Foundation and I learned a great deal from it, among other things how to ride a horse (which came in very useful fourteen years later, when I played Captain Nolan in *The Charge of the Light Brigade*). Being in front of camera didn't bother me at all. I'd been on stage often enough and I found the film-making process frankly boring. I preferred audience contact – quite a lot, actually.

I also continued to perform in a sporadic tour of *The Turn of the Screw* through several other European cities, until, in 1955, on the stage of the opera house on the Champs-Elysées in Paris, my voice broke, mid-aria, and my career as an operatic treble was over.

I'd been thoroughly briefed that this would happen, of course, but even shortly before my fourteenth birthday it came as a shock to have to face up to a new set of responsibilities. Ben wanted me to carry on singing. He was sure that I could make the transition to operatic tenor, provided I had the right training. Such was his faith, he was prepared to sponsor me through an English public school and the music academy in Florence. But I had already recognised that I didn't find the atmosphere of the opera world entirely congenial and, while Benjamin had never attempted to take advantage of me, there was no question that he and his partner, Peter Pears, and many of their friends lived in a world where homosexuality was the norm. I declined his offer, much to my father's chagrin and, as a result, alienating him almost completely. I've never really understood why he was so distressed by my decision, though I've since concluded that he saw it as the final rejection of his earlier influence over me as a boy singer.

In any event, my travels had made me restless and, at the end of the Easter term in 1956, my intermittent education at the Glyn School in Epsom was terminated by mutual agreement between the school and myself – although, as I recall, the initiative came from them. I'd been consistently absent and, I imagine, they felt they couldn't take responsibility for educating me if the situation was likely to continue, which, as far as I was concerned, it was, since I'd made up my mind that I was definitely going to become an actor.

As a result of my sacking, three crucial decisions were made: first, that I should continue my education, such as it was, at the Arts Educational School, off Portman Square in London; second, that I should move out of home – effectively chucked out by my disgruntled father – to live within daily travelling distance of the school, lodging in the house of a woman called Mrs de Mello in Streatham during the week and at my grandmother's in Woking at weekends; and third, that I should be put on the books of a suitable theatrical agent.

The first of many agents who have represented me over the years with varying degrees of enthusiasm was a lovely and, despite the pencil moustache and general appearance of a black-market nylon-stocking dealer, an unusually honest man called Johnny Wilcox.

Johnny had been introduced to my parents via Dafydd Havard, an actor who had appeared with me in *Five Clues to Fortune*. We had an interview with Wilcox in his slender, cluttered office in the upper regions of 186 Shaftesbury Avenue. A loft conversion above was home to artist and cartoonist Michael Ffolkes, with whom I was to spend many an hour playing with his pens and pencils and scrap paper. I'm sure I was a tremendous pest, but he was generous with his time and taught me a lot, particularly how to be loose and not to take the work too seriously; he was, after all, a cartoonist.

The 186 office also housed Songmart Music and, we gathered, Johnny had a variety of clients – actors, and singers and songwriters. Douglas Cardew 'The Cad' Robinson, Johnny told us proudly, had published his 'School Days are the Happiest Days' through Songmart Music. My father signed with him on my behalf and so, for the first time, I had a legitimate agent.

Johnny's agency traded under the name John Wilcox Direction, something of a misnomer, as far as I could see, since most of his clients seemed to be going in no direction at all, except possibly downwards. The tiny office would be filled to bursting with the motliest mob you could ever imagine outside a circus, crouched or lounging on faded, arse-worn chairs ranged around the bare walls, with Johnny's desk squeezed into one corner. His clients were treated like a family and the office was always inhabited by an extraordinary parade of people with incomprehensible aspirations to performance of one sort or another.

One of them, an old ham who went under the implausible moniker of Monty de Lyle, was a tall, gangling character with fierce buggers' grips tufting from his cheekbones, a waxed Hercule Poirot moustache and eyebrows that flared angrily (I should talk!) to go with them. Monty was very much the traditional type of actor, who boomed rather than spoke and wore tweeds even in the hottest of summers. He could never under any circumstances get a job, however many Johnny put him up for. He would announce his arrival at 186 Shaftesbury Avenue first by the clatter of his boots on the bare wooden staircase, then, as the door flew open, by booming, 'De Lyle, De Lyle, De Lyle,' several times, depending on the number of residents lolling around on the office chairs.

On one occasion, when invited to audition for a job in Bristol, his finances would only allow him to get there on foot. He walked the whole way to the theatre and, on being told fairly summarily that he hadn't got the job, turned round and walked all the way back to London. On his next visit to Johnny's office, still bristling with indignation, he told his tittering audience that the final ignominy had come as he crossed Hammersmith Bridge, almost back at his seedy lodgings, when one of the local whores stepped out from a doorway and greeted him with the words, 'Hello, cheeky! Fancy a bit of fun?'

Broke, jobless and rejected, he was still sure that, as a professional actor who had appeared five times in the West End twenty years before, he merited a great deal more respect. I was so young and innocent that I believed and sympathised. It was years before I recognised the appalling bogusness and self-obsession with which some people could remain convinced that they were still performing artists when they hadn't performed for years.

The aforementioned Dafydd Havard was a gaunt, gay Welshman who always looked a bit dodgy, I thought, but fortunately never preyed on me.

Peter Oliver was an actor who wrote the odd play or song and another tall figure, blond to ginger, with effete spectacles and a slight lisp. There were a couple of dwarfs, twins they might have been, who were always entertaining and never stopped chattering away.

Then there was a ventriloquist called Arthur May, who toured the seaside circuit, playing the ends of piers. He must have been about ninety, but had failed to learn, in all the years he'd been at it, that the audience are not supposed to see your lips move and that the dummy, in his case 'Claude', is supposed to have a different voice from the chap on whose lap he is sitting. As it happened, I developed a great relationship with 'Claude' and was allowed to poke my hand into his back and swivel his head about, propping him on my knee to Arthur's grinning approval.

This group and several others were all a constant presence at Shaftesbury Avenue, and when the office became too crowded, which it often did, we would repair to the local café and drink tea and have stale cheese rolls.

Talk about 'Welcome to show business'. Here it was in all its depressing glory, and I loved every minute of it. The office, with the two large windows looking out over the avenue, covered in once-white, now pale-nicotine sheers; the single desk, cluttered with junk; the battered chairs; and over all, the great cloud of cigarette smoke constantly hanging in the air like a pale grey fog.

In the interests of economy Johnny would light his Senior Service several times, taking just a couple of puffs with each match, and as he carefully stubbed it out would stare at the assembled mob over his pencil-thin tash and make plans for our future. I adored him and his girl-friend of long standing, Babs, who towered over John's slight frame – Little and Large, as it were. Many years later, I went to see them both, still together, in Brighton. Johnny was suffering from lung cancer. We went over the old days, the old faces, and he played the saxophone for me, a talent that had been kept under wraps but for a photograph in the office of him with a tenor sax to his mouth. I had never thought to ask about it then, but it seemed that was how he got into music publishing, through dance bands, and when they lost favour, he changed his course and fell, ultimately, into the agency business. From dance band to business. It struck me as strange that his career was so much like my father's and he was such a father figure to me.

A month after this fond meeting, he died, and I miss him still.

The Arts Educational School was an independent establishment founded by Grace Cone and Olive Ripman with the intention of giving its pupils, boys and girls, a normal academic education heavily supplemented with stage and drama skills – everything from ballet to singing, tap to acting.

To this day, I'm not sure who paid the hefty fees they commanded. I have a feeling that the Surrey County Council gave me some sort of scholarship as a result of my experience in *The Turn of the Screw* and *Five Clues to Fortune*. At the age of fourteen I was so much more experienced than any other children there that the school didn't know quite what to do with me. I'd been working in the theatre or entertainment of one sort or another since I was six. I knew the ropes and I'd lived and worked with a lot of adults, touring with them, with only my doting mother as a frankly ineffectual chaperone. But I did make a few friends, some very good ones over the two and a half years I was there.

During the week, I used to stay in my digs off Streatham Park Road, paid for by my sympathetic grandmother. Mrs de Mello, my landlady, was kindly and rotund, and usually had three paying guests, though I rarely saw more than one, a shoe salesman with a smart little tash who taught me to play chess and backgammon properly. Though I was but a little fellow, hardly yet in long trousers, I had spent a good few years in digs of varying degrees of cleanliness and quality and Mrs de Mello I recognised as being up there with the best.

One of my few friends from Tolworth, Peter Searle, attempted the move with me, but after a couple of weeks he left to go back to his removal job in Kingston and reclaim his long brown Pickfords coat, I imagined. I wished him well as he returned to his mum. My father had predicted that I too wouldn't last more than a month, which made me, of course, determined to prove him wrong.

I would take a tube up from Tooting Bec each day to Marble Arch, a few blocks from Upper Berkeley Street, where the school buildings consisted of a terrace of early 19th-century houses knocked together to provide the series of large rooms that were needed for classrooms, dance and theatre studios. The terrace has since been demolished, to be replaced by the Portman Hotel, and the school moved several times before it was permanently housed in Chiswick.

The buildings then were occupied by the school on a short lease and were already on borrowed time. They were full of narrow, rickety staircases, of which I soon learned to take advantage. If a girl I fancied was coming down while I was going up, I wouldn't let her pass until she'd given me a kiss. It wasn't subtle, but it worked.

While at least half our day was meant to be devoted to normal academic studies, I was delighted to find that this was very much the secondary purpose of the school – at least in those days – and all the children seemed to be enjoying their time there. A large proportion of the students were girls and most of them were intent on becoming prima ballerinas, like Alicia Markova, who was the school's president. There was, as a result, a strong connection between the school and the Festival Ballet and we regularly provided extras for their productions.

Although I was physically capable of ballet, I simply couldn't ignore a deep, no doubt cultural, conviction that it was a very sissy thing for a boy to be doing. So I objected strongly early on in my career at the school when I was required to turn out in tights and ballet shoes at the back of *The Nutcracker Suite* in the Festival Hall.

A very young woman teacher was charged with chaperoning us on Saturdays when there was a matinée as well as the evening performance. Her main task was to keep the boys out of trouble between the two shows by taking them for a walk somewhere nearby. This presented me with the perfect opportunity to register my disapproval by throwing my cap over the Embankment into the Thames. I knew very well that if I turned up back at school without my cap, there'd be trouble, for her and me.

Nevertheless, I never managed to avoid completely some involvement in song and dance, and indeed was required to indulge in it professionally several times in my later career. In my last year at the Arts Educational, one of the older students, Dorothy Bishop, was ordered by the cost-conscious, not to say tight-fisted, management of the school to coach us in a production of *The Fleet's in Port Again*.

The fleet's back in port, yo ho! yo ho!
We'll all have a jolly good time.

It was a great piece of burlesque which turned out to be a lot of fun and we all ended up in fits of laughter with Dorothy.

However, on the whole I wasn't exposed to too much ballet, and I was given every opportunity and encouragement to go out and do paid acting work. The school, as agents, took their cut on anything I earned, and I don't doubt this possibility was a factor in their giving me a scholarship, so I spent an awful lot of time away from school, working.

On the rare occasions I went back to my parents' home, my father seemed to go out of his way to make my visits as uncomfortable as possible for me, and my warmest memories of these unhappy occasions are of my mother thrusting illicit pound and ten-bob notes into my pocket when my father wasn't watching. As a result, I didn't go home often and tended to spend a lot of weekends in the more amenable surroundings of my grandmother's house in Woking.

I'd always spent a lot of time at Redstacks. Apart from the fact that Grandma Hemmings was inclined to indulge me, the place had a number of attractions for an inquisitive young sensation seeker. In the house itself, my grandmother's lodgers tended were always a source of amusement, although it seemed to me that they often took precedence over poor old Grandad Percy in the household. Peter Goodchild from No. 148 stayed my strongest connection with Woking, and it was he, through his outstanding prowess on the tennis court, who introduced me to the upper-middle-class milieu of Hook Heath Tennis Club and attendant mating rituals, dominated by pimpled boys from Malvern College or Charterhouse. My grandmother, presumably aware of the deprivation I'd suffered at home, thoughtfully encouraged me in making these new friends, while my father expressed his severe disapproval, not this time on the grounds that they weren't 'good enough', but because they were 'looking down' on me or wanted to know me only for my precocious fame and the slight celebrity that had followed *The Turn of the Screw* and early television appearances. It was obvious to me, however, that I was not considered a desirable catch by any of the mothers who oversaw these things, and I always felt that I was part of this group under false pretences.

At school, among the variously motivated kids, several from theatrical backgrounds (Hughie Green's daughter Linda and Toots, daughter of Margaret Lockwood), I became part of a gang of unruly lads, with Bernard Doe, a stout, spotty youth, Jonathan Swift, tall, handsome and highly fancied, whose father owned a newsagent's in Westbourne Grove, and Martin Baron. We were united in our loathing of the school uniform and our desire to foment insurrection.

We decided that we would eschew the school blazers with badges and caps that the rules demanded and wear only charcoal-grey suits. There was a showdown, in which the headmistress, Mrs Jack, told us we had to wear the blazers. We refused. Rather craftily, she got round the impasse by making us 'prefects', a hitherto unknown position at the school, and decreeing that the privilege of wearing grey suits attached to this status, though we still had to wear caps on the way to school, which I resented very much. In retrospect, I should have worn it backwards, like kids wear their baseball caps now (though to my mind they look bloody ridiculous).

*

But despite my preoccupation with rebellion and all the outside work I was doing, I managed to find plenty of time for the girls too. Slightly built and fresh-faced as I was, my voice had broken into an effective huskiness caused by chronic sinus trouble, and I acted with the confidence of a fourteen-year-old going on twenty. I was already roaming London like a street kid, frankly relieved to be free of my father's constricting influence, and already eager to develop my burgeoning interest in girls, and specifically my first big passion, Patsy Morton-Davies.

Patsy lived in Sydney Street, in a swish part of Chelsea, and for a few months – or was it weeks – I was besotted with her. My greatest achievement back then was to persuade her to come down to Woking with me and visit Granny Hemmings at Redstacks. The London to Basingstoke railway line ran nearby, within rattling earshot, and at the back of the house, through the orchard, past Grandad's old workshop, were the shunting yards where goods trains would be parked. I had learned a long time before how to sneak in there and climb into the wagons. It was in one of these, smelling faintly of some unidentifiable rotting vegetable, that I saw Patsy naked for the first time.

Curiously, or perhaps not, I never got so far with the one girl who truly entranced me for the next few years at the Arts Educational School.

Ann Thorn was six months older and in the same class as Bernard, Jonathan and me. She was tall, fun, strong, beautiful and just the right amount rebellious. She also had a lovely pair of breasts, from which I always found it hard to tear my adolescent eyes. When she first arrived at the school, a little after me, she started walking out with the dominant male of the class, Jonathan Swift, and I had to settle for adoring her from afar. It was in order to get to know Ann that I first became friends with Jonathan. With a great deal of subtle manoeuvring, I did finally manage to persuade her to come with me to see a film at the Swiss Cottage Odeon. The content and quality of the film became utterly immaterial to me when she allowed me to feel her magnificent young breasts. To cap this triumph, she turned to me and said she liked me more than Jonathan. All my Christmases had come at once!

That was about as far as it ever went physically, but despite my more advanced experience with Marilyn in the English Opera Group, I must have been content, because Ann and I became inseparable although I never did manage to go the whole way, despite spending a lot time thinking about it. However, we whiled away many happy hours together in her parents' house at 7 Clifton Hill in St John's Wood, laughing and chatting while we played backgammon. (It was one of those odd but pleasing coincidences that, years later, the same house was taken over by John Mackenzie, who directed me in a bizarre film called *Unman, Wittering and Zigo*.)

Ann, like me, was studying 'Modern Stage' at the school. At this distance in time I don't know why, as she didn't seem particularly committed to a life in the theatre and, as it turned out, never joined the profession. She was, though, always very supportive of my efforts at acting, heaping praise on me once after a workshop session (we didn't call them that in those days) in which Bernard, Jonathan and I had to prepare and deliver Cyrano de Bergerac's 'I thank you, and again I thank you, but no thank you' speech. She told me afterwards that my performance had so moved her she'd ceased to notice my grimy grey suit and could see Cyrano's massive proboscis on my face as if it were really there. That was encouraging.

'Modern Stage' also included tap-dancing, as well as traditional and ballroom – not skills of which I ever made a great deal of use in my subsequent career, although there's no doubt, as Mrs Jack once severely told me, they teach you poise and a way of holding yourself, which turned out to be very useful on stage and in the movies.

To a lot of my contemporaries at the school, I must have seemed like an orphan. I never introduced Ann to my parents, but I often asked her to come by train with me on a Sunday to visit Granny in Woking. She liked the large garden and the open country nearby, where she loved walking while we tattled and giggled and fooled around. In the summer, they were dreamy times: Franco Zeffirelli would have made much of us, strolling through daisy-filled hay fields, full of youthful innocence, every so often dropping down on to the soft turf to kiss and caress. I would do it all again tomorrow if I could

Once, though, it went badly wrong.

Through one of my part-time jobs, I'd managed to get my hands on enough money to swagger into the nearest Burton's and order myself a bespoke suit of what I considered great distinction and the last word in fifties cool. So proud was I of it that the day after I picked it up, I couldn't resist wearing it for one of our pastoral walks near Woking.

Ann, as usual, had run on ahead, pretending she didn't want to be caught, and I was chasing after her. It was only as I heard the sharp sound of crisp new gents' suiting being ripped that I realised she'd led me over a hedge that concealed a barbed-wire fence. I was beside myself with grief that I should have torn the suit on its very first outing. Ann, probably appalled at such an outburst over an article of clothing, could only placate me with a fervent promise to get it invisibly mended. God knows why I was wearing this precious suit out there in the middle of the country, but I was unbelievably upset.

On week days, after school we would often go, just the two of us or in a gang, to a coffee bar that had opened up on Baker Street, complete with a battery of steaming Gaggia machines, hissing and howling like banshees to produce the froth that suddenly everybody wanted. It seems extraordinary, now there's a Starbucks on every corner, that the London coffee bars should have been considered so hip, but in the late fifties whole movies were made about them. It was as if coffee had only just been discovered – which, I suppose, for a lot of us it had.

On the whole we had good innocent fun, walking through the parks in summer, going to the cinema in winter. There was not much boozing then. We might sometimes have a beer. But usually it was coffee, coffee, coffee.

The most depraved thing Ann used to do, thinking she was the coolest of kittens, was smoke pink, powder-blue and mint-green Sobranie cigarettes.

Sometimes we'd go on to see *Humph at the Conway* (featuring the acclaimed trumpeter and future chairman of *I'm Sorry I Haven't a Clue*, Humphrey Lyttelton), an ad hoc jazz club within the Old Labour walls of the Conway Hall in Holborn, though how on earth I got in, I can't imagine. They must have been very indulgent, or just desperate for trade. But I knew a lot of people there. I'd already extended my taste in music – and my talents, such as they were – to embrace the pop and rock coming out of Tin Pan Alley. Johnny Wilcox also had an interest and introduced me to that world. I loved the business and tinkering with songs, fiddling with lyrics, and astonishingly there were people, like Johnny 'Jingles' Johnson, who were prepared to humour and encourage me. I made friends then that I kept for a long time and worked with again when I started my own music company fifteen years later.

One of my few triumphs then, both musically and romantically, was to put my stamp on a song called 'A Very Precious Love', for which I wrote most of the lyrics:

Blow-Up

A very precious love is what you are to me,
A stairway to a star,
A night in Shangri-La . . . and so on.

I got a great kick out of telling Ann I'd written the lyrics especially for her.

As the school's own theatrical 'agent', Miss Fisher was producing a steady stream of outside work for me and, with all my other activities, my academic education was inevitably somewhat neglected. This didn't worry me (not then – it does now), although I loved studying and playing in *A Midsummer Night's Dream* for my English Literature O-level. In sharp contrast to my Cyrano performance, I took the part of Bottom, whose eagerness to please everyone appealed to me – 'I will roar you as 'twere any nightingale.'

But in between appearing as an Ovaltinee and in *Whacko, Billy Bunter, Dixon of Dock Green*, a couple of Gilbert and Sullivans and Otto Preminger's *Saint Joan*, I was put in charge of a school magazine, which also took up quite a bit of time.

I and the others in my gang who helped decided to call it *The Rebel*.

As soon as she heard, the headmistress called me in. 'You can't call this magazine *The Rebel*. You'll have to change it.'

Our only competition was a weedy publication called, I think, *The Philatelist*, so our alternative was renamed *The Sign Post*. We thought this was very clever because it was just as subversive as we had planned *The Rebel* to be, pointing as it did, in an arbitrary direction, suggesting 'follow our lead'.

It sold well, for 2d an issue, primarily on the strength of a single-page insert of vicious (and highly fictitious) gossip about the teachers, which was very popular. It soon knocked *The Philatelist* off its box. Our mode of production was to scrawl the text by hand with special ink on to a tray of gelatine. Once it had been hardened in the fridge, we pressed a blank sheet of paper on to the gel, then peeled it off. It was a very long job, but we loved it. And our success attracted a lot of contributors. I've wanted to run a newspaper ever since, but, luckily for everyone, I've never got further than writing sporadic pieces for various newspapers and magazines around the world.

Despite my rebellion against the uniform and other aspects of discipline, I enjoyed my time at the school and I've been grateful for what I learned there. Miss Jack, who ran the place by sheer strength of character, was an astonishing old-style battleaxe. She pounded the corridors with her hair tugged back into a ballerina's bun and a demeanour designed to command instant authority, if not terror. We were all expected to be petrified, but I found she was fine if you could get on the right side of her. I was certainly never quite as scared of her as the other children were and I would use some of my encounters with her to hone my acting skills. Several times she caught me all but fag in hand in the nether regions of the building, but when she tried to lance me with her gimlet eye and accused me of smoking, I rose to the challenge, producing an insouciant smile.

'Mrs Jack,' I would expostulate gently, 'how *can* you imagine such a thing?'

And even though I probably reeked of smoke, she chose to buy it – perhaps to encourage my acting.

I also learned the value of keeping a straight face under threat. We were being given a lecture once, on James Joyce – not a subject to tickle the fancy of a sixteen-year-old – and I decided to engage in an elaborate mime from my desk halfway down the class. I opened a fish and chip shop and, in complete silence, started to take mimed orders from other pupils sitting nearby. I carefully plucked the fried fish from the fat, scooped out a dollop of hot, sizzling chips from the fryer, then salted and wrapped them up before handing them to the waiting customer. Every time the teacher turned in my direction, I stopped instantly and assumed an air of rapt attention. He didn't catch me once, while the others just couldn't control their giggles and drew his wrath.

We did have some wonderful teachers, though, especially for drama. An actor called Anthony Sharp was one regular visiting teacher who had the great gift of being able to explain and transmit the skills we needed. Robert Morley, too, appeared from time to time to pass on his knowledge. We also went to the theatre a lot, usually the Old Vic, where I saw Richard Burton several times. I make no apology for being heavily influenced by him, and in my view his 1954 performance of Dylan Thomas's *Under Milk Wood* is still one of the finest spoken-word recordings ever produced.

The two ladies who had founded the place, Grace Cone and Olive Ripman, were distant, God-like figures. Miss Cone had two sisters, Miss Lily and Miss Valerie – all victims, no doubt, of the shortage of men after the First World War – who acted as general functionaries in the school. Mrs Jack, they tell me, went on for years running the school, eventually moving with it to a new boarding site that had also been opened at Tring. She must have been responsible for turning out a great number of theatrical figures during her reign.

Ann stayed at the Arts Educational School with me until we had reached the senior class and she took her O-levels in the summer of 1958, when I was still spending a lot of my free time with her. It was then that I felt the first stirring of what was to become a serious affliction throughout my life – an incurable urge to marry women.

At the age of sixteen I truly, deeply wanted to marry Ann Thorn; and she wanted to marry me.

I suppose then, and ever since, I craved the stability I thought marriage would bring – the sense of belonging to a family again, of which my father had effectively deprived me.

Although legally entitled to marry, we were, of course, absurdly young; but once again, the somewhat bizarre life I'd led allowed me to believe that I was capable of handling the challenge.

I was sure Ann's parents would not present any problem. I knew her mother liked me, often eyeing me as if I were the favourite naughty puppy. Ann's father, Bill, was a stern sort of man who liked to think he ruled his household with a rod of iron, although he could never have crushed completely Ann's tremendous spirit.

However, he must have been astonished when, thoroughly confident that it was a mere formality, I asked him if I could talk to him alone. He agreed, and I told him I wanted to marry Ann.

His face hardened in an instant. I should have read the signs.

'Aren't you a bit young?' he asked quietly.

'But, Bill, I can afford it!' I boasted, with no idea of what it would cost.

'What do you mean?'

'I've done a lot of work already, you know, and I've got £200 in the bank. I'm going places.'

He grunted and left the room without saying another word.

I had an inkling things had not gone well when, a little later, he walked back into the drawing room, where Ann and I were playing backgammon as usual. He looked at us with a thunderous face for a few seconds. We looked back with bland innocence before he withdrew once again without saying anything. But a short while later he was back, opening the door with unexpected ferocity, as if he'd been sure he would find us in a passionate clinch, or worse. We were still playing backgammon.

He couldn't restrain himself any longer. He glared at me with undisguised hostility before turning to Ann to say with a cold shaking voice, 'Get that boy out of here, and out of your life, now!' As Ann's lower lip trembled, he went on, 'Tell him to leave – I never want to see him again.'

That was the kind of man her father was and, apart from leaving home, there was very little she could do about it. Effectively, from that moment, our relationship was over.

At the same time, it wasn't helped by Johnny Wilcox, who also contributed to the debate. 'Listen, David. It's your career or that girl,' he told me with a world-weary gleam in his eye. 'You'd better sort yourself out and drop the girl.'

Between them, Johnny and Ann's dad put the mockers on what might have been my first and, who knows (though let's not be blinded by nostalgia), only marriage. But the idea of marriage still had a massively strong appeal for me. It didn't take long for me to find another candidate.

Nevertheless, the loss of Ann preyed on my mind for many months and, after I'd left the Arts Educational School and got a part-time job at Sa Tortuga, a café in the King's Road, I went back to St John's Wood and hung around outside Ann's house, hoping to catch a glimpse of her, which, luckily I suppose, never happened.

I heard that she went on to train as an occupational therapist – maybe the drama helped – and a year or two later, when her father took a job in the Philippines, she went to live there with her parents and didn't come back to England for seventeen years. It was 43 years before I saw her again.

6

Staging Posts, 1958–1961

When I finally abandoned my sporadic learning at the Arts Educational School in the summer of 1958, I wasn't yet seventeen. I'd worked so much during my years there, I had very little education to show for it, but I did have the grounding and the confidence to feel certain that I could go on and make a living as an actor. In fact, to anyone who would listen, I boasted that my ultimate ambition was to move into the production side of the business as soon as possible; that, I assured them, was where the real money lay.

To his credit, Johnny Wilcox took me seriously and behaved generously.

'Look, David,' he said during one of those rare moments when there was no one else in the office, 'you've done an awful lot of work over the last few years playing kids' parts. You're a man now – well, almost – and with all the experience you've already had, a whole new lot of roles are going to open up for you. I can see you really going places now, but I'm getting tired and I'm not the man to realise your true potential. If I was to do the job properly and give it the time it needs, I'd have to drop half my old clients. You know I can't do that – they're like family to me.'

Sad as I was about parting, I knew that I needed someone with more oomph, and perhaps the canny old boy was simply pre-empting the inevitable. In any event, it was he who suggested I went to Beryl Seton's agency, which I thought was very obviously a few rungs up the ladder from Johnny's. For a start, it was in a fairly grand building on the fringes of Soho. Beryl had her own personal office, the entrance to which was guarded by two beady-eyed women, a secretary and a book-keeper in an outer office. With the usual proviso that I shouldn't expect bloody miracles, she said she was sure she could find me plenty of work. In the meantime, I was on my own and I had to find ways of making a living until the jobs came along, or in between them when they did.

*

That summer I was short of money, as usual, and there was no immediate acting work in sight. With Alan Gunter, one of the boys I knew in Woking, I decided to apply for temporary work at Bentalls, the great department store in Kingston, which was Surbiton's much smarter neighbour. Our first job was in the store's customer car wash. With virtually no driving experience, we soon smashed up a car, so Mr Rowan Bentall decided to move me on to a less breakable commodity, plastics, in the hardware department. Plastic was the new household wonder then, admired with the same misguided enthusiasm as Brynylon clothing. Spurred on by curiosity and a desire to succeed, perhaps on terms that my father would appreciate, I sat down and wrote to all the suppliers, asking how they made their products.

Within a month, I'd learned a great deal about plastic, and I'd also found a large stock of gadgets in a stockroom. I asked if I could set up a stand to demonstrate them to the punters flowing by. To the surprise of the management, I flogged them all, clearing the entire stock. As a result, Rowan Bentall asked me to be in charge of the display of a hideous great plastic-injection moulding machine which was to be installed temporarily in the main sales area, the Wolsey Hall. It allowed the public to see an amorphous lump of plastic going in one end and spoons spewing out at the other, while all around the hall individual suppliers sold their wares from stands, demonstrating their durability. It was part of my job to site them and tell them where to go. The punters came flooding in to see how the goods were made and then to buy them.

The two-week exhibition went well, but afterwards I was put in charge of lifts – a serious demotion in my eyes. Two days later, I complained that I was bored to death. I was promoted to the job of floor walker – to the understandable resentment of some of the old hands – but shortly afterwards was offered a part in an episode of *Dixon of Dock Green*. I'd been there before, selling Yule logs at Christmas from a barrow – an archetypal crooked cockney with a heart of gold. I went to see Rowan Bentall again to tell him I was going to take the part.

'So,' he asked, 'what do you want to do with us?' An old-fashioned Englishman, he didn't consider acting a proper job, and he said he'd been hoping I might make a career with Bentalls.

But my mind was made up. 'I'm an actor,' I said with proud conviction. 'And that's what I must do.'

'I think you're making a great mistake, but off you go – and the best of luck to you.'

I'd had a great summer there and it did cross my mind that a life in the retail trade might suit me very well. I even talked it over with my father, who favoured a less risky option than show business. But, although I couldn't help being enthusiastic as long as I was at Bentalls, I knew that, at heart, I was a performer.

Curiously, however, there was another branch of performance that I learned while I was there. In the canteen at lunchtime, I used to watch a man called Brian Buzzing do tricks at his table, messing around with coins, making them appear and disappear in utterly convincing and mystifying ways. I badgered him relentlessly to show me how he did it and in the end he succumbed. I was an eager pupil and, by the time I left Bentalls, I was hooked on magic. The idea of being able totally to convince people that something had happened which had not was immensely appealing to me. After that, it didn't take me long to find my way to Davenports Magic Shop, which I carried on visiting for years afterwards whenever I could.

By now almost entirely independent of my parents, I'd moved out of my digs in Streatham and lived with my grandmother for most of the time I was working at Bentalls.

Once I started being sent up for more jobs through Beryl, Peter Oliver, whom I knew through Johnny Wilcox, suggested that I move in with him and his parents in Fulham, and I welcomed the change and the proximity to the King's Road and the West End. But that didn't last long and, workless, my resources were stretched.

Johnny had always looked after my money meticulously, but the allowance I received from him and then Beryl was never enough, so, though my mother crept away from Tolworth to see me once a week and sub me four pounds, I realised that I had to get a job.

Fortuitously, another of the Wilcox gang came to the rescue. Gerry Bozel was a nightclub singer, eagerly ambitious, talented in a Tony Bennett kind of way with fine pipes and great chutzpah. He was Jewish, and seriously so, and told me that his mother took in paying guests. She had a vacancy. Did I want it? I did.

And so began a fiercely Hassidic upbringing for which I was totally unprepared. Mrs Elboz (Gerry's real family name) ran a very kosher establishment and I was expected to conform, which meant going to *shul* on Saturday, observing Yom Kippur, wearing a *yarmulka*, the whole nine yards. I learned fragments of Hebrew, went to Jewish weddings and funerals – which seemed to take place weekly – and learned to trade and save. Mrs Elboz was widowed and during the week ran a stall in Berwick Street Market, stocked with fresh vegetables; on Sundays she had a stall in Petticoat Lane, selling costume jewellery. She was a large lady with a great heart, stern of countenance but funny with it.

I didn't have much to do with Berwick Street, but I threw myself into Petticoat Lane like a young man possessed. I loved every inch of it. Jellied eels at Tubby Isaac's, watching the world go by with a sly beer at my side, keeping track of the hustlers and the three-card-tricksters, the dodgy watches and the barkers, the rickers and the shills, all connivers in less-than-honest street trading and faces that I came to know well. The colour of it all, the banter and the sheer brazen bollocks from behind the stalls, voices raised in a bizarre harmony to attract the punters to buy rubbish – all of this appealed to me greatly, for they were actors, on stage for a Sunday morning, trying to fleece a bob or two.

The majority of these reprobates would meet just after midday. Pints would be sunk and the explosive chatter was ceaseless. Here, I could pick up a job for the afternoon, as a shill or a gofer, or get a job for the following Sunday, doing pretty much anything. We would play Spoof or Liars' Poker with dice, or settle in for Killer on the dartboard. But Spoof was my game, and I still play it to this day, given a mark who doesn't know me too well.

It was in Petticoat Lane that I learned the run-out from 'Greasy' Mike Nesbitt. After a great number of lessons in the finer points of this awful scam, which plays totally on the punter's expectation of getting something for nothing, I was allowed to work his stall so he could sit drinking. Not since my days in Bentalls' hardware department selling functionless gadgetry had I had so much fun.

But to celebrate my first summer of freedom, some instinct persuaded me to take off for a while and wander round Europe, with only a battered guitar and a few magic gimmicks to help me chance my talents in whatever town or back-of-nowhere village I ended up. It was in some ways a wonderful period. I started each day without any plans, simply allowing events and the people I met to direct my next move.

I found this complete abrogation of responsibility and being answerable to no one else very liberating. Unfortunately it was a frame of mind I found hard to abandon and in later years, when I was married or in 'permanent relationships' and sometimes popped out for cigarettes, only to reappear three days later, the current woman in my life was inclined not to see it my way and become somewhat scratchy. With time, though I still found it hard to see their point, I learned to accept that they held it and my unheralded absences tended to run to three hours rather than three days.

On this first peregrination I found myself singing – and wrecking my vocal cords to overcome the background noise of Germans quaffing litre steins of lager – in Bavarian *Bierkellers* one week and squatting beside my efforts as a pavement artist in Juan les Pins the next. The experience confirmed my belief that, on the whole, success in the performing arts relies at least as much on sheer bottle as on raw talent.

Back in England at the end of 1958, I found that Beryl was beginning to extract the odd audition for me, and had put me up for a part in *Noah's Ark* with Leo McKern, which I got. It was made in the studios at Alexandra Palace with an old triple-lens TV camera, which reversed directions and had to be compensated for. There was very little room for error in filming since at that stage in its development editing on VCR tape was very expensive and discouraged by the BBC. (One of the first performers to be permitted to break tape was the comic perfectionist and tricky customer Tony Hancock.) There were also odd small parts in odd small films – *Men of Tomorrow*, *The Wind of Change* – usually still as a schoolboy because, despite what I considered my worldly maturity, my most obvious asset was still my (hugely deceptive) cherubic face.

Beryl also found me my first jobs in provincial rep, which, whatever anyone says about the horrors, pitfalls and tedium involved, is a superb training ground for a young actor. And I was young, all right – still a slight and, on the face of it, youthful seventeen. At a high-Victorian theatre in a large northern town, I met Andrew Ray, another young actor, who became a great friend. He was the son of a well-known comedian, Ted Ray, who had made his name before the war and since on what we used to call the wireless.

For eight weeks Andrew and I shared a room in the spotless semi-detached, brick-and-pebbledash villa of a seasoned theatrical landlady called Mrs Wainwright. Mrs Wainwright had curly white hair, small silver spectacles and wore floral pinafores of a kind I've only ever seen on Rupert Bear's mother. Every day, before we headed off for the evening performance, she gave us a delicious high tea, of which she was very proud, and we were very appreciative, never leaving a scrap on our plates.

But we were both still at that stage in our lives when change and fashion were important, as much with drink as with anything else, and for some reason we were going through a sherry phase. I realise this must sound incredible now, but there was much more sherry about then. Besides, in the interests of time and motion, not to mention sheer economy, sherry gets you drunk quicker and cheaper than anything else on the market (apart from Buckfast Abbey Tonic Wine – ask any Glaswegian teenager). And there are a lot of very happy old ladies in homes all over the country who will still testify to the merits of good, old-fashioned sherry.

We favoured a dry *fino* variety and made sure we always had a bottle in the wardrobe, to hide it from our landlady's possible disapproval. After a week, however, we noticed that the sherry was going down rather fast, so naturally we blamed each other, and both denied it vigorously.

We concluded, with the steely logic of any of the mackintoshed detectives we were playing on stage, that if it wasn't one of us, it must have been someone else. We made straight for our nearest offy and bought another bottle. We drank enough from it to accommodate a good measure of our own pee and hid it seriously.

By the end of the next week, the level in the bottle had dropped again and gleefully we told all the cast what we'd done. They howled their appreciation, and from then on all you had to do to corpse someone on stage was to whisper as you passed them, 'Sherry's gone down again.' It was guaranteed to blast them away, and it became the season's running gag.

Routinely, we'd buy a new bottle take some out, top it up, put it back in its hiding place and, sure enough, a week later it had gone down, and we'd pee in it again. It was astonishing to me that someone as overtly respectable as Mrs Wainwright should not only be pinching her lodgers' booze but drinking it, and enjoying it enough to come back for more despite that fact that it was a good 50 per cent pure pee. But she was being so sweet and kind to us, I almost felt a few pangs of guilt, though not enough to stop doing it. Nevertheless the process – and the jokes – continued joyously for the rest of the season.

When it ended, we stood with our suitcases in the hall, saying, 'Thanks, Mrs W, you've been absolutely wonderful and you've cooked some lovely meals for us.'

Just as we were getting in to the taxi, she leaned through the window with her russet-apple cheeks glowing, and a tiny tear in the corner of her eye.

'Mr Hemmings, Mr Ray, you've been the nicest boys I've ever met in my life, and I've loved having you, so I do have one little confession to make.'

Andrew and I looked at each other, knowing what was coming.

'I've been going up to your wardrobe from time to time,' she went on, 'and taking a bit of your sherry, but I only did it because I do know how much you love your trifle.'

We tried to cover the green tinge that must have coloured our faces as the taxi drove away, while she waved a small lace handkerchief at us. At the station we met up with the rest of the company, who were going back to London. Andrew and I looked at each other again and we shook our heads. We couldn't tell them. They already knew that, without fail, we'd had three helpings of trifle every Friday night.

Back in London, Andrew and I kept in touch, and I soon found that he was as ready as me to try anything; he had the same mean sense of humour that thrived on seeing people in awkward positions, usually brought about through their own actions. He also liked to make a few quid, so when I suggested we should try and operate a few run-outs, as learned in my days with the Elbozes, around the bigger street markets, he jumped at the idea. He brought along a friend in the music business called Leapy Lee, who had his own brief fling with fame a few years later.

These bogus auctions were called 'run-outs' because that was usually how they had to end. We'd set up a pitch in Petticoat Lane, Bermondsey, Portobello – a trestle table, maybe – with a display of domestic goods and a van full of boxes behind. I'd stand on a wooden orange box behind the table and start intoning loudly at the passers-by – barking, as it's known in the trade.

'Now, ladies and gentlemen . . .'

If you barked with enough authority, it took very little time to gather a crowd of idle watchers – an audience of potential victims.

'Today,' I would announce as if it were a very special occasion, 'I'm going to offer you some of the best bargains you've ever seen or will ever see in your whole life.' It didn't do to undersell. 'We have been lucky enough to acquire a warehouse full of top-quality household products, which we can sell at prices you wouldn't even dream of.' I would pick up one of the assorted, more or less totally useless, saucepans made of wafer-thin steel and wave it around, banging it carefully from time to time in a way to suggest solidity and durability. 'Look at this – top quality, a set of five, ideal for the busy housewife who likes to cook. You know how your old man loves your cooking, almost as much as the other . . .' pause '. . . things you do for him.' A quick leer and a saucy laugh here. 'And, talking of beds, I've got this beautiful linen – sheets and pillowcases. Look, with posh little frilly bits too, just like they have in Buckingham Palace. And look at these crocks – you could have the Archbishop of Canterbury to tea with this lot. And these kitchen knives!' I would pick up a knife of implausible brightness and run my thumb along its soft, blunt edge. 'Phwaw,' I would gasp with a wince. 'You could top an elephant with that.'

It is a testament to the power of live performance that the crowds swelled fast as I proclaimed the merits of all this terrible crappolata. When I felt enough had gathered, including my stooges, Andrew and Leapy Lee, I launched into the offer.

'Now, ladies and gentleman, and that bloke at the back,' I added, nodding vaguely over the heads of the crowd. 'I'm going to put a package together for you at a price you won't believe. This tea set, this full set of chef's knives, a fully boxed set of cutlery and a set of five professional – professional, mind – saucepans. How much do you think that lot would cost you in one of the big, posh stores?'

One of my stooges – rickers they were called in the trade – would yell back, 'Twenty quid!'

'Twenty quid?' I would come back, appalled. 'You wouldn't get that lot for fifty! And I can see you haven't got twenty quid, but if you had, that's what you'd pay for this lot, is it?'

'No more'n twenty quid,' he would challenge.

'All right, but have you got ten quid? Yeah? OK, give me that ten and I'll hold it in my hand. Hang on. No, don't give me ten, give a fiver.'

My ricker would eagerly push his way through the crowd with a fiver in his hand.

'OK,' I'd say when he reached me. 'You said it was worth twenty. Never mind your fiver, just give me a quid – and that's it!'

An appreciative gasp burst from the crowd and another ricker would rush in for the same deal. I knew I'd got my audience then. They were all sure now that they were getting something for nearly nothing and there was surge of them, all waving their green pound notes, which I scooped up while a couple more helpers packed up cardboard boxes of the stuff we had paid pennies apiece for. As soon as the last punter had his or her package, we piled everything that was left into the van and fled before anyone had time to get home and try the stuff.

Once we'd exhausted the street markets, we started booking British Legion halls in crummy parts of suburban towns and would fly-post the area beforehand with ads offering 'Sugar at 1d/1lb'. That brought the punters in droves. Leapy Lee would wander around, giving out a bit of sugar, and then I'd start barking.

There were frequent hairy moments, though, especially if we stayed too long. Once, in Woking, we were just about to pack up when an early punter returned with some sheets she'd bought in a lovely boxed set. She pushed through the crowd waiting for their packages with a large limp rag in her hand and flung it on the stage. 'That's your double sheet, just washed,' she shrieked.

All the dressing had washed out, leaving it a limp piece of low-grade gauze that might have been used for making poultices.

There was an ugly scene as we were forced to give money back to most of the punters who were still there before we made a run for it.

Another 'business venture' in which Andrew and I helped Carol Elboz was a movable operation called Carols of Wembley. We would set ourselves up in department stores with a mini studio and a serious-looking camera and invite mothers to have their darling little progeny photographed for entry into a competition for the most photogenic child. I've been a dad since then, several (some would say rather too many) times, and I understand how irrational parents can become in gauging the merits of their own offspring. However, it amazed me as a callow eighteen-year-old how some mothers, heaving around infants that looked like Arthur Mullard on ugly pills, could feel that their little bruisers, no doubt o'erbrimming with other laudable qualities, might stand a chance in a beauty contest.

Perhaps they knew there were going to be no winners anyway. Our job, once we'd snapped them with a convincing display of professional know-how (which came in very useful a little later in my career), was simply to sell a few prints to the mums, and any doting grannies who happened to be present. It was a little dishonest – people who had hoped their junior plug-uglies were going to become stars were disappointed – but no one was seriously harmed and they had a lovely memento to go home with. And it was very easy.

These scams appealed to me enormously, not because they were crooked but because they involved, albeit without a great deal of subtlety, the art of deception, which fascinated me, and magic, which I'd been hooked on ever since I'd first seen it in the canteen at Bentalls. I was fascinated by the comparative ease with which the simple tricks could be achieved, merely by distracting or offering the victim's mind another focus of attention. It was at about this time, at a glitzy show-business party that I had wangled my way into, that I saw the famous magician Ali Bongo performing at close quarters. I was gripped by what he had done – an uncomplicated but mystifying manoeuvre involving a handful of salt that he was able to make appear and disappear on demand. I sidled up to him later and, without much hope, asked if he would tell me how he did it. He took one look at me and, either recognising a soulmate or anxious to get rid of me as soon as possible, slipped the piece of equipment – the 'gimmick' – he'd used into my pocket.

'Don't you tell anyone else about it, son,' he murmured conspiratorially.

By giving me this unsophisticated little bit of kit (which the rules of the Magic Circle forbid me to describe) he did me a great favour. I went on to find out as much as I could, shamelessly extracting lessons and tips from practising magicians until I was deemed good enough to apply for membership of the Magic Circle myself, although I never got around to formalising arrangements. I still derive huge enjoyment out of it; whether or not my audience does is, of course, another matter.

In the spring of 1960, on a two-week run at Leicester Rep, I met an actress a year or so older than me who was already an unmarried mum and was appearing there under the name of Jenny Lewes. Her real name was Genista Ouvry, always known as Genny. She had just been transferred by the impresario of provincial repertory theatre, Mr Barry O'Brien, from Bournemouth to play the lead in *The French Mistress*. I was playing Edmund, opposite her.

With my customary impulsiveness and, I suppose, with what a shrink would deem to be my underlying need for domestic stability, we met for the first time on a Tuesday and were engaged by the following Thursday. In part, my instant decision must have been influenced by the rapid consummation of our relationship, my first complete sexual experience since the girl in the English Opera Group.

When we proudly told the rest of the company, for some reason inexplicable to me then, they fell about with cynical laughter, pissing themselves to a man and woman.

We weren't deterred, though, and when Genny landed a job in rep for the summer season at the Theatre Royal, Shanklin, on the Isle of Wight, I quickly made my way down there to see her. The whole prospect of spending summer in a seaside resort with her looked very appealing to me.

While I was back home in Tolworth for a few days before returning to London, my father was more acerbic than ever about my career prospects.

'You're just playing at it,' he sneered. 'You won't amount to anything, doing a few bit parts here and there. I've told you to get a career, somewhere you might expect to end up a thousand-a-year man.' He had an extraordinary vision of this superhuman being who could command a four-figure salary and to whom all doors were open and everything was possible.

I tried to fight back, but it was hard. I was insecure enough about my prospects as it was, and I didn't dare tell him yet about my plans to marry Genny, let alone the existence of her son.

'Well,' I retorted. 'It so happens I've got a job for the rest of the summer, in the Isle of Wight.'

I hadn't yet, but I was pretty sure from my researches that I could. 'And then you can tell me what a waster I am.'

The row degenerated, once again coming very close to the physical battles we had had when he knew he was stronger than me. As it was, I still wasn't much of a match for him. That night I felt utterly forlorn and almost suicidal. I rang Genny in the Isle of Wight and found that just the sound of her voice helped to soothe me; she promised to do anything she could to help.

Actually, it turned out she was more worried than I'd realised. I must have come on a little stronger than I'd intended. That's the trouble with being an actor for most of your life: you get very careless about calling your skills to heel when once you've let them out of the bag. But I did manage to find a place for the season at the Pavilion Theatre, Ryde. Beryl Seton was very disparaging, even quite shirty, about my dogged-ness in going, since it meant missing out on a few more lucrative and, frankly, career-enhancing roles in *Dixon of Dock Green*. It was, in retrospect, by no means the last time I sacrificed a constructive career move for the advancement of my chronically dysfunctional love life.

*

Ryde was not at its best when I first made its acquaintance. As if putting my youthful optimism to the test, the rain was sploshing down as I stepped off the boat from Portsmouth. In front of me, a swirling mist shrouded the long, north-facing Esplanade, like theatrical ghost-gauze. Groups of tourists were stumbling along bravely with short, gritty steps, clinging to their billowing brollies like figures in a Lowry townscape.

Looking around through the lashing rain, I identified my theatre – a run-down edifice with a perceptible list to starboard and an undisguised rusty, wrinkled iron roof. I thought it must present an interesting challenge in the rain; worse in hail. Shouting at an audience to overcome the rattle of what would have sounded like rapid machine-gun fire could hardly be an encouragement to subtle performance.

At that time there were two repertory theatres on the island, one in Shanklin and the other in Ryde, this latter very much the dowdy sister, constantly showing her slip. There were in fact three theatres if you counted the small, non-professional but very enthusiastic company based in Ventnor, but the Ryde Pavilion had neither the kudos of amateur status nor the voluntary optimism and passion of a local dramatic association. A few weeks after I was well settled in, a group of us went to see one of their shows, *Peter Pan*. In this financially challenged production Peter and the children didn't fly but ran up a staircase, waving their arms furiously in front of a glitter-dust night sky that buckled in the centre. It was an enchanting evening, full of gusto and derring-do, and although the audience smiled at the costumes and the sets, there was nothing patronising in their applause.

We professionals loved every moment of it and only wished that we could have pleased our audiences as effectively. It was made even more magical because they had added this special Sunday night performance so that the other actors on the island could see it. Delightful. Bravely, they even fielded a live dog which, for once, was accurately portrayed by a Newfoundland and not, as is so often the case, by an Old English sheepdog. It slobbered liberally, as Newfoundlands will, while a handy member of the cast hung constantly at the ready with a tea towel.

That's what I call theatre.

But for now, and the next few months, the Pavilion, Ryde, was my theatre. It was Sunday, ten in the morning, when I'd arrived on the ferry. I didn't have to go to rehearsals until the following day for the new play, which opened on Thursday. I was to play Cadwallader, a Welsh police-man in Agatha Christie's *The Unexpected Guest*, a hardy old repertory staple. The character had only a few lines and spent most of his time squirming around in a doorway, flicking the pages of a notebook, looking Welsh and confused. Thus it had been decided, in the interest of economy, that I didn't need to be there for the first two rehearsal days. My ability to look Welsh and fumble with a notebook was taken as read.

The rehearsal schedule, I discovered, always took the same form: Friday, block acts one and two; Saturday, act three. Sunday was left free for learning the lines, so the actors could arrive on Monday morning more or less knowing them. (Or 'coming off the book', as it is known; or, far more intimidating, 'DLP' – Dead Letter Perfect – a rare occurrence indeed.) For the shorter roles, this was quite satisfactory: cleaners, policemen, odd red-herring colonels – easy-peasy. For the meatier parts, nobody ever got really to grips with the text until the dress rehearsal, and regularly frantic actors could be seen in the Ryde Castle Hotel bar, across the street from the theatre, with script in hand, postcard jerking down the page and lips moving frenetically in a soundless mutter. With their head inclined towards the ceiling, their eyes would stare wildly for a moment, then dart back to the page as the postcard moved down, was lifted for a quick peek – a bizarre pattern of behaviour, suggesting chronic addiction to absinthe.

There you have the answer to the question always asked of actors: 'How do you learn your lines?'

In fact, in my experience, it's a combination of slog-learning, with stage moves and contextual clues: the picking up of a prop; the natural flow of the character within the scene and the play itself – a landfill of sometimes odd and seemingly unfathomable information that, by osmosis or panic, or both, gets you there in the end. Unless it's Pinter, or Beckett, or N. F. Simpson, in which case it's all slog. Shakespeare, by comparison, is a gentle breeze. The rhythm and the sheer elegance of the language carry the actor along. It's getting the depth and reach of the character that's the tricky bit with Will.

On Mondays and Tuesdays, then, we rehearsed through each act; on Wednesdays, there were two run-throughs, all very stop and start, but completed in time for the current show's matinée, with a final run-through and photographs on Thursday morning. In the afternoon there was a dress rehearsal. The first performance was that evening, with nerves raw and stomachs churning bile.

This sequence was adhered to rigidly for all fourteen plays we did over the summer months. It was gruelling and horribly confusing, with a maze of plots and endings, characters and sets – all seeming somehow very similar, which led inevitably to moments of sublime disorientation. An actor might easily slip into a small section of last week's play, particularly if a cue happened to be close to one from the previous production.

These were all delights to come. For now I was confronted with the very dark and gloomy entrance to what looked like a cardboard warehouse. A poster announced *Bed Linen* by James Fish. A farce, apparently. I drifted around, looking for the stage door, which I found set in one side of the building from which emerged a sound of banging somewhere inside. I dropped my bag and whisper-footed my way along what looked like a narrow hospital corridor from the Great War, with peeling paint in aubergine and brown, and a vague smell of damp mingled with greasepaint. The backstage of all theatres in those days smelt the same, whether the Vaudeville, the Savoy, the Theatre Royal, Haymarket, or the Pavilion Theatre, Ryde. Different theatres each, to be sure, but shut the eyes and open the nostrils for a good sniff backstage and you'd be hard pressed to tell the difference.

I peered into a dressing room, seeing the familiar bare bulbs around mirrors that were propped precariously against the walls on trestle tables, with curly-edged postcards and photographs pinned to the frames. I peered at myself in the nearest, leaning on my hands among the make-up sticks and flannels, remover and powder. A moustache and sideburns were set with pins in a soft stuffed head, mounted on a base. I noted that the mirror reflection was by no means true. My chin swept floorwards as in a fairground attraction and to get a decent image I had to find exactly the right spot. So far, I thought, *nul point*.

My reflections were interrupted by a voice with a Hampshire accent from the door. In the mirror, I saw a very little person of around forty, but he grew about six inches as I turned and faced him directly. The mirror would have to go, I thought.

'What d'you want?' he burred.

'David Hemmings. Come to join the company. Here for the season,' I said. I was going through an adolescent, clipped-dialogue period, stolen from some recent movie. (Fortunately, over the years, it passed, though I admit to still saying things like 'V. good', an irritating hang-over from that period.)

'Not many last the *whole* season,' he observed, almost to himself. 'Sunday's a day off. Only the set boys in today. I'm Fritz, the stage doorman.'

He had a proprietary air about him and he rocked on his heels like Jack Warner in *Dixon*. He was obviously proud of his status as theatre owner by proxy. I learned later that he had been at this stage door for twenty-odd years. His face had the look of a piece of newspaper crumpled for the fire, so that you felt that, if you turned sideways and squinted, you could read it. This was topped by a round dome, bald on top, with three or four hairs Brylcreemed across it like Tooting Bec tram-lines. He wore a long brown grocer's coat with indeterminate paint smears on it, so I guessed he also worked the scene dock when pressed. We shook hands.

'Nobody in today, just me and the chippie. Where you be stayin'?'

'Shanklin. Friend there. My fiancée.'

He looked at me in sly disbelief. Even at my now relatively travelled age of eighteen, I looked as if I should be in short trousers and sucking a gobstopper. To demonstrate my maturity, I pulled out my American Pall Malls in their long red soft-pack, acquired underhandedly from Ruislip US Army base. Eccentric cigarettes were, at the time, another feeble affectation of mine. I banged on the pack expertly and a single cigarette popped out, which I offered to him. He eyed it with great suspicion, as if he were being sold a used car, flicking his eyes up at me from under thick eyebrows.

'Roll my own,' he said, then paused as I started to light up with my Zippo.

Another cool move, I thought, but he was not much impressed. Some people can flick open a Zippo and it looks as if the flame bursts forth instantly, magically. But it was a knack I had yet to acquire. Anyway, I probably hadn't filled it, because it stubbornly refused to light.

Fritz leaned through the doorway, holding an old brass tube-lighter with a dangling wick that he'd whisked from his coat, and thrust the flame to the end of my cigarette.

'Engaged, then? You don't look but a boy.'

'Yes. Engaged. Month ago. She's here for the Shanklin season.'

'Shanklin, eh?' There was a certain reverence in his voice, as if I'd mentioned the Vatican. 'And you here at the low end. That don't bode too well, do it? They're all snobs up there in Shanklin.' He paused to look at me closely. 'Hemmings, you say?'

'Hemmings. Yes.'

'I'll be back in a bit,' he said, and went off down the passage, muttering the word 'Engaged' to himself in wonderment and deep concern for youth.

'I'll be on the stage,' I called after him. I wanted to see it, see the inside of the theatre, get a bearing or two – just tread the boards.

For an actor, there is something utterly compelling about an empty stage with a silent auditorium in front of you. The imagination runs riot. You can almost hear audiences applauding and feel the spotlights in your eyes, blinding you from the faces in the seats. Even when no one is in, there is often a light spilling onto the stage, illuminating part of it flatly, brighter than the overhead worklight for the stage staff. Instinctively you move into it and breathe in the adrenalin that seems to have been bottled by a long succession of performers and then scattered liberally along the footlights.

I went to examine the stage setting for, presumably, *Bed Linen*. I sat in a deep armchair, which, since it was normally the case with reps, had probably been borrowed from a local antiques shop. Fritz came back.

'Thought so. Message for you.' He walked over with floppy Clarks sandals scraping across the stage and thick black socks bulging between the straps to hand it to me.

It was a note from Genny telling me her address in Shanklin. I deliberately hadn't organised any digs of my own, since we had a tacit agreement that I would stay with her, even though cohabitation in rooms was strictly forbidden. I had thought this represented an added challenge to spice up the coming months, a lot of ducking and diving and sneaking up stairs. The deviousness with which we conducted our relationship would have done credit to a John le Carré novel, though in truth I doubt that we fooled a soul. On our desperately meagre salaries, however (I was earning £7 a week, Genny £10), the fact that we could share a bed offered economic advantages as well as the more obvious tender creature comforts.

I thanked Fritz and wandered up to the bus stop, while the rain still splattered and the brollies still flapped in single file along the Esplanade, still Lowry-like as the wind cut through and dispersed the mist, whipping up whitecaps across the Solent. If I had been trying to design a backdrop for a French *film noir* I couldn't have done a better job.

Ryde needed the sun. I needed the sun – and I badly needed Genny.

*

Shanklin is very different from Ryde, more upmarket, less susceptible to day visitors. More Land Rovers and bridge, gin and tonics in the Bear Hotel lounge on Sundays.

Genny hadn't made her final living arrangements when she left Leicester, but she'd said in her note that she was staying in Deverall Road, opposite the Theatre Royal, where she was playing. Her landlady was a Mrs Worthington, no less, about whom, as the season progressed, there were to be many Noël Coward jokes, 'Don't let young Genny come of age, Mrs Worthington', being the least smutty.

As I turned into Deverall Road, off the main street, the theatre loomed at me, imposing, grey and in complete contrast to the shack at Ryde where I was to be employed. I saw at once what Fritz had meant. It had great sweeping steps leading to the front of house, with classical colonnades on either side. This was the real thing – serious stuff, I felt. I had to ask myself if I'd made a bad move and should have listened to my agent, but the deed was done.

'You'll regret it,' Beryl had said with a minatory shake of her head. 'Ryde is the pits. Barry O'Brien is the pits. You have TV offers this summer. You want to throw your career away?'

Clearly, I was in love, committed, dewy-eyed and just eighteen. The one-eyed trouser snake was in command, waving about in readiness for the battle of the Little Big Horn, where I was Sitting Bull. Thus I did not listen. My virginity was on offer here; I wanted eternal groping, not fame. Again, I sought out the stage door, which was open but with no Fritz lookalike. This was a much grander affair, with a glass booth and message racks, a telephone on the wall. I pulled a bit of paper from the rack and scribbled a note, saying, simply, 'Attention Jenny Lewes', and stuck it on my bag, which I left in the booth. I could hardly, after all, rap on Mrs Worthington's door, suitcase in hand, like a waif in search of soup and shelter, and sex.

The houses on Deverall Road were rather impressive, detached, with gardens at the front and rear. Vaguely Victorian, faintly oppressive. No. 11 had a tree in the front, which I assessed for climbability, though of course I had no idea which room Genny might have been given. Despite my reluctance, I finally plucked up enough courage to knock on the door and in moments a very large woman pulled it open. She was not large in the rotund sense, just tall and imposing, with shoulders like

Henry Cooper's. She had gimlet brown eyes which flashed with superhuman intelligence. I shrank back as if I had been sent to a headmistress behind whom a very sharp cane lurked. This did not bode well for the plan. This was not the unfortunate victim of senile dementia that I had probably hoped for. And this was a sighted person. Not a cane in view. No hearing aid. No luck. This was an Amazonian who could, I was sure, crush hormone-crazy actors found illicitly stair-creeping with one squeeze of a single hand.

'Yes?' she asked discouragingly.

'From the theatre,' I mumbled, lips drying, tongue swelling.

'Yes?' She smiled in sympathy at what she must have imagined was my shyness.

I was actually having a cardiac arrest. I had thought that the whole thing would be easy, that it might be fun to be so skulduggerous, but I had not reckoned with my own normal state of perpetual anxiety. The full realisation of what we were plotting, Genny and I, was thumped home by this charmingly terrifying gargantuan landlady. My groin friend was in retreat. Custer had won. We had not yet embarked upon the sixties proper, when life would have been a bunch easier and she'd have probably invited me in to share some Acapulco Gold. I thought I would compensate. I would simply ask for Genny. A sensible, mature approach.

'Yes, good morning.' I paused. 'Were you thinking of going to the theatre this week? Canvassing the local residents.' Fear and compromise don't drink together.

'Yes, of course,' she answered indignantly. '*Bell, Book and Candle*. I go to every play without fail. I have Jenny Lewes staying with me. She's in the cast, you know. Leading lady.'

'Yes. I did know. With the company myself.'

'Are you in this play?'

'No. Not this one. No.' A silence like thunder. Please let me fall into this deep ditch I am currently digging specifically for myself, I thought.

'Well, thank you. Enjoy the play.'

'I'm sure I will. Goodbye.'

I backed up the path, then turned hastily towards the gate, which creaked ominously.

She called after me, nothing but kindness. 'Mind the road,' she said. She sounded like my mother.

*

Finding Genny was the first priority and I was no expert on the high streets and by-ways of Shanklin. I went to the stage door to see if the doorman was at his post, but no luck. The place was seriously dark. My bag was still there, its note on top, untouched. The obvious answer, of course, would be the local hostelry. I was well aware that most landlords are mines of information. Actors do not go far at the end of a performance to find the first pint, so I thought it would probably be the nearest. They give little consideration for quality of service or winning smiles. Their simple requirements are proximity, speed at the pump or optic and a certain flexibility regarding closing times. It was pressing lunchtime anyway, but because of age restrictions, without appropriate friendly connections I was hardly going to be welcome in a pub. I'd probably have to suffer a Coke and a cheese roll, followed by a trudge up to the main road and a beer.

The Bear Hotel appeared to be the closest watering hole, about a hundred yards up the street. It sported a small front lawn with optimistic garden furniture sprouting sun umbrellas from white iron tables, now fending off the rain. Hotels have advantages for actors too, since the licensing hours can depend on residential status, easily acquired with a wink and a theatre ticket or two. Besides, I assumed, as far as the hotel management was concerned, actors were a jolly crowd who attracted additional custom.

The Bear tuned out to be an extended cottage, with no more than a dozen rooms. The bar possessed that special aroma, peculiar to pubs, of stale smoke and sour beer. It contained a clutter of dark wheel-back chairs on a thick, gloomy and slightly sticky carpet. The place was fairly crowded with what I took to be locals talking about property prices and traffic flow through the town.

Conscious of my age and more in hope than expectation, I ordered a pint of shandy, which was plonked on the bar immediately with no questions asked. Things were looking up, although there was still no sign of Genny.

I was munching my way through an unassuming cheese roll, trying to identify a likely person to ask about theatrical types, when through the murmuring council-meeting atmosphere a deep booming voice, RADA rich, carried across the room like an approaching storm. I made my way towards it with a fresh shandy – light on the lemonade this time – to discover its source was a woman of about sixty. I was sure she must be part of the theatre company.

She was a voluminous woman, with large heaving breasts and broad shoulders wrapped in a summer sarong more like a caravan cover than a dress. Her ample behind generously overlapped the meagre seat of the barstool. This was obviously my day for larger women.

During a brief pause in the almost unstoppable flow of her conversation, I introduced myself and discovered she was called Evelyn Gaye. I explained that I was an actor looking for another. Did she know Jenny Lewes? Was she with the company?

She wasn't, as it happened. She ran an antiques shop on the edge of town. But, she told me, she and her friends generally used another pub called the George. 'It's cheaper, you see.'

I offered her a drink, which she promptly accepted, a large vodka and tonic, no ice. She stirred it with a podgy finger, covered in rings of dubious caratage, and tipped it down in one. My wallet winced with pain. I soon gathered that she had been an actress but had retired and now knew all of the current Theatre Royal company quite well, including Genny.

'I do provide them with the odd piece of furniture for shows,' she said. 'And I take the trouble to get to know them all, sleep with some, if there's anything lively going,' she added simply. 'Of course, a lot of them have turned these days. Queer as coots. It's all very depressing. You're not a homo, are you?'

I shook my head emphatically. 'Not remotely. Engaged.'

'Give it time, love, give it time. You've got a good bum.'

Her audience laughed. I ordered a pint of best bitter. I liked her a great deal and, as the season progressed and I spent much of the time commuting between Ryde and Shanklin, I saw a lot of her. Her voice was certainly the result of a combination of vodka and Senior Service (which I thought, considering her age and lusty lifestyle, to be a rather well-named cigarette for her to smoke). The years she had spent belting out songs in Vaudeville – she had appeared at the Players' Theatre, a London landmark for traditional variety shows until quite recently – had certainly left their mark. Her voice reminded me of a description of Louis Armstrong's special timbre, something along the lines of 'old nuts and bolts with a little oil being shaken around in a shoebox'.

I have this strange and sometimes inconvenient gift for attracting 'characters', or perhaps I'm attracted to them – either way, it happens. So it was with Evelyn. She insisted on escorting me personally to the George, probably on the scent of further vodkas.

On the way down the hill, I told her the Genny story and explained why I hadn't been here for the first two weeks of the season.

'So you ended up in Ryde, eh? Lord, nothing like true love,' she said.

'Well, it can't be that bad – can it?' I asked anxiously.

'Shanklin's the place, love. Better theatre, better actors. Perhaps you can switch.'

'I'll be fine.'

It seemed no one had a good word to say for the poor old Ryde Pavilion.

Genny wasn't at the George, but a couple of other members of the company were. Evelyn was greeted with bows and much enthusiasm. I wondered if she had already managed to bed any of the current troupe. I doubted it. Charlie Cousins was a balding, red-faced fellow with a broad smile and acerbic wit. He had a younger man with him, Tom, who was thin and pasty, with sunken eye and flaccid hands. He looked vacant as he stroked my hand by way of a shake, while Charlie grinned and saluted with a limp wave from the forehead.

There was also a young girl, Alice, an assistant stage manager, I was told, with the slightly frenetic look of someone a little out of her depth, trying to remember what she ought to have done that morning but hadn't. Her notebook was on the bar, crumpled and bulging with dog-eared paper notes.

Charlie offered us both a drink.

The barman stared at me. 'How old are you?'

'Old enough,' Charlie intervened, 'for me to buy him a drink.' He turned to Evelyn. 'Where did you find him?' he asked peering at me with interest.

'The Bear. And keep your eyes off him. He's engaged to Genny. He's with the cast at Ryde.'

'Good God! Poor soul. You look far too young to be on your way out. They send actors to Ryde to die where no one can see them.'

'So they tell me,' I said weakly.

'Great arse,' Charlie went on, not stopping his perusal of the goods for a moment.

Evelyn pulled deeply on her Senior Service and slugged another vodka. It didn't touch the sides, as usual. A wad of notes came from her bag and was smacked onto the bar. She was certainly not short of a penny or two.

'More,' she said as imperiously as Edith Evans being Lady Bracknell.

Heads turned to the entrance as a comparatively elegant young man came in through the etched-glass doors. He was very well dressed, with a theatrical manner and a resonant, educated voice, demonstrated in a somewhat stentorian, 'Good morning. Drink, anyone? And a very good morning to you, Evelyn.' He looked at me. 'Who's this, dare we ask?'

Evelyn put an overprotective arm around my shoulder. 'He's mine,' she said. 'Finders keepers.'

'David Hemmings.' I offered a hand. 'Good to meet you.'

'You an actor? Are you joining this lot?'

Tony chipped in from somewhere deep in his personal closet, like a cold breeze. 'He's with you lot. Ryde.'

'I'm at Ryde. Paul Elliot's the name. How good to meet you.'

We became friends at once, and it was certainly good at last to meet someone from the same company. Paul had a wicked glint and a charming way about him. He gave me a rewarding back-slap.

'Are you *the* David Hemmings? English Opera Group, Benjamin Britten, television, all that?'

I was, I said.

'Good heavens! What on earth are you doing here?'

'He's engaged to Genny. He wanted to be near her. They're going to do the "for richer for poorer" bit,' Evelyn said, looking at me carefully.

Charlie added, 'He's trying out the latter first. Slumming.'

Tony had perked up at this news. 'Ben Britten, eh? Did he . . . er?'

'No, he didn't.' I had fielded this question dozens of times.

'Take no notice of the woofters.' Paul dismissively downed a whisky and water. 'But Britten? Boy, you're asking for it with this lot.'

The ASM spoke up, tucking a pencil behind her ear. 'David Hemmings. I think I saw you in *The Heart Within*, with Earl Cameron. All set in the docks?'

'That's right.'

While Evelyn got more drinks in, Paul Elliot took control of the conversation, outlining for me the shaky status of the Pavilion Theatre and its gloomy start to the season. 'Oh, they look down on us, but actually it's tremendous fun. Good laughs. There's a lot to laugh at, of course. You'll have a great time. Up here they take it all far too seriously.' He grinned with mischief and meant it.

Now, some forty years later, Paul Elliot is the king of the pantomime circuit, studding stages with Danny La Rues, comedians, soap stars and retired boxers every winter season. He keeps some 120 pantos on the stage around the country each year and is known as a tough taskmaster, a hard worker and generally brilliant. He has cornered the market, much like Jimmy Goldsmith did on a good day. But I still can't remove him from the context of the Pavilion Theatre. We lost touch during my long stay in America, but when we did meet up again, the first thing that we discussed was our days in Ryde. A welcome trip down the memory lanes of the Isle of Wight.

Genny at last arrived at the George, like a whirlwind, with the doors crashing open, a scarf about her hair, bemoaning the rain, breathless, carrying a parcel of meat. Normally she was quiet and, I thought then, unusually shy for an actress. I've since discovered, though, that most actors are fundamentally shy, hiding behind the walls of very private castles, staring out through arrow-slit windows with fearful and often tearful eyes.

They emerge from time to time, painted in brighter colours than the truth to 'strut their trade and charms on the ivory stages', as Dylan Thomas described, or better yet, on a non-performing day, like Eliot's Prufrock, 'to prepare a face to meet the faces that you meet'.

I have a vivid recollection of David Warner before he went on stage to play Richard II at Stratford. He was in a paroxysm of despair, with his arms wrapped foetus-like around his knees, his hands clenched in white-knuckle despair, quivering with fear. His eyes were fixed in utter terror on an uncertain spot, like a bush-baby caught in torchlight, until suddenly he heard his cue to step on to the stage, to confront his audience and the complicated role. He straightened, pulling himself up to his considerable height, and the character emerged from within him, like an alien. His shoulders dropped and he walked forward through the wings, full of confidence to spend the next two hours giving a legendary, fearless, captivating performance, leaving schoolgirls to swoon in the stalls as if they'd been touched regally in the nether regions of their collective souls. It was stunning stuff.

Genny was a genuinely shy, gentle and vulnerable person. She wasn't particularly ambitious, just very real, and I loved her very much. We were an unlikely couple, she older and with a child, me a gregarious enthusiast, although in truth shy too, but with an efficient defence mechanism as a result of my young days spent in the company of extraordinary adults. Genny was more down to earth, more rooted, with a set of responsibilities that I hadn't even considered yet.

'David!' she called. 'I've been looking for you everywhere.'

'And me you. How'd you find me?'

'Saw your bag and the note, and Mrs Worthington.'

'Lord, she's something. I was terrified of her. Lied to her.'

'She told me.'

'She told you I lied?'

'Of course. You said you were with the company. She knows *everybody* in the company. She keeps a list. Gives a party for the whole team at the end of the first week. And you asked if she was going to the theatre. She got you in one. Thought you must be looking for me.'

'Oh, shit. And she asked me to "mind the road" – what a twit!'

I pulled out a Pall Mall and took a working-man's-cooperative from one of the burning cigarettes in the ashtray.

'I see you've found the team. How did you know the pub?'

'Evelyn,' I said, putting a hand on my new mentor's shoulder.

'I picked him up, lost in the Bear,' she grinned.

Genny laughed, slipped an arm through mine and gave me a peck on the cheek. I pulled her close.

Quickly I ordered a round, with dry white wine for Gen, whisky and Stones ginger wine for me to chase my lingering pint. For a while we chatted on, getting to know each other, sewing the first threads of a rich shared tapestry that is one of the best elements of theatre folk – gypsies all, wandering minstrels, troubadours, a new audience daily, whether in a pub or a playhouse.

Things, I felt, were looking up. This was going to be a grand summer. Evelyn slurped down her vodka, while a telltale dewy mist formed across her eyes. Charlie was staring at Tony, who had found another life in the middle distance, thinking perhaps of what things might be like with Benjamin Britten. Paul encouraged the ASM, Alice, with her notes, producing perhaps, even then. Genny and I slipped away with a wave. The meat in her bag was seeping blood and, as it was for Mrs Worthington, she wanted to get it back as soon as possible.

Thanks mainly to Paul Elliot, I settled into the routine of the Pavilion, Ryde, in a remarkably short space of time. We had a 'good, solid' audience there, I was told, meaning from among the residents, not the tourists. The visitors came too, of course, and were very welcome. They would turn up for a night out or, if it rained, on a Wednesday or Saturday matinée, smelling of seaweed. But the locals were our backbone. They would fill the theatre for an Agatha Christie, slipping out of their B&Bs or their honeysuckled cottages and pottering eagerly up towards the pier. They wore hats, cardies and 'sensible' shoes. Most of the women had grey or even pale azure hair, and long, serious smiles as they walked up, hugging their husbands' arms. The men, ruddy from wind and whisky, generally wore frayed sports jackets and twill trousers, or suits for an evening performance. It seemed to me, then, like a parade of muted colours, warm comfort and friendship.

Elizabeth Bellows was around eighty and owned Polly's Tea Rooms, a small establishment with a couple of letting rooms over the top. It was known locally and appropriately as 'The Parrot' and no one ever found out who Polly was. Elizabeth said she had no idea. She was a determined season-ticket holder, a regular who would lurk on the planks that led to the stage door, as if lying in wait.

'Go on, David,' she would say, giving me a little nudge. 'Just tell me whodunnit?'

I would smile and give her a complimentary ticket for the inevitable friend. (We used to get three comps per night, four on matinées. One of the perquisites for being paid so little.)

'Elizabeth, you know I can't tell you that,' I would reply with feigned indignation. She was perfectly familiar with my standard line after each performance. 'And please, don't give away our ending . . . It's the only one we've got.'

But she knew I would give in, which is why she always pitched me in the first place. Sometimes, though, I tried to throw her off track. I would sigh in resignation, then bend to her ear and speak in a preposterous stage whisper from behind my hand. 'Look out for the one in the blue dress in the second act.'

And sure enough, Elizabeth, getting the better of me, would wag a finger. 'Well, I'll rule her out, for a start!'

It was a weekly game, she in her elegant finest and ready for the afternoon; I unscrubbed, just about ready to fight my way to my four-foot dressing room, a few paces away.

I shared this hovel, surprisingly, with the leading man, who had rich grey locks, an eagle profile and a chocolate voice. He was one of those 'actors, you know', as my father might have said, who strut and pose. He was a glorious cross between Oscar Wilde and Rasputin. His name, or, at least, the name under which he appeared to the world, was Richard de Novard (pronounced Novar in the French manner, of course).

For the very first performance we gave together, he appeared ten minutes before the curtain was due to go up, which meant, officially, he was late. He dropped onto a creaking bentwood chair and crossed one leg over the other in order to scrape some shoe-leather dust from the bottom of his boot, which he wiped with an elongated finger across the lids of his eyes, as eyeshadow. He dabbed a little blusher on his cheeks and a bit of baby powder under the eyes. The whole process took him no more then fifteen seconds.

Once satisfied, he reached into his portmanteau – a solid, battered object of well-worn leather – and dug out a Thermos flask which turned out to be full of vodka. He gulped some down and stood rigid for a moment, as if struck by lightning, with wide staring eyes, until he shuddered from head to toe, rippling like a dog shaking itself after a swim. He hurled a pair of Fisherman's Friends towards the back of his throat before taking another long pull from the flask, followed by another long, rewarding shake.

Finally, he acknowledged my presence. 'How's the house?'

'Doesn't seem bad.'

'Well, bollocks to them!' He strutted off to peer through the curtain edge by the wings, something that was considered thoroughly bad form. He was already in costume, having changed at his digs, to allow for his last-minute arrival.

I soon grew accustomed to this routine – it seldom varied.

One of the more endearing customs of the company at Ryde was a weekly game which we devised to add a little zest to our lives. It was played with an apple and the rules were simple.

An actor was chosen, usually the person who had lost the previous week, and before the curtain went up on the final act this character was given a small apple, a Cox's orange, say. It was then his or her aim to pass the apple, preferably without the audience noticing, to one of the other performers on stage, disguised by some natural movement, like a handshake. Should an actor holding the apple have to leave the stage for any reason, it had to stay with them until their next entrance. If, however, it was their last exit, they were condemned to keep it and had lost the game.

They would also lose if they dropped the apple and an intended recipient was the loser if they failed to accept it. The person holding the apple as the last line of the play was spoken was liable for a full round of drinks in the pub later that evening, since the apple game was invariably played during the Saturday matinée.

This was tremendous fun, not only for the cast, but also for the regulars in the audience, who had long since discovered the tradition and would will their various favourites to victory. On a particularly good 'pass', even in the most solemn of plays – which, thank goodness, were rare – a great cheer would go up from the crowd, followed by thunderous applause. This left the uninitiated in the audience deeply perplexed. They might consult their programmes to see if there was a note about the line or the move that they should have understood. We even thought at one point, since the apple game was often more popular than the play, of including the rules on Saturdays and offering a prize to the members of the audience who had guessed the outcome.

It was inevitable on apple days that the stage blocking we had been assigned, and often the dialogue too, went out of the window. An actor would suddenly rush across the stage for no apparent reason, saying, 'Let me shake your hand, Miss Marple,' or some such unexpected addition to the text.

A regular Saturday afternoon coach party even brought along their own apple to one performance and passed it down the seats to one another whenever it was passed on stage. Since neither they nor we had any idea of how many times the apple might be passed, it was perfectly fair.

It was no surprise that Richard de Novard hated the game, which naturally made him the focus of extravagant plots. Maids who had only one entrance, and that long gone, would suddenly reappear uninvited during a later scene, holding an envelope to cover the apple and pass it with fresh dialogue along the lines of, 'A message from Lord Bramley, sir,' before discreetly bowing out.

After a brief look at the envelope, the holder might mutter, 'Isn't that Maisie's handwriting?' and pass it to another character on stage, who would quickly pass it again, saying, 'Never seen it before. What do you make of it, Chloe?' Then Chloe, as a last resort, might ring for the maid, who was duty bound to return onstage and be given the blasted thing back. If a duster or some other object was handy to cover the apple, a pass could be initiated with, 'Take this filthy thing away.' Always a popular line.

In *A Clean Kill* by Michael Gilbert, a popular whodunnit scribe, the inspector, played by me, had to explain to the audience in an enormously long speech how the deed had been done with chemical detergent. The most recent victim in the piece had been Marchant, a seaman, played by Paul Elliot. Marchant had snuffed it some fifteen minutes before I embarked on this dissertation. He had wound up under a sheet, part-hidden behind the sofa so as not to distract the audience from the denouement of the play. He had also been passed the apple. Only the two of us were on stage now until the curtain came down, so I thought I was safe. However, halfway through an impossible stretch of monologue, well peppered with chemical formulae and the fatal results of mixing washing powder with whisky, a gasp issued, quite unscripted, from the sheet behind the sofa.

I heard a murmur spread through the audience but, as I was facing them, the source of their interest escaped me for a moment, until I paused and turned, only to find the dead seaman, Marchant, wrapped in a Woolworths white single, giving a fair impression of Lazarus. Down the stage he crept, elbow after elbow, gasping and moaning with plenty of guttural drool rising and falling in his throat. It was a great performance, and I could do nothing but stand there and look aghast.

By now the audience were in hysterics – at least, the regulars were. As for the rest, this must have seemed a last-minute twist on an already convoluted plot, but I could offer nothing by way of explanation, even though the audience were mine to command. There was uproar among the regulars as Paul made his way inexorably to my trouser leg. With a dying heave and rolling eyes, he passed the apple to me under cover of the sheet. He slid back down and lay across my feet with arms spread-eagled.

There was nothing more I could do. The drinks would be on me that night.

For this performance we received a standing ovation, rare indeed in Ryde, joined uncertainly by the baffled tourists. There was little point in explaining the plot now. The moment had passed. The curtain came down and they were still standing.

On that particular afternoon I didn't deliver my usual line, 'Please don't give away our ending . . .' As the apple game went, no one would ever see its like again.

7

Wedlock and Dylan Thomas, 1961–1966

Accustomed as I was to the mothers of the girls at the Hook Heath Tennis Club wincing when they saw me drift into view, I was pathetically grateful that Genny's parents were ready to put a brave face on our impending marriage, however young we might have appeared to them. Their daughter already had a baby, Dominic, whom they loved very much, and I guess, as far as they were concerned (and it was still only 1961), any husband was better than none.

To be fair to Mr and Mrs Ouvry, they did far more than I could have asked in accommodating us in our own wonderful flat (which, of course, I called the Penthouse) on the top floor of their rambling manor house. This allowed us to be close to them, which helped both with expenses and with looking after Dominic when we were working.

My father remained tight-lipped and unbending in his cynical attitude towards the marriage. He was vile to Genny about it, accusing her of simply wanting a father for her illegitimate son. He was scathing with me for being so weak as to be taken in by her.

The first of the four marriage ceremonies in which, over the next forty years, I was to appear as groom, was a slap-up white wedding at St John's Church, Hurst Green, in Surrey, on 25 March 1961. Fifty or sixty guests, smart Ouvry relations and more down-at-heel Hemmingses, with a few actors and my oldest friend Peter Goodchild, as best man, witnessed our promises and exchange of vows – all, as it turned out, of an ephemeral nature, but sincerely meant while they lasted. I had bought a book on wedding procedure, and Peter and I each delivered short, stuttering speeches that make me blush to recall. Thank God that no one in those days was around to capture them on film. Genny's father, Romilly, laid on a lavish reception at a hotel in Westerham and subbed most of the cost of our honeymoon – a week's falling over in the snow in Austria.

When we first settled in to our new life of wedded domesticity, I was determined to make the most of living in the unaccustomed splendour of Limpsfield Court, and I soon made a name for entertaining at the house, as well as arranging great gatherings in the local pubs.

The other members of the family weren't always happy about this but, on the whole, I got on with them well enough. I was a little in awe of Romilly Ouvry, who was a lawyer, precise, dour and somewhat uncommunicative, while his wife was an absolute charmer, and determined to deal with all the tribulations life had thrown at her with as little fuss as possible. I was very fond of her.

There were two brothers, as well, Jonathan and David, with whom I did my best to get along, but sanguine though I always am about my relationships, I had to acknowledge early on that I was never going to get anywhere with Jonathan. He was about to join his father's law firm and already had some of his father's aloofness. I remember calling him 'Johnny' once, as is my wont, and he exploded with affronted dignity.

'Never, ever call me Johnny,' he barked furiously.

David, by contrast, was a wonderful musician, a cellist, among other things, and thus altogether more circumspect, in the way musicians tend to be as they immerse themselves in music and don't really care what's going on in the world about them. I have long loved to lose myself at the piano, so I understood this very well.

But in general I was under no illusion that I was anything more than tolerated in the household and my efforts to engage in the upbringing of Dominic, for whom I wanted to take responsibility, were met with complete indifference by my in-laws. I think they took the practical position, always tricky to gainsay, that as they were paying the bills, they called the shots. However, I was determined to make the marriage work, whatever obstacles were thrust in our way, as much by the demands of my career as anything else.

Thanks to Beryl Seton, I was beginning to work steadily, if not lucratively. I was becoming quite well known among the London film crews and a few of the British directors who were working at the time. There was a lot of celebration and bottle-opening when I landed a part in an early English TV soap, *Home Tonight*, which was broadcast live at the same time as *The Archers*. Unfortunately, a few months in, it fell victim to a well-supported actors' strike (famously broken by the

Canadian comedian Bernard Braden) and the whole thing came to a halt. I lost my job, and the Ouvry parents, after a temporary respite, resumed their tutting.

I played a small role in a film called *The Wind of Change*, in which Donald Pleasence played the lead, and I managed to get a part in a play of folkloric tendency at Leatherhead Rep, which did something for my credibility, if not for my bank balance. I was finding that although most of our living expenses were being met by the Ouvrys, I had developed very expensive tastes, and I never, ever seemed to have enough money. Added to that, Genny announced that she was pregnant.

As I'd come to consider myself an entrepreneur first and an actor second, I decided that I'd better try and set up some enterprise that would keep me going between jobs. With great enthusiasm, and expense (I can't remember whose), I went out, researched and bought a small printing press, which I installed in our flat. I figured that as I still never seemed to sleep, I could use the small hours to set it all up, and ended up whiling away many long nights fiddling about with it. In the end, the only print orders we took were from family and friends, who got the work done either for nothing or at a massive, loss-making discount.

Meanwhile, I found myself spending more and more time in London. Living like the young country squire was all very well, I told Genny, but realistically I had to keep in touch with everyone in the business to get the jobs that were going. And I had to do what I could to supplement my income. I even did a stint as a DJ in those days – not a good one – and, worse, I adopted that mid-Atlantic accent which appeared to be a given at the time. It seems impossible to credit John Peel with once sounding close to Jerry Springer, but this is fact. Dave Holden was my disc name, and I would come out with lines like, 'This is your own DJ, DH, bringing you the best of the sounds around on wax and shellac – now here's my favourite pair, Sonny and Cher.'

Well, please! You wouldn't have wanted to know me. Thank heavens it was Holden not Hemmings who took the stick. And I must insert a word here about John Peel, the ubiquitous broadcaster, who seemed to find albums that no one else could find, and which were – to me – truly ugly. There were those who came to dread his long-running signature tune on the BBC World Service, promising the nastiest heavy metal tracks, one with the unforgettably tender lyrics, 'Loving you's a dirty job, and I'm the man to do it,' screamed with wide-open throat. It is fair to say, though, that in the early days he probably launched more bands that otherwise would not have got a listen than anyone else.

However, while I was in London with very little money, I didn't want to waste it on accommodation if I'd been out late, and I got into the habit of staying with friends – people I'd known from my days with the Elbozes: Leapy Lee, Andrew Ray, but more often than not girls who offered a little more than bed and breakfast.

I was sure there was nothing wrong with this, as long as Genny didn't find out, and I became an adept manipulator of the truth – to save her from hurt, I convinced myself. I also couldn't deny that I enjoyed running around with other girls. Dylis Watling was a nightclub singer who lived in a house full of artists, where I felt quite at home, and sometimes thought I should have taken my art more seriously; I couldn't have been any worse off than I was already. Amanda Reiss, then an actress who'd been in *The Rag Trade* and a couple of 'Nurse' things, was a few rungs even lower in the pecking order than me and happy to put me up for the night.

The year 1962, when the Beatles erupted into our consciousness with 'Love Me Do', was better for me. After a short run in a Pamela Franco play at the Theatre Royal in Windsor, I went down to Bristol for a couple of months to make *Some People* for Clive Donner. The film's message was encapsulated in the opening line of the soundtrack – 'Some people think that kids today have gone astray . . .' It was about youth clubs, vicars, shrinkable blue jeans, motorbikes and English rock'n'roll. Four teenage layabouts are talked into forming a rock group to keep them out of trouble, and I appeared as the first of several young pop singers I played in a bunch of low-budget movies that quickly slipped below the threshold of public consciousness. This was also the first time I'd worked with Ray Brooks, before *The Knack* thrust him into the spotlight. He became a good friend and got on well with Genny when she came to visit the set in Bristol, very pregnant. After that, he often came down to while away a few days at Limpsfield Court.

Another regular visitor was Peter Goodchild. Although he was younger than me, I envied his intelligence and perceptiveness. His life had obviously diverged from mine – it would do so even more when he went to study Russian at Liverpool University the following autumn – and sport had become a more dominant part of his life. But despite the fact that he had nothing to do with my life as an actor, because we'd shared so many adventures as kids, I found his company reassuring. He couldn't drive yet, so when there wasn't much else going on I would ring him and, if he was free, drive over to Woking to pick him up from Goldsworth Road. He would stay in our penthouse at Limpsfield for a week or two at a time. We played tennis and golf around the garden and we would make films on a crummy little 8mm cine camera I'd bought – an early manifestation of my aspirations to direct films.

On 13 April 1962, our daughter Deborah was born. I was astonished and utterly overawed by the idea of fatherhood. Paternal pride and a determination to be better at the job than my own father dominated my thinking for the first few months. It also made me want to try harder at being married, although Genny's postnatal lack of interest in the physical side of marriage was more than I could handle.

At the same time, I was feeling more buoyant about my career. *Some People* had been made with a small grant, or perhaps just a pat on the back from a Duke of Edinburgh Foundation designed to encourage young folk not to behave like the complete arseholes that nature intends and show how tearaways could go straight, if only . . .

As a result there was a reception for Clive Donner and all the cast at Windsor Castle, and however much of a rebel I might have thought I was, I was pretty impressed.

The euphoria was marred soon afterwards by the death of my grandfather Percy Hemmings, whom I loved and with whom I still felt a strong bond. Genny and I went over to Woking to be with my parents and do what we could to help with the funeral. I was almost overwhelmed by the effects of this first death of a close member of my family, especially one with whom I was sure I had a lot in common. After that, my parents, always strapped for cash, it seemed, moved in with my grandmother at Redstacks. In a way, this too was sad for me, because it was to Redstacks that I had gone to escape my father's excessive discipline, and now he was there all the time. But I had my own home and my own life now, and I refused to let it bother me too much.

Anyway, I was busy again. I'd been cast to play a small part in another rock'n'roll film, an early example of the work of that famously florid eater of dinners, Michael 'Death Wish' Winner. *Play it Cool* starred Billy Fury as a lip-curling Elvis look-quite-alike, with the busty baritone Helen Shapiro appearing as herself. It was one of those pictures that tried so hard to be hip it looked hopelessly dated before it was even finished. But I enjoyed myself, glad of the excuse to get away from babies and nappies, and happy to be working with Ray Brooks again.

This was followed by a rather bizarre little film called *The Painted Smile*, about deception and murder.

That summer, in anticipation of my 21st birthday, Genny and I were allowed – even encouraged – by her parents to hold a huge party in the grounds of Limpsfield Court. I was tremendously stimulated by the whole idea and threw myself into the organisation of it. Naturally, I asked everyone I could remember I'd ever worked with, and, in my naïvety, wasn't at all surprised when hundreds of them turned up – a crowd so diverse as to include Ned Sherrin, John Hurt, Gordon Newman, Patrick Garland and Tom Courtenay, along with a number of my shadier London friends and girlfriends, including – and this was probably an error – Amanda Reiss.

When the day came we faced a number of potential disasters. First, Romilly Ouvry had been taken to hospital and his wife was ill in bed. They insisted, though, that we go ahead. But it turned out to be one of those classic English summer days when it doesn't stop raining for 24 hours, and the whole party had to be moved into the main part of house, and the escapologist I'd hired at great cost had to do his stuff dangling not from a tree, as planned, but from the fortunately robust oak rails of the main staircase. The booze didn't run out and bouts of furtive groping were taking place in every nook and corner of the old house, not least, somewhat indiscriminately, by me, and the party, despite all the problems, was deemed a complete success and still lives on in the memories of large numbers of elderly actors and film people.

It's possible that the Ouvrys' thinking behind the party had been that if I could entertain my friends at home, I wouldn't spend so much time away from Genny in London. If anything, it had the reverse effect, although for a while I did make a little more of an effort to go home. I remember clearly one evening in the autumn of 1962, after a day etched grimly on the memories of all of us who were alive then, standing on Waterloo Station with Andrew Ray to catch a train home, listening to the news broadcast over the Tannoy that the United States and Russia were nose to nose in brinkmanship over what came to be known as the Cuban Missile Crisis.

We were truly frightened. We believed that there was a real threat to our safety and our security. Of course, this wasn't discussed as we approached platform 12. Rather, there was silence. We looked at each other, I recall, neither of us prepared to express our feelings. Other passengers on the train were silent too, staring in front of them in bewilderment and fear.

A few days later, the Russian ships carrying their nuclear weapons turned back, and we sighed with relief. The anxiety, however, remained and, with it, a lack of responsibility for the future which perhaps to some extent underpinned the libertarianism of the sixties.

I couldn't say if my party had a direct bearing on the increasing amount of work that began to come my way, but over the next few months and into the early part of 1963 I made several more movies, including another for Michael Winner, *West Eleven*. Here, I had the interesting experience of working with Diana Dors, who had the somewhat hyperbolic distinction of being Britain's answer to Marilyn Monroe. I also worked with Michael Crawford for the first time since we were kids, in *Two Left Feet*, a precursor to his great TV success as Frank Spencer in *Some Mothers Do 'Ave 'Em*.

Straight after that, I played yet another young pop musician in *Live It Up*, this time as lead for Lance Comfort. The tag line of this cringe-maker was, 'Yeah! Yeah! Yeah! It's got the new beat that beats them all.' Enough said, although slight as it was in my own memory, I was flattered when I bumped into John Lennon with the other Beatles a few years later and he told me how much he'd liked it – what a charmer! One bonus of the picture was that the costumes were designed by John Stephen (of Carnaby Street) and Mary Quant, giving me the chance to get my hands on one of her super, groovy black and white minidresses for Genny, who was doubtfully impressed. She was, understandably, getting fairly pissed off, living down in Surrey with two small children while I was spending most of my time in London, drinking at the Establishment and Raymond's Review Bar with Andrew Ray and Kenny Lynch, and still carrying on with Amanda Reiss.

In April 1963 I was very chuffed to be offered the lead part in a good stage play at the Royal Court called *Skyvers*, not least because I felt here at last was something artistically worthwhile to show my father, who'd always been at his most bitterly scathing when talking about the films I'd made. At this stage the play, by a West Indian schoolmaster called Barry Reckord, was being presented as a Sunday-evening, one-night-only 'production without decor' – a practice established at the Royal

Court by George Devine as a way of trying out new plays, writers and actors. The audiences tended to be people in the trade – other actors on their day off and critics – all of whom had to be members of the club, to allow Sunday performances and evade some of the archaic strictures on content by the Lord Chamberlain.

Although I was 21, I still looked young enough to play a fifteen-year-old tearaway in a comprehensive school trying to decide what to do with his life. It was a well-written, complex part which I found a real challenge compared with most of the movie acting I'd been doing. Feeling that I was making something of it, I invited my mother and father to come up and see the production in Sloane Square. I'd put everything I'd ever learned into the part, and was rewarded at the end of the performance by magnificent applause and a couple of curtain calls, thrilled that Dad had been there to see this obvious appreciation by my peers and the critics.

He came backstage afterwards.

'What did you think?' I asked eagerly, delighted that here at last was an unequivocal chance for him to show some approval.

'That was rubbish,' he hissed. 'Terrible performance.'

'But didn't you hear the applause? We took two curtain calls.'

'That doesn't mean a thing. They're other actors, aren't they, supporting one of their own – bloody sycophants!'

I was flabbergasted, and more hurt than I had ever been by his bitter refusal to concede any merit whatsoever in any of my achievements since the last singing competition in which he'd accompanied me. I'd been ten then; I was twenty-one now. My poor mother stood behind him looking on, distressed and helpless.

It was a small consolation, although it left me even more puzzled by my father's reaction, when all the papers greeted the production with great reviews. Even Bernard Levin found something good to say about my performance, and three months later the same production was given a proper three-week run at the Court, and very well received once again.

I see, by the way, from a review and an interview I gave the *Daily Telegraph* at the time (who ran the piece under the headline 'New play by Negro author'), that besides acting, I also played the guitar and saxophone and had spent a year singing in Austrian cabaret. I described my pastimes as 'painting, philosophy, photography and magic'. My taste for prestidigitation of the truth (or bullshit) was obviously already well developed by then.

Blow-Up

*

After a month spent driving to Monaco for the Grand Prix with a friend, John Crosthwaite, I got back to England to find that I'd been cast in my third and, as it happened, last film for Michael Winner, so in the summer of 1963 I set of for Torquay in balmy Devon to make *The System*. I was introduced to Oliver Reed, with whom I was to work (and carouse enthusiastically) on several subsequent occasions, lastly in 1999 on *Gladiator*.

If one has a proclivity for a sip on a warm day and others of a similar persuasion are at hand, trouble will ensue – not necessarily violence, but certainly exuberance – and so it was when Oliver and I first met.

Ollie was never a man you would miss – broad, intelligent, funny, frightening and deeply unpredictable. He could drink twenty pints of lager with a gin or crème de menthe chaser and still run a mile for a wager. His aim always was to be larger than his already oversized self.

I knew, inevitably, that I was in trouble when I awoke in a dazzling haze and found myself staring up into the face of a swarthy orang-utan who breathed a fiery Anglo-American tang of Jack Daniel's and Boddington's Best. This could only get worse. My tongue felt like an affectionate kitten that had fallen into a deep sleep, not to be disturbed, in my mouth.

I was also – and here's the good bit – hanging over a vicious set of spearhead railings sixty feet below while large drips of soda water splashed on to me from the orang-utan's neck.

The orang-utan was Reed, and he was holding me by my ankles, dangling me from a sixth-floor window of the Grand Hotel, Torquay, while being liberally sprayed with a soda siphon by a drunk and giggling Andrew Ray – all for a bet, for God's sake – and I prayed he wouldn't drop me.

'How do you like this, boy?' Ollie growled like a bear, and another squirt from Andrew's siphon dribbled off his chin on to my naked arse. 'Wanna come up, boy?'

Oliver had a grin that split his face like an early muppet, but with less of the charm. Miraculously, I was heaved back in, wet with soda and sweat, and handed a drink, which I'd never needed more.

At the time, I concluded that Oliver, for all his charismatic, cavalier efforts as an apprentice hellraiser, was inclined to bully anyone smaller than himself – like me. In truth, it wasn't until *Gladiator* that I stopped feeling physically threatened by him. Pathetic, I know.

But it was wonderful to have Andrew Ray to play with again, crawling around the Palm Court tea room while the band played and we staged a string of practical jokes on the less-than-youthful inmates; and I didn't mind at all that Andrew was obsessed with teasing Michael Winner.

Quite early on in the film we had snuck into Michael's hotel room to see what we could do to upset him. When we heard him coming back sooner than we'd expected, we hopped into a cupboard, which vividly brought back memories for me of sheltering fatuously from German bombs with my mother and grandmother under the stairs at Gravetts Lane. I could almost smell the mothballs.

Our director bustled in and we tried to hold our breath – not easy when we realised he'd brought a girl with him. We listened, stifling the guffaws, as he attempted to seduce her. When it was obvious that, if she was ever going to remove her underwear voluntarily, this wasn't the day, he was surprisingly philosophical in consoling himself.

'Oh, well. I'm a bit hungry, actually. I think I'll just have a bowl of Rice Krispies before we go back down.'

God knows how he didn't hear us; we were howling like gibbons and trying not to pee on his shiny suits in the cupboard. On the shoot next morning, we had a field day, hissing, 'Snap, Crackle, Pop,' on the flimsiest pretext. As it happened, though he knew this was directed at him in some way, I don't think he quite got the point, although it did presage his famous obsession with food in later life.

But although we liked to tease Michael, we knew that he was among the very best British directors of the time, and also a very efficient publicist for himself – and also, to a certain extent, for the British film industry – for very many years. I admired him and became fond of him over the years. *The System* was a good, well-written film about a group of lads from a seaside town who had hung around all winter waiting for the holiday season to start, when they would roam about and prey on the tourists, not nefariously, but looking for romance – well, sex, actually.

Oliver Reed plays a beach photographer who usually scores the best-looking girls, until he gets his comeuppance by falling in love with one who knows how to treat him. She goes at the end of her holiday, leaving him heartbroken and ego-bruised, while his mates – Andrew and I – hang around to cheer him up. This cool beauty was played by Jane Merrow.

It's well recorded that one of the problems of working on a film set is that you have to spend a very large part of the day sitting around, possibly reading, or, if you are of a sociable disposition, chatting. I love a long, rambling chat – several of them, back to back, if on offer – and I soon found myself engaged in a great deal of ramble with Jane.

Throughout the film, Jane and I talked and talked and talked, helped by the fact that we were billeted together for make-up, wardrobe and dressing rooms in the local cinema, where we sat in the front seats and laughed, and talked. Of such moments life-threatening stuff may emerge, for Jane's affections were changing. Not literally, not in any kind of sexual desire, but we got on well. She was nervous – an agoraphobic child – while I was chatty, kind of relaxed and easy. That was how I thought of myself then – a good-humoured sort of bloke, and easy to talk to.

She'd recently finished a relationship and this had hit her hard. It was obvious to me that she was suffering – whether from loss of love or loss of face, it's hard to say from here, but certainly from a hefty blow to her ego – and I felt, as a supporting actor on the set, it was no more than my duty to help her through it. I wouldn't perhaps have felt this duty so keenly if she'd been a little less good-looking, and the duty quickly became a delight, and tender words were easily supplanted by tender touch, until I realised I'd started something I couldn't stop.

Jane was about my age. She had worked on several films and was already quite well known, having just starred as Lorna Doone in a big television series. We seemed to be giving one another a lot of mutual support during a tricky time and inevitably we became very close. My fidelity was tested, and failed miserably. The production came to an end, but there was no question of letting that get in my way. Besides, tensions back at Limpsfield Court had set in, and somehow Genny's belief that the sun rose and set on D. Hemmings was waning fast. Tragically for her – though not much to the surprise of her parents – the obedient, responsible father she wanted for her children, and the consistent, reliable husband she yearned for for herself had not emerged from the ether of our powerful early love.

I phoned Jane and arranged to meet her at the White Bear in Featherbed Lane, Sanderstead, then a favourite pub of mine halfway between where she lived at her mother's house near Crystal Palace and my home in Oxted.

Genny had already sensed a change of mood in me; she knew this wasn't just another of my 'flings'. She was in any event already twitching about a letter I'd received from Amanda, which made it clear

I didn't spend my visits to her place doing the *Times* crossword (as I think I may have suggested). Due to one of the innumerable fiscal crises that seem to crop up at regular intervals throughout my life, I didn't have a car at the time and Genny agreed to drive me to this portentous rendezvous. She dropped me there, I gave her smile of tragic regret and went in to wait for Jane.

I'd made up my mind that I should leave Genny and I hadn't felt like taking anything with me. The problem with Limpsfield had been that everything there belonged to the Ouvrys – even, it seemed, Deborah and Dominic, whom I had adopted – and perhaps it was partly this feeling of complete powerlessness to affect events in the life of my family that propelled my departure – that and an incurable, restless curiosity.

But however possessionless I was prepared to be, there was, and still is, a side to me that dreads the idea of not having a place I can call home, with a woman on hand to look after me, despite my regular abuse of the comforts on offer. I certainly wasn't going back to Woking, and Jane seemed the best option; besides, I was now seriously in love with her.

She arrived looking strong, competent and just as beautiful as my overheated memory had painted her. I bought her a drink with some money Genny had lent me.

'Right,' I announced unequivocally. 'That's it. I've left Genny.'

Jane looked a little doubtful, not to say startled at this turn of events.

'She's just dropped me here,' I pressed on. 'I don't have a car, I've got no money and I've got nowhere to go.'

'But, David, you must have! You're a working actor. You must have made something this last year.'

'All gone,' I told her airily. 'Of course, there's more on the way,' I quickly added, sensing I'd overplayed the abandoned-waif card.

We talked about Genny, not unsympathetically.

'You should never have married her,' Jane said. 'You were miles too young to take on someone else's baby. And it's not as if she was pregnant with yours at the time.'

'But I really, really wanted to marry her,' I said. 'It seemed like the only possible option at the time, and, let's face it, her parents made it very easy for me – it suited them too.'

Jane looked at me with an expression I got to know very well over the next few years, shaking her head with a grin, as if she were indulging a small boy who'd been caught with his hand in the humbug jar. But she was more pragmatic than enthusiastic about my proposal; she was undoubtedly fond of me – at least enough not to put up much defence against the onslaught of my own determination to move in with her. We agreed that I would take over the spare room at her mother's house, and we set off with all my belongings in a small carrier bag on the back seat of her lumbering great Hillman.

Jane's mother was wonderful about my moving in and I loved her from the start. She completely understood the world in which Jane and I worked. She came from a long line of theatricals herself. Her father had been stage director at St Martin's Theatre for years and her mother had worked backstage there as an artist.

Jane's father had long since jumped the broom and lived with a second wife in London. He was the son of a distinguished medical professor at Cologne University but had fled Germany and the Nazis, arriving just before the war and changing his name from Mierowski. He too was an actor, although it was to his knowledge of seven languages that he resorted in order to scratch a living as a salesman during and since the war. Thus it was that Jane had grown up surrounded by the theatre and its particular terms of reference, which seemed to make her an ideal partner for an aspiring young actor like me.

I loved my new living arrangements. In a fresh rush of creativity, I threw myself into writing the script of my own play *The Seven Masks of Leo Blount*, which, inspired by *Skyvers*, I was hoping to see produced at the Royal Court.

To start with, we kept up the pretence that I was a lodger in Mrs Merrow's house, but as I wore down Jane's mild resistance and we inevitably became more of an item, she and her mother sort of accepted it. In the meantime, for Christmas 1963 we all went down to spend the holiday with her uncle, who had a hotel on the Isle of Wight, where I got on really well with all her family.

The following spring, Jane's mother wanted to sell her house and I jumped at the chance to talk Jane into moving into a flat with me. Her mother was shocked and upset by this proposal, because, astonishing as it may seem now, in the early sixties cohabiting was not generally an acceptable way to behave. Nevertheless, we found the flat at Elmhurst Court in Croydon which was to become our home for the next few years.

Once we had moved in and were indisputably a couple, I refused to be fazed by the fact that Jane had learned to act properly, at RADA, and had already starred in three feature films, as well as a major television series. She was, anyway, always massively encouraging in everything I did and, despite my continuing weakness for any opportunity to explore any fresh sexual adventure, we were very happy.

Genny was being paid attention by a new man and, not unreasonably, wanted a divorce. Blame and cause were more of an issue in divorces at that time, but Amanda Reiss's indiscreet note was produced and deemed to provide adequate proof of adultery, and I didn't contest the suit. I was banished for all time from Oxted, not allowed to see my children and not to come within a mile of the house, its drive or Limpsfield Chart Common even. The family had tired of the naughty puppy they'd taken in and it was no longer welcome. I understood that, but I don't think they had any idea how much I was going to miss the children.

Meanwhile, work – and income – were a little scarce. I did one more pop film for Lance Comfort, *Be My Guest* (which starred American rock'n'roller Jerry Lee Lewis, as well as Steve Marriot from the Small Faces) and a couple of television plays. One of these was a good Wednesday Play (remember them?) called *Autostop*, in which I was supposed to be wandering around Europe with a rucksack, while in fact I was wandering around the Devil's Punchbowl by the A3 at Hindhead in Surrey.

More prestigiously, though with peanuts for wages, I appeared on stage at the New Theatre, Bromley, with Brenda Bruce in a Ted Willis play called *Woman in Dressing-Gown* (which transferred to the Vaudeville in February 1964, where, having already appeared as a film eight years before *and* a television play, it died fairly swiftly, though not before providing me with some useful audition material for Antonioni later on).

As usual, at the same time I was casting around for ways of supplementing my earnings as an actor, and for a while I even found myself operating an illegal roulette wheel in Bermondsey.

Since I'd been with her, Jane had opened up another fascinating and, for me, endlessly engaging world. She'd lived in Norwood most of her life and had a lot of friends in south London. Among these was a former boyfriend and young actor, Simon Ward, whom she knew from the National Youth Theatre, and whose father, Len, was a well-known purveyor of pre-owned cars and a great character. From time to time he was kind enough to lend me cars, always elegant conveyances, like a Facel Vega HK500, flashy, roar-in-your-face kinds of motors that no one except extreme enthusiasts would be seen dead in today, with dash-boards like a 747 cockpit and panel fascias of pure walnut. They were over the top, without doubt, and not less than politically impertinent, even then. But for a working actor, kicking in a TV part here and a small film role there, with the kind friends that I had scattered round the East End and Dulwich – publicans, pool-hall owners, barmaids and bankers – it made a kind of sense.

Len Ward had a diverse network of friends and contacts, one of whom was Tom Daly, who owned Toby's, a boxing gym and drinking den in Leroy Street, Bermondsey. Tom had a son called John, about five years older than me, who already had a reputation for zealous deal-doing and was currently employed as a commission salesman by the Imperial Life of Canada insurance company. Len thought that John and I would get on, and asked me down to meet him at a pub in Walworth, and I felt immediately at home with the sharp, good-looking young guy I was introduced to.

As a matter of course, knowing it was a great ice-breaker and using a skill I'd been honing for the last three or four years, I picked his watch off his wrist without his noticing. It was only when I asked him the time, maybe twenty minutes later, that he saw it had gone. As soon as I pulled it out of my own pocket and handed it back to him, there was a gleam of appreciation and recognition in his shrewd, restless eyes, and a friendship started that lasted, with the odd hiccup, for the next forty years.

John came round to Elmhurst Court a few days later and sold me and Jane a policy each, then invited us to come down and see Toby's. I loved the place at once, John's dad, the camaraderie of the south London semi-underworld and the boxers.

I can't now remember whose idea it was that I should operate the roulette table, although it was probably mine. In those days the gambling laws were still very restrictive and few places had licences for gaming. If Toby's had applied for a licence, I imagine it would have been kicked out of court halfway to Peckham. But we devised a table with a top that would turn over with the flick of a lever from a fully functioning, 36-number, three-zero wheel and marked baize top one minute – flip – to a normal table, complete with bottles, ashtrays and glasses glued to the surface, in the event of an unannounced visit from the local plod, which, it has to be said, was fairly frequent, on account of the free-spirited nature of some of the regulars.

These regulars became friends who could get anything I needed on the cheap and warm side, and took me around the East End, introducing me to the Blind Beggar and other key venues frequented by the principal villains of the day. What triggered our mutual interest is hard to identify, but some of them became very great friends and were capable of astonishing loyalty. I suppose, in a very minor way, I became part of that world for the few months that I went in and ran the roulette at Toby's, which I loved with a passion – the excitement of an illicit activity, as well as the adrenalin buzz of gambling. Needless to say, like most of my business ventures, it looked better on paper than in reality, but it did at least tide me over until my next big part came along.

I was living life to the full, then, but this wasn't the sixties of the flash parties and the easy sex. This, for me, was the real sixties. Pip Perring was an example of bizarre reality. Working stolidly at the docks, running the family import-export company, he loved to meet me at lunchtime, when we would sneak into empty churches and spend an ecstatic twenty minutes blasting away on the organ, until someone came along and, if they didn't believe whatever cock-and-bull story we gave for being there, kicked us out. But Pip suddenly decided to leave his elegant and charming wife of 27 years and run off with a busty barmaid from one of our regular lunchtime haunts, the Anchor on Bankside.

Similarly my accountant, the highly esteemed Stanley Vereker, upped sticks one day, left his wife of twenty years or so and went off to be a sculptor – a good one too, a little like Giacometti, good but thin. And another friend, an infamous accountant, had the gall to ring from the Channel Islands to explain that he couldn't resist running off with large chunks of his clients' money, as well as another client's wife.

Jane and I wound our way through the sixties together, not with flowers in our hair but with a dog at our heels in Elmhurst Court. We didn't have a care in the world. We built our bookcases out of used bricks and planks of homely deal, had our friends and our life. And right up until 1966, I still believed 'Tramp' was the person by the railway station I gave a ten-bob note when I could afford to.

Andrea Newman would stop by and worry us to death about whether she could ever become a writer, not long before she wrote *Three into Two Won't Go*, and we drank Mateus Rosé by candlelight and told stories of plays and repertory while our Border collie, Jasper, lolled by the electric fire. Not the most natural of settings for a Border collie, but he liked it, and was quite unaware of the stardom he had missed in *One Man and His Dog*.

My next proper part, in *The Eye of the Devil*, was also an eye-opener for me. It was the first full-scale international, foreign-located film I'd ever worked on.

J. Lee Thompson was a legendary maker of big action movies – *The Guns of Navarone*, *North West Frontier* and *Ice Cold in Alex*. I'd also appeared as a sixteen-year-old in one of his lesser-known films, *No Trees in the Street*. His new movie was going to star David Niven (one of my all-time heroes), Flora Robson, Emlyn Williams, Kim Novak, Donald Pleasence, whom I knew from making *Wind of Change* five years before, and the comparatively unknown but totally ravishing Sharon Tate, who was the same age and had done about as much as I had.

Most of the film was made on location in Brive, in south-west France, among the vineyards of the Dordogne in the Château de Hautefort. I loved the setting and my part, which demanded skills in riding and toxophily. I had to be trained in archery, but to my delight found that all the hours I'd spent playing darts in pubs gave me a real advantage and earned me great accolades from my teacher. Even now I believe I could still remove a half-smoked fag from the lips of anyone mad enough to volunteer. But I found it odd that a young lad of 24, dressed in black leather and riding a white horse, albeit with my toxophilic advantages, should have been thrown together with such a distinguished cast. The older actors were astonishingly kind to me. Niv's charm was profound and genuine, despite the efforts of biographers like Graham Lord to puncture *The Moon's a Balloon*.

It was he who arranged that each of us would buy lunch at one of the local restaurants in strict rotation, and in such a way that he always took us to the most expensive, Donald to a slightly less extravagant one and me to a charming bistro with high standards and very low prices.

We'd opted for these external lunches as a result of a most unwelcome change in the production company's eating arrangements. Initially, local French caterers had been engaged and were producing sublime meals of a standard utterly unheard of on an English film set, served on checked tablecloths in candlelight down in the cellars of Château de Hautefort. Regrettably, the English crew had complained that they weren't getting mutton stew or boiled beef and carrots, so the lovely French cooks were exchanged for English moviecaterer Phil Hobbs or, as he was known, Swill Hobbs, and we started eating elsewhere.

Another of the delights of making this film was the opportunity to ride my white horse through the local countryside, sometimes on my own, usually with Kim Novak. She loved it too, and was always ready to come with me through the vineyards and along the small rustic tracks outside the town. We would stop somewhere to sit and chat, easily and at great length about almost anything, before remounting our horses and riding back to the set in perfect harmony and, to begin with, no hint of physicality, though I thought she was wonderful. It wasn't just that she was very fanciable; after a while, I began to detect that strangely attractive, wicked look in her eye that an experienced woman gives to an inexperienced man.

Of course, I had no idea how to approach what appeared to be on offer. She was a big star then, while I was a complete ingénu. As far as romantic encounters were concerned, I was quite at ease with Sharon Tate, who was more nervous and less experienced than me, and I was a little taken with her, but Kim was much more forceful, witty, knowledgeable and voluptuous.

However, I didn't dare make a move until she called me, a few weeks into filming. We were staying in different hotels in Brive, on either side of the main *place*. She asked me to meet her in the large, tree-filled park in the centre of the town. It wasn't a suggestion, it was a command, and, being the young man I was, a command that I knew would lead inevitability to possibilities which, of course, intrigued me.

It was dark when I met Kim at the park gates. She was dressed in a short white plastic coat with two black stripes and big buttons down the front.

'Hello, Kim,' I greeted her, no doubt smirking fatuously.

'Shall we go into the park?'

I didn't know for certain where this would ultimately lead, but I wasn't that stupid. We headed into the empty gloom of the park. When we had reached a suitably secluded spot, Kim turned to me and opened her coat. She was not wearing a great deal beneath it.

I now knew there was no question about the purpose of the meeting, but I think I was totally in awe of this woman who had suddenly invited me to indulge my fantasies, and my performance right there in the park was utterly hopeless. Nevertheless, she invited me back to her hotel and we carried on for a couple of days, but I guess I simply wasn't up to snuff, if I'm truthful, and she soon tired of me. I was 24; she was ten years older. I understood.

(Years later, I cast her in *Just a Gigolo* with David Bowie, by which time her life had changed and she was married to a vet in Northern California. She came to Berlin to make the film and was wonderful, and was a very happy, completely different person from the one I'd known in our 'Brive Encounter'. I still admired and fancied her, but I never thought – and nor did she, I'm sure – of repeating the experience, although I might have been better at it by then.)

Shortly after my encounter with Kim, when we'd almost finished filming, our producer, Marty Ransohoff, held a press conference, at which the stars of the film were present. Frankly, I can't recall what Marty said to upset Kim, or if it justified her reaction, but I have an indelible vision of her stubbing a cigarette in his one good eye, which led to an ugly scene, a failed press conference and Kim being sacked from the movie. The result of this was that I had to come back and make the whole thing over again, this time with Deborah Kerr, a very old friend of Niv's, whom he had put forward as a replacement. Thus I was paid twice for doing the picture twice, making it the most lucrative job I'd ever done.

We finished work on the film finally in early 1966. I came home to England and a degree of domesticity with the lovely Jane, whom, I discovered, I had missed enormously, despite my adventures; or perhaps because of them.

At the same time, I was given a sharp reminder of my earlier, and neglected, responsibilities when Genny phoned to say that my parents had asked her and Deborah, who was four now, to come over to Woking for tea. It was the first time they had asked, but my father, as usual, had made it relentlessly clear to Genny what he thought of her and her ill-fated marriage to me. I was well aware that my performance as father to Debs was derisory, and I felt colossal guilt that this had happened; but I was as mystified as ever by my father's extraordinary bitterness towards everyone who should have been dear to him. Genny and Deborah were never asked to tea again.

To compound a sense of dissatisfaction with myself, there were few job prospects floating around. However, it was at the end of the previous year, on a brief visit home between Kim and Deborah, that

Andrew Sinclair had first sounded me out on my views about Dylan Thomas. When I'd told him I was very partial to the Welsh drunkard, he had looked pleased, mumbled and spluttered something about the show he was devising. But for the most part, life continued with the usual ducking and diving, chasing after jobs at the bottoms of rainbows, playing in the East End with John Daly, who had become a firm friend by now, and sitting around in Chelsea with my luncheon companions.

I have never underestimated the value of a good pub, and I wasn't averse to spending a few hours at a time slurping bitter and playing darts in my local in Croydon, followed by a long walk and training session with my dog, Jasper.

In those days, for a while, before life became too chaotic, Jasper used to go everywhere with me, and I loved him. I could walk up Oxford Street with him, through the seething hordes of shoppers, and his nose would never leave my leg. And in a park I could stand 100 yards from him, put up my hand and he would drop flat on the ground. He was a real Border collie, a sheepdog able to do anything asked of him, a superb dog, the likes of which I've never had again. At the dartboard, I had a regular ritual which usually produced the right result. First, I would grasp the curtain and give it a tug to dry my fingers, then I'd take the darts in my right hand, pat Jasper on the head with my left, and play. And I continued to go through the same ritual every time I was about to throw a dart; in Jasper's absence, I just patted the spot where his head would have been.

One high point during this short lull was another chance to meet up again with my hero David Niven. Donald Pleasence and his wife had asked me and Jane to a dinner party at their house in Datchet, along with Niv and his wife, Hjordis.

I was thrilled to receive the invitation; I felt I'd really arrived. And to cap it all, I could drive there in my new car. I'd just blown nearly all my earnings from *The Eye of the Devil* on an Aston Martin DB4. We set off from Croydon in our best frock and tux, feeling glamorous as hell. I put the hood down and pointed the car down the A30.

The problem with less-than-new sports cars is that, like elderly racehorses, they are inclined to break down. That is the price of the vicarious glamour they afford. Halfway to our destination, the blasted car ground to a halt, steaming like a kettle on an Aga. While by nature I have an understanding of things mechanical, I do not possess the patience to be a good mechanic, and, in any case, I'd allowed exactly long enough for this journey to pitch us on the Pleasence doorstep dead on time.

I had also become, surprisingly, something of a snappy dresser when the occasion demanded, so now I was in an ensemble that I valued highly and was not remotely suitable for fiddling about with oily engines under the bonnets of temperamental motor cars.

I admit to leaping out of the vehicle, seriously considering murdering it on the spot. I was very, very distressed, and mortified when Jane described my performance to me in the calm aftermath of the disaster. There wasn't time, I thought, to call out anyone to help; besides, any memberships of motoring organisations I might have had had lapsed through lack of subscription. I had no choice but to dive in and try to sort it out myself, and, after an hour of vicious blasphemy, buggering about with bits of hose and a penknife that also had a screwdriver on it and the services of a helpful passer-by in fetching more water, we managed to get going again.

We arrived, utterly dishevelled in my case and in a state of advanced paranoid tension, just about as dinner ended. Of course, we were fed, but somehow the opportunity to shine had passed. Fortunately, though, I did keep in touch with Niv, and soon met his son, D. Niv Jr, who became a great friend and playmate.

Meanwhile, life in Chelsea, where I spent most of my spare time, was beginning to take on the flavour of the sixties for which it is so vividly remembered. I was an actor with too much spare time on my hands, and a lot of it was spent in restaurants, drinking and playing with others in a similar position.

Italian restaurants were the most chic, with white tablecloths hurriedly replacing the gingham check and candle-in-Chianti bottle bistros that we had become accustomed to. Pasta was in. White was in. Italians were in – well, Sicilians mostly (there is a difference), bell-bottom trousers were in, influenced, I'm sure, by Italian waiters, who always seemed to get the girl, with all that polyester swagging about the heel.

It was these blasted Italians, the lovely, minimalist Mario and Franco, and Alvaro, who enticed me to join a sort of 'Grappa' gang as the sixties developed and got into their full stride.

David Bailey and Peter Evans, in their fine book *Goodbye Baby and Amen*, attempted to define the decade with photos and platitudes.

While the book itself is pure coffee-table sixties, it misses the fundamentals of the time; and while paying homage to those who suffered it, enjoyed it and played a raucous part in it, they overlooked the fact that many inhabitants have lasted a little longer than their predictions. Still, none of us is perfect. My picture is in it, with one of my lovely wives, and from time to time we reflect on it with affection. She as elegant as ever; me dressed like a moth-eaten dog. What she saw in me beyond the fun I can never imagine.

I think, though, that the Italian restaurants were a hit because they were simple. No fuss, no formality. And you could find an essential sixties group around a table on a Saturday lunchtime in any of them, though mostly Alvaro's, a nourishing white venue, much favoured of a weekend, tucked away on a side street with handy parking, where we would slurp pasta smothered with indefinable sauces, galloned down with barely drinkable *vino rustico* from whatever obscure corner of Italy the owner hailed.

This was almost always a prelude to the afternoon footie, either Chelsea or Fulham, just down the street. The regular protagonists would be Dougie Hayward, tailor of Mount Street, witty and sharp; Ian La Frenais (who always for some reason called me 'Petal'), also witty and sharp; Tommy ('Still got the first pound I ever earned') Steele, not witty, sharp but frugal with it (never saw him pick up a tab – though did the gang try . . .); Ian McShane, quite witty, not sharp, but very good-looking with a wicked smile that could quiver a woman's knee at fifty paces; Dick Clements, unquestionably not sharp – or, rather, deceptively slow – not good-looking and a very bad tailor, but with a wonderful smile and somehow very good company. Some strange chemistry made La Frenais and Clements a perfect partnership in their various projects, Ian writing, Dick writing and directing.

But Alvaro held sway over all. He was, to put it charitably, a rotund man, and jolly, with a grin that split his melon head in two. He was the consummate Italian, born, I think, in Ilford, but more Italian than most.

As a late participant, I was invited to join the Bang Club, which involved most of Alvaro's regulars of a Saturday lunchtime and whose principal purpose, as devised by Ian, was to make friends look foolish.

Once a month, a person was elected 'victim', and the remainder had to hunt him down, preferably in circumstances that would cause maximum embarrassment. The hunters would then point their index finger with thumb raised and three fingers curled and say, or mouth, 'Bang!', at which point the 'victim' had to die in the most atrocious way possible – in a second. No hesitation was allowed, or procrastination. They had to die on the spot, no matter who the witness or how great the damage. La Frenais took out an entire desert trolley at the White Elephant, having been 'Banged', and several tables along with it. Few have topped this, and there can't be much more stimulating than to destroy someone's lunch by careering into their table, sprawled across a desert trolley like one of Clint Eastwood's victims across the back of his trusty steed. Of this you can be sure. Trust me – I'm an actor.

McShane suffered an invidious fate, though, at the hands of the Bang Club. As he was being presented, almost on bended knee, to Princess Margaret at the Empire, Leicester Square, at some première or other, from behind the silken ropes the rest of us stood up and, over a rampart of black-tied shoulders, as one we pointed fingers and mouthed 'Bang!'

Ian was caught, dead to rights, between the eyes. Eastwood would have been proud. Theoretically Ian should have fallen on the hapless princess, rolled her down a couple of staircases, taken Richard Attenborough and Judi Dench out with him and generally put the proceedings in peril and confusion. But he chickened out and disaster was, sadly, averted. There is, however, a sort of satisfactory conclusion to this short story. At the far end of the line, waiting patiently, was Vanessa Redgrave. She had not an inkling of the Bang Club, but, being sightless, assumed the guns – merely fingers, you realise – were the real thing. She clutched the person next to her – Bryan Forbes or Nanette Newman – and fainted dead away on the podium. All guns were then turned on Vanessa, as if she had been the target all along. But she revived in moments, as Redgraves will, to curtsy elegantly in front of HRH.

Alvaro, Mario and Franco weren't the only Italian food and style purveyors. They may have been the best known and patronised by the not necessarily rich but usually famous, and their charm was unquestionable. But there were others – Quaglino's, Fermi – and even Simpsons in the Strand had begun to put *fegato* on the lunch menu. Mr Chow, a confirmed Chinaman but with an eye to the trend, had a pasta chef demonstrate the creation of traditional *lumachine con cozze* in front of the customers every night, and it was soon widely agreed that Mr Chow tossed up some of the best Italian food in London.

*

David Hemmings

On Monday 6 March 1966, *Adventures in the Skin Trade* opened at the Hampstead Theatre Club for a four-week run, and to refreshingly good reviews. Since it was clear that the Italian restaurateurs had their hands so securely in the English pocket, it shouldn't have come as a great surprise that an Italian film-maker should set his sights on London as a location for a film that would exploit the excesses of the time in swinging London. That he should have come looking for cast in Hampstead was my little share of the serendipity that occurs in the movie industry from time to time. One moment you're drinking coffee and reading the vacancy ads; next thing you know, all the buses have come at once.

Antonioni's earlier films, particularly the trilogy *L'Avventura*, *La Notte* and *L'Eclisse*, are deservedly regarded as masterpieces. But *Blow-Up* has humour, despite the pretentious tag line plastered across the posters:

> *Antonioni's camera never flinches,*
> *At love without meaning,*
> *At murder without guilt,*
> *At the dazzle and madness of youth today.*

It stands in stark contrast to the mood of Fellini and Visconti and it is not Italian in the sense that their films are. Perhaps for this reason *Blow-Up* has become a cult movie, and is now a class work for universities and their ubiquitous film schools.

Maybe its humour looks odd, often unfathomable and, some might say, difficult to enjoy, but there is something eternally haunting about it, from the hand of a director who was able to encapsulate the spirit of what came to be known as 'swinging London'.

Was London really 'swinging'? I sometimes think I must have been too damned busy to notice. Some aspects of it almost completely passed me by – the rampant use of cannabis, for one. Marijuana, hash, dope, pot, weed, Lebanese Black, Moroccan Gold, Thai Temple Balls were only words to me. I'd already recognised how easy I found it to overdo the booze and was disinclined to extend my repertoire, except once . . .

📷 📷 📷 📷

Outside Scott's of St James's, the queues stretch mercilessly towards a pair of bouncers who look like they've been hired from the hippo lake at Longleat. There is another door – closed – where those who indulge in monster tipping can slide by. The music that blasts from within is fearsome, and not amusing: John Peel on a seriously bad night.

I am among the group waiting to get in, without partner, hoping that the night would provide. Beside me were the lads from Liverpool, John, Paul, George and Ringo. We'd met, long before, at Twickenham Studios, when I was filming some odourless B-movie and they'd said how much they liked *Live It Up*.

It starts to drizzle and boredom creeps up on us. John offers me a joint – not a joint in the normal sense of the word. This is Che Guevara's arm, Withnail's Camberwell Carrot. You must accept that I know nothing about drugs. This will be my first experience of any narcotic, other than aspirin (and booze, of course).

Once the joint is in my hand, encouraged, I take a deep, horrific pull on it. The lads tell me to hold it in, not to exhale too fast. I oblige and my eyes pucker, as do my toes and other parts of my anatomy. After a moment or two, my eyebrows seem to curl upward, a state in which they will be forever fixed. My peripheral vision begins to fail, so that life is seen as if over Glenn Ford's shoulder in *Up Periscope*.

How I manage to get to our table is a mystery. I am now blind and, I think, incontinent. There is a deep humming in my head that my lack of vision seems in some way to compliment, rather as a juvenile Alaskan whale, lost in a frozen ocean, hears its mother cry out through the icy depths.

This is not a great experience. I can hear the music, just, but like the bass notes from a neighbour's trannie, so low I can hear my knees break, and every vertebra in my spine rattles with a thump I'll never forget.

But I come round in time. Gradually, vision returns and I see dancers reeling about the floor. I've ordered (Paul, I think, tells me) a vodka and tonic, and it lurches towards me from the table. I reach at it with gratitude and, after what seems like an hour and a quarter, I make contact with the glass. I think I hear cheers and applause.

Paul suggests that I dance with a much-legged, elegant young female hovering by the table with an air of willingness. But I'm trying to focus on getting my drink back onto the table – a tricky task, since I've been transfixed by a beer mat, perfectly shaped and coloured orange, clean and pristine, I thought, and I'm purposefully trying to match up its edges with my glass.

When finally I've summoned up the energy to dance with this compliant female (and, frankly, not very well), I'm not even sure it's the same person I was aimed at earlier. But I fail further inspection or dalliance by falling into a deep sleep on a convenient sofa.

[📷] [📷] [📷] [📷]

I suppose it was about five a.m. before I'd fully recovered and woke to find a lovely brunette, with long hair draped across my shoulder, snoring like a breakfast kettle, arms fondly surrounding me, for all the world like lovers of old, though neither sex nor recognition had been part of our brief encounter. I slipped away without a word, just a gentle touch of lips on cheek for a 'thank you'.

I didn't know her name then, but I do now and we've spent some thirty-odd years in platonic friendship, which just goes to show what a judicious peck on the cheek can do.

Since those days, or, more accurately, since that night, I've rarely seen any of the Beatles. Ringo at the White Elephant occasionally, Paul at the Ivy, always friendly, like years ago. In the early days it all seemed simple and friendly. We were just mucking about in our own way. I certainly thank John, Paul, George and Ringo for their passing friendship, since in many ways we grew up together, unsure, suddenly lionised, but insecure for all that. And what a wonderful gift the four gave us – music to love, lyrics to treasure, bringing so much charm, humour and colour into all our lives.

When John gave me that joint, I was a part of the scene, so to speak, an ephemeral sixties person; but not really. I've probably only smoked a handful of joints in the three decades since: with Samantha Eggar, filming *The Walking Stick*, and a couple, perhaps, in Idaho. But that's about it. Booze has remained my drug of choice, and while the sixties were so flattered and inflated by media coverage, for most of us they didn't happen until the seventies, if at all. We had the opportunities, that's for sure, and those who could and were lucky enough reaped the rewards. I saw the sixties, I was part of it, and thank the Lord for that, but this is now and that was then, and the Devil take the Wildebeest.

Now I know that *Blow-Up* changed my life more than any drug could have done. Suddenly, from Croydon, from Jane, from Jasper, even, I was to be plucked away and thrust up into the big time; and I had nightmares about losing Jane and Jasper.

Jasper and I talked. He was not as articulate as Jane but I assumed he would miss me. Sadly, not long after I left, he was killed running under a milk float. I was so angry with him. 'If you had to get run over – please, you had great reactions – not by a milk float!'

But the loving that had gone on for so many years, nose to boot, couldn't end in posthumous recrimination. He was a dog that could never be faulted, and I cried like a wet September. I am very soppy where dogs are concerned.

I was desperate about Jane, too, and we talked, too. She was tearful. She had problems of her own, with agoraphobia and serious panic attacks, which I'd tried long and hard to help her over. Some people thought it was psychological but I was sure it was a clinical condition. Sometimes they were so bad she couldn't get on a train, a bus or a plane. I flew to Paris with her to see how she would cope; it wasn't promising. I knew it also augured badly for our future together.

Before I went to Hollywood, I was desperate to know that she would come out and join me. I persuaded MGM reluctantly to cough up an open ticket for her, though in the end she never used it for herself.

Besides, she said, she had a lot of work on, now and on the near horizon.

But, deep in her soul, I think she knew it was over between us.

8

New York to Los Angeles, 1966

A merican limousines of the sixties weren't as long or as loaded with gadgetry as the ludicrous white slugs you see slithering around the West End these days, transporting Posh'n'Becks to film premières or the winners of *Fame Academy* to the nearest McDonald's. In their time, though, they were excessive enough and I was young enough to be impressed with myself as I lolled on the maroon plush seats in the back of the silver monster that smoothed over the Queensboro Bridge the first time I entered New York.

As we neared the Manhattan end of the steel-girder corridor, the famous skyline began to reveal its detail in individual buildings and I was hit by the reality that this great city was about to absorb me into its hyperdynamic innards. I shook my head with a grin. Here I was, courtesy of MGM, to promote *Blow-Up*, on my way to Los Angeles, courtesy of Warner Brothers, to make *Camelot*, a Hollywood musical, and I was more than ready to take it all on.

But we'd just hit a blockage. I could tell by the colour of my driver's ears that he was getting excited. Suddenly, he was swinging the steering wheel furiously this way and that, when it was perfectly clear there was a mile of traffic in front of us, incapable of movement. Like most Brits, I'd grown up with a grudging acceptance of the propaganda that everything in the United States is done better than it is in the old country. My frustration at the hold-up was somewhat neutralised by my joyful relief that they hadn't cracked their urban congestion any better than we had. I took a closer look at my chauffeur – or 'shiny-ass', as they were also called, on account of the considerable wear to the rump of their 60 per cent polyester suits from driving or, most of the time, just sitting around on leather seats waiting for their inconsiderate charges to finish dinner.

My shiny-ass, I discovered, was called Manny Bellavoce, which made it sound as if he might be a Jewish choreographer who sang opera. He was a New York Italian, from Brooklyn. A navy-suited portly geezer, putting one in mind of pasta and Pavarotti, with a grizzled blue chin – not so much unshaven as a little overcast. His furry brows fell over his eyes like Lincoln's, and when he spoke, he had a habit of blinking long, camel's lashes. Beneath his wrinkled forehead, though, he wore a permanent shrewd grin, with a look in his eyes that said he'd seen it all before. Strangely for a man with an air of the camel about him, he was just about the same height sitting in the car as he was standing on the ground outside. With his thoughtful frown, he was Danny De Vito with a dash of gravitas, and I was inclined to like him at once. Certainly he knew the streets, and he spat like a camel too from time to time, ejecting a wad of chewed tobacco that bulged in his cheek like a cyst.

He'd been waiting for me at Kennedy at gate 22, holding up a banner marked 'David Heffing'. In my awe at setting foot on American soil for the first time, I'd been fairly diffident in correcting him. It couldn't have had less effect; he called me 'Dave' anyway, which I've always loathed but never had the heart to correct.

Confronted with the jam of vehicles ahead of us now, he sighed philosophically and leaned long and heavily on his horn.

'There doesn't seem much point in doing that,' I suggested in a tentative conversational sally.

'Tell you the trut', kid, no hoot, no snoot, not nowhere! Get cute. Lots a lead on the line. Don't rubber 'em, ya get to first. Got me?'

Not by a long way, I thought. It was my first experience of the tongue-twisting wonders of the American language, especially when tortured by powerful dialect. But although I hadn't got him, I did warm to him.

'Dis here's a bridge.' Perhaps to illustrate his point, he launched a pellet of tobacco-stained saliva out of the window at the skyline.

I felt desperately that I should say something sharp and witty, since clearly we *were* over the river – or at least, a stretch of murky water the colour of slurry, which gleamed threateningly far beneath us.

'A bridge,' he repeated. 'And that don't bear mentionin',' he added in a meaningful growl.

'Why's that?' I looked around anxiously, wondering what he was talking about.

'Dey sink 'em here. Drop 'em off like stones. Never see 'em again. Not even in the papers. Pull 'em down here in the early morning. Drop 'em out.'

With a deftness surprising in his chubby hands, he performed Harry Belafonte's trick from 'Island in the Sun', twirling his lighted cigar in his fingers and flicking it between his thumb and forefinger, way out over the beams of the bridge. Like a small brown body, perhaps.

I nodded to myself. America. Yeah. I was now definitely in at the deep end; first port of call on the far side of the turbulent pond that divides us.

After a mind-numbing period of stop and jerk, the traffic at last oozed slowly down the bridge. Almost as soon as we'd turned off it, Manny switched, probably unconsciously, into guide mode and settled into a tour that I hadn't asked for but welcomed when I recognised it for what it was.

The torrent of semi-incomprehensible words kept coming while I looked out at New York: Wall Street, Fifth Avenue, Times Square, 42nd Street musicals. He showed me the Statue of Liberty and Ellis Island, where his grandfather had arrived in 1923 with a few lire and a skinful of Mediterranean optimism. We turned uptown, cutting down to Third Street, past liquor stores with bars on the windows, manholes ejaculating steam from subterranean geysers and yellow taxis nose to tail for blocks; faces nervous and cold, bodies bent and huddled, like workers leaving a Lowry factory, crammed, busy, purposeful, all paranoid, it seemed, with darting glances and furtive hats. Woody Allens appeared around every corner, huddled in heavy coats, carrying tenor sax cases on the way to meet their shrinks. My heart raced in anticipation.

Even from the insulated comfort of the limo, it was obvious that this was not a city where people came to live; they came to fight, as if the entire length of this very tall place – all of it, from the Staten Island ferry to the Brooklyn Bridge – was one enormous Madison Square Garden. I wondered where all the losers went.

Manny would probably have said, 'They go to woik.'

He did not consider his driving 'woik'.

'You know what dis is for me? Dis is Disneyland. I get to run the rides and take the bucks. I get to nod at a few biggies, hover among the rich. It rubs off. I'm a good driver, got heat. Got enough. S'a pleasure drivin'. S'like warm socks and tortellini.'

There wasn't much to say to that.

His accent spilt from Brooklyn movies and, once I got the hang of it, I couldn't get enough of it. Some years later I met his mother and sister in a Brooklyn brownstone and they both were as Italian as Napoli, so I don't know where Manny's speech had come from. I never asked about it, but I suspected that maybe Mom's and Sis's were cadences of convenience – in New York it's convenient to be Italian, perhaps sometimes life-saving. Or Irish. Irish is good.

I wound the window down to breathe in and sniff up the atmosphere. Smells tend to seep into your consciousness unheeded, catching you by surprise so you suddenly find yourself whisked backed to periods of childhood unvisited for years – like damp, newly mown grass or the crisp smell of a winter morning, which always transports me straight to the Lake District. Now that I have spent a great deal of time in America, I've learned its smells. Like London's, they have become familiar and, like London's, they're not always pleasant.

US cities, though, have their own particular perfume of smoggy fumes and traffic, Naugahyde car seats, oversized, dribbling hamburgers and hot dogs, the sweat of baseball. There's always a lurking anxiety that breathing might cut you off in your tender years, leaving you gasping like a hippo. But for now this was very new to me. Very definitely, very excitingly different.

Manny, like many New Yorkers, felt it his duty to dispel any illusions I might have had about baseball. I then held the broadly accepted British view that it was about very overweight persons playing rounders. We did not ascribe to it the status of a religion. Manny tried to re-educate me on this point as we passed Shea Stadium with a reverence usually reserved by members of his family for the Vatican. His eyes left the road as he gazed at the portals of this hallowed place, his head turning back as we cruised silently by. I half expected him to make a sign of the cross; I'm sure he would have genuflected, if he could.

As it happened, I had heard of Babe Ruth, who could, I've been reliably told, point to a spot in the field and whack the ball there, and had done so for a legendary home run. It was also said that he liked a drink and sported a midfield bulge that reflected enthusiastic excess as it plunged over his belt towards his knees. More Buddha than Babe, some said. I asked my new friend the driver what he thought.

'See,' Manny mused, 'gotta let 'em know you're about, udderwise you ain't wort' nutt'in'.'

This blunt advice went straight over my head. I was a new boy.

Manny sniffed, looked up at me in the mirror and pulled his cap down on his head with a tight tug that left his eyebrows showing, a gesture peculiar, perhaps, to those who can flick a cigar butt a quarter of a mile. I felt like Damon Runyon without his pencil.

On the face of it, Manny Bellavoce was an unlikely prospect for a close friend in the way English people understand the term. Nevertheless, on that first day in the United States I already began to think he could be. As it turned out, I did get to know him very well over the years, and he became what I would certainly call a good friend.

Perhaps instinctively knowing he would appreciate why, I asked him if he would take me to the Algonquin Hotel. 'Please? I'd love to see it.'

At first, he missed the point. 'Sure, lotta hookers there these days. Ever had an American hooker?'

I tried to remember if I'd had any experience of American women. The closest I could come was Penny Fortune, an ex-Windmill girl and sometime bargain hooker around Old Compton Street, who came from Montreal. I rather liked her and she didn't charge me, so was ever after known as Penny Farthing, but I didn't think she counted.

'No,' I said.

'They'd break your balls. Specially the good hotel workers. Cost ya Christmas. Yeah. Break your balls.'

I explained that it was the famous Round Table at the legendary hotel that interested me.

'Dat's right, o' course! You're doin' *Camelot*! Round table. Algonquin. I got it. Sure. Hit the bar too. Good barman. Porevski, somethin' like that. He's OK, for a Polak. Get a Manhattan. He makes 'em great. Gotta have a Manhattan in Manhattan, right?'

'Right.'

We soon pulled up in front of the hotel on 44th Street, halfway between Fifth Avenue and the Avenue of the Americas. Manny ushered me out of the car and tipped the purple doorman for parking purposes.

At that stage in my life, I was by no means an aficionado of grand hotels, still suffering from a tendency to whisper when in large lobbies. A little time was to elapse before American Express would call to welcome me personally when I landed in their country.

When we walked into the Algonquin, I just stared at the place: the long staircase, the side lounge and the deep plush furnishings that spoke so eloquently of a past of cigarette holders and long conversations, brittle and fierce, witty and caustic. At the Round Table in the dining room, great critics, poets, columnists and editors had sparred.

The poetic injustice of Gertrude Stein could wreck reputations, and Dorothy Parker would out-snub them all.

'He has blue eyes,' she said of one popular entertainer. 'All eagles with blue eyes have small eglets.' (American's pronounce the word *egg*lets.)

She wrote some of her pithiest lines on Algonquin table napkins, often blurring the results with pink gin.

A poem of gluttony, one might suppose,
Would be when, with the coffee, the man ate the prose . . .

Was it also at the Algonquin that she was asked what she knew about horticulture?

All I know is you can take a whore to culture but you can't make her think.

I *wish* I'd said that.

Her liking for large pink gins suggests a hint of Anglophilia, so she couldn't have been all bad. Perhaps she just drank too many of them. As I looked around the almost deserted hotel, the brickwork, the marble columns and the tapestries – all unchanged since it was built in 1902 – and sensed the wit and laughter that had gone before, I thought how very English it must all have been, as if the Algonquin was a setting specially designed with Oscar Wilde or Noël Coward in mind, rather than F. Scott Fitzgerald.

I went to the bar and dutifully ordered a Manhattan. I sipped a thoughtful toast to the past glories which were, after a few more Manhattans, manifestly lingering in the very air of the place, but I wished I'd been there with Gertrude and Dorothy (wearing protective clothing, of course; I would have been a very soft target for those ladies' barbs). Also missing were the hookers, but I found I didn't mind. I had the impression that the real class acts in that department had long gone.

Manny and I had been touring New York all afternoon when he suddenly swung the limo up a side street and pulled over at a small bar at the end of a bridge on the Lower East Side.

'Hang for a bit, OK? I'll be back.'

He slammed the driver's door and disappeared in a few short strides. I peered from the car, across the pavement – sidewalk, I should say. The bridge arched away across the water and I imagined more bodies being prepared for a long-term dunking.

A few moments later he was back, with a fresh cigar poking from his jaw. 'Gotta say hello to a guy. You don't mind? There's booze in the back if you want some. In the cabinet there . . .'

Leaning through the window, he flicked a stubby finger at the back panel of the car, where, sure enough, well-stocked decanters and glasses were neatly arranged on small shelves. I watched him disappear and poured a drink for myself, but, on the grounds that one drink in company is worth three on your own, I soon decided Manny's bar over the road was a more appealing prospect. I let myself out of the limo and followed my shiny-ass.

📷 📷 📷 📷

I find iron stairs that lead to a basement bar. My spirits rise as I descend into this manifestly dodgy establishment.

There are some moves you make in life that remind you of other things you probably should not have done. Perhaps, for instance, you should not have told Christine Keeler you were in love with her.

As I make my way through a haze of blue smoke that hovers like dry ice about the place, trying to spot Manny, I already know that my mistake, which it surely must be, isn't that I'm scared or nervous about being here, but that we're not going to get out of a place like this before dawn.

Someone called Trudy, according to a sign by her elbow, is singing deep, romantic blues from a tiny stage at the back of the club, and the bar itself is lined with characters Runyon could have created. The whole place is littered with men who might have hung out with Bogart, hat brims over eyes, cigarettes drooping and ash on their lapels, with languid women whose dark-treacle voices issue from mouths picked out with three coats of lipstick. I find Manny and ask him for the keys.

'Why? Where ya goin'?'

'I'm going to lock the car. I smell a long stay.'

'Could be. Could be.' He grins with a smile that lights his face like a halogen lamp. 'You OK with that?'

'Let me lock the car. We're near a bridge.'

He hands me the keys and I go straight out to secure the car while I can still do it. In for a penny, I think, with no hint of regret.

Manny's 'friend' turns out to be an ex-boxer, charming in a 'dese, dem and dose' kind of a way, with swollen hands that suggest some of his fighting has been done without gloves. Hands that have been broken too often lose the ability to knit, so that bone grafts to bone and fists end up like four-pound hammers, which are great for fighting but useless for playing the balalaika.

Bundles of grimy green currency pass between Manny and his friend. I don't ask why. East London has taught me enough about bars like this. Shut up; don't stare. Don't smile; don't listen. Speak when you're spoken to and always keep your hand on a chair back. Keep your knife and your knuckleduster out of sight at all times.

I buy drinks with my meagre stash. All I have is my per diem spending money, which I've been given in advance. I order a stiff Jack Daniel's, which I detest, but this is America, after all. I sink a straight shot, no ice, no water. I've arrived in the country where every actor wants to work; I'm on my way to Hollywood, for God's sake, and, as that old pragmatist St Augustine said to his friend Ambrose, When in Rome . . .

Later I realise that, before I get to Hollywood, I have to get Manny home. The charm of the first few Harvey Wallbangers (please don't ask) has crept up behind him. His ex-fighter friend, known as Satchmo, from the size of his lips not his colour, seems uglier as the night wears thin. His face now looks as if Francis Bacon had painted it.

Manny – my shuvver, my shiny-ass – is sliding fast towards the underside of good health.

I try to be philosophical. I've been met in some style at the airport, ushered to a limousine longer than a Grand Union narrowboat and now I have to order a taxi to get my driver home. America? Have I lost the plot?

I also have to get myself to the Warwick Hotel, where I am booked for the night (which, naturally, I call 'Worrik' and everyone else calls 'Wahrwick'). I'm supposed to check in with the studio promotion people and let them know I've arrived safely. I gather up Manny and manage to persuade him it's time to leave. So it turns out, my first night in New York, I find myself driving a licensed limousine through the city at three in the morning, with a short and seriously uncommunicative Italian stretched out on the back seat.

The camel is dehydrating. I'm driving on the wrong side of the street, saved only by the fact that so is everyone else. I think of pulling up under a 'No Parking' sign, in the hope of being arrested, but I am very unsure of how to park the beast, let alone find a space to fit.

Suddenly, only two or three blocks from the getaway, I'm saved. An affronted Manny wakes, sits up with his eyes sparkling, totally appalled at what has happened.

'Jeez! Jeez! Stop this thing. You want me to lose my fucking licence? Pull over! Jeez!'

'I can't pull over.' I shrug.

'Just stop!' And he's opening the back door into the traffic. I stop. 'Jeez! What is it with you English? You fucking crazy? You just got off a plane wit' a straw out your mouth and ya think you got a hackney licence in ten fuckin' minutes. Jeez! I should break your knees.'

'Nice, Manny. Thanks. You were drunk.'

'Me? Do I look drunk. I ain't drunk! I'm fuckin' throwin' up here. You know the cost of this? This ain't some fuckin' cockamamy tin of fuckin' beans. I got a serious mortgage on this. I don't pay? People hang me by the balls from a bridge. Son of a bitch! Jeez!'

This to some extent explains Manny's obsession with bridges – suspension, cantilever and box girder. Maybe he would like to talk about them to Thomas Telford or Isambard Kingdom Brunel. Behind us the traditional hooting has risen to drown him out.

'You want to get in?'

'Too damn right. Yeah, I wanna get fuckin' in. Where're da keys?'

'In it, of course.'

'What were you doin' with the keys? Jeez! You stole the keys? In front of Satch? And you're livin'?'

'I locked it, remember.'

'Shit!' He's calming down.

'Sorry,' I offer.

'No shit.' He turns to face the cars stacked up behind us. 'Get lost, motherfuckers! I got a fuckin' madman in here!'

I slide along the bench seat in the front. He climbs in and settles his behind in its usual place, and we're off. I can truthfully say that I've never seen anyone revert to sobriety with such amazing alacrity. I've been around several who could fake it under confrontational and uniformed pressure, but now, as far as I can tell, Manny is genuinely in control. He regains his composure, with me in front beside him as I contemplate my undamaged knees, and bridges.

📷 📷 📷 📷

I had to give interviews from the Warwick for a couple of days, so I couldn't get out and about much. My previous films had not impacted greatly on the American consciousness and *Blow-Up* wasn't due to open in America until 18 December, in five weeks' time. As a result, the reporters and photographers who turned up knew practically nothing about me. The promotional department of MGM led me through a series of meetings and I was heavily stalked by William Morris, one of the leading theatrical agencies in the US. They talked big numbers, as agents will, and took me to lunch at the Friars Club, 21, the Four Seasons and Elaine's. I always insisted Manny was there. After a week it was considered the norm and he ended up on MGM's payroll for a long time after I'd left for Los Angeles.

Manny was my personal bodyguard and driver all the time I was in New York and he gave me the background on every place we went. He offered streetwise guidance that wouldn't have applied in London. This was New York, he said. This was the big time, the jungle.

The tigers will eat you sooner or later, his philosophy went, so in the meantime, go with the flow; take what you can while it's on offer, because it won't last. While it's there, consolidate, and be the biggest you can.

'Gotta flash neon, kid. Keep 'em blind. All I ever needed was to keep 'em blind. Dey never see me comin'. 'S'all I need. Shit.'

'That, and Harvey Wallbangers.'

He laughed. 'Yeah, yeah, kid. Dem too.'

We would sneak off to bars together, his haunts, some grand, some sleazy. I always preferred the sleazy; I guess they took me back to boyhood times and singing in tobacco-haze pubs with my dad. Sometimes we took with us the poor girl who had the stressful job of being coordinator for MGM's public relations and press office. She could drink with the best, though, laughed like a bassoon and we all had good times together. I was always amazed that such a thin person could down liquid in such quantities and produce a laugh that could have tumbled the walls of Jericho.

Back in New York a good few years later, I heard she went on to write, married and passed into suburbia in upstate New Jersey, from where no laughing bassoon returns.

The night before my flight was to leave for the West Coast, I received an unexpected parting gift. A girl – a woman, really – pitched up at the door of my hotel room. She was a truly voluptuous redhead in her thirties with supremely sculpted rather than colossal breasts and very white teeth. The teeth were the first thing I saw when I pulled the door open.

'I'm from Manny,' she said, flashing them.

'What from Manny?'

'Please, David.' She arched her eyebrows and shrugged her shoulders as if I were simple. 'I'm your American hooker. He told me you never had one.'

'I haven't. Come in.'

'You're leaving in the morning?'

'Yes. Los Angeles.'

'You're not busy now?'

'Nope. I'm delighted. Drink?'

She nodded and I went to the minibar, reconsidered and called room service. By the time I had ordered champagne and nibbles, canapés and olives, she was coatless and gorgeous. We spent the first half of the evening in fumbling foolery before we slipped down to the bar across the street, then to a little Italian restaurant. I ordered pasta and she had an omelette. I picked up my glass to propose a toast. She looked at me, and something in the last bottle of Bardolino helped me realise she was a seriously beautiful woman.

'Here's to the rest of the night,' she said.

'Yep.' I said. 'And to something else really special.'

She raised her glass. 'OK. What?'

I clinked with her. 'Here's to warm socks and tortellini.'

For a lot of English kids who have been brought up in the mistaken belief that Disneyland is a handy, terrestrial form of heaven where St Michael is played by Mickey Mouse, that fantasy world is the *raison d'être* of Los Angeles.

For a south London chancer with a large appetite for louche pastimes, the whole of Southern California seemed like Disneyland. It still felt absurd to me, even faintly immoral, that I was being paid to come here and wallow up to my neck in physical pleasure, warmed by an unfailing sun, with the opportunity to do just about anything that took my fancy without risk of censure. I'd been working, living and partying hard for the previous ten years in England, but I arrived in a frame of mind that from now on I was really going to start trying.

Blow-Up

*

I stepped off the plane at LAX and sucked in my first sample of the distinctive, 'LA Only' smell – the heat, with faint subtropical aromas and the fumes of traffic surging along the palm-treed boulevards blended into a pale peach smog, once inhaled, never forgotten. Russ Baker, a runner from the William Morris Agency, met me to take me to my hotel. I was booked to stay in the Chateau Marmont on Sunset Strip. Just the name and address made me tingle. To reach it, I cruised Sunset Boulevard for the first time, and the Strip, spawning memories of *77 Sunset Strip* and Efrem Zimbalist Jr – one of the finest names ever to grace a credit – Ed Byrnes and Cookie, comb in pocket. I couldn't resist a pull-over to take a look at the original location for the series, Dean Martin's club and restaurant, Dino's, on the Strip. I wasn't disappointed. The wooden arch, the drive in, just the way they were in every episode I'd ever seen.

I'd heard of the hotel where I'd been billeted, of course, its reputation and its extraordinarily eventful past. It had been built in the twenties, an unashamedly bogus 18th-century Loire château, with ivy-clad pillars and gothic arches on the outside, vaulted ceilings and hand-carved panelling inside. It was set in gardens that had grown truly sumptuous around the nooks and corners and Latin cabanas by the swimming pool. Under its ornate roof, Jean Harlow, on honeymoon with another man, consummated her affair with Clark Gable, and a thousand other stars canoodled.

Whatever I was expecting, I was quite unprepared for the reality of the place. It so reeked of Hollywood glamour and excess, it took a while for me to lose a permanent flush of excitement and for my pulse to slow down. I was, after all, just 25, single, healthy and about to become part of the high-octane motion picture business in the world's movie capital. I thought I was getting a sneak preview of heaven.

I'd been told that if I found myself staying on in Los Angeles, it would be worth trying to get a place for myself; and anyway, Warner Brothers, God bless them, weren't going to go on picking up my Marmont tab for ever. But for the time being, this was everything I'd ever dreamed of, since I'd first been thrust into the world of entertainment fifteen years before. I soon settled in and made myself at home. There was no question that it was a pretty quirky place, well accustomed to dealing with quirky clients. Amidst its bizarre architectural charms, the staff were more or less unshockable and ready to cope with the most extreme whims and fancies of sojourning stars suffering from any amount of self-delusion over their ranking in the stellar panoply.

I had no illusions about my own ranking, but I wasn't going to let that worry me. As in New York, no one knew who the hell I was when I first arrived in LA, although, thank God, there were one or two familiar faces among the guests at the hotel – Sharon Tate, who was just down the corridor, and Donald Pleasence, both of whom I knew well from *The Eye of the Devil*.

A room just along the corridor from Sharon housed a suave, good-looking individual of about forty, an extra/actor/entrepreneur sort of figure who seemed to be a permanent Chateau Marmont resident, endowed with some invisible source of income. He went by the name and style of Commander Ted Hartley and he was the first American I'd met who had what might be considered an English stiffness about him, with an East Coast accent that sounded positively clipped beside the vernacular drawl. In the end, he and I became good friends, though whether he was a commander or not, or ever had been, or was even called Ted Hartley, I never knew for certain, though was inclined to doubt.

The concierge had been visibly distressed by my meagre luggage, but I didn't stop to unpack it. I made a few phone calls, shivered at the soft California voices that answered and headed off out to pay a serious visit to Dino's, just a short way down Sunset Boulevard.

With an English disdain for climbing into cars unnecessarily, I decided to walk there. I didn't know then that generally the only pedestrians in Los Angeles are mad, fanatical joggers or those who can't afford a car; and cars are very cheap in the US. At that time too, in one of the LAPD's new initiatives to deal with youth crime, there was an evening curfew in operation for kids under twenty. I should have taken heed of what that might mean, though this didn't really get home to me until I suffered a horrible crashing blow on the back of my skull and felt, or rather smelt, an odiferous young hoodlum rifle through my trouser pockets for my empty wallet and make off with it.

I staggered about, with blood spattered like claret all over the already garish Hawaiian shirt I was wearing. I was dazed and cursing that anyone should do a thing like this in dreamland California, when Ted Hartley came to the rescue. The commander had seen what had happened and stopped to scrape me off the sidewalk and get me back to the hotel, where they patched me up and shook their heads at me for being so dumb as to walk around on my own in the middle of the night.

For a while after that, I thought it best not to go outside the doors of Chateau Marmont, so I stayed in and looked around for people to play with. The hotel was a favourite with most English actors working in Hollywood and a few other members of the cast of *Camelot* had arrived to stay there. Donald Pleasence, working on another picture, was staying in the room that Greta Garbo had always used. She had loved it, she said, because it was the only place where birds would sing on her window ledge, and the room had since been named after her.

I spent a lot of time by the swimming pool, canoodled a little with Sharon for old time's sake, did crosswords with Donald and played backgammon with the commander. A few days after my thief encounter, I was sitting as usual with Donald beside the pool. He could be very good company. Although he was one of the wickedest men I've ever met, a caustic wit with no mercy, I felt safe, he and David Niven having been so good to me on *The Eye of the Devil*.

All of a sudden I felt a pair of hands massaging my shoulder and a voice began to warble, in a familiar melody from *The Sound of Music*:

Crabs in my eyebrows and sperm on my nipples,
Left-handed wankers and perverted cripples,
Guardsmen who beat on my bum till it stings,
These are a few of my favourite things.
Up your jacksie, in a taxi, feeling low
I try to remember my favourite things,
Then I don't wank so slow . . .

The bony hands came away and I turned to see a sharp, wizened face embellished with a spiky moustache for the part of King Pellinore in *Camelot* – in real life, Lionel Jeffries. Lionel turned out to be an indefatigable rhymester of astonishingly low taste and vulgar inventiveness. I wish I could remember more of his oeuvre, for I soon appreciated that such ditties had their uses in whiling away the unavoidable empty hours that big-scale filming involves.

The part of Guenevere in Camelot was being played by Vanessa Redgrave. As it happened, this was the second of three films in a row I did with her (between *Blow-Up* and *The Charge of the Light Brigade*).

Vanessa, well connected of course, had fixed herself up with a house. We hadn't started filming and I hadn't seen much of her, but a week after I'd arrived, she rang me. There was an emergency, she said, and she wanted me for a stand-in.

Hollywood society, in one of its sporadic and highly visible out-pourings of sympathy, had decided to hold a massive gala evening in aid of the Aberfan Disaster Relief Fund.

On 21 October 1966, a massive and heart-rending accident had occurred in the small village of Aberfan, in the coal-mining valleys of South Wales. A waste tip, destabilised by heavy rain, had slithered down a mountainside one morning, first completely destroying a farm cottage, before enveloping and burying most of Pantglas Junior School and another twenty houses. Of the 144 people who died, 116 of them were school children. About half the children at Pantglas Junior School and five of their teachers were killed.

There had been universal shock and sympathy at such a completely unforeseen and almost unprecedented tragedy and support had flooded in from all over the world.

The Los Angeles event to help the village was being held at the Coconut Grove in downtown LA, and Tony Newley, at the height of his fame, was going to perform. I was such a new boy in town, I hadn't even heard about it or been canvassed to attend. Vanessa, of course, had been invited and had told her hosts she would bring our co-star in *Camelot*, the famously unpredictable Richard Harris. Richard had cried off at the last minute and Vanessa wanted a replacement. Would I come, please?

Sure I would, though I couldn't see how the tragedy would attract a serious attendance at a function out here in Movieland. When was it?

'Tonight.'

I winced. I'd had a tricky day.

Still recovering from the battering my head had taken from what, it transpired, had been a Coke bottle, I had dared to venture out that after-noon in my hired rag-top Chevy Camaro to go for a session with Clive Donner, who was living down in Doheny Drive. Since Clive had directed me in *Some People*, down in Bristol with Kenny More, we'd kept in touch, and now he was out here he'd tracked me down to the Chateau Marmont.

So far my only experience of driving in the States had been at the wheel of Manny's limo in New York, in the wee hours, and Californian boulevards take a little getting used to. I soon found myself floundering somewhat in the GM beast with bouncy-castle suspension. I had only a sketchy idea of where I was going, but I'd just seen Doheny Drive on the left. I thought if I didn't take my chance, I might have a ten-mile detour before I got back to it, so I turned into it, apparently from the wrong lane.

Almost immediately, out of nowhere, a police car wailed at me and I was forced to pull over. A cop jumped out, absolutely looking the part, as if he'd come straight up from central casting with all the LA cop characteristics you'd expect – square shoulders, yellow-tinted aviator glasses and a fuck-you demeanour. He told me to get out.

'Look here,' I said in my best Bertie Wooster. 'You can't do this. I'm British. Here's my passport.'

He wasn't impressed. 'Just get outa the car,' he barked, with a panicky edge to his voice.

I could smell expense in the air, and I was still living hand to mouth on my per diem. Indignantly, I prattled some more and didn't budge.

'Don't give me that,' he bawled. 'You just made an illegal left turn!'

He pulled out his gun and waggled it nervously at me.

'I say, is that loaded?' I asked with genuine interest.

'What are you? Some fucking wise-guy kid? Get out of the car!'

I didn't argue and climbed out. It was only later that I guessed, after all the flower-power hippie invasions of Sunset Boulevard, which had in part triggered the prevailing curfew, the cops were nervous of just about any man whose hair straggled over his collar. In fact anyone with long hair was viewed with deep suspicion, especially in a brand-new convertible. I had very long hair at that time and the hint of a nasty little beard. I was a natural target.

However, despite my initial display of pathetic defiance, my plea that I was from England, new in town and here to make a movie seemed to mollify him, although I had the impression he neither knew nor cared where England was. In the end he let me go with an angry warning. But all that gun waving had shaken me.

Back in the hotel that evening, I got Vanessa's call.

Despite my never-failing desire for good times, my first instinct was to look for excuses. 'But I haven't got a dinner jacket or tux with me.'

'Don't worry about it. No one will care.'

I stopped resisting. A fund-raiser in the Coconut Grove with a few Hollywood glitter folk was too tempting. 'OK, thanks,' I said.

She told me she was living at 13,957½ (or some such number) Sunset Boulevard.

'Great,' I said. 'I'm living on Sunset Boulevard too. I'll come and pick you up.'

I put the phone down feeling helpful and virtuous. I'd got over my encounter with the gun-toting cop and was glad to be heading out again.

Reassured by Vanessa's absolute certainty that it wouldn't matter if I turned up underdressed, I pulled out the only suit I'd brought with me to LA (in fact, the only suit I had in the world at the time). It was, even from this distance in time, a truly horrible thing, made to measure from the Burton's catalogue of painfully dodgy designs. Its particular feature was a pair of early-sixties reverse lapels, a bizarre collar treatment in which the top lapels pointed down below the tip of the bottom ones, and mine, to make it worse, were cut with a curve. In the interests of economy, the jacket had a canvas lining. Like something Gerry and his Pacemakers might have worn, the trousers were very tight around the ankle and the whole ensemble possessed no aesthetic merit whatsoever. I looked like shit in it, and I've never worn anything like it since. It would have become in time, I suppose, a period piece; curiously, the only man I've seen in recent years wearing anything similar is David Dickinson, and that was only on one of those 'Antiques Hunt' shows on television.

But for the Aberfan Relief Fund Gala, it was all I had to put on.

Vanessa had told me we were supposed to be there at seven-thirty for eight. I thought it might take half an hour to get to her. But even the number of Vanessa's place hadn't prepared me for the sheer length of the street on which we both lived. I simply hadn't appreciated that Sunset Boulevard is 26 miles long, running from downtown Los Angeles to Pacific Palisades, where, it seemed, Vanessa was staying. But this meant nothing to me and I didn't know where the hell I was going. I started looking at numbers once I was past Dino's on Sunset Strip; three-quarters of an hour later, I was still crawling along, looking at street numbers a thousand less than hers, and for the tennis club she'd told me to use as a landmark. Finally I found the club, and the house.

Vanessa said we were going to be very late, because we still had to get all the way back Downtown to the Coconut Grove. We shot off, with her trying to give directions, saying things like, 'Take Wilshire,' which I'd never seen. My Gerry Marsden suit, designed for the prevailing climate in Slough, not Los Angeles, was beginning to feel tighter and warmer.

David Hemmings as a
toddler.

With parents Arthur and Kathleen Hemmings.

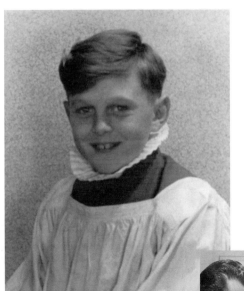

David Hemmings chorister: Chapel
Royal, Hampton Court Palace.

Right: David Hemmings:
Five Clues to Fortune, 1956.

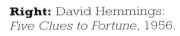

David Hemmings in the Piazza San Marco, Venice, 1954 for the première of *The Turn of the Screw*.

Below: Jenny Lewes (Genista Ouvry), 1960.

Bottom: David Hemmings and Oliver Reed: *The System*, 1963.

Inset: Kim Novak, Sharon Tate and David Hemmings: *The Eye of the Devil*, 1965.

David Hemmings: *The Eye of the Devil*, 1965.

David Hemmings
on the set of
Blow-Up, 1966.

Below: Vanessa
Redgrave, David
Hemmings,
Michelangelo
Antonioni and
Nathalie Wood at
the DGA screening
of *Blow-Up*, Los
Angeles, 1966.

Jack Lemmon and David
Hemmings on the set of *The
Great Hall of Camelot*, Los
Angeles, 1967.

Right: David Hemmings:
Camelot, 1967.

David Hemmings and Jane
Fonda in *Barbarella*, 1967.

David Hemmings on the set of
Alfred the Great, Ireland, 1968.

Inset: David Hemmings and Rory on the set of *Alfred the Great*, Ireland, 1968.

David Hemmings as Captain Nolan in *The Charge of the Light Brigade*, Turkey, 1967.

Blow-Up

[📷] [📷] [📷] [📷]

We finally reach the Coconut Grove at about half-past eight. It's a vast space, filled with a mess of people, all immaculate, bejewelled and in incredible order. I'm looking like a tramp with bad taste.

Vanessa hands me her glasses to look after. This is ominous; I know she can't see more than a few inches in front of her nose without them. I put them in my top pocket, where I've also lodged a sheet of loo paper, doubling as a white handkerchief. Vanessa and I find we're seated at one of the ten tables ranged around the stage, towards the edge of this glittering throng. Our table is occupied entirely by women, except for me. I soon gather that most of them are responsible in some way for organising the event.

Once I've sat down, trying for the moment to sink into a little quiet anonymity, I turn to see who my neighbour is.

On my right is Jean Simmons.

Jean Simmons, for God's sake! I gasp to myself.

I try not to flush, or draw attention to myself in any way. I know I look like crap beside everyone else in the room, all suited and booted, but I feel I must say something by way of explanation. I take a deep breath and go for it.

'I'm terribly sorry I haven't got the full kit and caboodle on tonight, but my trunk hasn't arrived,' I blurt out, with what sounds to me like pathetic transparency.

Miss Simmons gives me a long, withering stare before she speaks. 'Oh?' she drawls disdainfully. 'Trunk hasn't arrived? Ughugh.' She nods and turns away meaningfully.

Later – it seems an awful long time later – I manage to retrieve her attention. 'I'm, er, very new in town,' I try to explain, with a self-deprecating smirk.

'All right,' she concedes with barely disguised contempt. 'Do you play tennis?'

Visions of all my disastrous, humiliating performances at the Hook Heath Tennis Club flash before my eyes. 'Absolutely!' I chuckle to hide the quiver of doubt in my voice. 'I *love* tennis.'

'There's a small tournament at my house Sunday,' Miss Simmons declares, bestowing a broad, bogus grin on me. 'Why don't you come?'

'I'd really like that!' I agree heartily.

'Do you have a racket?'

'Of course, but it's in my trunk. I'm sure it'll be here by Sunday, though.'

'Along with your tuxedo? I do hope so. It'd be nice to see a new face around the courts.'

I am beginning to realise how little I know about local tribal customs – always a problem for a spontaneous adventurer. I know almost nobody in the room, and I have no idea what an Aberfan Relief Dinner in LA is supposed to look like, but I'm learning fast.

Our attention is demanded from the stage by a black-tied buffoon who turns out to be our compère for the evening.

'Ladies and gentlemen, it's wunnerful to see you all here, and we have some wunnerful, wunnerful guests with us this evening. May I introduce Mr and Mrs James Stewart.'

A follow-spot swings round and deposits a pool of light on a table on the other side of the room. Jimmy Stewart and his wife stand up.

I'm thinking, Fucking hell, Jimmy Stewart!

The compère allows us to wallow in our proximity to stardom for a moment before he goes on, 'Ladies and gentlemen, Mr John Wayne.'

John Wayne stands up.

I'm thinking, This is not possible! when the compère announces, 'Ladies and gentlemen, Mr and Mrs Henry Fonda.

God Almighty! I almost gasp out loud, and realise that I'm being embarrassing with my rubber-necking in front of everyone.

'Miss Myrna Loy,' the compère intones, with the reverence of a priest saying the words of consecration.

I think, Myrna Loy! Jesus, where the hell is she? The woman next to me stands up.

I hadn't said a word to her yet.

Bloody hell, I'm sitting next to Myrna Loy!

I lean back in my chair and swing to my left as if I'm looking for a waiter and it's the most natural thing in the world that I'm sitting beside this hallowed piece of Hollywood history.

It's all a deathly experience. I turn back and gaze at Vanessa, pleading for help, for a little conversation or something to make me seem less redundant at this table, but of course, she's so short-sighted she can't see me. She's chatting politely with her neighbours, while I'm just a blur to her. Somehow, I blag my way through the courses without much more communication than the occasional simper at the ladies either side of me.

The tension eases a little for me towards the end of dinner when everyone smokes – which wouldn't happen today.

I've not been making much headway conversationally, mostly sitting like a prune, though I have managed a brief chat with Myrna and I'm now talking across Jean Simmons to the woman who is our hostess for the evening. She's friendly enough, welcoming me to Los Angeles and asking how it feels to be at a table full of women.

Despite the aplomb with which I face life on my home territory, I'm aware that I'm not a well-travelled man and, frankly, am pretty naïve at an event like this. I know nothing of Hollywood etiquette and I'm very conscious that I'm not in control of everything I'm doing here. But I try to relax, leaning back with my drink, looking around and puffing away on an untipped Gitane.

All of a sudden, the strong black tobacco isn't delivering. I glance at the cigarette. To my horror, I see the flame's missing; suddenly I know it's in Jean Simmons's skirt.

Inside, I panic. I don't know how to deal with this, but I know I'll get a bollocking because, of all the people in the room, she isn't smoking. She'll know she's not to blame and I've got this bare-ended cigarette sticking out of my fingers. Quickly I grind it into an ashtray and, assuming an utterly fake nonchalance, start peering at Miss Simmons and, more particularly, into the folds of her skirt, trying to see where the flame has gone. This is difficult, gazing into your neighbour's groin, but I can't just stick my hand into her crutch and say, 'Excuse me, I think I dropped something down there.' Or, 'You look a bit warm, dear. Have a glass of water,' and then slosh it all over her thighs. That wasn't going to work. But I know this burning fag is somewhere in her skirts and I'm desperate to spot it before she leaps up in pain and anguish, with a burning sensation around her nether regions.

She gives me another of her scornful looks, as if to say, 'What are you looking at, sonny?'

I'm trying to shrug it off when there's a sudden searing pain on my right arm, in the crook of my elbow. Looking down, I see there's a hole the size of an almond in my Burton's suit. The canvas lining has been exposed as a brown oval, smouldering at the edges. I start flapping at it to put it out, while my arm is in agony. It's still hot and I think I'll have to spend the rest of the evening clutching it to hide it, convinced that it will start smouldering again at any moment.

While I'm still grappling with this painful indignity, our oleaginous compère suddenly reappears on stage. 'Ladies and gentlemen, we will now proceed with the sale of raffle tickets in aid of the Aberfan Relief Fund.'

As he speaks, a man looms purposefully right up behind me. He is carrying a massive box of raffle tickets, priced, I observe with horror, at $100 each. I cringe. I've got precisely $25 on me, and nothing else with which to pay for them.

I look at the stack of tickets with a shrinking stomach. Am *I* supposed to buy this lot?

'Ladies and gentlemen, to sell you the raffle tickets we have two wunnerful young stars from England, over here to make *Camelot*. Miss Vanessa Redgrave and Mr David Herring.'

Fuck you, you obnoxious little shit!

This is all I need. I can't go out and sell tickets in the Burton's suit with a hole and a scorched canvas lining. I look around at everyone on the table with a sick grin.

'This looks like a jackets-off job to me.'

I shed the beastly garment with relief and a little self-congratulation at my quick thinking. I nod at Vanessa, who's also on her feet, and off we go. I start with the Stewarts and the Fondas, and after that things move pretty fast. I sell all the tickets, somewhat to my astonishment, without having to buy any myself.

I sit down again at the table, thinking I've handled the whole potentially cringe-making episode rather well. I clutch for a wine bottle to top myself up, under the impression that the worst is over. I don't care any more if Jean Simmons has already written me off for appearing altogether too dodgy.

Myrna Loy is otherwise engaged and never gives me another look.

But there are further indignities in store.

With a great hoo-ha and a flourish, large and painstakingly decorated cakes are carried in and placed at the centre of each of the top ten tables. These spectacular confections, which look, I have to say, appallingly like a series of collapsing slag heaps, are going to be auctioned off to the occupants of the tables.

The compère oils up to the first table.

'Well, what am I bid for this fan*tas*tic cake? $500? $600? $1,000? Ladies and gentlemen, thank you so much!'

The second table, not to be outdone, bids up to $2,000 for its cake.

By the time it gets to the table before ours, they're bidding $9,000! I've still got only $25 in my pocket.

The compère has reached us now. He gazes at me with a horrible leer. 'Jesus Christ – a table with one man and nine women, what an evening you must have had, Mr Herring!'

'It's been wonderful, thank you,' I lie.

Many eyes are on me. I am still in my shirt sleeves, but I'm fairly pissed by now and I don't give a shit.

'So,' he says. 'What am I bid for this last fantastic cake?'

I say, loud and clear, '$1,000.'

Jean Simmons, almost as quick, says, '$2,000.'

I turn to her quickly with a gesture of largesse. 'Miss Simmons, you must have it, of course. I don't really like cake that much.'

But she's not going to get lumped with it either and sharply passes it on to the next bidder. It's bid up round the table and, to my supreme relief, gets knocked down to our hostess for $8,000.

Shortly afterwards, by waving extravagantly from my side of the table, I manage at last to catch Vanessa's eye. She agrees that it's time to go and stands up, instantly knocking over someone else's wine glass.

While everyone is fussing about this, I turn to say goodnight to Jean Simmons, who is also on the point of leaving.

She inclines her head slightly. 'I'll see you for tennis on Sunday?'

I've been hoping she's forgotten. 'Thanks. But you haven't given me your address.'

'We-ell . . .' she drawls, thinking it over. 'I don't think you play tennis, and I'm certainly not going to give you my address.'

With that, she drifts off into the moonlight, and we never meet again. I pick up my charred and rumpled jacket and take Vanessa home.

[◎] [◎] [◎] [◎]

9

At the Court of King Arthur, Autumn 1966–Spring 1967

In the weeks that followed the Aberfan Disaster Relief Fund Dinner at which I felt I'd managed to convince Hollywood I was a complete klutz, I was aware that I hadn't made many new friends from among the eminent stars gathered there. They were, I had to accept, completely indifferent to the charms of new young British actor David Herring. I wasn't surprised when Jean Simmons failed to get in touch to reinstate her invitation to the tennis afternoon; I was bloody relieved.

Apart from my coterie of friends within the wacky purlieus of the Chateau Marmont, I still hadn't ventured out much with anyone new. The efforts of MGM's publicity people to generate interest in *Blow-Up* had not yet impacted on Hollywood's consciousness, or opened for me the Pandora's box of goodies which I was sure lurked somewhere within its heart. But my new agents, William Morris, showed no symptoms of discouragement.

William Morris had opulent offices on El Camino Drive in Beverly Hills, in a stark, modern building with deep-pile carpets and an inescapable odour of decomposing scripts of unmade films, which I didn't recognise at the time. Of course, over the years it has become very familiar, like the smell of old forgotten books. In a sense, William Morris were my new family now, despite their unsartorial habit of wearing ties with short-sleeve shirts. Practical in the California heat as this may be, I can report that from the first day I was escorted into the Morris offices, I never once succumbed to this appalling dress code.

This new family of mine, this anthill of activity – theatrical agents, literary agents, music agents, secretaries, runners, assistants to runners, mailboys – was presided over by the head ant, the seriously homuncular Abraham Lastfogel, a kind though very little man who carried his surplus pounds with tenacity, vitality, and possessed a digit-crunching handshake. He had been in charge since the forties, and despite searching the premises diligently over time for a photograph, painting or some documentary evidence of the original William Morris, I never found one, though I presume he must once have existed (outside the late 19th-century British Arts and Crafts movement).

Abe was no more than five foot three at full stretch, wore size six-shoes and boasted the best client list in Hollywood. It is said that when Natalie Wood (one of his clients) became irritated with the producers or director of a film she was making, she would petulantly throw off her coat, stamp on the ground and yell, 'I want to hear the patter of tiny feet around here! Get my agent!'

But by the time I joined the Morris office, Abe was hitting fourscore, his tasks were more conceptual than practical and he spent much of his day at the Hillcrest Country Club, where I often joined him. He normally had a half-dozen or so guests, mostly Hollywood power brokers of some sort, or his table, always the same one, would simply fill up with whoever was around that he knew.

There could be tennis players, golf professionals or actors with obscene tans, often, it seemed, with a large pair of breasts peering over their shoulders. These dormant mammaries belonged to young ladies who, I noted, all sported radiant teeth, so uncommonly even and immaculately white that I half expected an animated starburst to flash momentarily from an upper incisor. They spoke rarely, thank heavens, and then only to describe in enthusiastic detail perhaps the joyous experience of being crowned Miss Truck Driver, Detroit, or Crocodile Queen, Swamp City, Florida. I guessed that sooner or later most of them would end up draped over the rocks at Hugh Heffner's Playboy mansion, engaged in aspirational fornication. I didn't pay them a lot of attention, but it taught me to keep my mouth shut. My deeply nicotine-stained teeth could never have stood the competition.

Every one of the studio executives who hung out there was short, as if Abe Lastfogel had imposed a height limitation at his lunches, like a ride at Disneyland. You could have swung a scythe at five feet five over their heads and not one member of the executive group would have been harmed. These gatherings were full of light bonhomie, gossip and, I suspect, as much bullshit as similar gatherings in Hollywood have always been and always will be.

I soon learned that *every*one has a script which they are absolutely on the point of producing, or acting in, or for which they are 'putting the last pieces together'. It's this oil of dreams of imminent fantastic success that keeps the Los Angeles wheels lubricated.

Nevertheless, at Lastfogel's table all seemed glitter, and my English accent went down well with the available bright-fanged concubines. But due to my extremely limited wardrobe, my impecuniousness and my complete inability to master the mind-numbing intricacies of either washing machine or ironing board (I could iron, but I couldn't unfold the bugger of a board), I couldn't appear with knife-blade creases on white trousers as worn by everyone else, and with my long hair and my scrawny beard, which I was struggling to grow for *Camelot*, I looked less than stunning. No one seemed to mind, or dared to disapprove. For Abe had taken me under his wing, by inviting me not only to the Hillcrest but also to his home in the Beverly Wilshire Hotel, around the corner from his offices.

I found it hard to see how someone could live in a hotel for twenty years or so, until I met Abe's wife. She had been, in some distant, pre-talkie past, a supreme vaudeville artiste, singing and dancing across America. She was made-up with alarming excess, but in a strange way had remained exceedingly glamorous. She still had that effervescent quality of the absolute show girl: all bust and guts; glory or nothing. You could imagine her singing for the troops, or hammering the stage of a saloon in Moose Droppings, Montana. An Ethel Merman in *Gypsy*, all dolled up and ready to roll with the next train. Or alongside Louis Armstrong as he sweated over his supreme trumpet, while she clutched the mike to her chest in the single spotlight at Hollerin' Harry's Jazz Club in Livingstone County, Louisiana, singing torch songs until dawn, when the sun dyed the bayou deep purple and the alligators slid silently back to the slime. I can imagine it now, because I've been there and seen it. I wish I could have seen her then too.

I guess that Mrs Lastfogel hadn't changed a great deal since those touring days, but hotel living had become part of her soul, and while Abe loved to argue with producers, he never disagreed with his wife. So there they were, occupying six vast rooms in one of the most expensive hotels in Beverly Hills – for twenty-odd years, no less. I was aghast at the opulence; the sheer terror of the bills filled me with dread as I wondered how Jane was coping back in England with the upkeep of Elmhurst Court. I was very conscious that I had never seen a gilded lion, four foot high, in Croydon, nor heavy Baroque gilt chairs in such abundance.

On my first visit to the Lastfogels' vast establishment, finding myself surrounded by red-flock walls that tainted the air like asbestos, a terrific thirst came upon me and I asked if I could have a drink.

'Help yourself,' Mrs L said, in a voice with the sonic qualities of a shaken tool box.

She waved a hand vaguely at an array of decanters on a tray. Since none contained a clear colourless liquid, like the vodka I craved, I sniffed a few of them. They all contained sherry. I was shocked, and, as I looked around carefully, I detected other signs of non-existence here in this elegant hotel suite, as if it had been preserved, but not lived in; the expectation of imminent departure seemed to permeate the place. There was a kitchen but it contained no crockery, no tea towels, few implements or any of the other normal accoutrements. It was very bizarre but, eager to drink my fill of this crazy town, I was willing to embrace anything new, no matter how foreign it seemed.

When I was shown the Trunk, I began to understand. This massive seafaring coffer had lurched on steamers and trains and riverboats for decades. It was covered with labels to every destination you could think of, cardboard packet cards, some torn in half, others intact. The whole leather box, with brass fittings and locks, and rawhide straps around to hold the top secure, was beyond elegance. It was magnificent. It stood alone, base down, barely squeezed into the enormous wardrobe that was Mrs L's own, where no gowns hung on rails, no scarves, nothing. Only the trunk occupied it.

And it was from here that Mrs Lastfogel dressed every day, sending less-than-perfect garments to the hotel cleaning service. They arrived back neatly folded but were always returned to the Trunk. Some were dresses from the twenties and thirties, thin and elderly; others were fresh and sprightly, delivered from Rodeo Drive. All were kept in the Trunk.

Mrs L still lived the vaudeville life in her own imagination, for she was as old as Abe, and I wondered, as I was shown these precious insights, whether she could sometimes be glimpsed gliding through the corridors of the staid Beverly Wilshire, decked in a boa and slinky sequined skin, singing some long-forgotten torch song, as she had done those many years before.

There was no question that the Lastfogels were extreme eccentrics by any measure, and I hugged them to my bosom, along with the rest of the people at the Morris office. And for me, in those early days in Los Angeles, somewhat discombobulated as I was, a little home life, even lived from a trunk, was a most welcome thing. And I hoped very much that Mrs L's warmth towards me would last for ever, but sadly this was not to be.

I have never played the piano well – I tend to play 'at' it, rather – but I was hosting a party for the Lastfogels a few years later at Cumballs, an elegant club near Venice Beach in Santa Monica. I had managed to persuade Mrs L to sing, to my ham-fisted accompaniment, two classics, 'As Time Goes By' and 'One for the Road'.

The performance was a miserable failure, made more poignant because dozens of enthusiastic and influential guests were there to witness it.

Besides that, restricted as I was to the key of C major, I just couldn't handle one where she was more comfortable, with the result that her voice sounded like a Malibu rock slide with a little surf-on-shingle thrown in.

To be fair to her and me, we'd both been playing fast and loose with Old Kentucky Bourbon for some hours; perhaps it was now taking its revenge. Richard Harris summed it up afterwards with wry Paddiness, 'Y'know, the piano is not your forte.'

Since I was hosting the party, I was forgiven by my audience. Mrs L, leaving the small stage after a performance that could only be described as gruesome, was not. My sanguine hope of creating an atmosphere of late-night promise had been trashed. The Lastfogels left in haste; neither Abe nor his wife ever contacted me again, and I never so much as sniffed a glass of Old Kentucky after that.

The finances at the William Morris Agency were run by Roger Davis, the most rigorous of chancellors, and Lenny Hirsham, the individual agent assigned to me, was known for having discovered, among others, Clint Eastwood. Lenny was tall: Eastwood came up to his shoulder; Lastfogel to his hip.

In November, when I'd been in LA only a short time, it must have been Lenny who asked me along to a party being held for Teddy Kennedy at Peter Lawford's house, down on the beach below the promenade at Santa Monica. I didn't discover if Peter was hosting the party; I don't recall seeing him there on that occasion. Nor did I learn until many years later, when the whole extraordinary saga unfolded, that Jack Kennedy had held his trysts with Marilyn Monroe in this very house. Peter Lawford, the go-between, had lent it to him for the purpose and, being married to a Kennedy, had kept shtum about it for many years after the event.

At this party, though, unlike the Coconut Grove bash, there were a lot of people with whom I could feel immediate empathy, some of whom became friends for many years, many even to this day. For the most part, inevitably, they were film people – directors, writers, musicians, actors even.

Tom Mankiewicz, who wrote the screenplays for the early Bond films, became a very good friend as a result of this gathering, as did Jack Haley Jr, director, producer and one-time spouse to Liza Minelli, whose father had played the Tin Man in *The Wizard of Oz* and who was going out then with Nancy Sinatra; Evie and Leslie Bricusse, who wrote the lyrics for *Stop the World*, *Dr Dolittle* and *Pickwick*; Quincy Jones and Steve McQueen; even Frank Sinatra. And this party led inevitably on to others – many others.

But, for me, by far the most significant encounter of the evening was with someone then virtually unknown – a stunning, flawlessly beautiful young actress. Like me, she'd been inveigled to the party by her agent. Stan Kayman, who handled her at William Morris, had big plans for his client and had sent a limo to pick her up and drive her here directly from LAX, where she'd just arrived.

The first moment I saw her is as clear to me now as it was then. Across the broad space of the sunken living room, from where I sat on the back of a sofa between two vast picture windows which overlooked the ocean, I had a sudden vision of two shining aquamarine orbs beneath a cloud of shimmering copper hair. For a second, in a way which, until then, I thought existed only in the most slushy of Barbara Cartland's novels, our eyes met and locked onto each other as if we'd suddenly been joined by some kind of indestructible conduit along which surged a current of instant understanding and overwhelming attraction. It seemed, frankly, too good to be true, and when a moment later the vision had gone, I wondered if it had been real. But then, in another glimpse, I saw her disappearing into one of the many powder rooms that are placed strategically in the houses of movie industry party givers.

I followed at once, leaving enough time for a girl to do what a girl has to do before I opened the door and stepped in.

She had her back to me, facing a large stage dressing-room mirror, touching up her mound of backcombed, lustrous auburn hair. I stood behind her and moved my head to one side until I could look over her shoulder and see her face in the mirror.

'Hello,' I said, with what sounded to me like crass banality. 'I'm David Hemmings. Who are you?'

She smiled with a flutter of her false eyelashes and a faint nod that confirmed all that I had gathered from that first long glance across the room.

'I know who you are,' she said. 'I'm Gayle Hunnicutt.'

After that we walked and talked, in and out of the house, on the terrace, meeting all sorts of new people, who, as it turned out, were soon to become part of both our lives. And in the process we started getting to know each other.

Gayle had flown in that evening from San Francisco, where she'd been staying with an old friend from her home town of Fort Worth, Texas, who had decided to marry a basketball coach from Northern California and was now a kindergarten teacher in the tiny community of Twain Harte – which must have offered a hilarious contrast to Gayle's life as a budding movie starlet in Los Angeles.

I soon discovered, though, that Gayle was unlike any of the women I'd met so far in Los Angeles, and a world away from the bikinied floozies who showed up at Abe's lunches in the Hillcrest. Although she was an actress, I had the refreshing impression that she was in the business at least as much for the art as for the glamour, an outlook that appealed greatly to my own ambivalent attitude to the whole pantomime. In fairness, I should admit that I was also there for the obvious promise of sexual adventure, which she, quite clearly, was not.

Her background in Texas had been very conservative. After a period at the Texas Christian University in Fort Worth (TCU), she'd been awarded a Regent Scholarship to the University of California at Los Angeles (UCLA), majoring in English. When I met Gayle, she had graduated the year before, 1965. 'A's she'd been on a scholarship, she'd had to maintain a four-point average, straight 'A's all the way through the four years of her course. Being a conscientious, well-brought-up gal, she'd had her nose down in her books, living in her sorority house on campus with sixty other girls and very little time for dating. After graduating, she'd shared a house in West LA with three girlfriends from UCLA, one of whom she also knew from Fort Worth.

Gayle told me she'd wanted to be an actress from a very early age, but feeling that this was somehow inappropriate for a strictly nurtured daughter of a warm but strait-laced southern family, she imagined that in time she would outgrow the unseemly urge which was so alien to her genes.

When she was eighteen, she had played Elizabeth Proctor in *The Crucible*. It was a serious role, which confirmed to her that she too was serious about acting. She told them back home in Texas that this was what she wanted to do with her life; it was an option unheard of in the family and they tried to tease her out of it.

But the urge persisted through university and beyond. When one of her housemates went for an interview to be a secretary to the director Roger Corman, king of the B-movies, who started so many careers, she didn't get the job, but she told him, 'One of my friends wants to be an actress. Will you meet her?'

He said he would and Gayle went along. As a result Corman gave her her first film part – in *The Wild Angels* with Peter Fonda, Nancy Sinatra and Bruce Dern (whose daughter, Laura Dern, starred in *Jurassic Park* thirty years on). The film was about Hell's Angels; it was made in LA and out in the mountains behind Palm Springs with a gang of real and terrifying Hell's Angels. Gayle was an angel's moll, with a scar down her face. She was scared stiff most of the time, she told me, but she survived and earned her Screen Actors' Guild card.

In complete contrast, after that she acted in a play – the PhD project of a Hungarian student at UCLA – at the Cahuenga Playhouse, where she was spotted by a Warner Brothers talent scout. She was asked right away to come in and meet Pandro Berman, one of the great figures in Hollywood casting.

Berman called Max Arnow, an agent known for discovering new talent in an industry that sucks up talent like a whale swallowing plankton. Max was in his sixties, but took Gayle under his wing with enthusiasm, and he got her her first outing on a TV series, *Mount Roberts*, followed by a guest spot on the *Beverly Hill Billies*. The producers of *BHB* wanted her to appear regularly and offered to create a new part for her. Max, very wisely in my view, talked her out of it; Gayle becoming famous for being a Beverly Hill Billy sort of defies credibility.

However, he let her take a cameo role with Helen Hayes, a great actress, in the first *Movie of the Week* made by Universal. She played a wild Italian girl who spent a lot of time frolicking in frilly black lingerie and lacy suspenders. Gayle's description of it made my mouth water, but she primly assured me that there had been nothing sexy in the part;

she'd just been playing an innocent, madcap girl. But, as luck – or serendipity, as I like to think of it – would have it, George Peppard came along to the studios to look at a screen test of another actress and, having arrived early, was invited to see the dailies of Gayle's scene.

He told me later he'd made up his mind in a matter of minutes. 'That's who I want to star in my next picture.' The film, *PJ*, was due to be made in January 1967, and the day I met her, Gayle was still waiting to hear if she'd got the part.

The following week there was a party at Steve McQueen's estate in Brentwood – a very big party to celebrate a clutch of Oscar nominations for his latest film, *The Sand Pebbles*, which he'd made with Candice Bergen and Richard Attenborough.

Joan Collins had asked me, among a crowd of others, to drop in to her place for a drink on the way to the McQueen party. Joan was very much at the centre of the English expat community in Hollywood then. She had been up at Chateau Marmont with one or other of my fellow guests and I'd already met her there, along with Samantha Eggar. Almost the first person I saw when I walked in was Gayle. She had come with Stan Kayman and his date, Simone Zorn, an interesting French journalist. Gayle and I immediately made for each other, delighted that we were going on to the same party later.

The McQueen mansion was a classic movie star's lair, perched way up a hill behind massive security gates and a forest of arboreal rarities. They'd decorated the place for the party like a ship, with nets and rigging all over the place. It was hard not to be impressed, and the buzz of impending glory was inescapable. Everyone in LA thought Steve was going to win the Best Actor Oscar (although, when it came to it, Paul Schofield won with *A Man for all Seasons*).

I found I already knew quite a few people at the gathering – some of the British contingent and others that I'd met at Peter Lawford's, who were quick and kind enough to introduce me to several more Hollywood regulars. But mostly I wanted to talk to Gayle. She was a little nervous, since Stan had told her he'd asked a friend from San Francisco as her blind date, and we couldn't help glancing down the hill in trepidation as each new limo crept through the gates and wound up the long drive towards the mansion, until one arrived carrying Frank Pimento, her date. I was naturally a little pissed off, but

Frank turned out not to be an attractive man in any way I could identify, and I relaxed. There was a lot of marijuana smoke in the air and, though I didn't partake, I soon slipped into the mood, which suited me very well.

Gayle, on the other hand, didn't really seem to know what was going on; she was still, as they say in Texas, 'so green you can't put her on the ground for fear she'll sprout roots'. I found that very endearing and, frankly, pretty unusual at a party such as this, but it seemed she was still a very old-fashioned person.

So, between forays among the wonderful cast of characters on offer, I spent a lot of the party dancing with her, desperately trying to persuade her back to the Chateau Marmont with me, until she announced that she should do the honourable thing and leave with her date.

Gayle liked Stan's friend, Simone, and Frank, she told me, was a really nice guy, if not her top choice of date for her first really big Hollywood party – not, she felt, a suitably glamorous accoutrement for an aspiring starlet at such an event. But he was courteous and attentive to her, and she felt she owed him no less, whatever her more basic instincts might have been urging her to do.

This is the kind of consideration I've always admired, although I find it hard to sustain myself. The trouble was, that night, Gayle feeling compelled to leave with the ugly bugger, left me feeling like a self-satisfied early bird who's just had the worm whipped from its beak.

But she was adamant. 'I'm supposed to be with this guy' – who by this time was absolutely legless. 'I have to go home with him.' Not 'home' as in going to bed, I knew, but going in the same limo.

However, I knew it wasn't what she really wanted to do, so, despite the obvious disappointment of not getting her back to my place, I didn't feel too short-changed. Later, we learned that Frank was gay; Stan was his boyfriend and was trying to cover up, as if anyone would give a shit these days. Simone was obviously just a beard.

Gayle might have gone, but I was nowhere near ready for bed. I went back into the party, where I succumbed to an invitation to play poker with Peter Lawford, Sammy Davis Jr, Efrem Zimbalist Jr and Tony Newley.

Although the guys could not have been more friendly – indeed, I saw a lot of them all while I was in LA – things did not go well on the gaming front that night. I was becoming desperate and, in the final round of a heavy hand, I found myself left in with just Sammy Davis Jr.

📷 📷 📷 📷

I think my hand's good. I think it's better than good, it's great.

I look inscrutable, and stare at the singer to see if I can read anything in his dark, unblinking eye.

He stares back; I carry on staring. I can read nothing; his eye is totally blank. He could be holding a royal flush or a pair of twos for all I can tell.

He goes on staring, until he growls, 'You're looking in the wrong eye, kid. That's the one with the warmth. It's made of glass.'

I have completely forgotten about Sammy's famous glass eye. I don't suppose he is giving anything out with his real one either, though, and after he's forced a few more raises from me, he lays his cards down and cleans me out.

📷 📷 📷 📷

The day after Steve McQueen's party, with a bulldog tenacity Churchill would have admired, I continued my pursuit of Gayle by ringing her. She was also being hotly pursued by Mel Ferrer at the time and, in her charming naïvety, asked me up to Universal Studios to meet Mel on the set of *Wait Until Dark*. His wife, Audrey Hepburn, was there too, looking so amazing I could hardly take my eyes off her.

Well, I thought – like a greedy little boy with the run of the sweet shop – Mel, old chap, why don't we just swap this around and I'll have a wondrous affair with Hepburn, and you can take Gayle where you want?

But that wasn't to be. I would probably, in any case, have been punching above my weight in that household. Besides, Gayle and I were getting on sublimely. When I'd first met her at Peter Lawford's, she told me she had just moved into a new house, a redwood A-frame on the side of the canyon at 819 North Beverly Glen Boulevard, between Sunset and Mulholland. She asked me up for a drink there. It was an enchanting place, with a timber deck that projected over the hillside and always seemed to catch the sun. All around was green, with deer coming down off the Santa Monica Mountains to graze in this magic spot. One end of the house was all glass, so that the sun shone in with a wondrous glow on the redwood interior.

In December 1966, when I'd known Gayle only a couple of weeks, Antonioni's final cut of *Blow-Up* was being shown. It was the first time

I'd seen any version of it. I had no idea what I would think of it or what the reaction would be. Partly to impress, partly for support, I asked Gayle to come with me to the Directors' Guild of America on Sunset Boulevard to see it. They held regular screenings there of new movies likely to be of interest to members. Although at that stage *Blow-Up* hadn't had much publicity, Antonioni was at the height of his powers and reputation, and word had seeped out among the Hollywood movers and shakers. As a result, the cinema was packed that evening with other directors and people from the industry.

I hadn't seen the Maestro since my brief visit to his cutting room in London a few months earlier. He was wearing his customary chic sports jacket and dark grey trousers, with an open-neck shirt and an Indian silk scarf wafting around his neck. His brow shrouded penetrating brown eyes, in which, for the first time, I even detected a hint of nervousness. Once I'd sat down, with Gayle on one side and him on the other, I noticed he was rattling his foot on the stairwell and pulling his hands through his hair, while his head wagged from side to side like a demented pendulum. Carlo Di Palma looked depressed too, lurking moodily with a tight 'Why am I here?' rictus scratched across his face, as if by a drunken girl in make-up.

I was sweating and nervous as hell. Gayle tells me, although I have no recollection of it, that I fiddled with a coin the whole way through the film, flipping it ceaselessly back and forth across my knuckles, muttering, 'They hate it, they hate it.' She was truly worried about my state of mind if the picture bombed.

I was already sure it would.

I was appalled by what I saw. I thought it was slow; I thought it was boring. I'd seen barely a foot of the movie previously, as Antonioni had always been so secretive. While he was making it, the whole thing was in his head and he certainly never had any need to tell me what he was intending to portray or how he was going to do it. But I had hoped it would all become clear in the final cut. Now I just wasn't seeing it.

When the film ended, there was an extraordinary silence for a few moments. I felt myself grow rigid with disappointment and bitter shame. It's strange how long these silences can seem. Suddenly, though, it was over and the whole audience erupted, apparently overwhelmed by what they had just witnessed. I may still have not understood the picture, but it turned out that enough other people had.

I guess, looking back, that it did capture the zeitgeist, and thus became a period piece, but its predominant theme is less temporal – the elusiveness of reality. Life is about constant change and nothing has eternal reality; appearance deceives, and we can never be sure that what we have seen did actually happen.

In the cinema, people appeared from everywhere to congratulate the director, pumping his hand and patting his elegantly clad shoulders. They were all over me too, yanking my arm up and down, while cameras flashed, with warm smiles and fine comments from everyone. Gayle, having watched me fidget disloyally during the film, was speechless, her mouth agape, never having had much idea that she would be on the right side of 'up', so to speak.

Nor had I.

But now we were out in the entrance lobby, crushed by the mob, fêted by the soothsayers, the magazines and the autograph hang-arounds, those who will have you sign a card which they'll then sell on for a buck. Now, with Antonioni, I was suddenly the hero, glowing in the beam of Hollywood's spotlights.

I didn't particularly want this; I didn't crave it. But I was unquestionably thrilled that the film had worked, and over the very many years since I've come to respect the kindliness of this bizarre, brave little movie. I did not appreciate the joy of making it enough at the time, cocky and arrogant as I was, but now, in spite of my first knee-jerk response, it has claimed me as a friend. Antonioni was irascible, for sure, difficult, dogmatic and sometimes plain plug-ugly to work with. But he was also fatherly, like Britten, trustworthy, caring, and a man into whose hands I felt I could safely place my aspirations.

It's potentially wearisome to describe a complete life spent in front of the camera, the familiarity of the studio floor, the camaraderie, the mud. But some high points have to be acknowledged and to have had the pleasure of working with the Maestro is undoubtedly right up there for me. After all, it changed my life and it gave me the wherewithal to move into regions I hadn't even thought of – sometimes down, sometimes sideways, to be sure, such are the perversions of life as a jobbing actor. That I did not make better use of this advantage is not, after all, Antonioni's fault. The launch pad had been primed. I was in Hollywood. The great hall at Camelot beckoned. And, for a moment – for such things are very fleet – I looked down from a height that only the lucky or the unhealthily rich ever get to reach.

*

If the evening was a turning point in my life as an actor, it was also a turning point in my relationship with Gayle, who, despite many subsequent tribulations as a result of my own seriously dysfunctional behaviour, is still a good and loyal friend.

Being an old-fashioned southern girl, even after four years at UCLA and a couple as an aspiring actress in Hollywood, Gayle was still steeped in Texan codes of honour and morality. While I admired this and was attracted by it as another aspect of her unexpected and tantalising innocence, I was anxious to show my admiration by consummation. And to my great joy that night, for the first time, she agreed to come back with me to the Chateau Marmont.

It wasn't until after Christmas, when Gayle heard she'd definitely got her part in *PJ*, that I met some of her family in Fort Worth, and realised just how strong her southern roots were. Her grandmother Mrs Darling-Love Bows was from Georgia, and they don't come much more southern.

She was 97 when Gayle introduced me to her. I asked her if she remembered the Civil War.

'The War between the States?' she corrected me. 'Not directly – it ended in 1865 – but my parents remembered it well.'

'What sort of impact did it have on your family?' I asked innocently.

'Well,' she drawled, 'pretty bad. We lost all our slaves.'

In the end, I became quite fond of them all, even Gayle's very proper, much-travelled and hawk-eyed Aunt Hazel Hunnicutt. I'm not sure, though, that the feeling was ever mutual.

I'd been in Los Angeles for a month or so before, finally, the cast of *Camelot* was assembled on stage 5 at Warner Brothers, the largest sound stage in the world. Only later would the James Bond stage at Pinewood surpass it. A heady thought. But there it was before us: the Great Hall at Camelot. Courtesy of John Truscott, the production designer, who also, somewhat unusually but equally brilliantly, designed the costumes.

John had put together a set that was so large that technicians had to squeeze between the real walls and the constructed manifestations of the castle interior. Barely an electrical cable could thread its way through the narrow space between truth and Truscott's cinema reality. Naturally, when Jack Warner first saw it, sensitive to the colossal investment he had in it, he growled gently, 'Listen, you people, I want to see every fucking inch of this on the screen!'

If you've seen the picture and you're one of those people with the ability to retain every line of dialogue in a movie, you will recall that I'm given the task of realising this promise. Mordred's specially added line, 'Wonderful place for parties!', followed by a vast, wide, over-the-shoulder shot from my point of view, taking in the whole massive construction, was inserted deliberately to appease the accountants, and to fulfil Jack Warner's brief.

Warner Brothers' Great Hall of Camelot was unquestionably magnificent. Visitors gasped as they walked in. We all gasped, agape, tiny figures gathered on our first day. Richard Harris, complete with crown and eyeshadow, Vanessa Redgrave, Lionel Jeffries, Laurence Naismith, fully wigged and bearded as Merlin, Franco Nero (or Franco Zero as I liked to call him; though Vanessa didn't) and me. We hovered, a mixed bag of actors waiting for our orders.

My advice to anyone foolish enough to aspire to membership of the fraternity of film actors would be this: 'Don't learn to act, learn to wait. Acting is easy. Waiting is much harder.'

And we waited.

Our director, Joshua Logan, would have been the first to own up to having a small cold sip of a warm afternoon, but his past achievements went before him as testimony to his talent. He had, after all, directed *Picnic, Bus Stop* and *South Pacific*, cold sip or not. He had seen Marilyn Monroe naked, which looks good on anyone's CV. No need to read further. Josh was certainly no novice ingénu, nor talentless tyrant, and we were looking forward to submitting to his skills – except perhaps for Richard, for whom submission was not a natural posture.

The whole assembled company, the players and the crew, were ready to do his bidding. It is a fine, rare moment when all are ready and willing, when every smallest piece is in place, like a Friday night before a Saturday wedding, with napkins folded like swans.

So it is on a film set, that first day, when the enthusiasm and the adrenalin could be bottled, when all are bent on a common task, waiting only for the hand to guide.

As if on a cue, our heads all turned together to watch appearing from behind the Round Table – yes, *the* Round Table – the man himself, Joshua Logan. Nedda, his wife, was with him, though, perhaps in recognition of studio etiquette, a little behind him. His figure, like the table itself, was inescapably circular. He was balding, full of face, with a band of tufted hair above his upper lip and chubby cheek add-ons that bulged by his ears like a hamster's fodder bags. It was popularly rumoured that in these the booze was stored.

Nedda, despite following Josh by a step or two, held herself with dignity. Square-shouldered and slight of stature, she had the air of a woman well in control, with a power tool for a smile. The steady gleam in her eyes suggested that she did not suffer anyone gladly, and fools not at all.

They stood before us silently, also taking in the vast walls of Camelot. Josh seemed lost in a dream for a long moment, drinking in the fantasy, breathing in a sense of movie and the smells of fresh paint and endless stipple, applied as if Laurence Llewelyn-Bowen had been allowed to run amok for a month. Indeed, on closer examination, Camelot was not yet dry, and the fine work-lights picked out the damper spots, making them glitter and sparkle, as we all hoped the movie would, once the shooting was over.

Logan coughed and cleared his throat. He had smoked with true commitment for decades, washing down the nicotine with whisky. His voice was heavy gravel – rubble, even – being poured from a road builder's truck.

'Well,' he drawled, fumbling with his moustache. 'As you can see, this is the Great Hall of Camelot.'

We knew that. He knew that. I wondered, momentarily, if this was his first visit.

'I thought . . .' He paused for a very long time. 'I thought . . .' he repeated, though now a little hesitantly. 'I thought . . . Richard, that you might come in from the door?'

I wondered which of the seventeen doors available he had in mind.

After a few moments' silence, Josh laughed. Moisture seeped on to his brow.

The crew were still poised.

Logan looked around, and where he looked, we all looked. If he was after inspiration, so were we.

Except Harris, who stood erect and firm, with an Irish grimace of insolence which only he could have produced.

Vanessa stared at her feet.

Franco Zero sneezed as he tugged at a scarf around his neck. He had a cold, but then he always had a cold. Over the many years since in which I've worked with Italians, I've come to acknowledge that they do hypochondria very well, and not just on the football field.

As Logan carried on staring nervously around the Great Hall, Harris looked at me with a half-clenched hand tipped to his lips, as if clutching a glass.

Did he mean he thought that Logan had already had a few drinks, or that we should go and find some for ourselves?

Logan interrupted my conjecture. '*Or*,' he said, with directorial emphasis, looking hard at Richard, 'maybe we could find you sitting on the throne . . . After all, you are the King!' He glanced around uneasily for affirmation, waving his outstretched arms in a wide arc that embraced us all. 'After all,' he repeated, 'you are the King!'

He chuckled deeply, as if he had suddenly, and with great profundity, stumbled across the Holy Grail. But his body language did not confirm it.

The modest silence and inactivity turned abruptly to busyness. Where the crew had stood poised and ready, they now found things to polish. Papers were rustled, wooden finger-wedges piled neatly, lenses, already pristine, were cleansed a little more.

Suddenly Josh turned on me and fixed me with a kind of stare that I only remembered from the playground bullies of my early youth. 'And why don't you . . .' he said. But before the end of the sentence emerged, his voice trailed off. He wiped his sweaty brow with a quivering hand as he sank into Sir Gawain's chair at the Round Table with panic in full rout.

Nedda did not move a muscle.

'God!' he cried out suddenly. 'God, won't somebody help me?'

It was clear to me that this was not a wholly well person, whatever his past credits.

The silence that followed was profound.

It was so quiet, given the enormousness of the set and the grave responsibility for the film to be made, you might even have heard a smile.

Logan wasn't well, but the anxiety was not his alone.

Bloody hell, we've all been through it! First day at the new job, heavens – we were all as terrified, every one of us.

But Richard stepped towards me with his clenched-fist-to-the-lips gesture, without comment and with a nod that drinkers know. We left the set without flourish and walked swiftly from the alcohol-free studio compound to pass the time until things were sorted out in Camelot.

*

Across from the studio's back gate, Richard and I had discovered a small truckers' bar, the Cauldron, which from time to time we used as an alternative to the commissary (Hollywood jargon for a canteen with tablecloths). It had the advantage of allowing us to sneak out in full costume for a beer at lunchtime. Californian bars are notoriously gloomy and it took several minutes with a sweeping motion of the hands in front of you to find anything resembling a barstool. We were, of course, still in full costume, Richard with crown in place and I in Mordred's dreadful purple-and-cerise leather suit. But it was 1967, very dark, and no one seemed to notice.

We drank Budweiser in this sleazy bar. It was a sawdust-on-the-floor, shotgun-under-the-counter kind of place and we both liked it a lot. Strange, but it is in such a manner and in such places that big friendships are forged. We laughed until it hurt, trading stories, never once talking film. Richard aired his Machiavellian wit, while I slapped my thighs at my own jokes.

The Cauldron served hamburgers so greasy they had to be eaten over a bowl to catch the drips, as we learned after several reprimands from the wardrobe department. I guess the locals had seen this sort of thing before – a ne'er-do-well in cerise leather and a king in full regalia, eating burgers, both slightly pissed, passing an afternoon. That's Hollywood.

Peter Foreman, the Camelot gofer, sought us out and told us that there would be no shooting that day. Logan apparently was not well.

'Well, isn't that a shame?' said Richard. 'What are you having, Foreskin?'

Inevitably after that, this impoverished second to the second to the first assistant director was always referred to as 'The Skin'. And, because his job entailed being yelled at constantly and from afar, cries of 'Skin!', 'Skin!' or, as in golf, 'Fore!', 'Fore!' would often be heard echoing across stage 5. Poor lad. Fortunately, young as he was, his mother didn't know he was out. He took it in good part, though, and insisted on calling Harris 'Dick', which Richard loathed, so Foreskin got his own back.

The only other alternative drinking hole to the Cauldron was the Tex-Mex bang opposite the front gate, and therefore a bit unsubtle, since the Warner Brothers Studios were dry. Any booze discovered on the lot was deeply frowned upon and cause for dismissal, certainly for crew. (Although there may have been wine in the executives' restaurant, that was by invitation only and hardly relaxing.)

Finally, Harris and I decided that we ought to have our own cache – for emergencies only, of course. We were always able to smuggle supplies in, using the time-honoured conveyance of the prop van. I have never known a film set anywhere in the world where, by shiftily creeping up to the back of a prop wagon with a thirsty look, you wouldn't get a dram or a beer. Our problem was disposal of the empties. As luck would have it, outside our small caravan/dressing rooms, right by the main stage door, there were two portaloos for our personal use, one for Richard, one for me. We decided to share one and use the other as our repository.

Of course, after emergency had followed emergency, our empties were almost level with the loo seat, helped by guests, crew and other odds and sods having quite quickly discovered where the bar was.

Jack Warner took great pride in showing off the Great Hall and the Round Table, and would take small gatherings on to stage 5 at a moment's notice. He would come in through the back doors, closest to his offices, pass the table and the throne room, then make the long walk up the body of the Great Hall itself, showing off its vast size and height.

To be fair to those who created it, to see the set fully lit, with all the knights in full regalia and armour and Arthur at the head of the table (though it was round so all would be equal), with a horse or two hoofing it across the stone floor of the hall itself, sweating and carrying a messenger for the table, was an experience. The set had no equal, either in size or in quality.

Richard and I were away from all that, momentarily, when we had had an unusually quiet afternoon, chewing the fat, going over dialogue or ideas, sitting in chairs outside our vans, letting the valley smog fill our lungs. We talked of Ireland, fresh air and Guinness from the Liffey, and how late we might finish that evening – the normal intellectual nonsense, saving the world, passing the time.

Until Warner suddenly emerged through the side door to the stage and we hastily slipped our tinnies inside our costumes. He was followed by a dozen or so unmistakably Japanese people – distributors, we discovered later. Caught short, a rather elegant woman rushed to the portaloo and pulled open the door. The clatter of beer cans and the clink of bottles would, I imagine, have been heard in San Diego.

The young lady was instantly swept up by Richard and escorted to the other loo, leaving me to face Warner. But a slow, incredulous smile was all that came from him, as if suppressing a genuine guffaw.

'You'd better get craft service to clean this up,' he said as Harris came around the caravan towards us. And then, as the distributor went back to join the parade, hitching up her Nippon variant of Mary Quant slacks and the group toddled off, Warner whispered from the side of a grinning mouth, 'This bar is now closed.'

If you get the impression that life on a film set is nothing but beer and a couple of fingers of rye now and then, you'd be wrong – not entirely, but you would have missed the point. The work is hard. Intense concentration is needed and certainly doesn't allow you to get pissed out of your tree and then get through – let aside, remember – four or five pages of dialogue, in the way that guys who work heavy machinery can have a pint at lunchtime and still keep it under control, because they have to.

But these were the sixties, and everyone went to the pub for lunch, or the studio bar, especially in England, France or Italy, where the caterers would put wine on the table for those who wanted it. I once did a film on an English location in a small manor house beside a river about thirty feet across. On the far side was an appealing pub, tables at the riverside, cosy, beamed and serving real ale. To get to it by road required a journey of a mile up a gravel lane to join a minor road, 200 yards of dual carriageway and another gravel drive for a mile back by the river to the pub.

When the grips and the riggers arrived to set towers for the lights that would stream in through the downstairs windows of this charming manor, the first thing they did with their planks and scaffold poles was to build a bridge. The entire crew, come lunch, could walk across and sup up. That wouldn't happen today, now that booze, like cigarettes, is out of fashion.

I like a pint at lunch, preferably a PoG, but poor Richard gave up the booze and he told me, thirty years later when we met on the set of *Gladiator* in Farnham, there wasn't a day went by that he didn't miss the lunchtime break in filming, sitting in costume, on a barstool in a local, chatting over a bevvy.

As *Camelot* shuffled on, we all did our best to look after Josh. Richard Klein, the director of photography, nursed the material and Josh to bring to the screen perhaps not the greatest musical ever made, but a creditable one none the less. For Harris, it was a dream fulfilled, and as we know it was a role he was born to and would have happily played to his death.

Jack Warner had asked everyone he could think of to play the role. But he hadn't thought of Harris.

Burton had turned it down without hesitation. 'To play a king,' he'd said, 'is to pretend too much below me . . . at least in a moving picture.'

But the truth is more likely that Warner didn't want to pay him enough. 'Warner is a little fart,' Burton said. 'But at least I fart with my voice. And I have a strong voice.' He was not to play the role.

Similarly, Robert Goulet, who had a fine voice but a dull humour, said, 'I have lived it . . . I have been the king on Broadway, or, more likely, Burton's prince.'

Warner, it is well documented, asked Goulet to kneel in front of his desk, which Robert duly did, fully expecting the role to be grafted to his soul. Not to be. Warner took a paperknife and tapped him on each shoulder with it. 'Arise, Gullet, I ain't no queen, and you ain't Arthur.'

As you might imagine, there was a pause, a long eclipse. But Goulet emerged the winner. He didn't get the role but he did get to keep the paperknife.

Harris, however, was to prevail, not by the normal means of agents, managers and package brokers, but by guile. He had been canvassing Warner for months. In his own words: 'That little leprechaun will be the start of me.' And in many ways he was right.

The two could not have been more different. Warner was a charismatic 56-year-old, stumping up a mere five foot two. Harris was the rugby hero, the Limerick star of tough and booze, six foot four, with Irish eyes and a threatening demeanour that could dominate most. This was a prize fight in the making: Harris had the reach, but Warner was the head of the largest distribution company in the world, certainly, and was watching with glee as the crumbling studios of MGM sold off real estate and Judy Garland's shoes.

Warner was a leprechaun, yes, and with plenty of Blarney, but he was having trouble finding an Arthur for *Camelot*. Harris knew he was right for the role. He knew, despite his reputation, appalling as it was, that he could really make it his own.

It was true. I was with him through the film, pocketed with him almost, and saw him on stage in Hawaii, Seattle, Los Angeles and Chicago. He made the role his own. After all, not every Tom, Dick or Harry can be an Arthur.

'I stutter slightly, I know, but I'm Irish, so I don't think as fast as my tongue. I mean, have you ever met an Irishman who thought before he spoke?'

But as an actor he thought a lot, and he could sing . . . just.

After seeing the preview, paperknife in hand, Goulet said, 'I could not have done better, but I might have carried the tunes with more accuracy.'

Although casting directors had begged Warner to see Harris, they were all refused.

Warner hated Harris as a casting idea. 'He is a drunk. This is a dry studio,' he objected. 'Why would we want an Irishman playing a King? You want a goy to play Moses?'

But Harris would not lie down – although, actually, to get the job, he did.

Creeping ever closer to production, with millions of dollars at stake, Warner still did not have a lead. He did not have Arthur. He tapped everywhere, but no one out there came to mind.

In the slip of an evening Harris had bribed the security men to let him in to the studio lot. He had explained what he wanted to do. Sleep in front of Jack Warner's door. He curled up at about eleven and was still snoring deeply at six in the morning, when, prompt as ever, Warner arrived. He stepped over the rubble without a word and immediately picked up the phone and told security, 'Get that fucking tramp Harris off my doorstep.'

Harris stood up in the doorway and stared at Warner, who grimaced over his unlit cigar.

'I know . . . you wanna play Arthur,' Warner said.

'I'm the best you'll get,' Harris said with total conviction. 'If you don't like the first day, fire me.'

Now this was a hell of a gutsy challenge. Richard, who had made no heady mark on Hollywood thus far, was staking all.

Warner looked up and lit the unlitten. 'I think you're an asshole. No. I don't think . . . you are a pain in the proverbial, and you do a San Francisco on my stairs.' Here a heady breath. 'Fuck! Get yourself to wardrobe, go to make-up, and don't speak to me till I take my hands from my eyes at the preview.'

Thus Harris became Arthur.

I'm glad he did. I loved working with him – Richard's sheer unpredictability gave potential excitement to every day. And we became almost close; close enough that on one, very rare, occasion I was able to persuade him to change his mind, although Richard was never one to take other people's advice willingly.

We were going through a sticky patch in the making of *Camelot* and I'd come round to talk to him about it at his house in the Hollywood Hills. I found him outside; he'd clambered out of a window and shuffled along a very narrow balcony which overhung the swimming pool.

He stood up to his full height. 'I'm going to jump.'

'You can't do that. There's no water in the pool,' I blurted, though I guessed he knew that.

'I don't give a fock,' he growled. 'Go away from me!'

I got the impression he wasn't sober.

'Fockin' Warner Bothers,' he muttered. 'Fockin' Hollywood – the people here are all fockin' arseholes.'

I managed to clamber up on to the balcony myself and edged my way towards him. I was very nervous. I didn't like danger; I'd resisted all invitations to ride in Steve McQueen's Cooper S.

'Do you really want to do this?' I asked the muttering Harris.

He must have heard the note of desperation in my voice. 'No, I don't,' he leered. 'Let's have fockin' drink.'

I don't suppose he was serious about jumping, but this was Harris and I'd learned never to second-guess him. And, curiously, he never forgot that I'd talked him back.

It was soon after that that I introduced him to Jimmy Webb, a songwriter I'd met with the Bricusses. In fact, I think I suggested that Richard should sing 'MacArthur Park' – an insane combination and a most unexpected hit. Jimmy and I became great friends after that.

There was no question for me that making *Camelot* was a completely new experience. To start with, come Friday I would ride a studio bicycle with my name emblazoned along its side to a small kiosk adjoining the accountants' block. There I would be handed a wedge of dollar bills, for which I had to sign. I had promised myself that I would save these per diems so that I could go back to England with a suitcase full. This promise proved to be an empty one, like the suitcase.

After all, life was momentarily rich and there was so much to do and check out. I was busy with jazz clubs and deep-cellar, sleazy bars (always a favourite) containing elderly torch-song pianists who always had a giant brandy snifter on the piano where one could stuff a dollar or two; poker nights; Californian shirts with vast collars; cowboy boots and Levi's; restaurant after restaurant on La Cienega, or the Polo Lounge at the Beverly Hills Hotel, or, better yet, the bar at the Hotel Bel-Air, tucked away behind a slender bridge over a long lake, where swans greet you and where Harry Nilsson and I, perched on stools in our favourite corner, shared large brandies and talked of music.

In other words, I was busy with all the kit and shit that makes Los Angeles what it is. And now that I had settled a little after my early misgivings and mishaps, I was determined to enjoy every morsel of this unique city that nips from suburb to suburb in search of a centre.

As a new face in town, I was invited to a mad variety of things, from flower-power gatherings with the Mamas and the Papas to elegant dinner parties with Jack Warner, or casual, friendly get-togethers where, say, Danny Kaye cooked Chinese food for twenty (brilliantly, by the way).

On the set, though, the actual filming was gruelling. After his nervous start, Josh Logan had settled too, with loyal support from Richard Klein and the rest of the crew. But, as always, front office (i.e. Warner) wanted speed.

I appear only in fits and starts, and my one musical number, 'The Seven Deadly Sins', was cut at an early stage, so for me it wasn't so bad. For Richard and Vanessa and Franco Nero, however, it was painfully hard.

Richard was also in a continuous dialogue with Warner about the nature of the relationship between Lancelot and Guenevere. Richard believed that their relationship should not be consummated and that Arthur's intense grief and confusion was caused by jealousy and the possibility that it might be. Warner totally disagreed, and insisted that they did the business – several times, if he'd had his way.

Memos flew back and forth, and there was much yelling and recrimination until Warner and Harris could hardly face each other in the commissary. Many of us (including me, although I agreed with him) urged Richard to leave it alone. It would not be above Warner, I thought, to let Harris go, and he would probably have enjoyed it, given that he'd never wanted him in the first place. That being the case, it seemed a trifle stupid of Richard to complain so vociferously about whether or not Franco gets up Vanessa's underskirts in the gardens of Camelot.

As the early days went by, the feud continued, and had to be resolved.

Richard was sitting on the edge of the steps that led to his throne, thumbing a script, staring out at the Great Hall. The crew was gathered, ready for a final rehearsal, when suddenly the heavy tread of a front-office footfall echoed past the Round Table and confronted Richard.

'Warner's office, now!'

Everything happening on the set ground to a halt with furrowed brow and an unquiet silence.

Richard caught my eye, then flicked to the round bespectacled man, removed his crown and said quietly, 'We're in rehearsal.'

'Now!' spectacles repeated, thrusting a tense jaw at the king until their faces were inches apart, then took the crown from Richard's hand and strode off with it. He was wearing short sleeves and a tie. I rest my case.

Richard and I followed him to the main stage door and we sidled out into the blinding California sunlight. Short sleeves and specs was gone. Richard turned to me and shrugged.

'Ah, well, shit! It's my own f-fault,' he said dismally.

There really was no reply to that, and he strolled off with a backward wave towards what we all imagined was a red card. He looked so much like a cuckolded king, hunched and shuffling, a momentary lapse from his normal twinkling mode, that I thought, as did many others at different times: he *is* King Arthur, and there isn't a soul on the planet who could better him in the role.

Jack Warner met him at the steps from his office with thunder on his face, and, Richard observed, he had his lifts in, which was always a bad sign. Warner grabbed him by the arm and marched him to the studio gate, where guards grovelled appropriately. They walked outside, across Encino Street, and stood together on the sidewalk in front of the Mexican restaurant opposite the gate. Warner pulled Richard's arm.

'Look up,' he said, 'and tell me what that sign says.'

'Warner Brothers,' said Richard with a shrug.

'Right, right,' said Warner slowly, with emphasis. 'And when it says "Harris Brothers", they needn't fuck. Until then, they fuck!'

He dumped the crown in Richard's hand and crossed the street, leaving Richard amazed, but smiling.

When he got back to the stage, or rather to our caravans alongside it, he whispered, 'The king is dead! Long live the king!' and we cracked open a couple of Budweisers from our illicit store.

'The bloody little leprechaun beat me,' he grinned. The twinkle, and Arthur, were back.

Blow-Up

*

It hadn't taken me long to recognise that whatever doubts I might have had about *Blow-Up*, even after its glorious reception at the Directors' Guild of America, it had suddenly, literally overnight, turned me into a star. There are those who say you can judge your current status in the stellar stratosphere in Los Angeles simply by logging the number of phone calls that come in each day – even each hour. The phone in my room at the Chateau Marmont increased its ring rate from half a dozen a day to getting on for twenty an hour. My market value, much ramped by Abe Lastfogel's team, had abruptly catapulted to heights un-dreamed off a less than a month before back in England. For years I'd been impressed by people moaning about the tax they'd paid and how they planned to avoid it in future, but up until now I'd had little cause to trouble the taxman; indeed, my principal objective had always been to make the kind of money that would have interested him.

Thinking how cleverly pre-emptive I was being, I decided I needed some sound fiscal advice, and in my view the smartest financial man with whom I had any empathy was John Daly.

Before I'd left England, I'd talked to Jane long and hard about her coming over to join me at some point. Of course, there was a large part of me that wanted her to, and that was why I'd made sure that MGM supplied a ticket – in those days in real terms about ten times more expensive than now. But because I also felt that it wouldn't necessarily be the greatest thing to be tied to anyone while I was in LA, when I rang her tentatively to discover if she was still thinking of coming, I was quite relieved when she said she just couldn't face the flight. Her panic attacks were as strong as ever, she said, and besides, she had several roles in hand and there was talk of a part in *The Lion in Winter*, alongside Peter O'Toole and Katharine Hepburn. I didn't blame her for wanting to hang around and see what happened. At the same time, if I'm honest, I think she'd made up her mind that our relationship was over, and when I told her I was hoping John Daly might be able to come out and see me, she volunteered her ticket without any prompting from me.

John didn't want to give up his day job but I persuaded him it was important and would be worth his while. Within a week or two, he'd arrived to join me at the Chateau Marmont. It was his first visit to the States, but, like a typical self-reliant south Londoner, he refused to acknowledge any sense of awe. The first evening he was there, I'd been invited (and told I could bring John with me) to Jack Warner's place as a B-list guest, which meant we didn't qualify for dinner, but only drinks after the A-list had finished theirs.

I walked in with John and he immediately recognised Mel Ferrer. He'd never met Mel, of course, Mel not being a habitué of Toby's gym in Bermondsey, but that didn't preclude an effusive greeting. Unfortunately, however, while swinging up a hand to say a glad hello, he swiped a bulky crystal glass vase from its tiny podium. It fell to the marble floor beneath Jack Warner's table, at which about twenty people still sat, and shattered noisily into several thousand tiny pieces.

With well-honed, lightning reactions, John threw his hands up in a gesture of pure innocence. 'Mel! How could you have done a thing like that to Jack Warner's beautiful vase?'

Mel was caught off guard, and was shrugging his shoulders in bemusement while John pressed home his attack and turned to Jack Warner. 'Good God, Jack,' he said, 'is this how your guests normally behave?'

Thus, with a splendid display of true cockney gall, he managed to pass the whole thing off as Mel's fault – which tells you a lot about John Daly. He is undoubtedly one of the world's great wrigglers, which can be as useful in Los Angeles as it is in Peckham. Frankly, though, I'm in no position to criticise, because I was the same. We were both to some extent wide boys in the old sense, which I don't necessarily consider a derogatory term. Throughout my life I've always had more fun from the wide boys than those officially employed to entertain us. In any event, it didn't take John long to settle in and find his level, and he's lived in and out of California ever since.

By this time I'd made friends not only with every maid and Latino gardener at the Marmont but also with the management. I had cajoled them into letting me into a huge three-bedroomed suite which I shared with John, and which soon became the scene of much partying and bad behaviour. Sharon Tate was still there, although with Roman Polanski hanging around, and Ted Hartley, and there seemed to be an endless stream of visitors. John loved it from the start and was as happy as a pig in a wallow. The hotel didn't seem to mind what we did. Once, for instance, I asked if I could take over the switchboard for a while, and had a blissful couple of hours telling puzzled Hollywood agents and gossip writers that they'd got through to Scotland Yard or the back gate at Buckingham Palace. If I'd stopped to think, I might have found it odd that the worse we were, the more the hotel indulged us.

And in Hollywood generally I found very few people trying to tell me what or, more importantly, what not to do. You'd have thought, for instance, that anyone would have tried to talk me out of putting on an evening's celebration of the poet-boozer Dylan Thomas at a Beverly Hills nightclub; but they didn't. I've no idea how I persuaded Jack Hanson to let me take over his place, the Daisy, to stage my medley of Thomasania, largely based, frankly, on Andrew Sinclair's *Adventures in the Skin Trade*, but he did. Once I was committed, though, I went for it – we had harp music and scenery to provide a suitably Welsh backdrop (though not, as someone suggested, a reconstruction of the Aberfan tip) and, to my amazement, a large Hollywood crowd turned up. I could hardly believe some of the faces I saw in the crowd, even, in a dark corner amid a pall of smoke, a droopy-eyed R. Mitchum. At the end of the show the audience was so bewildered it couldn't stop applauding, which was strange but very gratifying.

I loved the Daisy and was there pretty much every night when there was nothing else going on. I did another little show with Jane Asher, and Jack let me DJ there occasionally too. Happily I'd learned a few new techniques since my first attempts at this profession. As was my habit, I liked to get involved in everything that was going and Stuart Whitman knocked me out one night because he felt I was being loud and getting a little too close to a woman he thought he was closer to.

Perhaps an even more extraordinary indulgence I was granted was being allowed to record a dozen tracks for a projected album. I first had to suffer a little humiliation to achieve this. Having talked our unfortunate record producer into taking me on, he asked me along to the studios for an audition to make sure I really could sing. John came too – for immoral support.

I can't imagine that it was a very impressive performance. The angel purity of my childhood voice had long since been scarred by singing in *Bierkellers*, as well as by tobacco and whisky. We had also been carousing particularly hard the night before and I was relying heavily on cigarettes to keep me standing. I coughed and croaked my way through a couple of songs, told the producer about various other ideas I had for the album and, more importantly, told him that before I started recording I wanted an advance against royalties of $10,000, in readies.

I held my breath. Frankly, it was a bit of a bluff. I would probably have taken a postdated cheque for two grand, if it came to that. The trouble was, although I'd finished shooting *Camelot* by then, all my per diems seemed to have evaporated and I still didn't have any money. But I really did not want to arrive back in England boracic lint as usual – not now, after all the excitement and hype over *Blow-Up*, which had just won the Palme d'Or at Cannes, while my face was plastered across the side of every double-decker bus in London.

Above all, I wanted something to show my father.

Thank God, the record company bought my bluff. They gave me the ten grand and over the next few weeks I popped into the studios now and again and laid down some tracks, some of them perfunctorily written by me in the car on the way to the sessions; none of them remotely memorable. The resulting album was entitled, regrettably in my view, *David Hemmings Happens*, which turned out to be a complete misnomer, both musically and commercially. It has been variously described as 'GBH of the eardrums' and 'music to have surgery by'. But I had my package of $10,000 (worth about £200,000 in spending terms today), which worked like a charm, just to look at, whenever I was feeling low.

I had been seeing an increasing amount of Gayle and we were by then what American tabloids like to call, with quaint euphemism, 'romantically attached'. I badgered her into letting me half move in to her house at 819 North Beverly Glen Boulevard, where we ceremoniously slung out the cardboard benches and tables which Mel Ferrer had been kind enough to buy for her as a moving-in present. Gayle and I went out and bought a tilting bed, new sofas and chairs and wardrobes, and Gayle had the place decorated with the money she'd earned from *PJ*.

I loved those few months in North Beverly Glen, going back there several times over the next year or so. In the little supermarket down the hill I'd bump into Tom Selleck, though I didn't really get to know him until years later, when I directed him in dozens of episodes of *Magnum, P.I.* In 1967 he was still making commercials.

We were having an extraordinary social life then too. It seemed to me an awful long way from Toby's gym and Elmhurst Court, Croydon. Steve McQueen, as big a star as there was in the world at the time, and his wife, Neile, became great friends. On a Sunday, instead of drinking beer and playing darts at the White Bear in Sanderstead, I'd be drinking cocktails and talking music in the bar at the Bel-Air.

We would invite people to dinner and they'd bring with them, unannounced, some amazingly famous faces – Paul Newman, perhaps, or Bob Mitchum – which took some getting used to. It was bizarre but, looking back, I can only guess that these people enjoyed the 'loony Limey' and the Texan Belle, both in their mid-twenties, both brimming with youthful optimism.

10

Charge!, 1967

I'd been in Los Angeles less than six months when I came back to England after making *Camelot*, but I already knew they'd been absolutely the most significant months of my life. I was still just 25, but where I'd left England an ingenuous and comparative unknown, I arrived back wiser, a little more cynical and a public figure. My mugshot was on posters all over London, *Blow-Up* was a hit, albeit of the cult variety, and suddenly an awful lot more people were asking me to dinner.

One of the first things I did was head for Croydon. Most of my meagre collection of possessions was still at Elmhurst Court and, of course, I wanted to see Jane again. It was sort of soothing to be with her after the frenetic activity of the past few months, but I realised it was going to take a little time to wind down from the excesses of Los Angeles. And I really didn't feel I wanted to live in Croydon any more, so I rented half a house in Brompton Square as a base while I started work on my next movie, *The Charge of the Light Brigade*, which was scheduled to begin shooting mid-April.

Jane seemed ambivalent about my being back. She had been subjected to some press speculation over our relationship and had stalwartly told them that, although she hadn't been able to get over to LA, she was still expecting us to get married. Now, she was pleased to see me and thrilled that *Blow-Up* had been so well received, but she felt that I'd moved on and what we'd had didn't seem relevant any more. She knew I'd had the odd affair in the months before going to the States, and of course the whole Linda Estall Cole episode had come and gone while I'd been making *Blow-Up*. I'd already explained that Linda had just been a way of working off some of my childhood fantasies and my resentment at having been so shunned as a kid at the Hook Heath Tennis Club. Not much of an excuse, but it was largely true. I managed to persuade Jane to spend some time with me, although I could see she wasn't convinced. Then, with my usual perversity, I asked her if she would help sort out the pile of press cuttings I'd brought back from the States.

'You'll see an awful lot about this person Gayle Hunnicutt,' I told her airily, 'but don't take any notice. It was just a put-up job by our agents at William Morris, you know, for publicity and all that.'

I left her with a stack of assorted newsprint and went off for a costume fitting for *Charge*, but a couple of hours later she rang me.

'This is ridiculous, David. Half the Hollywood press have got you married off to her already. You'll have to move on. It's obviously over between us.'

I think it was a hard decision for her, because we still got on very well in many ways and we'd shared a lot together over the past three and a half years. However, although she was probably right, I couldn't bring myself to go and take all my stuff from Elmhurst Court. I went back a couple of times and hung around there, trying to remember how life had been when we'd first moved there – it seemed like a century ago. Quite soon, though, Jane took the initiative, packed up all her stuff and moved out. And that was that. Our lives moved on in different directions, although I did see her from time to time, and I was bowled over by her in *The Lion in Winter* when it came out the following year.

With no Jane, and Gayle back in the States, and the after-affects of *Blow-Up* reverberating through London, I found no shortage of entertainment or people to play with. When I told one of them, Soraya Khashoggi, how much I'd loved bombing around in the drop-head Silver Cloud in *Blow-Up*, she lent me hers and murmured something about giving it to me. I was very tempted but, on the other hand, it might not have taken much for Soraya's husband, the formidably opulent Adnan, to misconstrue the gesture and, perhaps, have something unpleasant, and possibly painful, done to me, so I declined.

But this short, heady period came to an end when my professional life was taken over by Tony Richardson and *The Charge of the Light Brigade*.

When I first went to discuss the film with Tony, who was to direct, and Neil Hartley of Woodfall Films in Mayfair, I was thrilled to be offered the role of Captain Nolan. Everything about the film gave it the air of a

British classic – the subject matter, though viewed from a deeply unglorious perspective; the principal cast: John Gielgud, Trevor Howard, Harry Andrews and Jill Bennett – a roll-call of dramatic excellence; and, above all, the script.

My part as the renegade young captain was one that I loved and soon learned backwards. The screenplay was beautifully, sparely written by Charles Wood, and I read it with glee. It contained, in my view, some of the finest lines in cinema, dialogue that captures the period and attitudes to war with subtlety, grace and style.

Wood had shown us a whole new approach to dialogue in *The Knack* and for *Charge* he wrote in a mystical way, with short sharp sentences and what I call 'fly-away buttons'.

'He would do that. Would.'

Or, from Trevor Howard, 'I saw you, sir. Saw you. Black bottle. Drinking beer, sir. In this mess. Saw you.'

Lines like these look odd on the page and are tricky to deliver – they can come out like gunfire or stumbles – but in the hands of Gielgud or Howard they were like droplets of pure colour on a backdrop of Victoriana. Charles Wood, along with Robert Bolt, will always get my vote for the finest screen writers we have produced.

In Bolt's *A Man for All Seasons*, for example, Paul Schofield, as Thomas More, turns to Essex, played by John Hurt, who has just betrayed him for the Stewardship of the Welsh. As Essex stops by More, with the whole gathering in the Hall of Justice looking on, More knows that this is his end. There is no help for him.

Robert Bolt gives Schofield a priceless moment.

From a crumpled, seated posture More looks up questioningly at Essex and says, 'A man might sell his soul for the *whole* world, Essex, yes.' He pauses briefly, then with gentle incredulity. 'But for *Wales*?'

A wonderfully understated piece of writing, the put-down acts like a knife through Essex's heart.

Similarly, in Charles Wood's screenplay for *Charge*, while I'm riding off, as Nolan, to take the infamously misunderstood order to Cardigan and Raglan, the order that will cause the massacre of the Six Hundred (or most of them), Gielgud watches me career down the cliff slope at breakneck speed but with vicious skill.

He turns to Airey and observes, 'I don't like that man, Airey. He rides too well. He knows too much.' He pauses and, with a perfect Gielgud long-suffering, wistful elegance, goes on, 'It will be a sad thing, Airey, when war is waged by people who know too well what they are doing. It smacks of murder.'

On the first day of costume fitting and preparation in England, I'd been picked up from Brompton Square in a spotless Humber Hawk by a chauffeur wearing a cap and cockade who'd been booked by Woodfall Films. He was about my age, a little taller, with sandy/orange hair and Michael Caine glasses.

'Morning, sir,' he grinned with an engaging lift of one eyebrow at the woman – a not entirely unknown young actress – who had exited the house with me.

'Morning. I'm David Hemmings. Who are you?'

'Danny, sir. Danny Wiles.'

From that very first day, driving to the studios, Danny and I found we understood each other's sense of humour very well and after that I made sure he carried on driving me for the rest of the production in England. We became very good friends, and have been ever since.

One reason could have been that Danny had the uncanny ability always to seem as if he were up for anything, without ever completely going over the top. He was what you might call a very useful safety valve for me in many of the more volatile situations we found ourselves in over the next few years. He was a bright London lad, born in the midst of Soho, where his mother and father had three tobacconist's shops, one on Carnaby Street, since long before Lord Kitchener's Valet moved in, and two on Beak Street, where he lived, and still does, in a flat over one of the shops.

The cast and crew of *The Charge of the Light Brigade* all met together for the first time at Heathrow before boarding a plane to Ankara. It felt like the start of a great adventure with a gang of chums and I found myself looking forward to what was going to be a long shoot, with several months of it on the Anatolian plain of central Turkey.

I knew a lot of the crew and among the cast was my good friend Peter Bowles, who'd played my agent in *Blow-Up* and with whom I'd spent many an hour while Antonioni had buggered about with lights and sheets of smoked glass. Vanessa Redgrave was also in the film, the third in a row that I had made with her. I was delighted. We'd been through a lot together on *Blow-Up* and *Camelot*, and although she was now deeply involved with Franco Zero, including carrying his baby (although she may not have known it at that stage) I still loved her like a sister. With us too was the elegant Mark Burns. He'd been in *The System* with me, but it was on the plane that day that we first really began to know one another.

Mark was ecstatic about being cast in *Charge*. After leaving the tutelage of the monks at Ampleforth he had become a cavalry officer and he'd read Cecil Woodham-Smith's *The Reason Why* regularly since he was fourteen. Tall, blond and handsome, he looked the very picture of an honourable, vulnerable Englishman. He was also a fine and knowledgeable horseman. He could have been made for the part of Captain William Morris, a handsome and innocently heroic young man. Over the six months we worked together, we became very good friends.

Turkey is not a place that most of us involved in the production of *Charge* will happily revisit, although we actors in many ways had a wonderful time and fared a lot better than the poor armies involved. The choice of Anatolia as the location was more than purely geophysical. For one thing, the Turkish Army maintained one of the few household cavalries still in existence, the Presidential Guard, which was bound to be helpful in duplicating the famous Six Hundred and the Charge itself. The Turkish government had offered Woodfall/UA the services of its local army to act as Russians; they were also providing horses and equipment, and generally overseeing the smooth and efficient control of its personnel.

The cast and company had been housed in Ankara's finest accommodation, the Buyuk Ankara Oteli. On our arrival at the Buyuk, we were summoned to view a march-past by what would become 'our' light cavalry, historically a combination of the 11th Hussars and the 17th Lancers.

Dutifully we lined up on the balcony of the presidential suite. Ataturk Boulevard stretched out below us, the Ataturk Palace at one end and the Ataturk slums at the other. Everything in Turkey, particularly in Ankara, is named 'Ataturk'. This is not, you can imagine, the Champs Elysées, even on a bad day. Howard, Gielgud, Andrews, Richardson all immediately adopted marching-past roles with the greatest of reverence as they saw the formation of troops and cavalry coming towards us.

As they drew closer it was clear that the forward rider had been on a horse perhaps once or twice before, where the rest obviously had not. Stirrups were lost, the cavalrymen were slipping from side to side, most grasping their pommels with white knuckles. We hadn't until now imagined our lancers or hussars to be swarthy, and we'd expected them to possess some inkling of horsemanship. As they passed beneath the balcony, a barked command, 'Eyes left!' echoed across the avenue. There was some confusion initially over which direction this meant. But as we waved enthusiastically at them all, they waved back, which did nothing to help their already precarious balance. Those that fell off struggled manfully to remount without breaking stride – struggled, but without success. After a few tries they opted to walk with nervous dignity alongside their mounts.

This introduction to filming in Turkey would go down in all our private histories and even spawned a play (by Charles Wood) on its making. After the march-past Richardson decided to give the entire company a pre-film pep talk, delivered from a small stage at one end of the bar.

Film units fresh from a long flight are not receptive to seriousness, and anyway the march-past had banished any thought of solemnity. Tony stood up. He was a long, gaunt, beanpole of a man, with a reedy voice and a gentle lisp. When he laughed, his entire head would tilt back from the upper jaw, leaving the lower to display a magnificent set of teeth. Now his hands flailed characteristically, while beside him, backing him up, were the lean Neil Hartley, producer, and other executives. We were all seated around the dance floor. The spotlight was on our director. He had a glass of champagne in his hand. We were all drunk.

Before Tony could speak Tom Buchanan, the flushed, rotund boom operator and a divine humorist, rushed to the centre of the dance floor.

'All those who can't tap-dance are queer!' he yelled, and proceeded to clatter out an appalling version of the first-time step.

All over the room feet were banging the floor. Tony's remained still, and so did Neil's. This appeared not to be a great way to ingratiate oneself with a new director.

Gielgud was more philanthropic. He leaned across to Trevor Howard, long since oblivious to the proceedings, and spoke quietly. 'Personally, I never travel with my tap shoes.'

With more hand action, Tony took control, as directors should. 'Thank you for the demonstration, Mr Buchanan. We are all now clearly aware that you cannot tap-dance.' He grinned widely and the top of his head fell backwards.

*

Not only was *Charge*, in my view, a very superior picture in many ways, it was also an astonishingly eventful film on which to work. Sixty miles from Ankara in Anatolia, the action was intense and always unpredictable – inevitably, I suppose, when a cast of thousands of men, women and horses is involved, but as in all film-making, there were lulls . . .

📷 📷 📷 📷

Lunch is late. We are into meal penalty: it's fifteen minutes past the agreed official union time. Producing meals on location in Turkey on any day is a complicated business; the catering set-up, like hairdressing, make-up and wardrobe, is housed in one of several cavernous zinc huts that have been built for the company five long, hot, sweaty miles down the valley in the dusty plain. Here, in what is known with some irony as Base Camp, also live the armies – hundreds of extras, uniformed as soldiers, eating, sleeping and looking very bored.

Today, perversely, shooting has been plagued by a lurking, plum-black thundercloud, the bogeyman of all cinematographers, who prefer high light, consistent clouds that remove contrast and make it easier to enhance faces with discreet, judicious lighting.

Now the first hint of rain is misting the camera lens and coating the horses with a slight sheen, like sweat, though not John Gielgud's mount, which happens to be made of wood, complete with saddle and tack. More reliable than the real thing for a close shot, it stands on a platform which allows Sir John to be mounted without actually having to ride. Behind him wait the Six Hundred, fidgeting with a jangle of bits and bridles.

This morning has been a purgatory of inaction. 'Hurry up and wait!' is the standard cry on a film set on a day like today, just as it might have been in the prelude to battle.

Our grandly styled director of photography, David Watkin, rarely moves from his chair and waves at his gaffer spark with an imperial air. He won't shoot if he doesn't consider conditions perfect. He has spent most of the morning glumly gazing through his pan glass at the louring sky.

Tony Richardson, director, is distressed, flapping his arms and shaking them from his shoulders in irritation. He does the same whether he's happy, laughing or angry. They dangle and flail around, with hands that look longer than his forearms twitching with nervous energy, like Leonard Bernstein exhausted suddenly in the middle of the

'1812' but still making an effort to conduct from his hips. This quirk of Tony Richardson's is well known.

His artistic flair is without question, but he can be sarcastic, with a brittle, wounding wit. He'll have his way, come what may, and suffers fools not at all.

I've observed that most directors have idiosyncrasies of some kind. J. Lee Thompson tears strips from the call sheet, then twirls them ceaselessly; others scratch or fiddle with viewfinders, or dangle their watches low on their wrists. Claude Chabrol cannot discuss a scene without an unfiltered soggy-ended Gauloise drooping from his lips. Some, like Michael Winner, insist on using a loudhailer when they are eight inches from your head. Antonioni, of course, had his tic. Worse, the rotund and otherwise delightful Richard Zarafian had a disquieting habit of farting immediately after he said, 'Action!' as if he'd used every muscle in his body to ejaculate the word.

Richardson is currently in angry mode. He's arguing with Watkin.

'I must shoot,' he entreats. 'We're way behind schedule and damn the weather.'

'You can't.'

'Don't tell me I can't. I will! I must shoot!' The arms flap.

'It won't come out.' Watkin is unmoved, staring up at the sky.

'It'll be perfect.'

'It won't match. It's dreadful. And it's going to rain.'

'I like the rain. I *want* rain! We have to shoot!'

'Let's break. Isn't it lunch?'

'Of course it's fucking lunch! That's why we have to shoot. I'm going to shoot it.'

'Go ahead, then. But you won't use it.'

'I've got Gielgud on the horse. I've got to shoot!'

As he stomps off across the muddy desert floor, there is a slice of lightning, a clap of thunder and the clouds release their load.

Richardson stops in his tracks and stares heavenward. 'Shit!' he bellows at the sky. 'Shit! Shit! Shit!'

'Lunch!' yells the AD.

Suddenly everyone is dashing through the rain, covering cameras, leaping into trucks, skidding off down the valley with their thoughts focused on food.

The rain, at first a drizzle, becomes a downpour while Gielgud, always the professional, waits patiently on his wooden horse, huddled in a blanket and weatherproof, under a brolly reading a book through half-glasses, quite content.

When he hears, 'Lunch', he expects to be removed from the artificial horse and escorted elegantly to the catering tent. This does not happen. Soldiers tramp by and assistant directors, anxious to rally the crowd for their meal, seem to ignore him.

Gielgud looks over his glasses at them, but they are gone as fast as they pass. He gazes around, resigned. This awful desert, soaking up the rain, stretches before him, miraculously emptied of actors, extras, crew, soldiers, publicity mavens and all other living creatures. Water dribbles from his hat.

Mini-Mokes and Land Rovers hurtle past, carting everyone to cover. Still Gielgud waits. The horse is too high for him to dismount without help, and there is no help. He settles back to his book, like a gentleman in his club, quite content.

An assistant director, late and hungry, hurries past in an open jeep. 'It's lunch, John!'

'Yes, dear boy. Could you . . .?'

But the vehicle races on in a spray of mud.

This is an extraordinary scene – an actor of such renown, left dripping, soaking, momentarily friendless for the sake of a lunch box. For those who believe the life of the film star leads only to glory, take note of Sir John's predicament in the Turkish desert.

All this I watch from the redoubts, the Russian gun positions high above our Valley of Death. John is half a mile away, surrounded by light and reflector stands, a camera, covered in plastic to protect it from the rain, still points at him. But now, besides him, there is not a soul in sight.

[◌] [◌] [◌] [◌]

It's impossible to be with a group of wits the calibre of John Gielgud for as long as we all were privileged to be without harbouring tremendous envy. Most of the young and certainly less experienced members of the troupe listened raptly. Early on, before shooting proper had started, I was sitting in the bar of the Buyuk having a drink with Mark and Gayle, who'd come with me to Ankara for the first few weeks, when Gielgud glided by. We asked him to join us, which he did with apparent pleasure. A moment later, his fellow star, the gruff, square-jawed Harry Andrews, marched across the far side of the room.

John regarded him with one of his long, ambivalent looks, and as Harry exited the room, he leaned forward very slightly. 'You'd never believe,' he murmured, 'that beneath that rough, tough exterior beats the heart of a little old woman.'

Throughout filming, in the bar, on the set, between takes, over dinner, there was seldom a moment when one or other of us wasn't repeating some new Gielgud quip.

Jill Bennett, for instance, was rumoured to be having a 'relationship' with Tony Richardson. A certain amount of 'corridor creeping' is the norm for a film unit on location and let no wife left at home believe otherwise. Much of it is only rumoured, but sometimes it really does happen. Tony's moments with Jill were never to draw light but the word persisted nevertheless. Gielgud relished this and was quick to mention it whenever Richardson's name came up in conversation.

During the shooting day, since we were so far from usual facilities, we were allocated tents which were also part of the set. Jill Bennett had one which happened to be close to the area that housed a dancing bear that figured in several sequences. A most benign and charming creature, it had become a kind of mascot to the unit and was allowed pretty much free access.

Jill was changing, getting ready for a new scene, when the bear pulled loose from its stake and stumbled into her tent, collapsing the guy-ropes and generally causing havoc. She screamed in fear and anger and, half dressed, stumbled from the crumpled canvas on all fours, followed, naturally, by the affectionate bear.

Gielgud looked at the scene as we all rocked with laughter. 'Oh, Mr Richardson!' he cried. 'How could you? And in your motor coat too!'

Charge had additional attractions. The impossible armies were not wise to the ways of film-making and didn't understand much of what was required of them. They had, of course, to be provided with costumes and appropriate weaponry. Those who had to make the trek up from Base Camp every morning were inevitably bored and truculent. First the Turkish infantry, playing the Russians, were decked in grey greatcoats provided at enormous expense by wardrobe. Our technical supervisor, John Mollo, whose meticulous eye for detail, from boots to buttons to bridles, was legendary, was alas also responsible for historical accuracy. Turkish soldiers are apparently not known for loyalty to their superiors and clearly John Mollo did not rank at all.

During the hike to the location, Russian greatcoats being long, cumbersome and very hot, the Turkish/Russians, using the field knives supplied, cut what they considered to be oversized coats back to a more comfortable length – about an inch below the knee. It only took one man to start the process and the rest followed, joyfully hacking and pruning their overbearing garments, rendering them historically inaccurate and visually worse than imperfect.

At the same time a new game was invented. It seemed the Turks were eager to test the guns provided. Blanks and wadding, while not deadly, certainly made a fair old 'bang' and could, if one was so minded, create considerable destruction to the papier-mâché hats that had been provided by John Mollo and his team. The sport was thus:

Take papier-mâché helmet.
Place on top of gun.
Fire gun.
Papier-mâché helmet top blows off and is destroyed.
Lots of litter in desert.
Lots of high Turkish laughter.
No hats on cavalry or lancers.

John Mollo and his team tried to dig themselves into a small grave at the end of the valley. Meanwhile, Richardson called over the most senior of the Turkish Brigade, now without hats but with smoking rifles, and the Russian contingent, with coats with extraordinarily ragged edges dangling around or just above their knees.

The valley too was draped, at this point, with remnants of grey cloth. And I don't mean just the odd spot but a long trail of old scrabbled coat-tails transformed the valley into patches that looked like grey droppings, as if an army of super-rats had come to conquer, then been caught short.

The sight left John Mollo weeping.

The stuntman charged with creating a convincing portrayal of people falling off horses, dying, being shot or shooting others was

Bob Simmons. He had also been responsible for a number of Bond movies and was a much-touted stunt coordinator class act.

I am naturally suspicious of stuntmen who look as stuntmen should. Bob Simmons wore black – black Stetson, black boots, black shirt, black jeans and, as I recall, a low-slung black gunbelt. In my view, this clearly branded him a 'baddie' and, in spite of his reputation, he looked ridiculous. Heavy sweat and black have an affinity it would be wise to avoid. But make no mistake, I'm referring here to a major talent – someone revered in the film industry as a 'top man'; a man who talks as if 007 is in his pocket and couldn't take a step without him. I discovered, far less illustrious than Sean though I might have been, that I could manage the odd step on my own, to the extent that I decided very early on I wanted to ride myself in every scene in which my character was mounted. Everyone except Tony tried to talk me out of doing the famous gallop down the gully – we had on the unit, after all, a brilliant horse double in Dicky Graydon – but although he would undoubtedly have taken it a little faster, I have never regretted my decision (or the fact that I didn't fall off in that particular scene).

Mark and I had been summoned to the Anatolian plain location after the infamous opening march-past to review our horses. Most of the animals on offer, the property of the Turkish Cavalry, were fairly ordinary-looking individuals, a lot of them apparently of American origin. I was allocated a pretty, grey but distinctly Arab horse, called Urma (whose double in the English shots had a very different-shaped nose, to those who notice such things). I tried mine and was happy with it.

Mark on the other hand, being a kosher ex-cavalryman, was more picky. He rejected everything until finally a magnificent, if historically inaccurate, bay English thoroughbred came striding over the ridge beneath one of the stunt riders, who protested that it was for his use.

Mark stood his ground. It was the bay or nothing, he said. It turned out that it was the commanding officer's horse, but Mark got it, and he and I spent many happy hours roaming across the plain on the two best horses on the set.

While we were there, Bob Simmons was in full command of the Turkish Cavalry, doing reverse cross-rides, which required sixty horses on one side to rush at full gallop towards sixty horses on the other, each line crossing with a foot or so to spare. Elegant stuff, if correctly executed. However, riding skills were at a minimum among the seventeen-year-old conscripts.

The practice of getting a horse to fall in an appropriate spot, perfectly gauged for the camera lens, is also a tricky business.

In the old days, several countries, Spain *per ejemplo*, favoured the 'Running W'. It may interest you to know how this charming trick was done, next time you happen to catch an old western.

Stick a handcuff round the horse's foreleg and put a wire on it (that's what the W stands for). Position two stakes about five hundred yards apart and run the wire from the horse's foreleg to an eye-ring that runs around the wire. Dig a deep hole to take a stake with a hook at its top that will jerk the horse's leg out from under him at any point you like, preferably at full gallop. This is ideal for the camera as the horse collapses into the dust and its rider affects a suitable fall, while the horse's leg is pulled unmercifully backwards, breaking it 50 per cent of the time.

Great shot! Looks wonderful! Dramatic! Add a cry or a snort or a whinny from the horse and the sequence is there. Good work done by all.

What is not on film after the shot has been completed is the horse being dragged ignominiously off the field of vision with his or her limp, fractured leg trailing lamely behind and the shot through the eye that puts the horse out of its misery.

In those days, Turkey, like Spain, accepted the use of 'Running Ws'. The acting body of the film, however, did not. Always a champion of causes, Vanessa Redgrave led us all into strike mode until the practice was forbidden during the film.

I agreed with her and admired her for making a stand, though I didn't always agree with Ms Redgrave's position on some other issues, much though I cared for her style. I couldn't reconcile decorating one's Hammersmith house to resemble Leningrad railway station, complete and replete with brochures and propaganda on a rack for handy dispensing, while at the same time harbouring Dom Perignon in the fridge upstairs.

While I fell off my grey innumerable times practising for shots, I managed to do it without injuring myself. Mark Burns, altogether a superior rider, fell off only once and promptly broke his wrist. This meant a quick trip back to Blighty for him. His return a week later, much welcomed by me, was made more memorable by his description of the changes that had taken place in London in the few short months we'd been away.

All the girls, he said, drooling a little, were wearing tiny miniskirts and skimpy T-shirts, cannabis was everywhere, and here was the Beatles new album, *Sgt Pepper's Lonely Hearts Club Band*.

A group of us gathered around a record player in his room in the Buyuk and listened with amazement to this ground-breaking collection of tracks. At first, stuck out here in a Victorian time warp, we just didn't get it, but by the time we left I'd heard it so many times, I loved it and I realised what a milestone album it was – which, almost forty years later, I still believe.

Mark also brought back a pleasingly bizarre single, 'A Whiter Shade of Pale', by Procol Harum. Our Turkish driver had a trixy little record player in his car that could handle 45s, up to a point, and we played it continuously driving out to the set. By the end of the first trip, I knew the tune and every word of it (although I still don't know what they mean).

There are those who nominate 1968 as *the* defining watershed year in the cultural history of the 20th century. But for me 1967 was the year when people knew that things had changed, and changed for ever. I might have said earlier in these ramblings that I was never truly conscious of 'the sixties' happening, but if they did at all for me, it was unquestionably in 1967 more than at any other time.

Meanwhile, back in Turkey, working with Gielgud on *Charge* continued to be a special experience. The stories told about him were legion. Although some may have been apocryphal, I found him immensely witty, deeply talented, of course, but imbued with a natural sense of humour that constantly made one smile in his company. Only two others I've known in my career had that particular quality – David Niven and Donald Pleasence. Niven's humour was divine, Pleasence's wicked, like that of a demented elf. Gielgud's humour captured both. He could be wicked about others, or, if not wicked, certainly irreverent, while being at the same time engagingly self-effacing.

He used to amaze his acting contemporaries at Stratford by doing the *Times* crossword in record time. He would finish it by folding up the paper with a drawn-out sigh of satisfaction and the long-suffering look of one who has been presented with a task too infra dig to be contemplated, while the rest of the company struggled on, enmeshed in the riddles for hours.

On one occasion, it was about two in the afternoon and a single clue was eluding everyone. Finally, having admitted defeat at the hands of the cryptographer, they snuck to Gielgud's bag and pulled out the paper to find the answer to the impossible 15 Across.

Gielgud's answer was GLISTHFANE, fitting perfectly with the answer to 11 Down, which, in Gielgud's version, was HARGRIPE, the clue for which was 'Pugilist's container (5, 3)'. The correct answer, of course, was MATCH BOX – a long way from HARGRIPE or, one supposes, HARGR IPE. On further review, the entire crossword was filled with odd, often non-existent words placed at random with no relation whatever to the clues posed.

The rest of the company decided to lay a trap. The following day, they asked John what the answer to 7 Across was. 'We're stuck here, John. What's "Around an Oak" . . . five letters?'

'Easy,' said John. 'Why don't you think? It's SPADE.'

'Doesn't fit with 3 Down,' said the company to a man, smiles on their lips.

'Of course it does,' Gielgud huffed, 'as long as you've got SWADENPLORT!'

He knew they knew of course, but it didn't faze him for one moment. He would simply thereafter finish the crossword and openly leave it in plain view for those who cared to look.

Tony Richardson's physician was Patrick Woodcock, a charming and erudite fellow who came out to visit us in Ankara while *Charge* was being made. And, since the Buyuk Ankara Oteli was the only game in town, it was also the tourist centre. Why anyone would want to tour Ankara is beyond comprehension, at least mine, but tourists there were.

While talking with Gielgud in the bar one afternoon, Patrick Woodcock, who spoke very elegant English, was confronted by a woman from Oregon, USA, wearing what looked like a dead grizzly on her back. She'd been listening to their conversation for some time, it appeared, with clearly no idea who John was. She sidled up to the bar and touched Woodcock gently on the arm.

'Please excuse me,' she said, presenting a broad furry back to Gielgud, 'but I've been listening to you in raptures. You have the finest English speaking voice I've ever heard. I just had to tell you that.'

Woodcock flushed. Gielgud remained stoic. She slipped silently away.

After a long pause, Gielgud put hands to glass in a ponderous way. Then, with his customary sonority and the weight of English sarcasm on each of the two syllables, he spoke: 'Charming.'

The Grizzly Oregona was to be outdone, however, by an American tourist from Iowa. Having 'done' Ankara in his first eight minutes there, and suffering the remainder of a two-week stint, he had discovered *Charge* and came out to visit the filming almost daily. He was very short, very bald – in the style of 'let's take this one hair I have left and spread it over the top'. He didn't bother anyone, didn't impose, merely hung back behind the lights and observed. He took a few photographs, but otherwise, after a while, became a kind of mascot. He'd sometimes get caught snacking from craft services and soaking up the atmosphere of the film set, but he rarely spoke.

Richardson was giving a dinner party for most of the cast on the night that our mascot (we never knew his name) was leaving the hotel. He came over in a viscose plaid jacket and white trousers, with his single hair neatly groomed for departure.

'I want to thank all of you for allowing me to watch the filming,' he said with charm and enthusiasm. He went on, addressing Richardson, 'I think you're doing a wonderful job. I hope the film is a big success and I'll be the first in line to see it. It all looks so darned complicated, but then it must be incredibly difficult to make a Viking film so far from the sea.'

We didn't disillusion him. I hope that he was first in line, and that the Vikings amused him as much as he did us on his last night in Ankara.

As usual, I was finding time between shots lying heavy on my hands and soon lapping at my very low boredom threshold. When I met a journalist called Nick Luddington, who ran an English-language paper called the *Ankara Daily News*, I couldn't help letting drop the suggestion that I should write and illustrate a regular diary of events on the set. Nick went for it and a daily column called, with irony and literal accuracy, 'Free of Charge', was born.

I would drive sixty miles into town after we broke at two each afternoon and spend a few happy hours relaxing, really, by producing my cartoon and a thousand-word column to go with it. As I never had much need of sleep, the evening's work and the drive back to be on set at six in the morning were no great hardship to me. I was amazed and, frankly, flattered by the interest everyone was showing in me and my work. As far as the population of Ankara was concerned, it seemed I was just about the biggest star in the world – the biggest, at any rate, to be working in Ankara that year, despite the presence of theatrical heavyweights like Trevor and John.

On the whole, we all found the Turks very supportive of the film company, not surprisingly, I suppose, in view of the revenue coming in from it, but not everything went smoothly in our relations with the locals.

Peter Bowles had decided, with Alan Dobie and another member of the cast, that it would be more amusing to move from the hotel in Ankara and take a private house in the residential part of the town. It was worth doing on such a long shoot, and he had his wife, Susan, coming out from time to time. I said I'd move with him, but Tony Richardson, with quite unnecessary caution in my view, decided that I should stay at the hotel, so that he could 'keep an eye on me'.

I ask you! As if I were a wayward teenager, not a top international movie star!

Peter found quite a grand place to rent, which was alleged to have once been a Swedish Embassy house. There was evidently some confusion, though, and the landlord was disappointed to find that he hadn't let it to John Gielgud, as he'd been told. However, Peter moved in and, as I preferred it to the hotel, I spent a good deal of my time there with him. But the owner of the property, who turned out to be a German of Turkish nationality, remained resentful and started stalking the house to spy on us. When we discovered this, we thought it very bizarre but, as we were all moving on soon, we didn't worry too much.

Towards the end of shooting in Anatolia, filming had moved to Istanbul, leaving only a small second unit behind to do a few sequences out on the plain. Gayle had come out to join me, as she had done a few times during shooting when her own schedule allowed, and we decided that instead of flying across to Istanbul we would hire a nice big air-conditioned Cadillac and go by road.

Susan had also come out to join Peter and we spent the last few evenings together. A couple of the other actors who had shared the house were involved in some of the second-unit shots; Peter and his wife were going to fly with them a few days later.

I was down at the company's office in the town, organising the finer details of our own journey, when we received an ominous phone call from Peter Bowles.

'I've just got back to the house,' he said, 'and found this German chap who owns the place scaring the daylights out of the women. He says he didn't get his rent last month.'

I checked with a company accountant still in the office who confirmed that the rent had been paid up to date. I told Peter and he rang off. A few minutes later he was back.

'Look, this chap just won't accept it. I don't know what his problem is, but he's gone outside into the garden and rounded up a gang of men to cut off the electricity and gas. Now they're all standing round the house, brandishing scythes and things, saying we can't leave until the money's paid.'

'What about your staff there? What do they say?'

'They're all scared as hell – no use at all.'

It must have been very unpleasant for Peter, but the film company seemed reluctant to get involved since the principal production people had already left for Istanbul. I said I'd go straight there in case there was something I could do.

I could see a commotion as soon as I came within sight of the house and I admit to thinking twice before pulling up to get out of the car. A few moments later, I wished I hadn't.

The German, looking ready to murder the first person who opened his mouth, stormed up to me, clutching, for some reason, a roll of garden hose. Like everyone else in Turkey, he seemed to know exactly who I was, and I noticed a sort of manic gleam in his eyes.

'What you come here for, Mr Hemming? You want trouble too?'

'Excuse me,' I mumbled, thinking conciliation was the best approach.

Before I got any further, I was answered with a powerful jet of cold water from the German's hose. I'd had no idea it was connected and the torrent came as a terrible shock. I was utterly bewildered, frightened by this display of naked lunacy and completely sodden.

With a burst of fear-fuelled strength, I managed to push my way past the irate man and staggered into the house at a run, slamming the door shut behind me.

'What the hell is going on?' I asked Peter.

'God knows! The man's mad. It's like something out of Kafka. Thank God,' he suddenly broke off. 'The police are here.'

A moment later the hammering on the door suggested that the local constabulary were not necessarily on our side. The Turkish house boy managed to tell us that the police couldn't come in if we didn't open the door. We followed his advice and tried to ignore the banging and shouting that came from outside.

Poor Peter hated situations like this. He had three youngish women with him – Susan and two of the other actors' wives. He was extremely embarrassed. As we'd all been to a party at the British Embassy a couple of weeks before, I decided to ring them. When I got through, I told them Peter was in trouble and trapped in his house.

I was answered with classic British diplomatic noncommittal unflappability, but a short while later we were extremely relieved to see a Rolls-Royce Phantom V with a Union Jack fluttering at its prow cruise into view and disgorge two Turks – lawyers, by the looks of them.

They stopped and talked with the fuming German, whom they seemed to know, before one of them carried on up to the house. We let him in. He established who Peter was and that he was officially the tenant of the property.

'We do have a problem,' he said in good English but with a strong Turkish accent. 'The situation is this: the man who owns the house says he has watched all of you in this house get very, very drunk. He's seen you through the windows drinking a lot of whisky, and this man –' he nodded at me – 'attacked him with a knife and attempted to murder him. This is a very serious accusation, attempted murder.' He now turned to face me directly. 'You will be arrested and you will be put in prison until you're tried, which could be in six months or two years' time.'

My stomach turned to liquid. I felt hideously impotent. We were in crazyland – beyond Kafka – and I was really frightened now.

I was an actor, here harmlessly making a movie and, incidentally, watching millions of dollars being poured into the local economy, and now this was happening. It was totally inexplicable and beyond comprehension. I had not a clue what I'd done to put us in this position, but if I'd got us into it, it seemed up to me to resolve it.

I walked straight past the lawyer and out of the house to confront the German and call his extraordinary bluff.

As soon as I reached him, one of the minders grabbed my arm and yanked it viciously up the middle of my back. The next thing I knew, there was a gun at my head. Now I was seriously terrified – one tweak of a finger and I'd be an ex-actor, brown bread, a former person.

I looked at the impassive lawyer, the cynical policeman, the mad German, and screamed back at the house, 'For God's sake! Help me!'

By now a large crowd of people had gathered in this quiet, smart suburb of Ankara. Word had evidently got about that a major drama was in progress. The embassy lawyer in the house came out and was joined by his colleague, the senior policeman and the German, while I continued to stand quivering gently at the end of a gun barrel.

After a nightmare that lasted maybe a minute or two, the lawyer beckoned me and I was released to walk with him back to the house, where Peter and the women were waiting with their eyes popping out of their heads.

'All right,' the Turk said to Peter. 'We make some progress. The situation is this. If your friend Mr Hemming will go down on his knees on the sidewalk of the street outside, where everyone can see, apologise to the proprietor and beg his forgiveness, he will be let go of all the charges.'

I was flabbergasted and weak with relief. If it was play-acting the loony wanted, then I was his man. If he was going to get some buzz out of my making obeisance in front of him in public, that was fine by me. It sure as hell beat two years in a Turkish jail.

Peter was looking at me with horror and disgust that, in order to extricate him from the mess, I should be required to humiliate myself like this. He wouldn't have done it, and he certainly didn't expect me to.

'OK,' I said. 'Let's get on with it.'

I went outside and, in full view of a large murmuring crowd, knelt in front of this absurd man and apologised for something I'd never done and would not even have remotely contemplated doing.

When that was over, the Turk from the embassy followed me back into the house.

'Now,' he said to Peter, 'all of you must clear out of this house immediately. Walk out now. You don't have time to pack or bring anything. You must come in the embassy car and leave now, or you'll all be arrested.'

In stunned silence, we all trooped out of the house. I was allowed to take my car; the others piled into the pack of the Roller and were swished away. Superficially, as an act of courage on my part, the episode doesn't rank very high. And yet, in a way, it took more bollocks to get down and grovel in front of the madman, in full view of a swarm of goggling Ankarites, than almost anything else I've ever done. If anything, Peter was more put out than I, and we didn't discuss the event again for many years.

*

I invited Peter and Susan to join us in the Cadillac we'd hired to take us back to Istanbul the following day instead of flying. There were a few more scenes to shoot there, and after the rigours and responsibility of filming a major part in a big movie, we hired a 66-foot schooner called the *Janako* to relax on for the rest of our stay.

Still fired up by the sheer physical excitement of filming *Charge*, and in this romantic setting, I guess it was inevitable that I should have asked Gayle to marry me.

There was much merriment and hordes of guests were coming on board for dinner most evenings. It was a wondrous interlude which I wish could have lasted far longer, but it was just an interlude, before the whole film company, cast and crew flew back to continue, para-doxically, filming the earlier scenes of the story in England. All too soon, we were back in London.

Beyond the battery of press photographers who greeted us at Heathrow eager to snap Gayle and me since we'd announced our engagement in Turkey, I spotted the cockaded cap of the excellent Danny Wiles, waiting nonchalantly beside his Humber to drive us to London. He greeted us warmly, congratulated us and received a kiss from Gayle in return.

It was on the way up the M4 that I asked him if he'd be interested in working exclusively for me, full-time. He took his eyes off the road for a moment to turn round with a look of surprise and pleasure on his face.

'It'll cost yer!' he said.

Feeling quite flush for once, I matched what he asked for, and he arranged to let his partner run their hire business while he joined Hemdale, the new company John Daly and I had set up, primarily as my driver. I loved cars, but I didn't enjoy the physical restrictions imposed by driving.

To celebrate my new chauffeur, after a few days back in London I went out and bought myself an Alvis, a great hefty old-fashioned open sports car with a manual gearbox and no power steering. Danny loathed it; he thought it handled something like the *Queen Mary*. Danny soon became more than a chauffeur – he was what you might now call a valet/PA – a sixties version of Jeeves to my Bertie Wooster. He would arrange my diary, organise meals, even cook if he had to, or act as butler in the flat. He would play darts with me in the pub, although he refused to lose when I ordered him to, and when I wasn't using it I'd let him take the car to visit his various girlfriends dotted around London.

I also told him he didn't have to wear his cockade cap any more. 'The only cockade we want round here would be some kind of aphrodisiac. For all I care, you can wear a sari when you're driving, just as long as you don't smash the car.'

I'd arrived back in England knowing that my life had changed irrevocably as a result of the success of *Blow-Up* and my new rapport with Hollywood. I was also sure that I was, at last, within clutching distance of serious quantities of wonga which would need some handling. I'd already asked John Daly if he could help me in looking after my affairs and he'd proved very useful in Los Angeles.

I would never read scripts, yet by the end of my sojourn there they were arriving by the barrow-load almost daily. I would ask John to read them and tell me what they were about; then, armed with his synopsis, I'd go off to meet producers and tell them all about the script, the plot and what was good or bad about it. I'd busk my way through the meetings, often with John beside me to prompt from time to time.

One of the big Hollywood producers was keen for me to do a picture with Natalie Wood. I loved what I had seen of it. I met Nat and she was charming, but for some reason the guys at William Morris were being a bit iffy. We prodded a little and they reminded me I was under contract to Warner Brothers for four more pictures after *Camelot*. They had me contracted at $4,000 (less than I'd been paid for *Camelot*) for the next picture, $7,500 for the next, then $11,000 – whichever way you looked at it, not a lot when I was now being offered at least ten times that for a picture. John suggested that we show the contract to the producer who wanted me.

The producer wasn't impressed. 'That contract's not valid. They can't pay you less for the second film than what they paid you for *Camelot*. There's a Screen Actors' Guild rule that there has to be an uplift.'

John took the contract back to William Morris and told them, probably not very politely. They were appalled by this cocky young Englishman coming to tell them that the Warner Brothers deal wasn't valid when they hadn't even realised it themselves.

John volunteered to go and tell Warner's their contract was void. A little sourly, they released me. As is often the case, though, for some reason the Natalie Wood picture never happened, which was a shame, as I really fancied her and had felt I was making a bit of headway.

However, when John and I had arrived back in England in the spring with my *David Hemmings Happens* $10,000 and a couple of contracts in hand, we had decided to set up Hemdale, whose basic function was to handle my earnings as tax-efficiently and productively as possible.

It's true to say that while John was money savvy, taxation wasn't his strong suit, but he did know an extremely clever accountant called Derek Dawson, who was very clued up. He talked to him, they came back with a plan for Hemdale and we took off.

Although the company's first function was to manage my affairs, we soon found other actors wanting to join us. The concept was quickly developed into a sort of agency-cum-management company for several other stars, some a good deal more prominent than me. We weren't the first to specialise in the field. Another British organisation had been set up a year or so earlier which had British actors as eminent as Richard Attenborough among its clients. A scheme had been devised to give them convertible loan stock in the company, which attracted lower taxation than a future salary. It was a clever tax device which we also used.

Once Hemdale was up and running, whenever I wasn't working on a picture I liked to go to the office every day and see what was happening. I enjoyed swanning around playing the young tycoon. The press had already latched on to the idea and liked it, and I began to believe I really was a successful, shrewd financial operator. I had a very clear image of how a young tycoon should behave, and behaved like it, although in truth most of my contribution to the operation of the company was spending its funds (which, I reasoned, I'd generated in the first place).

Fortunately, though, as the contracts rolled in, so did the funds, and John, with Derek's advice, was kept more seriously busy trying to grow the company as fast as he could. I didn't always know for sure what was going on, but I trusted John, and the figures looked fantastic. I was always throwing ideas at him, of course, and had some firm views on how things should be done. One of my first contributions was to tell our secretary/receptionist that I wanted her to log all incoming phone calls. I wanted to know how many there were, who they were and why they'd called. I felt, rather as I had in the Marmont in the weeks after *Blow-Up* launched, that we could accurately judge our profile by the number of calls we received. I was also responsible for our bat-wing Hemdale logo. John never liked it, but on this at least I stood my ground and it stayed.

At John's suggestion we recruited another member to the team to handle publicity and PR. Nigel Hutchinson had been the London press officer for Walt Disney and came highly recommended. He also was quite happy to join in the frankly louche lifestyles of the company's founders and was spectacularly successful at publicising (with some degree of control) both my activities and those of the company.

John started off running the business out of temporary premises, but we knew we should sort out more permanent offices. I'd recently met a property-dealing racing driver called Michael Taylor and told him that John and I needed premises. A few days later, he rang to say he had the ideal place for us – which just happened to be an investment property belonging to his wife Charlotte, former deb and star of the gossip columns.

John and I went to have a look at the offices at 39 South Street in Mayfair and said immediately that we'd have them. Michael took us back to his house in Chester Street for drinks to toast the deal and we met Charlotte for the first time. While I was there, I mentioned that I also needed a flat and they suggested I have the place they'd just vacated in a lovely cobbled lane behind St George's Hospital (now the Lanesborough) called Grosvenor Crescent Mews. It was a decent-sized flat, a few brisk steps from a Hooray Henry pub I liked called The Grenadier. It was also directly over Lilo Bloom's riding stables and I loved the idea of the horses clattering across the cobbles. I even found that the faint ambient whiff of horse dung appealed to the nature-lover in me.

I took a short lease on the mews house and, when I discovered that Charlotte was an interior designer, I naturally asked her to do up the place. Luckily my *David Hemmings Happens* money was still more or less intact, though over the next month or so she managed to make a serious dent in it.

Almost as soon as we'd got back from Turkey, Gayle had to go to the States to work, while I had a few more months' work on *Charge* to do in England. The earlier scenes in the film were made in studios at Elstree and on location in some wonderful settings. The wedding scene was filmed at Dyrham Park, near Bath, and the intimate family scenes – the more romantic moments between Vanessa and me – at Michael Redgrave's family home, a handsome Jacobean house beside a heavenly lake. It was lovely to be working with Vanessa again in this wonderful setting, and between shots she and I strolled arm in arm along the garden paths, happily singing together. Dressed in high Victoriana, it felt quite the right thing to be doing.

*

I was very excited and really looking forward to seeing Gayle again, and determined to give her a good welcome when she returned to London. Charlotte Taylor used to drive around in a beautiful metallic-bronze convertible Mercedes and I begged her to lend it to me to collect the Texan Belle on her first night back.

Before I could stop myself, I'd told Gayle it was mine, which impressed her. She was less impressed to discover that all the grand addresses I'd given her when I'd left LA were not current residences – nor had been for some time, if ever – but, thank God, she loved Grosvenor Crescent Mews and tentatively agreed to move into Brompton Square with me until the house was ready. She felt safe, I suppose, in the knowledge that it was a long way from her parents and her formidable Aunt Hazel Hunnicutt.

When she bought herself a furry rabbit and moved that in too, I guessed she was planning to stay.

"FREE OF CHARGE"

By David Hemmings

I find it necessary to bring my colleague to task. Tuesday an article headed "This Time They All Came Back" was run in our paper. It dealt with the filming of the charge itself and was inaccurate.

Even now a search party scours the the hills for the well-known Welch special effects coordinator Dai Namite.

On this occasion Namite, inventor of the controversial "Horse launcher" had adopted a suggestion from the camera department to use marshmallow cannonballs to avoid injury. He refined this further by developing a round merangue and filling it with strawbery jam thus achieving instant blood. Unfortunately Dai had been asked to impersonate an officer in the charge and had to run the gamut of these gore bombs himself. Incensed by the heavy sugar fire, his horse reared and threw him whereupon he was hurriedly carried off by a passing swarm of red-backed Demerera flies, a sweet Turkish delicacy in their own right.

"He'll be back after the banquet," said a local insect specialist.

The sweepstake on the first to reach the Russian guns was won by C. Mitten who correctly drew "Dolmus" a riderless horse from the 17th Hussars.

Editors note: "Inaccurate" says Mr. Hemmings of our article on the charge. If he had not been so all-fandangled impatient he would have found out we were right. Dai Namyte did come back and his series entitled "Life Among the Red-backed Demereras, Ole," starts next week in (of course) the Daily News.-N.L.

The Charge of the Light Brigade, 1968

11

Gayle, 1967

One of the first things Gayle and I had to do once she was back and our engagement was still being splashed all over the British newspapers was to drive down to Byfleet, where my parents were then living, to introduce them to my new fiancée.

I wasn't looking forward to this meeting, at least not as far as my father was concerned. I knew he wouldn't be encouraging. It was cowardly of me, I know, but I asked John Daly to come with us, to provide some back-up.

When we arrived, my parents' small house was spotless and my mother had all her best china and silver laid out for tea in the front room. As I'd feared, my father was standing there as tight-lipped and severe as ever. There was no escaping the tension that always seemed to build up between him and me. I was mortified for Gayle when he virtually ignored her. For the first half an hour or so, nothing was mentioned about our engagement, until, aware that this would probably trigger my father's pent-up resentment, I said, 'You haven't congratulated us yet.'

'Congratulate you?' my father sneered. 'On making a fool of yourself again?'

'What are you talking about?' I snapped back, trying to keep a hold on my own flaring anger.

'What about the others? What about Genny? How did that end? And look what you did to Jane. She was a lovely girl and ready to wait for you when you went to America, and what did she get in return?'

'But, Dad,' I tried to reason. 'She chucked me out – I didn't chuck her, and Genny's parents won't let me near Deborah. That's not my fault. And, you know . . . I've moved on.'

'A girl like her,' he said, nodding at Gayle, beautiful, clever, composed and already a blossoming movie actress in her own right, 'she's only after your money, now you're famous.'

At this crass display of bone-headed rudeness I could only see red. He'd been gratuitously nasty to Gayle for no reason, and all my resentment of his vicious unkindness about everything I'd ever done boiled over. Fuming, I bellowed at him, picked up the entire tea tray and flung it at the wall.

I'm not proud of this. Gayle was horrified and my poor mother was devastated with embarrassment and hurt, but what followed was even worse.

My father and I, as if by tacit agreement, went out into the tiny garden and started trying to punch each other. It was an ugly and ridiculous manifestation of his absolute refusal to accept that I'd succeeded where he had failed, and my frustration at never being able to earn his approval for anything.

Within an hour of our arrival, we had left and I vowed, as I had many times before, never to see my father again.

A few days later, in sharp contrast to this mortifying experience in a suburban Surrey villa, Gayle and I were invited to dinner in one of London's grandest houses. Among the guests was the iconic ballet star Rudolf Nureyev.

I had never met the dancer and, not being an aficionado of the ballet, I'd never even seen him dance. I knew not much more than that he was pre-eminent in his field and didn't mind being seen in public in very tight, contour-revealing leotards. I had also gathered that he was much admired by women, and I was, naturally, a little alarmed to see that Gayle had been placed beside him for dinner. When I observed that he had an intensity which positively burned in him and was powerfully magnetic, I was a lot more alarmed, especially when I saw he was all over Gayle, and she seemed to be lapping it up.

Without an opportunity to shine, I found myself growing very jealous. I overdid the supremely good claret being liberally sloshed into magnificent glasses which held about a pint of the stuff and I could feel myself sinking into regrettable, wine-fuelled truculence.

When it was time to go, Gayle was still full of the little Russian prancer.

'What's so wonderful about him?' I asked.

'He's so beautiful!' Gayle enthused with Texan forthrightness. 'And clever.'

'If he's so lovely, why didn't you go home with him, then?' I grumped.

'Don't be ridiculous,' she exclaimed with disbelief at my ignorance. 'He's not interested in women – except professionally.'

'What?' I asked, astonished, and conscious, not for the first time, of the drawbacks of not reading the gossip pages. 'Is he a woofter?'

'Oh, for God's sake,' Gayle said, a lot more advanced in English liberal attitudes than I. 'He's a genius!'

This was a cue for a long grumble as she drove us home in the Alvis.

When we got back to the house in Brompton Square, I staggered in, still fuming, feeling that, even if Nureyev was gay, she still shouldn't have flirted with him; it made her look indiscriminate.

The discussion was going nowhere as we undressed to get into bed. I was already naked when I declared that I'd had enough and was going out for a drive.

At that stage, Barbara Castle's breathalyser bags were relatively new and we hadn't trained ourselves to accept the imposition of drink-driving laws.

Gayle grabbed all my clothes and locked them in a cupboard. And handed me the car key.

'Fine,' she shrugged in her best southern drawl. 'Y'all go on and do what you want.'

'Fine!' I came straight back. I stormed out of the house carrying the car key and nothing else – not a stitch of clothing.

I walked all the way down Brompton Square and was about to climb into my Alvis when two policemen accosted me. I was just alert enough to explain that I'd been thrown out of the house and I was simply going to sleep in my car. Even in my drunken stupor, I could tell that they didn't believe me, until, God bless her, Gayle arrived with a blanket which she chucked over my back.

'Sweet dreams!' she called over her shoulder as she walked back to the house.

The police chuckled (they don't any more), thinking I'd suffered enough, and since I'd promised not to go driving they left me. I woke, stiff and shivering.

Hunnicutt 1, Hemmings 0, I thought.

I didn't have to do much checking to find that the chances of Rudolf seducing my future bride were indeed very slim, but inevitably some nosy neighbour, no doubt disgruntled by the interruption of a night's kip, had told the papers about my naked stroll and I found myself still answering questions about this entirely innocuous incident five years later.

While I'd been away in Turkey, John Daly had been relentlessly busy with Hemdale. I congratulated myself on my choice of partner in this venture; there was no question that he had all the attributes of a real-life mogul. He was loving it too, winkling out deals from all over the place, looking at every proposition, however obscure, that was brought to him. Naturally he chucked most of them out, but he clearly had a nose for hidden bargains.

I was impressed to find that we were in negotiations to buy Isleworth Studios, and had already bought a 5 per cent stake in the recently formed Welsh commercial TV station Harlech, which caused a lot of speculation among journalists who were unused to the idea of actors sullying their hands with finance (of course, David Frost had already pioneered the notion that the talent could operate the medium too, but it was still comparatively rare). Nigel Hutchinson had a field day: no harm being exposed in the financial columns as well as in the gossip and showbiz pages. It was John's plan that we should fatten up the business as fast as possible so that we could float as a quoted public company, with all the financial advantages that provided.

I was still enjoying myself as a young tycoon, but I could already see that my way of doing things conflicted with John's, in the sense that once I'd told someone I was going to buy something or take a particular course of action, I hated to go back on my word. I took the view that if you said things without meaning them, you might just as well spew wind and steam.

In between all this activity at Hemdale and preparation for my next film, in September Gayle and I were invited to the Sorrento Film Festival, where the magical atmosphere of the Tyrrhenian coast worked its charm on us. In fact we were so taken by the place and the romance of it all that, almost before we knew it, we were standing alone in a strange little stone folly in the beautiful monastery town of Ravello, exchanging home-made vows of love in our own private marriage ceremony.

There was nothing legal or formally binding about it – that, I guess, was its appeal – but to us at the time it felt as convincing and real as any wedding ceremony could. Nevertheless, knowing how cynical people can be, and how the press would have loved the story, we decided to keep it completely to ourselves.

When we returned to London, I started immediately on my next film, *The Long Day's Dying*, directed by Peter Collinson at Shepperton Studios and on location on the heathland around Aldershot. Danny Wiles was back on duty, delighted that the Alvis (or Tank, as he called it) had been replaced. I was well aware that it had always been a compromise for the Rolls-Royce on *Blow-Up*, which I really wanted, and it had been only a matter of time before I spotted another one for sale – a silver Mulliner Park Ward, Chinese-eye Silver Cloud III convertible, custom-built and ordered by Mike Todd for Elizabeth Taylor. I loved the car, even driving it myself, and it became a good friend for several years before, eventually, Diana Rigg bought it for her boyfriend, the director Philip Saville.

The new film, like *Charge*, was a less-than-flattering picture of war, this time the Second World War, with Tom Bell and Alan Dobie playing the other main parts. Mine was a demanding role, for which I had to be as fit as I've ever been. Danny was amazing about it. We were driving back and forth every day from Brompton Square, and if I was due on the set for seven, he'd pick me up at half-past four. We would be down there at five and do a hard cross-country run together, every morning, wet or dry, sometimes in the pissing rain. We'd come back covered in mud, with basic facilities on the set which offered only a cold bath – absolutely not an option these days.

We also had a technical adviser, an ex-Sgt Major called John Williams, in charge of musketry and whiz-bangs, a great character and an endless source of challenges. Once when we got in from our run on a particularly foul morning, he was asleep in a chair in the dressing room. Because I always slept so little myself, I was inclined to resent other people falling asleep on me. It was also extremely unusual to find John in a position where he wasn't in complete control of himself and everyone around him.

I leaped at the opportunity to stick a few cigarettes between his lips, under the headband of his cap and clenched between his fingers and light them all. I picked up an old 303 rifle, a prop we'd used that day with a magazine full of blanks, and loosed off out of a window.

John did not budge an inch. He simply would not allow anyone to see that he wasn't ready for the shot, or show that he was remotely fazed by it. Maybe he'd opened an eye and sussed it just in time. In any event, there was no way he'd have let himself be seen as a shivering wreck. After a moment or two, he opened one gimlet eye and shot a withering glance at me as he removed unwanted cigarettes from his person. 'Put that fucking thing away,' he growled, 'before you do yourself a mischief.'

Another of our locations was a good-sized though fairly derelict house which Peter Collinson had bought in a prime part of Shepperton. We were filming there as well as using it for dressing rooms. At the end of the film it was blown up, having already saved Peter a fortune in sets.

Peter managed to shoot the whole film in seven or eight weeks, which with the technology available in those days was very fast, doing only one or two takes for each scene. This was in welcome contrast to some of the more extravagant directors I've worked with, who could insist on fifteen or twenty takes and still feel they hadn't got it. The quality of Peter's film didn't suffer. *The Long Day's Dying* went on to take the Best Picture award at the Barcelona Film Festival. There were those who thought it an outstanding film and that it would have won a Palme d'Or, but fate moved in to knacker our chances when the technicians went on strike in Cannes that year and there was no festival. It remains, in my view, one of the best pictures I ever worked on.

Meanwhile, Gayle was flitting back and forth across the Atlantic. She was doing some television work in the States, and also trying to reassure her family that she wasn't out of her mind to have become engaged to a young English actor who'd made his name frolicking with naked girls on *Blow-Up*. She wasn't helped in this by one of my many indiscreet moments in a New York nightclub.

Richard Burton's ex-wife, Sybil, and her new husband, rock'n'roller Jordan Christopher, ran a club called Arthur, flavour of the month when Gayle and I were there in October 1967. I'd hung out there several times with Andy Warhol, Lester Persky and François de Menil, and we always shared the same round table with Sibyl.

We'd arrived in New York with me straining at the leash to hit the town as ever, but Gayle said she wanted to freshen up and have a zizz.

'Fine,' I said gallantly. 'I'll be at Sibyl's or 21 or Elaine's. I'll go to Elaine's first and leave a note on the door to let you know where I am if I've gone on.'

At Arthur, I found myself sitting beside Earl Wilson, one of NY's most heavyweight and hard-nosed gossip columnists, whom I knew well. Despite his reputation, he had an insidious charm.

'Tell me,' he said, wrapping an arm around my shoulder, 'when are you and Gayle going to get married?'

A little drunk, a little jet-lagged and suffering from chronic big-mouth syndrome, I couldn't resist the opportunity to electrify him, by showing him that there were a few stories he missed. 'We were married last month in Italy.'

His jaw dropped, rather unattractively, on to the table as I told him the story, missing out the vital piece of information that there had been no priest present to validate the event.

The story seemed to hit every newspaper in the world overnight. God knows how much Earl made out of it, because at that stage we were rapidly becoming a sort of poor man's Burton and Taylor, on the front pages of the tabloids most of the time.

Gayle's parents put a brave face on it, but she was concerned that they were very disappointed not to have been involved in a big wedding for their only daughter.

At the same time, I found I'd painted us into a corner. It was clear that suddenly to come out with an announcement that it was all bullshit wouldn't have endeared us to the press, and at that stage I still thought it was important to keep them happy (though these days, I couldn't give a gerbil's jacksie what they say), so we went along with it.

Back in London, Grosvenor Crescent Mews was ready for us to move in. I had also taken a lease on a houseboat called *Mayflower Two* at Chiswick Mall, not far from the Cherry Blossom roundabout. It was a sort of bolt hole, much prized by friends engaged in extramarital relationships. I spent some time there myself the following year, where I found something detached and otherworldly about living on a river in the middle of a mighty city, and my few short sojourns there gave me a taste for river life and canals that I never completely lost.

But for the last part of 1967, Gayle and I lived in Grosvenor Crescent Mews, which we both enjoyed. The charm of the horses clip-clopping out to Hyde Park was slightly marred by an incredibly powerful stench of horse dung that emanated from a new ventilation shaft Lilo Bloom had installed. I was forced to pour cement down it, which solved the problem, and fortunately she never found out – at least, she never complained.

About a month after we'd moved in, there was slight drama when winter rains began to fall. A hitherto undiscovered leak in the roof ruptured into a large hole and, while we were out for a day, almost completely flooded the flat. Gayle and I came home to find her precious bunny floating precariously in its basket and we all decamped immediately to the top floor of Charlotte and Michael Taylor's house in Chester Street.

I was occupied then with preparations for *Only When I Larf*, in which I was starring with Richard Attenborough and Alexandra Stewart, with the added bonus of working on location in Beirut. I was also finding that my business activity consisted mainly of having lunch, a skill in which I'd had much practice, chiefly at the White Elephant, often with Niv's son, David Niven Jr, who had become a good friend and was an indefatigable game player. Our visit to Deborah Kerr at the Connaught was typical of his sense of humour.

From somewhere, God knows where, he'd found a complete Laplander's outfit in bright reds and greens, including a tall pointed hat that tied under the chin and shoes with curly toes and tassels. We wondered what we could do with it. Go to Tramp, perhaps? Then David reminded me that his father was staying at the Connaught. So was his old friend Deborah Kerr, and suddenly the idea of teasing her was very appealing.

David Jr went to see her and told her that a reporter from the *Lapland Gazette* was very anxious to interview her. He easily persuaded her to see him, on the grounds that he was a bit thick and it would be a kind thing to do.

Naturally, I was the idiot who was going to wear the outfit, confident that Miss Kerr wouldn't recognise me through a screen of make-shift Nordic face-fungus, despite our brief time together on *The Eye of the Devil*. When I was ushered into her suite by a Connaught skivvy, Deborah looked at me with deep suspicion. But although I'd made a movie with her, living next to her for a month or two, she did not apparently associate me with this balmy Lap reporter.

I swiftly got into character, waving a spiral-bound notebook I'd borrowed from reception at the Connaught and blathering in a terrible bogus Scandinavian accent. Inevitably I pushed it as far as I could, egged on by both Nivens, who were standing behind her, wincing painfully with suppressed laughter. The questions became more absurd, the accent progressively more ridiculous, but it still took her twenty minutes to be sure it was a hoax.

'This is bullshit! Hemmings, why are you playing this extra-ordinary game?' she demanded haughtily, while the Nivens were pissing themselves.

I loved the whole thing. I'd always loved real-life play-acting, creating scenarios where most of the cast are unaware that they are taking part in them. I'd done it as a child and I'd done it often since, as a young actor before *Blow-Up*, when David Warner was just beginning to make an impact at Stratford and I went to stay with him.

It was during his performance in *Richard II* – astounding and ground-breaking in its time – that to relax from the great tension it created in him, he would join me in some wonderful practical jokes, where we simply used the real world as our stage and set. On one occasion when David wasn't on stage, we sprayed the entire theatre with sneezing powder from Davenports Magic Shop and sat in the circle listening to a cacophony of sneezing and spluttering that built up to a crescendo. It was horrible really, the whole place in a state of shit and derision, until the actors on the stage suddenly found themselves playing to what sounded like a herd of elephant seals during the mating season.

Another time, we found a suitably quiet pub; I walked in and ordered half a pint. A few minutes later, David came in with a newspaper under his arm and ordered a large Scotch, then sat down beside me. We didn't acknowledge each other, as if neither of us knew the other from Adam. He opened his paper and began to read. I immediately picked up his glass and drank half his whisky in a single gulp, unseen by David but in full sight of the barman. I returned to my half-pint and David glanced up. He looked at his glass, observed that it was half empty and said to the barman, very politely, 'Excuse me. I thought I asked for a double.'

'That was a double, sir.'

'Does that look like a double to you?'

The barman, getting flustered, looked at me. 'Do you two know each other?'

'Certainly not,' we both expostulated.

'Well, I saw you. You just drank his drink!'

'No, I did not,' I denied vehemently. 'I'm drinking beer. I hate Scotch! I wouldn't touch it! How dare you suggest such a thing!' I picked up my glass, walked up to the bar and slung what was left in it over the barman.

As I retired, David jumped to his feet. 'Excuse me! I still haven't had my double Scotch.'

The barman, still dripping, had no choice but to top up his glass.

It was all a little cruel, I suppose, and I was lucky not to be hit, or have the police summoned, but it was always a challenge to see how far you could push it.

One weekend I came up with one of my favourite women, a very funny, very good-looking girl from the BBC make-up department called Natalie Calf, with whom I was in the midst of a wondrous affair. We met up with Suzy, another girlfriend of hers and David Warner again.

This time Natalie and I went into a big, busy pub in Stratford, ordered drinks and sat down. Soon afterwards, Suzy burst in, looked around the crowd until she spotted us.

'There you are!' she bellowed indignantly. 'What on earth are you doing with that woman?'

The entire pub became deadly quiet.

I looked up, appalled, gulping like a guilty goldfish. 'Wha –?'

'And do you realise,' Suzy went on, glaring at Natalie, 'I've got your husband here.'

At which point David came in through the door.

This was a major dramatic soap-opera moment. It was *'Coronation Street* comes to a pub near you'. Everything was on hold: the barmen stopped serving; the fruit machine was abandoned.

All focus was on Warner, who threw back his head and declaimed like Donald Wolfit, 'You cad!'

'How dare you call me a cad, you bloody oik!' I returned, finding my voice.

I jumped up and, for a moment, we squared up to each other, bristling, though neither of us ventured a punch.

Everyone else was backing away, ready to witness the fight, when David walked up to the bar.

'Barman,' he said, 'where's your soda siphon?' He spotted one, grabbed it, strode back to where I stood and aimed a healthy jet straight at my face. He turned to Natalie. 'As for you, you cow!' he bellowed, giving her a good drenching too.

Natalie and I stood together defiantly, dripping like drowned rats, while I drew myself up to my full height, such as it was, and announced, 'We are in love, and before everyone in this pub, we declare our love, so sod you!'

With that we walked out of the hushed pub, while David turned around, walked up to the bar and plonked down the siphon.

'Thank you very much. D'you know something? You can never, ever trust a woman.' He then turned to Suzy, purportedly my wife, offered her a drink and sat down in a corner to canoodle and snog with her while everyone in the bar gazed on in shock and horror.

I loved these scenes, like short plays within a play that required a kind of burlesque, larger-than-life style of acting. And once again it was the creation of illusion, the skilled deception that pleased me so much. Doing it with Natalie and David, who were as addicted as I was, gave us a huge buzz, and was a major source of entertainment. One of the downsides of becoming famous after *Blow-Up* was that this sort of game became impossible – at least in England – even in later life, when I'd changed, I'd have said, beyond recognition.

Another friend I made while sitting around having four-hour lunches in Mayfair was Niv Jr's young PA, Linda Agran. She had worked at Jane Merrow's agents and had had to field a string of press questions about my goings-on with Gayle while I'd been in LA making *Camelot*, so naturally she was a little wary of me, but the ice was broken and I've known her ever since. She became an important television producer who gave me several big parts – God bless her. With Terry Donovan and David Bailey, we'd carry on after lunch at Muriel Belcher's Colony Room – incredibly, one of the few places you could legitimately get a drink in the middle of the afternoon.

Above all, though, I was enjoying every minute of being in demand. I found I could get away with a great deal of bad behaviour, and revelled in it. This was not always to the liking of my new 'bride'.

In December 1967, Gayle and I flew to Beirut when filming on *Only When I Larf* moved there. She had been delighted with a beautiful ring I'd bought for her in Tiffany's when we'd been in New York a couple of months earlier, but my somewhat cavalier attitude to our relationship was upsetting her. The tension between us was building and came to a head when I threw the ring out of the window of our fourteenth-floor hotel room on to the shingle beach below. The noisy row escalated until I ended it by storming out of the room and not coming back.

Of course, I hadn't flung the ring anywhere. I might have been angry, but I wasn't that stupid. For once I'd made practical use of my magic by palming it, but Gayle was convinced it had gone and spent many hours down on the beach searching for it and looking very miserable. I'm ashamed to say, I didn't tell her she was wasting her time until a lot later.

Things did not improve, and in any event Gayle had to leave Beirut because she was needed in the States to make *Marlow* with James Garner. Meanwhile, part of my job meant spending a lot of time kissing Alexandra Stewart, a task which, I admit, I was finding easy and enjoyable. One particularly vivid clinch in the sea was splashed all over the papers in England, but this can't have upset Gayle too much since she and Alexandra became friends, even spending that Christmas together in the South of France – both of them a long way from me.

12

King Alfred in Ireland, 1968

Beneath my normally exuberant surface I was missing Gayle, but I was too busy, and too damned proud, to admit it, even to myself. Besides, there were a lot of people and projects to take my mind off what had happened between us. The press hadn't made it easier for us, although I'd decided the best strategy was to come clean over the Ravello 'wedding'. It was a lot simpler to deal with the breakdown of a marriage that had never existed in the first place.

I've no idea how Gayle dealt with her family in Texas over this, but I knew enough about them to appreciate that they would have found the whole business very discomforting.

However, I had another hurdle of my own to get over before I could resume the rest of my life. *The Best House in London* was to be my second picture for MGM and, unlike Warner Brothers, they had a good contract to use me for a great deal less than my prevailing market rate. There didn't seem to be anything I could do to get out of it. I was peeved and frustrated at this; it seemed such a waste of time when we were working so hard to build up funds in Hemdale. If I was annoyed, John Daly was livid, and applied himself frenetically to finding a way round it as he had with Warner's. It wasn't long before he came up with an idea.

'Listen, H, about this MGM deal,' he said, with a shifty look that I knew well presaged a new wheeze or fiddle of some sort. 'Why don't you play *both* the lead roles in it?'

It so happened this made perfect sense within the plot of the film.

'Great, so you mean I'll knock off two of the movies I still owe them under contract instead of just one?'

John bit his lip and nodded. 'Something like that.'

I rang Carlo Ponti to tell him I'd like to play both parts, and Ponti, no doubt thinking he might be able to save some money, loved the idea, and I was soon being fitted up with costumes for the two roles.

Five days before shooting started, John suggested we go out to the
Canaries for a quick break and to pursue some other deal he'd found.
From there he announced that we were going to serve a notice on MGM
to the effect that I would get my contractual amount for the original part
of 'Charlie', but for the other role I would receive my full market rate,
approximately twenty times more.

'But, John, they'll go mad. The big companies loathe being messed
around by actors.'

'Maybe, but they won't have any option but to agree, now things are
so far down the line.'

As I'd predicted, MGM went berserk, and I could only sit in my hotel
room chewing my fingernails into extinction while we waited for their
answer. I was sure I would never work again.

But, as John had predicted, MGM had to give in. Eventually they
agreed to compromise, paid me handsomely for the two parts in *Best
House* and tore up my existing contract. I would work again, it seemed –
just not with MGM. After Philip Saville had done his worst with *Best
House*, I didn't mind, not at all.

My album, *David Hemmings Happens*, had been released and, not
surprisingly, sunk without trace into the quicksand of pop ephemera.
However, its existence did provide me with vague musical credentials,
and I was invited as a guest on Pete Myers's *Late Night Extra* on Radio
One. I foolishly let slip that I had once done a little DJing in my
chequered past and was offered the chance to take over the programme
for a session. It happened, and it wasn't the greatest success.

Among other guests, I persuaded Warren Beatty to come on. He
puzzled the handful of listeners by answering all my questions
inexplicably with the same three words – Chicken Chow Mein. It didn't
make for great radio, and I wasn't invited back.

Why I let these things happen I don't know, but it really had seemed
like an amusing idea that would be fun. And to those who said
Hemmings should stick to what he knew, I was inclined to ask, 'Please,
tell me what that is. I'd love to know.'

I was, however, given another crack at broadcasting later that year
when I was invited to take over a TV show called *Sunday Night People*,
in the former *Eamonn Andrews Show* slot and fairly prime-time. That was
fun. I asked if I could design the set, and was given a fairly free rein to
do it. It consisted, for the most part, of large plastic-covered cubes,

referred to by one of my guests as giant Lego blocks. Sammy Davis Jr agreed to come and staggered onto the set, making sure he tripped over all the cubes. He was draped with cameras in a kind of homage to *Blow-Up*, which was typically kind of him and went some way to paying back the money I'd lost to him at poker in my early, green days in Los Angeles. But although my show seemed to go well, I wasn't asked back for a repeat of that either. Any pretensions I might have had to become the new David Frost, or even the new Simon Dee, looked ill-founded.

In April, towards the end of making *Best House*, Dougie Hayward, my old friend from the Alvaro's Bang Club days, rang me to say that Gayle was in London. He told me that he had asked her to come with him to a party that was being given for Joan Collins. If I wanted to see Gayle, I should be there.

I was amazed and in fact a little alarmed by the excitement I felt at the prospect of seeing Gayle again, and this confirmed to me that seeing her was exactly what I wanted.

It was early evening, still daylight, and people were drinking and dancing around, a lot of friends of Gayle's and mine, and I soon spotted her from behind, chattering away and looking, once I saw her profile, as wondrous as ever. I carefully made my way towards her, keeping behind her so she wouldn't see.

I realised that a lot of people in the room had noticed me there and knew I hadn't seen Gayle for a while. The volume of chatter dropped a little and people were looking at Gayle. I could tell from the way she stiffened very slightly she knew something was up. By then I was almost behind her. I reached forward and ran a finger gently down her spine.

She spun round, our eyes locked and I knew at once the magic was still there, whatever we might have said or felt about each other in the heat of our break-up in Beirut.

We talked for the next few hours, trying to work out what had gone wrong. Her parents, of course, had been very upset by the reports of the fake marriage, and there was no doubt this was a big problem for her. But we followed up our reunion with a dinner the next evening and a night of warm reconciliation at Grosvenor Crescent Mews. It was wonderful to be back together again, but, after what felt like only a few days, Gayle had to go back to LA to do some final shots for *Marlow*.

I was desperate to follow her. Quite apart from other considerations, I was getting pissed off with *Best House* and being locked in at

Shepperton Studios day after day. I also felt a nice long dose of Los Angeles would do me a lot of good and remind a few American producers that I hadn't already expired. In anticipation, I asked Gayle to look for a house we could rent there for a while, before I had to start work in Ireland on my next big film, *Alfred the Great*.

However, the management of *Best House*, mainly in the form of the producer, Kurt Ungar, who no doubt sensed my restlessness, were very reluctant to let me out of their sight during the week and most insistent that I shouldn't be allowed to escape to the States at the weekend. I allayed their worst fears by pretending to let drop that my US visa had run out and it would take weeks to get a new one. Then, in a splendid manifestation of serendipity, I was asked to make a prestigious television commercial in France for Foster Grant sunglasses, with a massive fee attached. It transpired that they wanted me, plus my silver drop-head Rolls. Kurt agreed that I could do it, as long as I did it at a weekend and was back on the set at seven as usual on Monday morning.

Danny gleefully aimed the car at the Friday ferry and Paris, while John Daly and I followed on an evening flight.

The filming was taking place not far from Paris and there wasn't a great deal to it. A couple of what Danny called 'French-Onion Johnnies' would be standing at the side of a typically French road, probably lined with poplars, and I would pull up in the Rolls with the lid down and say, 'Excuse me, could you tell me the way to Versailles?'

They would answer, 'That way,' with an appropriate jerk of the thumb, at which, with a curt, anally retentive English nod, I would drive off, while they gazed after me in wonderment, saying, 'Was that not David Hemmings in those Foster Grant sunglasses?'

Memorable stuff – or it might have been.

We drove out to the shoot next morning, but I hadn't let on to John and Danny that I had other plans. I was there long enough for the crew to set up the shot, but they were taking their time over it and I told them I couldn't hang around; I had a plane to catch to Los Angeles, immediately.

John, seeing a large fee slip down the plug, was very grumpy and wouldn't help. In the end, I managed to persuade the bemused producer of the commercial to drive like the proverbial orang-utan with a frontal lobotomy and a death wish to Orly, which we reached just in time for my flight.

The next morning I was climbing out of an LA cab at 819 North Beverly Glen Boulevard, clutching a massive bunch of daffodils. Gayle nearly fell off her balcony in astonishment, but she was alone and pleased to see me, which was what I'd most wanted to know.

I flew back to London that night and turned up, a little red in the eye and a few minutes late, at Shepperton on Monday morning. We never got the money for the ad, though.

The minute *Best House* was finished, I headed west for a month or so of jollies with Gayle in LA. I asked Vincent Fleming, my trusty stand-in and drinking companion, if he'd like to come along to help out, but he said he'd be homesick, and Danny jumped at the chance to come instead.

I'd rented Lauren Bacall's house in the Malibu Colony, which I'd always liked, right on the beach, next door to Deborah Kerr, as it happened, and just along the strand from Katharine Hepburn and Burt Lancaster.

Gayle was in her element in the Colony. She had a gift for networking and soon she seemed to know everybody; or at least, when she organised our parties, everybody seemed to come, and it was a great privilege to see so many Hollywood stars scoffing our food and mopping up our booze.

There was some work to do while I was there – a couple of *Rowan and Martin's Laugh-In*s, one with Raquel Welch, as well as the première of *The Charge of the Light Brigade* and a quick trip to Rome to do my small bit with Jane Fonda in *Barbarella* directed by Roger Vadim. I had to make love to Jane by pressing the palm of my hand against hers, while intoning a password, which was my great contribution to this bizarre, cultish movie. I suggested the name of a village in North Wales. Jane loved it and it was a treat to see her bubbling away as she tried, successfully, to spit it out . . . 'Llanfairpwllgwyngyllgogerychwyrndrobwll-llantysiliogogogoch!' In between times, I refreshed my friendship with the Bricusses, Tom Mankiewicz, Steve and Neile McQueen and the rest of the crowd. This time I left LA confident that I had established my presence and knowing whom I could trust.

It seemed as if I'd scarcely arrived back in London when Danny turned up at the mews in a Land Rover he'd bought for me somewhere up the Edgware Road, to load all my personal possessions into it. When I told him this was all I owned, he was appalled.

''Ere, H, you're a big star now. You've gotta have more than this!'

But I didn't, and we headed off happily to catch the Fishguard ferry on the way to Ireland and County Galway, where I was to be based for the next four months while Clive Donner battled with *Alfred the Great*.

I was already in the bar of the Great Southern Hotel, Galway, when Danny arrived in the middle of the night. I summoned him to have a drink with me and the lovely red-headed daughter of Lord Killanin, one of the backers of the film and, more usefully, a Jockey Club steward at Galway Races. One of Lord K's sons, Redmond Morris, was also third assistant director on the picture. A gang of us sat up all night to launch the new production, until the dawn turned Galway Bay a glittering pink.

'Right!' I said to Danny. 'I've got this fantastic house. Let's get down there now and unload my stuff.'

He blinked in protest, but when he saw my castle he was as excited as I was.

Oranmore Castle stood proudly right on the edge of the bay. It had been let to me by Anita King, a cousin of Winston Churchill's, who lived nearby. It was basically a medieval house connected to an ancient square keep. It was the first time I'd been inside the place. The house had been well modernised but the real excitement came when I opened the door into the great hall of the castle itself – a massive hall with a fireplace as big as a hanger and an oak table ten yards long – which obviously hadn't been used for years.

I turned to Danny. 'Right, I want to live in here!'

'You're having a laugh, aren't yer?'

'No, no, it's fine. There's the kitchen. The table's all right.'

There was a spiral staircase up to ten derelict bedrooms. It seemed absurd to be in a place like this and waste it. I put Danny in charge of making the rooms habitable for all the guests I'd just decided I was going to invite over. To give Danny his due, despite all the customary Irish procrastination, he did a grand job.

Clive Donner was directing *Alfred the Great*. The best one could say about Clive as a director was that he'd had a lot of experience and, frankly, just one hit – *What's New, Pussycat?*, which, unlike *Alfred*, at least started life with a good script. However, I'd enjoyed working with him on *Some People* six years before, and we'd first talked about *Alfred* when I was in LA for *Camelot*, so I was thoroughly prepared.

Clive had located the shooting of this tale of Saxon kingship in the Celtic landscape of County Galway for its comparatively uncluttered background, as well as the frequent rainfall for which the west of Ireland is noted. As it turned out, 1968 proved to be one of Ireland's driest summers for years and a lot of time was spent filming beneath the water hoses of the local fire brigade. On top of that, it was a large-scale production, not unlike *Braveheart* thirty years later, involving several hundred students, grimy and be-flead, playing the Anglo-Saxons, and a contingent of the Irish Army playing the invading Danes. It was a major logistical challenge, and the biggest-budget picture made in Europe that year.

Clive also had a huge replica of a Saxon white horse etched on to the side of a Galway hill. He was very proud of it and valued it as a useful symbol and reference point in the narrative of the film. Before shooting had got under way, he took me up in a helicopter to fly across the set and the surrounding country which he planned to use. He became lyrical as we flew over his precious horse and, in his enthusiasm, turned to the patently hard-nosed chopper pilot.

'So, what do you think of our white horse?'

The pilot shrugged a shoulder decorated with bogus RAF gold tabs. 'It's all right, I s'pose.' Perhaps realising a more specific opinion was required, he squinted at it a little harder. 'It looks like a dog.'

I tried not to laugh. Unfortunately, he was right.

The principal set lay about a dozen miles from Oranmore, and was a splendid and thoroughly convincing Anglo-Saxon village of conical, thatched wattle and daub huts.

Physically, *Alfred* was a difficult film to make, not helped by Donner's technique – an indicator of his lack of confidence in his own vision. In complete contrast to Peter Collinson's directing style, he would shoot dozens of takes for almost every scene. While this was irritating for me, it was a lot worse for my long-suffering stand-in.

Vince was getting very annoyed, because he'd be plunged into a vat of water and made to hang around in it for hours at each take. He didn't have a very forgiving temperament and tried to persuade me to pull rank with Clive and insist on him not doing all these takes, but I could see that the poor director had enough problems already. Inevitably, tension built up between Vince and me, but I saw no point in moaning; better just to get on with it, hit the bar at the end of the day and down a few vodkas.

I'd learned much earlier in life, and I must have mentioned already that, for an actor, most filming was excessively boring, sitting around for hour after hour, in full make-up and costume, primed for the order to kick bollock and scramble. With some directors, like those who wanted twenty takes of everything, the tedium was greatly increased. You could sit and chat to your co-actors, and members of the crew who didn't happen to be busy at the time, but on a long shoot you soon found that you'd exhausted most potential conversations.

I was working with people I liked on *Alfred* – Michael York (who also happened to be a Hemdale client) was there with his wife, Pat; Colin Blakely and Alan Dobie, who'd been in *The Charge of the Light Brigade* and *The Long Day's Dying*; and a very young Ian McKellen played the marsh boy who burned the cakes. In those days it was unusual to make a film with two young leads, and in this case my female co-star, playing the Lady Aelswyth, was the lovely Prunella Ransome (whose handmaiden was Sinead Cusack).

Actors becoming emotionally or at least physically involved with co-stars of the opposite gender is always a potential source of worry (and headlines) for film-makers. It's an easy trap to fall into, but it doesn't always happen. On *Alfred* I took the view that if Prunella was game, so was I. I tried to convey this early on in our first scripted kiss, when, in the tradition of the great method actors, I felt I could give a more convincing performance if I indulged in the real thing. I was wrong. I was brought up sharply by her indignant squeal and a very sore tongue. Prunella found it hard to forgive me. Regrettably, although I tried to explain my motives, relations between us remained strained for the rest of the shoot.

These were all reasons to seek eagerly any outside sources of amusement in the evenings and at weekends during filming – anything to stop the brain from shrivelling up like an unused appendix.

Almost from the start I was ringing up friends in London and persuading them to come over and enjoy my castle. I loved playing the king, holding elaborate house parties with dinners in the great hall. I was also constantly trying to think of things to do to fill up a weekend.

Naturally, gambling formed the backbone to our social life: many, many hours were passed playing poker and a dodgy version of shoot pontoon called 7½. One of our neighbours was an obliging and frankly opportunistic bookmaker from Galway Town called Ginger Murphy. He also owned a pub in town, which provided an alternative venue. It wasn't surprising that the locals needed no encouragement to come up and join in, and we thought it would be a great idea to hold our own Donkey Derby. Danny went into Galway to hire a dozen donkeys and several of the local families provided their own. The first assistant director on *Alfred* was a tall, lanky individual called Brian Cook, who opened a book for the day, and a gang of tinkers came along with a very athletic donkey, more like a well-bred mule, which cleaned up for them, and left us serious losers. However, the casino that we operated in the castle that night recouped most of our money.

Another time we were coming back from the set and we stopped in a pub which had a rack of shot guns on display. I asked if I could take a look. The landlord pulled some down for me. I held them up, peered along the barrels and tried to look as if I knew what I was doing. Of course, I'd picked up a few pointers from staying in country houses, but I hadn't really got a clue. However, that didn't stop me buying two of them on the spot at £100 each – a lot of money in those days – and taking them away with me.

A good few open acres were attached to the castle and, the following weekend, we bought a launch trap and held a clay pigeon shoot against the village, who came up en masse for it with their own shotguns.

I had another spending spree in a fishing shop, coming home with a complete collection of rods, reels, flies and creels, which led to several long, boring and ultimately fruitless hours on the banks of a local river. I have a suspicion that we were always directed to the water where there was no risk of our depleting fishing stocks.

One of the more memorable aspects of life at Oranmore involved the dogs. During my life I have had relationships with many dogs, starting with the excellent sheepdog Jasper, who had fallen at the hands of a Croydon milkman. But there have also been Stanley, Heathcliff, Cathy, Isabella, Hindley, BBD1 and BBD2 (Big Black Dog – vast Newfoundlands), Sooty, Sweep and Hobbs (and not forgetting Tom Courtenay's Gus).

One of the most special, though, was Rory the Irish wolfhound. He was, to put it unromantically, an extra on *Alfred*, acquired by the film company as my character's constant companion. It was soon decided that the best possible way for the dog and me to bond and thus give a portrayal of a relationship that would truly convince was for him to come and get to know me by living as my own dog in the castle.

He genuinely became my constant companion for the whole of my lengthy sojourn there and was the star of the show. Needless to say, I grew very fond of him. He had his shortcomings, of course; he was only human. He would down a pint of Guinness in two seconds flat, and rape a woman in five. He was enormous – his shoulder came up to my belt and his head to my nipples. You never want your nipples snarled at by an Irish wolfhound, on that you can trust me!

The other new dog in my life was a greyhound. Conveniently sited for those on the unit who enjoyed live racing, there was a busy greyhound track in Galway and we visited it regularly. Brian Cook and I had a lot in common – we certainly seemed to spend a great deal of time at the dogs and drinking together – and on one of our forays to the race track we got into a serious discussion with Ginger Murphy. Ginger could have sold a hairnet to a slap-head and it took him about five minutes to talk us into buying a canine athlete for ourselves. Brian and I became half-owners of this animal, a bitch named Red Fury (perhaps after Billy Fury, whom she closely resembled), and within a week or two it ran under our names for the first time at the Galway track. Amazingly, and against all my understanding of the odds in such situations, it won.

Brian was ecstatic. 'We've got to get this dog back home and run it at White City as soon as bloody possible,' he crowed in drunken glee for the next four hours.

We'd paid £350 for Red Fury and we did take it back to London, where Paul Preece trained it at Wimbledon and it won two races and a substantial profit for us. Brian, unfortunately, was hooked and got totally carried away. He bought another dog for £650 (six weeks' wages) and it broke a leg on its first run at Youghall.

Many expeditions and many excesses filled our spare time in Galway, shared with and encouraged by an inexhaustible stream of visitors. And this pleasure was even enhanced by the knowledge that next door to us was a nunnery where nuns from across Ireland came for their holidays. They must have been mystified and thrilled by all the activity.

I was less confident of giving such universal satisfaction when Gayle announced that her formidable Aunt Hazel Hunnicutt had expressed a wish to come and visit me in Ireland while she was in Europe for her annual grand tour. For years, I gathered, Hazel had been shepherding groups of young Texan debutantes (I'd no idea there were such things) around Europe to further their cultural education. Now, in view of the somewhat erratic course of my relationship with her niece, I had the impression she was coming as an ambassador for the Hunnicutt family to warn me off.

Since we'd made up earlier in the summer, I'd suggested quite often to Gayle that we might re-establish our marriage plans. She was still being a little coy about the idea, reminding me of the horror of the Beirut Bust-up. But, I felt, I was on the case and was reasonably certain I could bring her round, provided Aunt Hazel didn't decide to put her iron-shod Texan hoof down.

It mattered very much to me that we gave Hazel the best possible impression when she came to stay. After all, with the advantage of being, albeit *pro tempore*, master of an impressively sited Norman castle, it would be a poor show if we couldn't. I was still very nervous about it and rushed around in a frenzy, telling everyone to clean the place up, hide all the booze and, above all, once our guest had arrived, to refrain from swearing, farting, belching or being sick.

Danny drove me in the Rolls to meet her at the airport and we brought her back for dinner at Oranmore. Dinner was as good as we'd ever done it, the massive table glowing in the light of huge candelabra and half a ton of peat stacked and glowing in the fireplace. I sat in my carved throne at the head of the table, as kingly as you like, and placed Hazel to my right, as instructed by Gayle.

To start with, because I had the distinct impression that she was here to give me the chop, I did everything I could to show her what a decent, caring sort of a chap I was. After dinner we talked.

'Honey,' she said, using the word somewhat deceptively, 'our family does not blame you for what happened last year and all the mess that followed. We blame Gayle –' she turned on me with an eye like an icicle – 'because Gayle was brought up to know better.'

'To know better than what?' I asked, trying to suppress a dangerous tremor of indignation.

'To know better than to marry some bum actor,' she declared, as if it were obvious.

That, I felt, was going too far. I drew myself up on my baronial chair and raised a pair of indignant eyebrows. 'Excuse me! Some bum actor? Here I am, entertaining you to a sumptuous dinner in a fine medieval castle, and you're calling me a bum?'

She backed off a little, allowing me to return to my charm offensive, and the evening ended more or less a draw – not settled but better than a full-blown rout.

Hazel seemed more mellow in the morning, the sound of surf and the magical Galway air, perhaps, doing their stuff. But I felt we needed to find some powerful distraction to help her achieve a more favourable perspective on my plans to marry Gayle.

I thought I would combine two pressing objectives. Our dog, Red Fury, was running that night down the road in Galway and I was very anxious to see it run. Over dinner that evening, with relations a little smoother than on day one, I floated an idea.

'Have you ever been dog-racing? You know it's the national sport here. You really should see it while you're in the Emerald Isle.'

I explained to her how all the local gentry liked to relax by racing their finely bred greyhounds, how King Edward VII himself as a young man had patronised this noble sport, and, furthermore, we had a very fine dog of our own running later that evening. Perhaps she would like to come and watch?

She rose to it like a trout to a mayfly, all gung-ho to come and have a look at this cultural phenomenon. When we arrived at the track, I was a little uneasy about how she might react to the appearance of the local 'gentry', but she didn't seem to notice.

'Do you think you might like to have a bet on our dog,' I ventured, 'just for interest's sake?'

'We-ell,' Hazel drawled, 'I don't truly approve of gambling, but if it's the custom in these parts, I will just this time.'

I put the money on for her and pointed out the dog to her. 'That's it,' I said, 'that skinny one – number five.'

At the 'Off', the dogs shot out of the traps after the bogus hare (or 'phoney coney', as I translated it to my guest). Red Fury raced straight into the lead and was still there as they came off the last bend. I glanced at Aunt Hazel and, to my amazement, she was totally committed, on her feet, on tiptoes, with eyes popping like organ stops, yelling at the height of her husky voice, 'Come on, the Five!'

I do not deny that Red Fury's second win went a long way to adjusting Aunt Hazel's view of the bum actor, but by the time she left a couple of days later we were on the best of terms. As far as she was concerned, there could be no objection to my continuing to see her precious niece.

*

Of course, Gayle came over to Ireland several times, which kept the flame going, and between her visits there was no shortage of other guests to keep me busy. Charlotte Taylor was staying with friends in the next county and came to spend a day or two on the set.

Lester Persky was a friend of Truman Capote's and a regular visitor from Los Angeles. Although he later started Persky-Bright, which went on to produce some big hits, like Warren Beatty's *Shampoo*, at that stage he was a gay, witty hustler of great charm and, it must be said, persistence. He had paid me (or John) a lump of money as an advance against my doing *Adventures in the Skin Trade* on screen for him – always an iffy proposition and ultimately consigned to that eternal purgatory which is the resting place for 99 per cent of movie ideas. He developed a habit of following me around wherever I was filming, always providing entertainment and an excuse for a party.

One weekend, without warning, Mia Farrow turned up. She'd asked John Daly to bring her over from London so that she and I could see each other again to follow up a couple of times we'd met in Los Angeles. Her marriage to Frank Sinatra was on the wane and I think she was wondering what the hell she'd done to get into it. At the same time, the success of *Rosemary's Baby* was bound to have made changes to her life. She was a lovely person, clearly striving to sort herself out, and it was wonderful to see her for the few days she stayed before heading back to London, where she was filming.

When David Bailey came to stay with Penelope Tree and a few other models, I got so excited after a long dinner that I insisted on climbing twenty feet up the wall of the great hall to a large niche where I could sit and play the guitar. It was a hairy climb at the best of times and a typically dangerous caper. Normally I could have done it without mishap, but I was already quite pissed and, when I'd almost reached the spot, I leaned out to grab a sturdy-looking flagpole on which to swing myself the last few feet and it snapped instantly. I crashed down on to my baronial throne and smashed my face.

I found I'd broken a few teeth and one was pushed up through my lip, poisoning my sinuses. Michael and Pat York, who were there too, insisted I went straight to hospital and I ended up sporting a very unattractive mask until my face had healed. It was also clear that my teeth needed serious reconstruction and, in a spirit of maximum cooperation with my director, I alerted my dentist and caught the next plane to London. Clive had no choice but to shoot around me until King Alf was back in business and able to grin without shame some three weeks later.

Living so close to the blue waters of Galway Bay, it was hard to resist the urge to put out to sea now and again, but the castle appeared to possess no suitable vessel. Coming back from the set one day, we were speeding past a little yard with a beautiful open boat for sale.

'Pull in, Danny!' I yelled. 'Let's have a look at that.'

I jumped out, followed by a sceptical Danny, and we went to inspect a fine, old-fashioned clinker-built boat, complete with a new outboard motor.

I turned to the beaming Irishman who owned the yard and was obviously gathering himself up for a serious sales pitch. I grinned as I stole the wind from his sail.

'That's a lovely boat. I'll have it. Send it down to Oranmore Castle as soon as you can, please.'

When we got back from work the next day, our new little craft was bobbing about in the water, tied to a stone jetty at the bottom of the castle walls. I couldn't wait to try it out.

'OK, Danny, get your captain's hat on. We're going to sea.'

'But, H,' he protested, 'we haven't got any fuel.'

'Siphon some from the Roller.'

'No, no. It's got to be two-stroke.'

'Well, there's bound to be some in it anyway. Let's try starting it up.'

With a frankly insubordinate shrug, Danny clambered into the boat and pulled the starter cord. The engine quickly spluttered into life and, within a minute, was singing as sweet as a canary on speed.

'There you are,' I crowed. 'Come on. Let's get this thing out to sea, where it belongs.'

'There's not enough two-stroke,' Danny moaned.

'Of course there is,' I insisted.

We headed out into the bay and I was loving it. The evening sun was gleaming on a quiet sea and a gentle in-shore breeze rippled our hair and the surface of the water; two miles behind us, the castle keep stood majestically and I felt on top of the world, King Alfred of Oranmore. It was a heady fantasy as I proudly surveyed the scene over the steady drone of the outboard motor.

Phut, phut.

Silence, but for the lap of small waves on the clinkered sides and the mewing of gulls high overhead.

For a few moments we drifted, with Danny still perched in the stern, wallowing in Schadenfreude.

'Don't forget you've got Anita and Bill King coming for dinner tonight,' he told me unnecessarily.

I hadn't forgotten. Anita, who had inherited the castle as part of her late father's Castle Leslie Estate, was to be an honoured guest that evening, with her husband Bill, a yachtsman who had twice attempted to sail around the world in the wake of Francis Chichester. We had also asked several other guests, to make something of an event. And here I was, adrift in Galway Bay and getting further from the shore with every minute on the ebbing tide.

'Where are the oars?' I asked.

'Search me,' Danny replied.

This was beginning to look embarrassing. I couldn't swim – I'd never had time to learn – and we really did need to get straight back to the castle.

'I tell you what,' I said with conviction. 'You can swim, Danny. You tie the bowline round your waist, hop in and head for the shore.'

Danny grimaced, but I think he accepted that we hadn't got any other option. With a grunt, he peeled off a few surplus clothes and plopped over the side. A moment later he was scrabbling frantically to clamber back on board.

'Hey, what are you doing?' I called indignantly. 'Get back in!'

'The bloody water's full of jellyfish!' Danny spluttered. 'Get in yourself!'

I peered over the side and he was right. The sea at this point was awash with purple-pink, see-through blancmanges with vicious-looking long tendrils.

'Oh, God,' I groaned. 'We should have brought those oars.'

'So we should,' Danny said with deliberate flatness.

We carried on drifting for a while, not even daring to put our hands in the water to paddle towards the shore, for all the good that would have done.

I was worried that, through my own recklessness, I was going to miss my own dinner party, again. I was jerked from my reverie by Danny yelling his head off.

'Ahoy! Hurry up!'

I looked up and saw with intense relief that Vince had managed to acquire another small boat from somewhere and was heading towards us with, as far as I could see, all our dinner guests on board, including Bill King, the great seafarer. I cringed with shame at our absurd predicament as they drew up beside us and we clambered on board. The little boat rocked precariously.

''Ere, why don't we get back in our boat and you tow us?' Danny suggested.

We tried it, but it seemed that the rescue vessel, small as it was and already loaded to the gunwales, simply didn't have the power. We had to chuck a kedge anchor over the side of our new boat and abandon it until we could come out with some fuel to bring it back.

When dinner was over and all our guests had gone home happily, I couldn't sleep, as usual, but this time I was worrying about my lovely boat, floating around on its own in the bay. I was sure the time to get it was high tide – four in the morning, according to the charts.

At my suggestion, Danny had gone out and got hold of a can of two-stroke during dinner. The boat Vince had borrowed was still outside, tied to the jetty. I looked at my bedside clock, set to ring at six. It was just coming up to four. No time like now, I thought, to go and rescue my boat.

Danny was less enthusiastic when I shook him awake, and even less so when we nosed our way cautiously through a thick dawn mist, but we found the boat eventually, filled the fuel tank, and Danny brought it back. I decreed that it should never be allowed out without the oars. In fact, I'm not sure that it was ever used again at all – at least not by me.

There's no question that *Alfred* was ultimately defeated by the short-comings of the script and, in my view, Clive's uncertain directorship, despite the quality of most of the cast and crew, but it also provided me with one of the most memorable and enjoyable shoots I've ever done and will always have a warm spot in my memory.

13

The Hemdale Years, 1968–1969

In London, what was now known as the Hemdale Group was growing like Jack's beanstalk on steroids. If I felt I was losing control over what was happening, I refused to admit it. I found it incredibly exciting to see this new corporate entity emerge from the first sketchy ideas for the business with which John Daly and I had started it. I felt like the proud father of a baby I had helped to conceive and who was now growing into an independent being with a life and will of its own.

We billed ourselves as:

HEMDALE
A new force in the entertainment industry
Artistes Management/Film Studios
Film Production/Public Relations
Music Publishing/Film Distribution
Property Hire/Merchandising
Finance/Artistes Agency
Travel/Music Recording

In autumn 1968, after I'd been away for months in Ireland, the private company Hemdale was reversed into a small quoted public company called Perben Foods. Before the takeover, Perben's shares were valued at six shillings, with Hemdale valued at £350,000. After the deal had been done and trading in the company (renamed Hemdale) reopened on 14 November, the shares traded at seven shillings and sixpence and rose to ten shillings. I owned 220,000 of them.

I felt quite pleased with myself, having arrived back in London the previous spring with nothing more than my *David Hemmings Happens* money. Of course, I'd been working hard, but I had to acknowledge that John had done an amazing job.

We now found ourselves operating Perben's existing businesses, including a small chain of restaurants called the Golden Chef, in sites as diverse as Hammersmith, Stoke-on-Trent and Preston, and a string of working-men's clubs, big operations in the north of England which had the muscle and the audiences to bring in major stars to perform live for their members.

We soon found we needed a whole lot more management than we had and over the next few months a motley selection was gathered to fill the space. Danny Wiles was shifted sideways from looking after me into running some of the restaurants. My father, still adamantly refusing to acknowledge my fairly obvious progress, had been brought out of retirement to take responsibility for some aspects of the business. I suppose, at the time, I felt that it was a way of showing him that I harboured no ill-feelings for the way he'd treated me over the years, but more likely, perhaps, it was the result of a subconscious desire I'd had all my life to please him and in some way to allay his chastisement.

Needless to say, he never thanked me for giving him this sinecure of a job which, after a series of financial hiccups, he badly needed. Realistically, he was probably a lousy choice, but John agreed and on board he came.

The agency side of the business was booming and, besides Michael York, a lot of other hot, young actors like Peter McEnery had joined, as well as other disparate celebrities such as Jean Shrimpton.

In fact, Jean, a staggeringly beautiful woman who was London's top model before Twiggy appeared, had come to us earlier in the year, at a time when Gayle and I were apart. Naturally, I couldn't resist the chance to take her out and examine her at close quarters. We went out together several times and she even stayed for a short while, but she presented me with a problem I'd not come across before. She was so beautiful and such an icon, I found it almost impossible to perform. No wonder her stay was short (or maybe, once she heard me recycling my own jokes, she thought it time to move on). Since Gayle had been back, of course, apart from the odd blip, I'd been focusing all my attention on her, and I was hoping that, when we got back to Malibu, I might be able to clinch the marriage plan.

Before Danny started working for Hemdale full-time, he came out with us to Malibu and moved into a handy little apartment alongside the house. Gayle seemed happy to be there too, but I still hadn't persuaded her that we really should get married as soon as possible. Whether she still harboured serious doubts or was simply trying to discipline me, I'm not too sure, and she's never told me, but she certainly knew how to create tension in a way that would have impressed Michelangelo Antonioni.

Finally, one night, coming back from a party at Steve McQueen's where I'd been particularly effusive, she told me she now would like us to marry, the sooner the better.

I was, frankly, ecstatic. When I got home, I was so excited I ran straight through the house, through the French windows on the other side, across the terrace, over the beach and plunged into the sea, still wearing the immaculate tuxedo and black tie in which I had started the evening.

When I came out, refreshed but still tingling, I went around to Danny's hutch and hammered on the door. He opened it and blinked blearily at my sodden dinner jacket.

'Come on, Danny, let's have a drink!'

'Wha'for? What's up?'

'We're going to get married! Gayle's said yes.'

'Fantastic!' Danny declared, awake at last. 'That does deserve a drink.'

We drank a toast to Gayle, and me, and marriage, and I asked if he'd help us organise it.

'When do you want to do it?' he asked, suddenly wary.

'Next week?' I ventured.

'Oh, my Gawd! You are 'avin' a laugh, aren't you?'

It was inevitable, given our taste for the flamboyant, that the real wedding, when it finally happened, on 16 November 1968, should be a spectacular and extravagant event.

We soon agreed on a venue when Jack Hanson, who owned the Daisy, offered us his beautiful Beverly Hills mansion, a classic neo-Texan bungalow with an enormous swimming pool and beautiful gardens that fell away down the hill.

Gayle insisted it had to be in the open air and she wandered around for hours before she decided the ideal spot would be the rose garden – a horticultural confection of pink and white, with a wonderful view of the mountains beyond. Pink was to be the dominant theme. That was OK by me; I feel perfectly comfortable with pink.

Danny, with the unwise advice that money was no object, was dispatched to muster most of the things we needed. He'd already learned which buttons to press in Hollywood and he did brilliantly. I don't remember if it was he or I who tracked down the pink-dyed doves that Gayle was so keen to have released after the ceremony, but they were duly delivered, and fluttered off pinkly right on cue.

I couldn't believe the guests who showed up, but the extraordinary thing was that Gayle and I, in our short Hollywood careers, seemed to have made a lot of friends, and they all came along to support us.

Tom Mankiewicz was my best man; Leslie and Evie Bricusse's four-year-old son, Adam, was ring boy; Steve McQueen was an usher; and the Mamas and the Papas sang at the reception.

It's not really possible to judge one's own wedding day from the guests' point of view, but for us it was a beautiful, magical day which neither of us has ever forgotten.

Our first idea for a honeymoon was to go to Peru and take in a few Inca ruins, but Leslie Bricusse persuaded us to come to Acapulco for the film festival. This was an attractive option as Gayle and I both had films being shown – *Marlow* and *The Long Day's Dying* – in the ancient stone fortress where the screenings took place.

The Bricusses had a house in Acapulco and the festival put us up at Las Brisas, where the pinkness of our wedding was reflected in the hotel livery. They even had us flown in from the airport in their pink chopper.

Leslie was busy down there working on *Scrooge* for Albert Finney, but he dropped everything to look after us and gave us a wonderful introduction to Acapulco. We went back and stayed there as often as we could.

It was on a subsequent visit that I witnessed the last word in sartorial correctness. If I hadn't seen it I wouldn't have believed it possible that anyone could be concerned, on aesthetic grounds alone, about what should be worn while dispatching a poisonous snake. But the supremely groomed and famously elegant George Hamilton had a house just below the Bricusses'.

One morning, we were sitting on the deck having breakfast and looking out over the bay – and a lovely view it is – when we saw George come on to the terrace below in a silk dressing gown to sniff the morning air. Suddenly, invisible to us, we heard his wife Alana's shrill, southern tones: 'Sna-ake! George, there's a sna-ake!'

'OK, honey. I'll deal with it.' He walked back in to the house. For a short while, nothing more was heard, until Alana screamed, more shrilly, 'Sna-ake!'

Leslie, intrigued rather than alarmed, got to his feet and picked up the nearest pseudo weapon he could find – a badminton racket. We then scrambled down the hill to find Alana gazing with horror at a small thirty-inch snake with a bright-red head.

'That's a coral snake,' Leslie said. 'Watch out. It could kill you!'

'Ah know!' wailed Alana.

'What's George doing about it?'

'He's gone to change,' Alana said.

As she spoke, Hamilton emerged, handsome and gilded as ever. He was dressed like Stewart Granger in *The Last Safari* in immaculate kit, with long, polished brown boots and knife-edge creases in the trousers. He was putting on a broad-brimmed khaki safari hat, with a tall chocolate and white feather stuck in the band.

He must have seen me looking at it. 'That's an eagle feather,' he explained.

Alana, already seriously alarmed, snapped, 'Fuck the eagle feather! Kill the fucking snake!'

Before George had finished making the final adjustments to his snake-slaying outfit, Leslie had darted across the terrace and whacked the serpent with a vicious back-chop, breaking its neck and his badminton racket.

George shrugged. Now he no longer needed the safari suit, he went back into the house and re-emerged a little later in his dressing gown.

After a couple of weeks in Acapulco, Gayle had to get back to work in LA, leaving me with Leslie and Mia Farrow, who seemed to be spending a lot of time around at the Bricusse house, although she and Frank Sinatra had a house nearby. It seemed that Mia and Frank were no nearer sorting out their marriage than they had been when I'd seen her in Galway earlier in the year. I was enjoying myself – the non-stop party mood of the place appealed to the child in me – and I decided to stay on for a few more days.

There was a big party to mark the end of the film festival, after which it was my turn to introduce the others to the Donkey Club. This was a fairly weird establishment which you could have felt you'd fallen into by mistake while on some hallucinogenic drug (or so I'm told). There was a dancing cabaret performed by some amazing girls, and an MC who looked just like Laurence Olivier in *The Entertainer*.

I was by then very drunk indeed and felt I'd like to talk to this chap. I climbed up on to the stage, to find that he'd gone, so I settled for a short stint in the chorus line. This was going quite well, until we struck out on to an apron walkway that projected into the audience. In an effort to earn the girls' approval with my ability to high-kick, I lost my balance and tumbled off the podium and on to a table of frankly ungracious men from Red-Neck, Tennessee. They were utterly unconcerned that I appeared to have done some serious damage to my back.

But I made it back to my table, where Leslie, Mia and I sat around thinking up headlines for the papers next day. Later, they carted me back up to Las Brisas in one of the pink Jeeps they supply to residents.

For a few months after our wedding and Acapulcomoon, we settled down to life in the Malibu Colony. On the whole, the glamorous residents of this bizarre community were very welcoming. We saw Deborah Kerr and Peter Viatell next door on a regular lunchtime basis, when I would feed Gayle's new dogs, which were to feature large in our lives for many years, on the table. They were Yorkshire terriers, very young pups, whose mother had a milk disorder, so I had to feed them with milk through an eye-dropper. One dog fell off the table and I had to rush it to the vet, who was famous in Malibu for being the kindest vet you could ever meet. Yorkie pups are so small – about the size of my forearm – we spent most of the night until four in the morning trying to find a vein in which to put adrenalin. We managed it, and the pup grew up to be the largest Yorkie I've ever seen.

The vet, Jack Forsom, became an important influence on me and, although I haven't seen him for years, hardly a week would go by when I wasn't reminded of what he taught me. He would take in birds with broken wings or that had somehow been damaged, or dogs that had been run over by trucks, and he would put each bone together. Over the next year, when I was in California, I used to go to work with him every day I could. He was as kind to me as I was subservient to him and I absorbed a lot of useful knowledge about everything, from dogs and cats to racoons and seagulls. I was very fond of animals and I enjoyed it.

For about two years before he arrived in Malibu, Jack had lived out in the woods, in a cave in the Northern Rockies. To begin with, he stayed there, absorbing the atmosphere and living the simple life, but he started holding a sort of vet's clinic in the cave he had partially prepared for himself.

Extraordinarily, one morning a bear sloped in with a bleeding paw. He allowed Jack to pull out a great splinter from his paw and the bear, three times his size, limped off back into the forest. After that, for the next year, in his little nest miles from anywhere, animals used to come and he would treat them – a fawn's broken leg; a racoon with a busted jaw; a coyote with gunshot wounds. They just used to pitch up on their own and settle down beside him, as if word had got out that there was this guy who could actually look after you, and he treated them and looked after them. He had gone to the forest because he wanted to be among nature and, somehow, nature understood. He was a remarkable man and I loved working with him.

I had of course kept in contact with most of my Hollywood playmates from the previous year, and for Christmas Leslie Bricusse asked us up to his house in Beverly Hills, where Mia Farrow was now staying. A week after Christmas Leslie and Tom Mankiewicz provided me with one of the great treats of my life when they and Nancy Sinatra took me with them to the Capitol Studios, where her father was going to record what was expected to be his next big hit.

The musician in me was jumping at the prospect. As it happened, I'd met Frank once or twice with Mia, but I'd not heard him sing live.

When we reached the famous circular studios, I realised it wasn't a matter of 'OK, Frank, we've done the backing track, now get your cans on, get in the booth and lay your vocals over it.' There was a hundred-piece orchestra assembled and Frank was going to stand in front, working with them. This was a full, live performance I was going to see.

Frank turned up, not talkative that morning, and wearing a trilby, you'll be amazed to learn. He walked up to the mike and, once the orchestra had started, he was effectively conducting them, although phrasing his own voice as always a long way behind the beat. Sinatra's strength was that he could fall off the back of a melody and still keep it together, spreading a song, as an actor might (and Frank was a good actor too).

The first take was superb, utterly magnificent; it was hard not to get down and worship. But it wasn't good enough for Frank. 'No,' he said. 'I want to do it again.'

He recorded the song a second time, this time with the great swoop, an octave and half, without a stop or a breath between the phrases 'I did it my way' and 'Regrets, I've had a few'.

It was a spellbinding moment, and I still can't hear this – the definitive version, at the birth of which I was present – without a serious shiver up my spine.

Even the orchestra, every one of them, couldn't help a spontaneous reaction. Musos generally, when in character, are not known for being the most charming people and don't normally grovel, but this time they prostrated themselves and gave Frank a prolonged standing ovation. He acknowledged it with a curt nod and stalked out of the studio. I was tingling for hours afterwards and wasn't in the least surprised that 'My Way' went on to be indisputably Sinatra's greatest song.

In one of those bizarre coincidences, 35 years later I found myself playing the part of Sinatra's manager, Mickey Rudin, to Dennis Hopper's Sinatra in an Australian film called *The Night We Called It a Day*, based on the true story of a disastrous tour of Australia Frank made in 1974.

At this distance in time, and at a stage in my life when I have finally discovered the emotional and practical benefits of fidelity, it's hard to see how I let myself drift so easily into affairs with other women. Usually, I suppose, it was a matter of convenience, or judgement impaired by booze and a penchant for the line of least resistance.

When I came back to England in early 1969 to make *The Walking Stick* with Samantha Eggar, Gayle stayed in Los Angeles to follow up some projects there. Living on my own in London, in Grosvenor Crescent Mews, my profile was higher than ever, thanks to *Charge* and Nigel Hutchinson's skills as a publicist, and I quickly dropped back into my old routine of clubbing and playing, while working hard at the studios.

The Walking Stick required many days of filming, sometimes intimately, with Sam, and Sam was a very alluring lady. Of course, I knew her, quite well, from my first days in LA. She was at a loose end and we spent a lot of time together; it was almost inevitable, in the absence of a little woman at home, that we should end up in bed, and quite often.

Once again, I justified my behaviour on the grounds that as long as Gayle didn't know she wouldn't be hurt and no harm would come of it. OK – I don't do discretion very well, but Gayle was in Malibu.

When my beautiful new wife joined me in London, she had, she said, heard an inkling of a rumour about me and Sam. I tried to reassure her – I think successfully – and when I was with Gayle, I was determined not to continue what I'd started with Sam.

Blow-Up

We decided it would be a treat to head off to the country for a romantic weekend in the Lake District to clear the air. Gayle was very excited; she spent hours packing, with everything matching, and we drove away in a little blue drop-head Merc I'd bought her for a wedding present – known as Molly the Merc. We found an idyllic pub where we ordered lunch, when, for some reason – a kind of inverted guilt – I felt I ought to phone Samantha. I told Gayle I needed to contact the studios and went off in search of a phone.

The pub was a bit of a labyrinth but eventually I found a pay-phone and was soon reassuring Sam that I would see her soon and – well, you know – I didn't want to hurt her either. That was always a problem for me – I hated upsetting people, or saying 'no', and in the end usually caused far more damage than I would have done if I'd said 'no' in the first place.

What I didn't know was that the call box was right next to the table where I'd left Gayle, with about a quarter of an inch of cracked oak panelling between us. When I got back to our table, Gayle was looking at me, pale and quivering, as if she'd seen a multitude of particularly aggressive ghosts. I wondered what on earth was wrong with her.

'David,' she tried to whisper, then gave up, as if she'd been struck dumb. She was trembling uncontrollably and tears were beginning to steal down her cheeks. She picked up a paper napkin and wrote on it: 'I heard every word you said. Just take me back to London.'

I felt the blood drain from my face – it was an alarming sensation. I had been caught, as it were, bang to rights, and yet I hadn't meant everything I'd said to Sam; I was just trying not to upset her.

But Gayle, I could see, was utterly devastated.

Silently we went back to the car and I aimed it down the old A6 to London. Without looking at me again, Gayle curled up in the well of the passenger seat and cried for the six hours it took to get home. At least she'd found her voice again. She kept whimpering, 'Why? I don't understand why,' over and over again.

I was full of remorse.

Gayle still had few friends in London and there was no one she could turn to for support. She also came from a frankly strait-laced background, conservative and monogamous. Her father was an old-fashioned honourable man and she simply had no way of dealing with this kind of situation.

I was determined to sort it out as best I could. But I was still working with Samantha. When it came to it, it wasn't so easy just to turn it off.

After a few days back on the set at Elstree we were doing the auction scene as a two-shot. Derek Till was directing. Vince Fleming, my stand-in, was hanging around by the door and saw my Rolls-Royce drift into view, with Gayle in the passenger seat.

He rushed in to warn me, 'David, David . . .' But it was too late.

Gayle walked straight into the middle of the two-shot in front of an entire crew poised for action and turned to confront Sam. 'I understand you're having an affair with my husband. I think we should talk.' And she went on to tell her, as the Texans say, 'how the cows eat the cabbage', and how she wasn't just an actress, she was also a Regent Scholar at UCLA. It was fair enough. She was very frightened and lonely and needed to assert herself in any way she could. She made a good job of it too.

The entire crew cracked up, because it was a bold and brilliant move. I couldn't fault her for having the guts to do that in front of an entire crew and 200 extras.

When she'd finished with Sam, we went back to my caravan, where we sat and talked for hours. Gayle felt that, while filming went on, I was trapped in a relationship with my co-star; it would always be like that and she couldn't take it.

It wasn't easy for me to face up to this obvious truth; it was not a pleasant moment.

Sam and I broke up, although we've been good friends ever since and I still love her to pieces, in a platonic way. She became my lucky charm; I've included her in a lot of projects and she's always done well for me.

We were able to put Samantha and *The Walking Stick* behind us while we moved to a new flat among the tree tops in Ennismore Gardens and made plans for *Fragment of Fear*, in which we were acting together for the first time, a lot of it on location in Italy around Sorrento.

This welcome interlude in the summer of 1969 was interrupted by various mishaps, not least when a tube train which had been hired to make a scene in the film crashed into the buffers and I lunged across the carriage to try to stop Gayle from flying through a glass door. Gayle was knocked out and she, I and ten extras were taken to hospital. She had bruised her face a little and I aggravated an ankle already knackered from playing baseball in Hyde Park. The result of this was that, for the royal première of *Alfred the Great*, I turned up on crutches, which evoked a characteristically sardonic reaction from Prince Philip.

The following month, on 9 August 1969, a far more sinister event shook the world, and Hollywood in particular, when the hippie Charles Manson and his 'family' broke into the house in Malibu which Roman Polanski shared with his new wife, Sharon Tate, who was eight months pregnant, and murdered her.

I had, of course, known Sharon for several years and I was very fond of her; we'd shared our first big picture, *The Eye of the Devil*, and I'd been to see her and Roman in the very house, just a month or two before. It was horrible to know that she'd died the way she had, and that I could conceivably have been there when it happened. The event left a nasty chill for the next few months, and I still think what a great loss it was that Sharon died when she had a hell of a lot yet to give.

I was able to commiserate with friends at first hand when we went back to the States for a while that summer. Leslie Bricusse asked us out to Palm Springs with George and Alana Hamilton, and while I was lounging around by the pool there I took a call from London, confirming preliminary arrangements for the first film I intended to produce myself, and there, lying beneath the waving fronds, I felt that the next phase in my career was about to begin.

But because of that trip to Palm Springs, I might never have made it back. George had announced one evening that he didn't want to go to bed late because he had to be up early for his first flying lesson. I leaped at the idea. More than anything else on earth, I suddenly wanted to be able to fly. George went, Leslie went, eventually, and they left me, half-cut, sitting there fantasising about flight.

George had brought down all his flying manuals and left them with me. I didn't go to bed or to sleep that night. I sat up until George reappeared, by which time I'd read every page of the manuals, several times over. I was confident now that I had the theory of the thing completely wrapped up.

'Can I come with you?' I asked George.

'Sure, if you want.' He obviously didn't think I'd get a lot out of it, but I really wanted to see if my reading of the theory was right.

We drove out to the airport where the little trainer (the plane, not the chap) was waiting. Soon the instructor appeared and said he'd be happy to take me up for the ride.

Once we were up – and it was my first ever trip in a small aircraft – I soon realised that George, skilled though he was in other areas, was not really pilot material. He'd been given the controls, but it was clear to me that he was beginning to panic. I thought if he stayed with the joystick very much longer, we might find ourselves in a terminal dive. Sensing an opening, I asked if I could fly the machine for a bit.

The instructor agreed and I took over. Much to my delighted astonishment, I found the *actualité* seemed to match the theory, and within a few minutes I was happily flying the craft on my own. The instructor was pleasingly complimentary and George pleasingly disgruntled, although at least I wasn't allowed to land it, and we all lived.

14

The End of the Sixties

Over the few years of Hemdale's existence, we had diversified hugely and involved ourselves in a frankly absurd range of activities, some profitable, some barking mad, most to some extent entertaining and, in the case of Henri la Motte, all three.

Until its sad demise a couple of years ago, booking Wembley Stadium for an event was a traditional and popular act of entrepreneurial machismo. We had hired it to promote an appearance of Evel Knievel, in which the bikerobat would leap an uncountable quantity of red double-decker buses in pursuit of a new world record, with live commentary by Ed 'Stewpot' Stewart. To fill the stadium's 100,000 seats at a worthwhile price, we knew we had to offer something more than just Evel. We let it be known around the world of random entertainment that we were searching for acts and, on very strong recommendation, booked one completely unseen.

The day before the event, we were getting worried that we hadn't even established what equipment this act required, although we'd been told they would bring all they needed with them. Around lunchtime, our receptionist announced that two strange characters had come to see us. They were ushered into the office, each with a large pack on his back and carrying a bulky, battered canvas holdall.

One was a tiny bruiser who could have been anything between 65 and 85, with rosy cheeks, massive biceps and motionless blue eyes; the other looked twice his height, with a long, limp moustache, a ten-gallon hat and a voice like a scrap-metal truck on a stony road.

'Good morning, sirs. Zees eez Henri la Motte and I am 'is manager.'

John and I gazed at the bizarre duo, enchanted and united in our fascination.

'Hello.' I nodded. 'Just remind me. What do you do?'

'Henri la Motte, he jump 'ead first from a tower of 150 foots into six inch of water.'

I leaned back, trying not to laugh at an appalling vision of this tiny little old man diving 150 feet headfirst into a puddle. I held my hands six inches apart. 'Are you sure you mean six inches?' I asked doubtfully, but not wanting them to deny it now.

The manager nodded vigorously.

'And what equipment do you have?'

The tall man nodded over his shoulder at his backpack and kicked the holdall on the ground beside him.

'But what about the tower?'

Henri moved for the first time since he'd come in. He leaned down a few inches to unzip his bag, pulled out a section of bright steel tube and quickly fumbled out a short, thin strut, which he slipped through a pair of holes in the tube. He held it upright and put one foot on the strut and mimed the action of scaling the narrow shaft hand over hand.

'For 150 feet?' I gasped.

'Of course.' Henri spoke for the first time in guttural Gauloise.

We hadn't filled Wembley Stadium, but there was a respectable crowd gathered to watch the diverse selection of acts we had assembled. We had billed Henri la Motte as the penultimate event, to precede Evel's flight across the buses.

The 60,000 punters, ranging from small girls in pigtails to wrinkled old gritters in leather jerkins with Harley-Davidson wings tattooed on their biceps, had not been excessively appreciative of what they'd been offered so far. There was a faintly discontented murmur among them as Henri's manager assembled a small blue plastic pond – something like a kids' paddling pool – at the base of an implausibly spindly metal shaft, anchored by six guy ropes and topped with a tiny platform. The pool's sides consisted of six panels held together by Velcro straps and was ceremoniously filled with water to a depth of six inches.

I sat beside Stewpot in the commentary booth, gazing at the scene with disbelief and a stomach churning with more butterflies than I'd ever experienced before going on stage myself. What Henri la Motte proposed looked utterly impossible and I was having terrible guilt pangs at ever having booked this hara-kiri madman.

But it was too late to do anything about it and, at a nod from me, Stewpot leaned in to the mike.

'And now, all the way from the French Riviera, in an unbelievable display of death-defying skill and bravery. Henri la Motte will dive 150 feet into six inches of water. Ladies and gentlemen, Henri la Motte!'

From the famous Wembley tunnel emerged a tiny figure clad in a silver lamé cape which swept the ground behind him, and a red, white and blue body stocking. He strutted across the turf to the tower, stopped and bowed extravagantly to the four points of the compass, while the cynical rumbling of the audience became an incredulous murmur.

I looked from the little fellow to the platform perched at the top of the pole. It seemed to me the first challenge would be getting Henri to his platform. But Henri displayed no such misgivings as he swept off his cape with a showman's flourish and discarded it carelessly beside his pool – his imminent resting place, it seemed to me – and began his ascent of the pole.

As he neared the top, his rate of climb decreased; so did the noise of the crowd. By the time he stabbed a short leg over the side of the platform, with what looked to me in my now paranoid state very much like an arthritic jerk, the whole stadium was in silence, apart from the odd bellow of 'Come on, 'enry!'

Henri pulled himself up and stood with his short legs apart as the pole quivered under his minuscule weight. I could hardly look at the tiny pool below him. It seemed quite absurd to expect him to land in it at all, let alone live afterwards.

I'd wanted to provide our expectant punters with a spectacle, of course, but not a public suicide – a snuff act. And besides, would we be liable if he did kill himself? Were we adequately insured? Would we be deemed accessories after the act?

Henri was displaying amazing confidence in his own indestructibility. He spent a moment or two acknowledging his audience, crossed himself, lifted himself on his toes and, to an excited female squeal from somewhere in the crowd, dropped headfirst from the platform.

There was a loud gasp from the crowd.

Immediately Henri bent his torso up into the traditional shape of a swallow dive. In the few seconds it took to reach the ground he became almost horizontal, and hit the middle of the pool in an absolute belly-flop. The six panels that composed the side of the pool burst open and flattened to the turf as the few gallons of water in it were dispersed over them.

I hadn't breathed for several seconds. I still didn't when I looked at Henri's homuncular frame prostrate and unmoving in the wreck of the pond.

'Shit!' I managed to whisper, struck by the appalling thought that if Henri was brown bread, we couldn't really put Evel Knievel on and all the punters would want their money back.

A second later, the tricoloured leprechaun had sprung to his feet and the audience erupted into wild cheers of wonderment, relief and sheer admiration at Henri's display of courage and bravado. I was never strong on physics, but it seemed that somehow the water, provided it was able to disperse under pressure, had broken his fall as effectively as a three-foot cushion.

I can't even remember Evel Knievel's act now. Whatever he did, after Henri's spectacular feat, it was a complete anticlimax. And I haven't seen or heard of Henri la Motte since.

This side of working with John was always entertaining, but, although I wouldn't have owned up to it, I was beginning to find my role in Hemdale fairly nebulous. John used to try to make me feel important by letting me announce various developments in the business, even when I wasn't entirely clear of the details. It was only later that I realised, rather naïvely, that he'd been using me as hack bait, not altogether unreasonably. He had always said the value of my presence (apart from generating funds) was as the organisation's front man.

I was, as I'd been since Hemdale's inception, spending a lot of my time when I wasn't working on films at the South Street offices. It was from there that I conducted my social life, as I continued to lunch most days at the White Elephant or Tiberio's, but I was reminded sharply of a past which I'd let myself overlook when my first wife, Genny, rang me out of the blue and I invited her up for dinner. I introduced her to John, of whom she clearly disapproved, and took her out to discuss my daughter, Debs, who was now seven, although I hadn't seen her since she was two. After going round in circles for a while, we decided at that stage there was no point in my getting involved, but I felt wretched about it afterwards, and for many years until, finally, thank God, Debs and I did meet up again.

My relationship with my business partners wasn't going well either. Somehow everything I did seemed not to fit in with John's vision of what Hemdale was about. He resented my drawing any more than the minimum of my earnings that poured into the company. Derek Dawson was John's man, not mine, and I could make no impact on him. To make matters worse, my father, whom I'd originally asked in specifically to keep an eye on my interests in the company while I was away filming, seemed always to side with John and Derek in any disagreements. Our internal squabbles were reported in the papers, the financial pages and the gossip columns, to such an extent that the next time I appeared on the *Simon Dee Show*, that ambitious though genial halfwit asked me, 'So what's the story on Hemdale? Is it true that everything isn't sweetness and light?'

'God, please don't ask me about Hemdale!' I responded with, I thought, an admirable display of discretion.

The next day, the share price was halved. I lost, on paper, a great deal of money; and so did John. He wasn't happy. Derek Dawson publicly announced that there was absolutely no problem, but it seemed there wasn't a lot we could do to repair the damage.

As it happened, Simon Dee paid heavily for asking indelicate questions and was drummed out of his high-profile though increasingly slippery slot. Soon after my interview, he disappeared from our television screens and sank almost completely out of sight, only to reappear a few years later in a piece in a gossip column, which revealed that he was living in the basement of Billy Murphy's shop, the Emperor of Wyoming, at the bottom end of the King's Road. The shot accompanying the piece showed a man seriously undernourished and carrying a good covering of stubble. He was barely recognisable as the chirpy presence who had for several years epitomised the spirit of the sixties on television, poor chap.

The following year, 1970, after a business relationship that had lasted barely three years, John and I parted company. There were several reasons.

Hemdale had been set up primarily as a tax-shelter company. In the old days of socialist ideology (before pragmatic socialism arrived on the wings of a Blair) income tax had been allowed to rise as high as 98 per cent. Hemdale's big idea was based on clients buying into the company through a plan for converting income to loan stock. But another similar operation, Constellation, were tactless enough to blaze their success across the papers – even naming their clients – and HM Inspectors of Taxes didn't enjoy having their faces rubbed in the loophole (if you'll excuse the mixed metaphor) in a piece in the *Evening Standard*.

A new ruling was included in the next Finance Act, 'Thou shalt not transfer income into capital', and the Inland Revenue were able to stop the gap. From that point of view, Hemdale had lost a substantial part of its *raison d'être*. However, John was unconcerned; he'd already moved on and set his sights, ultimately, on film production. I also wanted to run my own life. I had a number of friends in the City and for a while I looked at ways of taking the company over myself. In the end, I was left with no option but to take my money out of Hemdale, after John and Derek had deducted what they claimed I'd already had.

It was a messy, unseemly business, rather like and in some ways worse than a divorce. This was exacerbated by quite unnecessary behaviour on their part.

On one supremely embarrassing occasion, Brian Cook and I, with Gayle and Brian's wife, Pat, were in the Rolls on the way to see one of the greyhounds run at White City. I pulled in to fill up at the garage in Park Lane where I'd had an account for years, only to discover that the account had been closed by Hemdale. After that I found various credit accounts and charge cards had been summarily terminated without any reference to me. The repercussions of this went on for some time and two years later even the laundry Gayle had used for years shuffled their feet and admitted that they hadn't been paid since John and I had split up.

Since then, of course, large quantities of murky water have flowed under Albert Bridge; our earlier relationship and shared adventures in south London, Toby's gym and Chateau Marmont overrode our differences, and inevitably we became good friends again.

Hemdale went on to create a new investment and tax scheme for actors, SIFA (Secured Income for Artists). In time John also fulfilled his ambition to produce movies and for a dozen years Hemdale was a recognised presence in the industry, in Britain and the States, with a hand in a string of big films like *Terminator* and *The Last Emperor*.

For my part, I was trying to see my career in terms of directing rather than acting and was putting out feelers wherever I could. As an actor, there always seemed to be several jobs in view, most prominently Stanley Kubrick's Napoleon picture.

From the start, Stanley showed great interest in casting me in the title role. His developing script – what he let me see of it – suggested that it would be up to the extraordinary standards of all his previous work, and I felt it could be the big, serious part which I badly wanted after the disappointment of *Alfred the Great*.

I spent a lot of time with Stanley in the famous seclusion of his house in Hertfordshire. After our first meeting, he dispatched a large pile of books on Napoleon to my address and summoned me back the next day to discuss them, before sending me away with another great pile. We talked exhaustively about Napoleon and how he should be presented, but I spent almost as much time playing ping-pong with him and teaching him magic tricks, which he loved.

Stanley had a truly eccentric mind, which, I suppose, was fundamental to his vision and genius. He also had an astonishing capacity to absorb, analyse and retain information, and he expected people around him to do the same. It could be very exhausting but was always stimulating. It was, for me, a tragedy when *Waterloo* was released that year, with Rod Steiger's powerful and convincing performance as the little general, although it was completely at odds with what I had intended. Naturally, although you'd have thought that anyone would know Stanley's version of Bonaparte would be quite different, his studio developed severe cold feet about the project and pulled the rug on it. It is on a foundation of others' such whims and misjudgements that movie careers are constructed.

With the intention of taking control of my own future this time, I formed a new film production company with two friends, Gareth Wigan and Stanley O'Toole. The company, Wigan Hemmings O'Toole, rented offices on the first floor of a Slater Walker building at 39 Charing Cross Road and set up a project to make a picture called *Unman, Wittering and Zigo*, adapted by Simon Raven from a wonderful play by Giles Cooper.

As well as producing the film, I had the lead part in it. It was about a boys' school, which we set in North Wales (with a hint of Llanabba Castle). I play a young master who has just arrived at the school full of enthusiasm, but the pupils turn out to be something like the kids in *The Midwich Cuckoos* and my character's predecessor has committed suicide by throwing himself off the cliffs. It transpires that this is the boys' preferred method of disposing of people they didn't like. In the end, my character is carried to the edge of the cliffs and thrown over.

It was a short play but it made a very good film, a little like *If* . . . and was well directed by John Mackenzie, who also went on to make the excellent *Long Good Friday*.

*

Before we'd finalised arrangements for *Unman*, I'd also been offered a part in a film about Rimbaud, to be made on location in Ethiopia. To our great delight, Gayle had become pregnant in the new year and I asked if she would rather go to Ethiopia or North Wales.

Perhaps not surprisingly, she opted for Wales, and we went up to live there while I was making the film. The place we'd been allocated was a modern, suburban house in Llandudno and absolutely not up to Gayle's standards, so she promptly hired a taxi and headed for the hills. In a very pretty valley at Llanrwst, near Betws-y-Coed, she spotted a lovely place called Maenin Abbey farm. On spec, she knocked on the door to find that it was owned by a family called Vaughan. She asked if they knew of a house in the area which we could rent for six months. The Vaughans told her they'd just done up an old stable block, and they would quite happily move in to that and let us have the farmhouse.

I have very fond memories of our time in Wales. There was a good crowd on the production and Danny Wiles, who had left Hemdale by then, came back to drive for me. With Gayle being heavily pregnant, I did find myself inadvertently enmeshed in a dalliance with our female art director, which caused some complications and a few clothes to be thrown out of windows, but I was just as excited about the arrival of our first child.

On 23 September Danny came in a panic to find me to say that Gayle had been taken to the cottage hospital in St Asaph and was about to have the baby. I raced back to find our new son had already been born, delivered by Dr Parry Jones. Vince Fleming and Mike Guest, our second assistant director, were already gathered around Gayle's bed when I reached the hospital.

It was a long time since I'd been involved with babies at close quarters and I realised I would find it hard to make the necessary adjustments to my life, although I was determined to. We decided to name the boy Nolan, after my character in *Charge*, and we set about letting everyone know. An unexpected early visitor was my father, who seemed prepared at last to accept Gayle now that she'd produced a grandchild. My mother of course was thrilled, and they said they would come up and stay for a couple of days.

But if my father was as pleased as he'd said on the phone, he didn't show it once he arrived in Wales. All through Sunday afternoon after a lunch, with a happy buzzing crowd filling the house, he sat in an armchair, looking as if there was a nasty smell under his nose, while he unravelled a large ball of knotted string he'd found. For three hours, he didn't raise his eyes and would only answer with a nod or a grunt.

I found myself wondering, as I had hundreds of times before, what it was that made him so prickly, so uptight and cheerless. Although I was very happy to see Mum, I'm afraid I wasn't the least bit sorry to see the back of my father when they left.

In 1971 I got my first chance to direct a full-scale feature film, *Running Scared*. I wasn't going to act in it, but Gayle was, and our first choice for the male lead was an up-and-coming actor a few years younger than me called Robert Powell. I didn't know Robert then, but I'd been impressed by what he'd done on television. He came round to see Gareth and me at Charing Cross Road and we decided give him the part before he'd left.

I think, even then, Robert and I recognised that we shared a lot in common. Among other things, we were both highly competitive, particularly when it came to bar billiards, snooker and darts. In fact, over the years we worked together, if ever we found a game that involved one person competing against another, we tried it. It was that recognition of one another's nature that first attracted us to each other.

Robert was one of the few people who consistently beat me at most pub games, and he admitted that for a while he'd had to earn his living from pool, playing at his local in Hampstead – a hustler, as well as a pub darts champion.

We both liked pubs too. There is a wonderful levelling effect about an English pub – a home from home that means you could be the biggest star in the world, but if you don't respect the egalitarianism of the local, you won't be accepted as part of that special, warm coterie.

When it came to directing a film, I thought I knew a lot more about the job than I did in practice. Nevertheless, I learned quickly.

Some of the location work on *Running Scared* was done at the great canal junction at Braunston, which implanted in me a love of waterways that I've never lost. Indeed, only a short while ago I found myself with great delight appearing on a TV documentary about our own local canal, the Kennet and Avon.

I also loved all the technical challenges thrown up in making a movie: devising ways of achieving illusion required the same mind-set as creating magic tricks, which meant that film-making was like indulging in a favourite hobby and being paid for it.

Telling actors and actresses (in this case my wife) what to do was also a new challenge. Gayle, of course, was as compliant as you'd expect a red-blooded, independent Texan girl to be, but we got there in the end. With Robert, I found I had the most tremendous rapport. After a take, I didn't need to say anything; I'd simply give him a look, he would nod, and we'd do it again, as if he understood instinctively what I was looking for and what he hadn't delivered. After two or three takes, I'd nod, and we'd move on. It was really curious, and somehow incredibly life-affirming, to feel so close to an actor you're working with.

In London, with Nolan becoming a little boy instead of just a blob, Gayle was working as hard as I was. She had been asked to star in a major six-part BBC TV adaptation of Henry James's *The Golden Bowl* – a superb part which she played with strength and beauty, working again with Barry Morse, who'd been with us on *Running Scared*.

But she'd also found time to throw herself into the English social scene and life had become a long string of parties, grand dinners and weekends in Woburn Abbey (where I'd made *Five Clues to Fortune* about twenty years before). In fact, one of our closer friends, Lord Plunket, who was Nolan's godfather, was also an equerry to the Queen. I met the Queen through him, and other members of the royal family at various royal premières, and was occasionally asked to lunch at Buckingham Palace. Once, with the Queen, the Duke of Edinburgh, David Gentleman, whose paintings I love, Patrick Plunket and Arnold Weinstock, I found myself sitting next to Princess Anne, whom I found, if it isn't treasonous to say so, surprisingly alluring.

It was Patrick who arranged that we should be on the inaugural flight into the new airport on Mahé in the Seychelles, when Her Majesty was there to perform its official opening. The Seychelles were for most practical purposes unknown until then; there had been no planes flying in and it took weeks to get there by sea. I was also asked to produce a documentary about the event and the islands suddenly finding themselves with a gateway to the rest of the world. Once there, I made preparations for the royal visit and the official airport opening. I organised the whole tour and worked out the route so I was able to film it to best effect.

Blow-Up

The Queen stayed on board the magnificent old royal yacht *Britannia* while she was there and Gayle and I were invited for a reception. We set out in a launch behind the Seychellois prime minister, Jimmy Mancham, and were greeted with great cheers from the crew. I met the prime minister, who was very encouraging about all the plans that were already surging through my head.

I adored the Seychelles on sight – the lush tropical vegetation and sublime white beaches; the people, physically beautiful and as yet uncorrupted. I was totally seduced by the archipelago and started an affair with the place much as I might have done with a woman – an affair which was to last a year or two and which still lingers warmly in my memory.

Gayle loved the beauty of the islands, but the remoteness didn't entirely appeal to her. This wasn't improved when she discovered she had an allergy to coral and couldn't swim in the sea. But it was too late; she developed a nasty ear infection and went home before me. She needed to get back anyway to start work on *The Golden Bowl*.

Returning from the Seychelles with some regret, I promised myself I would go back as soon as I could and develop some of the ideas I'd had about what could be done there. In the meantime, I went straight into the thick of business with three new projects in hand and a new music management company I'd formed, always eager to retain a connection with an activity that I loved.

To help out at Wigan Hemmings O'Toole and Marzius Music, I recruited a new secretary, Prudence de Casembroot, whose credentials were impeccable. She had been a publicist at MCA records, where she'd met the talented and likeable Tim Rice. She'd become deeply involved with him and they'd lived together for a couple of years while he was writing *Jesus Christ, Superstar*.

Despite her Dutch surname (which means 'cheese and bread'), Prue was an English upper-crust girl in the classic mould. She wasn't as striking as Gayle and nor did she possess her iconic beauty, but she was unquestionably attractive, with soft, humorous brown eyes and long, fine dark hair. In addition, she brought to the office an infectious air of efficiency and fun. She had an absolutely natural flair for getting quite boring tasks done as if they were the most exciting things that had ever happened to her. As a man who has always had great difficulty with dreary details, it was a big relief to me to have someone I could rely on totally to look after them. And as can often happen when a woman sets out to make herself indispensable to a man, gratitude turned to affection, especially when this paragon also possessed an impressive pair of well-sculpted breasts.

I can't make any excuses for the affairs I had all through my life until I met my current love, Lucy, but I think, finally, I understand the reasons.

Of course, no man, however faithfully he might run his marriage, would deny that the idea of sleeping with another woman occurs to him fairly regularly, and I have been no exception, but more than that I have always loved women's company, and the very business of flirtation I find incredibly stimulating, almost like a drug. In addition, as a result of my slightly odd childhood, I've always wanted to please people and loved the idea of romantic relationships.

I know, of course, that over the years the damage and upset that my philandering has caused probably outweigh the joy I (and, I hope, my various partners) derived from my relationships. But at the time, as they occurred, I simply never had any choice; and that's the truth.

And so it was with Prue. It was only when I asked if she could come with me, as my secretary, on my second visit to the Seychelles in early 1972 that I slept with her. Frankly, beneath the waving palms and within earshot of the lapping Indian Ocean, there was absolutely no option.

I was out on Mahé again with a pleasingly assorted bunch of individuals. On the one hand, there was a small film crew, who were to help me complete my documentary on the islands, and, in addition, a pair of businessmen I'd met and with whom I hoped to buy some land on the archipelago. In fact, I had in mind to buy a whole island, North Island, which, as its name suggests, lay above Mahé, beyond the island of Silhouette.

Richard Syme was an adventurer who had ridden to England from Spain a few years before and had somehow persuaded the Seychelles government that he was the right man to report on the scope for commercial land deals there. I was put together with him, and he in turn, at a memorable meeting at somebody's house in Wilton Crescent, introduced me to the impeccably suave William O'Shei.

William was a property developer at the time, buying houses by the dozen in east London, doing them up and trading them on, and, by the look of it, doing very well indeed from it. In the early 1970s, property dealing was a very popular occupation among members of the upper middle classes who in former times might have been soldiers or vicars. At dinner parties you'd often meet people who had some old warehouses or derelict dockland buildings that they were busily trying to sell on, without there necessarily being a real end user for them.

It reminded me of the black marketeer who, after the war, was charged with selling orange juice so old that it was no longer safe to drink. The judge castigated him for purveying a product that might have caused serious illness to anyone who consumed it.

The defendant protested indignantly, 'But, m'lud, that juice was never for your akshul *drinking*. It was jus' for buyin' and sellin'.'

Of course, when the music stopped on that particular boom, an awful lot of people were still holding parcels of property that nobody wanted and caught terminal colds as a result. Not William, I'm glad to say, who had by then become a great friend.

We flew out to Victoria in the Seychelles together – Prue and I, William and his wife, Joy (forever known as Joybells), with dancing blue eyes, blonde hair and the longest legs I've ever seen. Also aboard was Harvey Herman, working on the report for the Seychelles government, who for some reason had a false ear, and Harvey Harrison, my cameraman and a great character, whose own front teeth were missing as the result of filming in a small plane as it crashed. By the time we stopped to refuel in Nairobi, they were known, for convenience, as Harvey 'the ear' and Harvey 'the tooth'.

Since air travel was still something of a novelty in Mahé, there was quite a crowd of locals gathered to see our plane land. We were met by a Major Christopher Bonn – a man best described as enigmatic – whom I had asked to help coordinate the purchase of North Island, which William, Richard and I had agreed to buy as a syndicate. I was booked into a charming hotel called the Northolme, where I managed to bag the best room, right at the top, which was known as the Crow's Nest. Also staying at the hotel was a man who ultimately, I suppose, had been my landlord in various of the London flats I'd lived in – Lord Chelsea, better known as Charlie, who shared a good few sun-downers (and sun-zenithers, for that matter) with us.

When we were all unpacked and ready, we met up for a few drinks with Charlie on a palm-shaded terrace overlooking the bay. It was blissful and none of us would have wanted to be anywhere else. As dusk fell, we decided it was time to bathe in the rose and aquamarine ripples of the placid ocean. The water was heaven and we stayed in for half an hour or more before easing out and drying ourselves off. We were soon back beneath the palms on the terrace, beckoning a waiter to take our order for more drinks. He shimmied up, with an anxious smile on his face.

'Have you just been swimming?' he asked.

'Yes, it was absolutely wonderful,' I told him.

'Mon Dieu!' he said with consternation. 'Didn't you know there's a hammerhead shark that comes around here every evening about this time to feed?'

All our eyes jerked up to look at the bay and we shivered. Sure enough, there was a large triangular fin slowly carving its way through the glittering surface of the water.

After that, we were more circumspect in our approach to adventure. One day we decided to cross Mahé. The distance from east to west was only about 36 miles, but the road, such as it was, passed through some dense, virgin forest and we hired an open Jeep to make the journey. William drove and I sat beside him, with Prue and Joybells in the back. In the forest, the women (and I) were appalled by the sight of the most gigantic spiders' webs I've ever seen. The spiders themselves were visible everywhere in the trees: they had a huge span, with small bodies but very long legs.

As we reached the edge of the forest on the far side, William, who had kept his cool admirably until now, suddenly screamed and started flapping frantically at his side and shoulder. 'Shit!' he howled. 'One of those bloody webs has got caught up on my arm!'

And I guess he thought the web's spinner was even now crawling up to bite a chunk out of his neck. But however hard he slapped, he couldn't seem to rid himself of it.

'Pull up,' I suggested sharply. 'Or you're going to drive off the track. Then get rid of it.'

He stopped and, to his deep humiliation, discovered that what had been flapping against his arm was not a giant spider's web but his shirtsleeve, which had become unrolled.

We all howled with laughter and teased William without let-up for the next few days, and for ever after, any unwanted intruder was known by me as a 'Sleeve'. Years later, when William and Joy had moved to the Bahamas, they named their boat *Sea Sleeve*.

There was almost another very embarrassing incident – at least, it would have embarrassed me. William, however, seemed remarkably relaxed when he discovered that Joy had left in the loo a bag containing fifteen hundred quid in cash that she was supposed to be looking after for him. Needless to say, when she went back, it was no longer there. She was horrified and utterly devastated that she should have done something so stupid.

Later, at dinner that evening, when Joybells happened to have disappeared again, the manager walked over to our table and asked William if he could have a word. A few minutes later William reappeared, grinning madly. An officer from the US base on Mahé, who was dining at the hotel, had found the bag containing the money and given it to the manager.

We instantly ordered a case of champagne and sent it over to the American, but we decided for the moment not to tell Joy, who was on her way back to the table.

After dinner, I was happily performing a few tricks. The others were new to my magic and apparently enjoyed it – at least, they were refraining from the groans my older friends usually made. For my third trick, sitting next to Joybells, I asked her to give me a five-pound note, which, after much embarrassed wincing she did, while the others looked on in stony silence. I told her I would see if I could change the fiver into the fifteen hundred she'd lost.

She gave me a sickly, resentful grin, which slowly changed to astonishment, then relief, then hysteria as I pulled more and more money out of sleeves and pockets and other people's ears (not Harvey's false one), until she realised with a great rush of relief that the money had somehow all come back. It was a sublime moment.

When we left the Seychelles soon after that, Prue stayed behind to wrap up a few details with Richard Syme, and I arranged to return there in a couple of weeks. Joy and William were sitting behind me on the plane and, with profound serendipity, I found myself sitting next to Pat Booth, a model I'd known vaguely and fancied rotten since she'd first appeared in the sixties.

The plane burst a tyre taking off at Mahé and we were warned that when we arrived at Cyprus a few repairs would have to be made and we would have to stay overnight. The pilot managed to land us rather scarily, but Pat and I had already established en route a sort of 'Here we are together, isn't this wonderful!' rapport and, once we'd all been escorted to the local airport hotel, I rather boldly said to the desk clerk that we were husband and wife, so we were given a double room.

It was, as they say, just one of those nights when everything clicks. It was funny, exciting, passionate and joyful. She was a supremely confident but at the same time ego-boosting sort of a bird, as well as possessing pert, lovely features and a body that would have won prestigious prizes for conformation.

I guess we knew it was a once-only affair, but when we arrived at Heathrow we really didn't want it to stop just yet, so the four of us headed down to Brighton, where William and Joy agreed to buy Countdown, Pat's shop in the King's Road, and Pat and I had a magnificently wicked weekend. And then it was over, never to be reprised, with no regrets on either side, only warm memories.

I took a deep breath and phoned Gayle to say I was home.

15

Hush Heath and Gayle
Warnings, 1971–1974

G ayle was pleased to see me and was very excited because she had found a perfect London apartment for us on the top two floors of a building in Bolton Gardens, a leafy street in South Kensington. Since the previous summer, our only permanent home in England had been Hush Heath Manor, a magical Elizabethan house near Goudhurst in Kent, which Gayle and I rented, staying in Chester Street with Charlotte and Michael Taylor during the week. We'd been told about the house by Patrick Plunket when the former owner, a hat designer called Otto Lucas, had been suddenly killed in a plane crash and his partner now wanted to let the house.

Gayle and I both adored Hush Heath and were keen to make the most of the place. We immediately started to fill it with the fluffy creatures of which she was so fond. There were a golden retriever, a lamb and a goat, all of whom slept in front of the fire. The goat thought it was a lamb, the lamb thought it was a retriever and the retriever thought it was both. Our son, Nolan, loved the space and the garden, and it was all very idyllic.

But Gayle was very busy making *The Golden Bowl* and, as she'd developed a taste for doing things in the correct English way, she was adamant that Hush Heath should be properly staffed. I'd had no idea until then that, when people grumbled about the difficulties of finding good staff, they were serious. I suppose I'd thought it was just a silly affectation. I soon learned. In the year or so that we were in Hush Heath, we never really cracked it.

We started off with a butler/factotum called James, and his wife, who cleaned. He told us he had been batman to a Guards officer during the war and he looked the part. When he came for his interview, he admitted that he had been an alcoholic, but swore that he was now recovering. I realised from the start that there were going to be problems, but almost immediately the house was filling up with guests for weekends of non-stop entertaining and we had to make do.

In any case, he could be quite impressive. In the morning, all my clothes would be laid out and he would advise me on which tie or socks to wear; and his wife was a brilliant cleaner.

I've often observed how tricky the Christmas holiday can be. This is usually attributed to personal tensions and expectations and so on. Mostly, I suspect it's to do with excessive booze. For Christmas 1971, Charlotte and Michael Taylor came to stay with their offspring, Emma and Luke. They arrived on Christmas Eve, amused at having been collected from the station by a drunk butler in my Rolls. I was quite angry about it – I didn't want the car damaged – but I didn't want to create a scene just then.

I'd also taken the precaution of hiring a cook for the holiday, so Gayle could relax and enjoy herself. This backfired rather distressingly when the cook came into the drawing room before our first dinner with a potato in each hand and said, 'What do I do with these?'

I spotted Gayle biting her lip with barely controlled rage when, perceptive and tactful as she is, Charlotte stepped in and offered to take over the cooking. Next day, she set about preparing a great Christmas lunch and, as she seemed to have everything in hand, at about half-past twelve I suggested a visit to the pub. Michael was almost as partial to a session in a country local as I am and took very little persuading to come out for a swift preprandial pint.

I don't suppose I've ever had a swift pint in my life, and certainly never a single one, or unaccompanied by a little something to give it bite. Thus it was that at about a quarter to four we lurched back into the house unashamedly plastered. The logs in the fire were bright, glowing embers. The remains of lunch, bar two places still set, were spread around the table.

We tried to make light of it as best we could.

'Oh-oh! Are we in trouble?' I asked humorously.

Gayle answered with a sort of strangled gargle. I could tell she wasn't happy.

After that there were many tricky moments with James and it was only a matter of time before something went horribly wrong.

I'd invited an important group of producers down to discuss my next directing project, *The 14*. Obviously, I'd promised to feed them, and we sat them to lunch in the lovely old dining room. We sat, and we sat, and we sat, rather as if Antonioni were directing us and trying to build a little of his famous suspense.

Finally, I went out and put my head round the kitchen door with a few crisp expletives of encouragement. A few minutes later, James shuffled in, manifestly, inescapably drunk, and served the soup, which was cold. It wasn't meant to be cold, but we were all trying to be civilised and my guests and I took it in our stride.

The soup should have been followed by beef. Instead, James carried in only a tray of vegetables, and as he walked through the door he held them up and announced that they were boiled beyond recovery, and to emphasise his point, now pissed beyond redemption, he sang 'Beyond the Blue Horizon' at the top of his warbling and not very accurate voice.

He served the vegetables, and my guests, not disguising their doubts about getting a proper lunch, gazed at their plates in horror.

'James,' I asked a little nervously, 'where's the beef?'

'Beef? Beef?' he expostulated. 'I thought you were all vegetarians.' He stared around the room wildly, before stumbling out.

Cringing with embarrassment, I followed him a while later, only to be told that he had gone down to the village local to finish what he'd started.

He managed to get back from the pub later without my seeing him, took one of the cars and disappeared with his wife. About three hours later, he'd smashed it up with his 'wife', who turned out not to be, and we discovered that he'd not been in the army at all but in the Merchant Navy, which may have explained why, when he was sober, he was so good. He disappeared without trace and I never heard from him again.

The episode didn't give a good impression to all the people I'd asked to lunch, but it's worth pointing out to those who suffer paranoia over this sort of event that *The 14* did get made.

And despite these shortcomings, living in a country manor was immensely appealing to both of us. The summer months in particular provided a wonderful opportunity to entertain our friends. Every week-end would be a house party, with elaborate charades after dinner and viciously competitive and invariably drunken croquet tournaments after lunch, along with every other country house pursuit we could find.

But, although we had both enjoyed living in Kent, there was no doubt that it wasn't hugely convenient for two busy people in the film industry. A London base was essential and so I agreed that we should go ahead with Bolton Gardens. Almost immediately after that, I had to head back to the Seychelles.

William O'Shei, Richard Syme and Harvey Herman had put together a report for the development of the Seychelles, as requested by Jimmy Mancham, who took it on board with enthusiasm. It recommended that they let Mahé go to the dogs of tourism but preserve and restrict development on all the other islands. A lot of the ideas proposed were taken up by Mancham and, after he was elbowed out in a coup, retained by Albert Renée.

I'd also seen the first draft of the report drawn up by Richard Syme and Harvey Herman regarding the development of North Island for tourism. Earlier, altruistic plans for an artists' colony had been abandoned, but the report's recommendations were in no way over-exploitative. They were, however, not to happen, at least not in that form, or at our hands.

When we'd got back to England, William, who had become the prime mover in putting the deal together, asked us all to cough up our share of the ante. It is amazing how many lovely, fantastical ideas founder when, in the end, hard cash has to be produced. I dithered; Richard dithered. William rang me and asked, as everyone was hesitating, if I'd mind if he just went ahead and bought it himself and sorted out the syndicate later. I was trying to buy Bolton Gardens at the time, so I told him to go ahead.

He rang Christopher Bonn and said he'd buy North Island, only to be told that some Germans had turned up with the cash in a suitcase. So much for Bonn, I thought, not entirely surprised, but William took it very hard. He was livid. He immediately started to sue, on the grounds that under the Code Napoleon, which held sway in the Seychelles, once the seller had agreed a deal he couldn't back out. Frankly, it was a long shot and he lost, though his QC advised him to go to the high court in Mauritius, where he'd certainly get it. But, by that time, the massive financial crash of the early seventies had happened, and William didn't need the hassle, or the expense, and all our plans and dreams for North Island were dead in the water.

Thirty years later, the island is being operated by company called African Adrenalin.com and I've never been back.

*

However, my third visit within nine months to the Seychelles was not prompted by the North Island deal. I'd been asked to direct a film for ORTF French Television, one of a series called *Les Histoires Fantastiques*. This one, *Mermaid with Oranges*, was going to star Yul Brynner. I was looking forward to working on the island of La Digue, and the islanders were very excited about seeing Yul Brynner.

The day before he arrived, we got the kids to paint the school house white and projected *The Magnificent Seven* against a wall to give them an idea of who was coming. He arrived next day in a pirogue, or dug-out canoe, and didn't take the ox cart provided. Dressed entirely in Magnificent Seven black as usual, and as cool as ever, he walked the full length of the main street, followed by 200 kids and most of the population of the island to the house where he was to stay. He was an absolute star and the people loved it.

He loved it too. Making that film was, I'm sure, one of his better times.

I had also used the opportunity to re-meet an old lover when I'd heard that Linda Cole was living in East Africa. I invited her to play the part of the mermaid in the film. This turned out to be not such a good move since, while I thought I was doing her a bit of a favour for old time's sake, she thought she was doing me a favour by allowing her legs to be squeezed for hours on end into a hot, narrow tube of scaly rubber to represent her mermaid's nether regions.

Sad to say, in the perverted way of our industry, we'd just finished filming when we discovered that the production company had gone bust. Yul was never paid at all. I had to pay Linda out of my own pocket, as well as all the hotels, caterers, extras and goatherds who'd taken part. It left me a lot less well off.

In the end, sadly, it was the débâcle of *Mermaid with Oranges* that put the cap on the whole Seychelles and North Island project for me.

In England I was preparing the next film I was to direct. *The 14* was a wonderful, true and moving story about a family of fourteen children from Birmingham whose parents had died. The local Social Services had an obligation to find foster homes for them, which meant inevitably that they'd be split up – and they were utterly determined not to be. The film attempted to show what they went through and the reactions they met with in the adults and officials they encountered. Eventually, a single home was found with a Cornish farmer for seven of them, but when his wife died, the complications began again, and were still not resolved.

In an unusual arrangement, the film production company set up a trust fund for the family that would benefit from a proportion of the profits of the film.

We reset the story in London, with Jack Wild, already well known for his Artful Dodger (*Oliver!*), in the lead role. As I'd always enjoyed working with children, making this picture was a great delight and I was amazed and gratified by some of the performances we were able to evoke from these kids.

The producer was a man called Frank Avianca and Brian Cook, my dog-racing mate from *King Alfred*, joined me as first assistant director. While it was fun and rewarding to make the film, it wasn't easy to retain the children's attention and enthusiasm. We set up a temporary studio in Willesden, north-west London, and I would arrange all sorts of treats and outings for them. (In fact, I often did that sort of thing for my adult cast and crew in future films, because I found that it gave a greater sense of cohesion and teamwork to the company.) We would have boules tournaments on the stage, or I'd take them all go-karting or stock-car racing. Once I took them all down for a day out at Hush Heath, where minimal damage was done. They loved piling into the back of my new black Rolls and playing with the car phone – then an astonishing novelty.

One of the advantages of filming in a makeshift London studio was that it was easy for friends to drop by. On one occasion Patrick Plunkett looked in with a friend of his, Lord Colin Campbell. We all ended up playing darts in a scruffy little pub in Kilburn High Road and were very late for a smart dinner at Le Mirabelle. The truth was that finishing off a series of competitive games of darts in a north-west London pub was just as important to me as getting into an overpriced nosebag in Mayfair.

I was very proud of *The 14* and, when it was released in the summer of 1973, it was fairly well received, though not as well as I'd hoped. It nevertheless earned me a Golden Bear for Best Director at the Berlin Film Festival.

Later that year it also gave me the opportunity to visit Johannesburg, where everyone was being very enthusiastic about the film. MGM, who were distributing, also asked me to open their two new luxury cinemas in Hillbrow. South Africans, being somewhat isolated then, were hungry for any prominent film person to visit and I was being seriously pumped for ideas and initiatives. At the cinema I gave a speech in which I promised (almost) that I planned to come back and make a film in South Africa to help and encourage local skills and talents, by bringing top technicians and establishing a rapport with the local industry.

'I have a strong feeling about people coming into a country, taking what they need and going away. One should be able to leave something behind, to foster talent and interest within the local industry,' I was quoted as saying, so I suppose I must have said it. I'm afraid I never had the chance to return and fulfil these promises – much though, now, I would like to have done.

While I was there I was also booked to open a José Feliciano concert in a ghastly venue called the Carlton Exhibition Centre, which I did with a speech that lasted all of thirty seconds.

I had taken Prue de Casembroot with me, as 'assistant', to Johannesburg, which only added to the prevailing confusion in the public's mind over my marriage with Gayle.

Frankly, if the public were confused, so was I.

Gayle and I had made a film together called *Voices*, which I also directed. She earned some good reviews and was, I think, pleased with the performance she'd given me as director. She was by now very occupied with other projects and had firmly established herself in Britain as a screen and TV actress. She was happy here, and adored Nolan, but she was becoming increasingly impatient of my adventuring. She understood perfectly well what was going on between me and Prue, who'd quite often baby-sat for us in her early days at the office. As a result, Gayle knew her quite well and reluctantly began to perceive her as more of a threat to our marriage than any of my other passing affairs.

The tensions between Gayle and me grew and, deeply though I regretted hurting her, I was pathologically incapable of delivering the kind of reliable fealty she craved, and certainly had a right to. When the press reported in May 1973 that we had split up, they weren't, for once, entirely wrong. I was spending more and more time with Prue and, in an exciting little interlude that was to have profound reverberations nearly two decades later, I met an astonishingly vivid, clever and bewitching sixteen-year-old called Tessa Dahl. She and her mother, the actress Patricia Neal (her father was the author Roald Dahl), were guests on a Russell Harty TV show in 1974. So was I, although I have absolutely zero recollection of what I said or anything that happened in the studio. However, I still have a very distinct memory of what followed.

Tessa and her mother succumbed to my invitation to dinner, and from there it was but a short hop to Tramp. Tessa's independence and her sharp perceptive wit, especially in a girl so young, were very arousing and, brushing aside the possibility that I was practically contemplating a crime, I asked her to dance. The kissing on the dance floor and a positive response to my straying hands encouraged me to think that here was a prospect worth keeping an eye on. It was inevitable, when she was a little older, that we should respond to our strong physical rapport. I loved seeing Tessa on and off over the next few years, until she'd had enough of my shilly-shallying and went off to have lovely babies and get married.

At the same time, my professional career was becoming somehow unruly; it was as if I were steering it in an old KwikSave trolley. There seemed an uncontrolled randomness to what I was doing.

There was a film in Venezuela, a true celebration of disorganised polyglot film-making, during which I found a snake living in my hotel room. The result was a picture so unsure of its own identity it was released under four titles: *No es Nada, Mama, solo un juego*; *Lola*; *It's Nothing; Only a Game* and, for no obvious reason, *Beyond Erotica*.

There was the first of several visits to Italy to act for various aspiring Fellinis and Antonionis, among them Dario Argento, in *Profondo Rosso*, a.k.a. *Deep Red*; *Deep Red Hatchet Murders*; *Dripping Deep Red*; *The Hatchet Murders* and (why?) *The Sabre Tooth Tiger*. It could be said that there is often a connection between the absence of quality in a film and the number of its aliases. One of the most memorable quirks of film-making in Italy was the strange attitude to sound that I'd come across working with Antonioni. All Italian directors, it seemed, had no interest in reproducing what could be described as live sound. They recorded no audio track when shooting and were very uninterested in accurate syncing when they dubbed on a voice track afterwards. Despite my experience with the Maestro, I never really got used to technicians and carpenters hammering, whistling or even singing while we were filming, but nobody else gave a damn.

Prue and I arrived late at night in Turin before the start of filming *Profondo Rosso*. We'd come by train (my preferred form of transport) and there were no restaurants open. The receptionist in the hotel in which we were billeted shrugged a shoulder and sent us around the corner to a tiny lorry drivers' pasta bar. The place was arranged in booths, four to a table, and we had to sit in one already occupied by a single, very small man.

As soon as we had sat down, he leaned forward and regarded me with piercing black eyes. 'You are David Hemmings, no?' he asked, with his nose twitching slightly.

I often find this embarrassing in what you might call domestic situations and it was the last thing I wanted at that time of night, but I agreed that I was, and yes, I had been in *Blow-Up*.

He asked a few more questions, before, a little to his surprise, I asked him what he was doing. He told me he was in Turin to see the factory that made his 'stuff'.

Incorrigibly inquisitive, I couldn't help asking what sort of stuff. I suppose I expected him to say frothy-coffee makers or exhaust flanges for Fiat Cinquecentos or Lambretta horns.

I perked up like the proverbial war horse to a blown bugle when he said he had special juggling clubs made for him which would turn into bunches of flowers and burst into flames in mid-air. This was something in which I could be very interested. I ignored Prue's heavy sigh as she realised we would be here until I had extracted every last drop of potential from this suddenly fascinating little chap.

He was called Pepe – a Spanish performer from a long line of travelling showmen. He had just been attending an annual convention of jugglers in Milan, where, he admitted without great conceit, he had won the first prize.

'How?' I asked, longing to know.

'Not with my clubs.' He lifted a shoulder and reached across to pick up my coffee spoon. He inspected it for a moment, twiddled it about, balanced it across his finger to find a point of equilibrium and held it up in front of his face. 'OK – I show you.'

He flipped the spoon up, spinning it vertically high above his head, and as it dropped back down, caught it by the wide end, right on the bridge of his nose, where it remained standing upright.

I was flabbergasted. This trick may not look much on the page, but you could practise it for ten years and never crack it, there are so many variables, as well as the need to develop a small crease in exactly the right place on the bridge of your nose.

Naturally, I insisted that he teach me how to do it there and then. It was a good two hours before I admitted defeat and showed him some of my own tricks, which he was polite enough to admire. And, in the meantime, he told me some of his family history and invited me to join him in his caravan as it continued on its never-ending journey back and forth across Europe with his small circus.

I was very tempted by the idea of no responsibilities and probably a goodish supply of the spangled, ample-breasted Slavic women I'd often noticed hanging around the circuses that visited Surrey in my youth. In fact, I probably said yes.

It's hardly worth saying that I never saw Pepe after that night, and my resolve to find him and commence the life of a peregrinating magician had weakened enough to allow me home at the end of the film. But it was a good little fantasy for the few days it lasted.

In England, perhaps as a result of *The 14*, I was asked to direct a couple of episodes of a popular children's horse'n'country TV series set in Yorkshire called *Follyfoot*. It was a charming series of a type we could do with now, and I enjoyed the bucolic values in contrast to Turin and *Profondo Rosso*.

After that, the making of *Juggernaut* with Richard Lester wasn't too demanding either. Mine wasn't much of a part, as sidekick to a world-famous bomb-disposal expert played by Richard Harris. Half the action takes place at sea, where Omar Sharif played the captain of a ship threatened by a bomb, and Mark Burns his first mate, all filmed on a gigantic ocean liner the Russians had just bought from Germany and renamed the *Maxim Gorky*. United Artists had rented space on the liner to make the film while it was engaged in its sea trials, when they spent a lot of time cruising around near Iceland, looking for a serious storm – which, Mark told me with some passion, they found.

Mercifully, all *my* scenes were shot in the studio in England, where my hairiest moment, and the only time I got to see Mark, occurred when Harris and I were parachuted into a water tank posing as the North Sea in Pinewood, and Mark had to come out in a lifeboat to pick us up.

This short snap of adventure filming, though damp, was perfectly safe. My experience in the altogether calmer, if shark-infested, waters of the TV series *Mogul* turned out to be far more hazardous than I could have imagined. I'd agreed, as a favour to a friend, to make a 'guest' appearance in a scene in one episode.

📷 📷 📷 📷

There is a wedding taking place and I am cast – you've guessed – as the official photographer. (With hindsight, it makes me cringe to think I should ever have concurred with such a naff idea, but there it is.) Part of the action requires a well-trained Great Dane to disrupt the wedding by grabbing my arm and shaking it between his massive jaws until I drop my camera. (Perhaps it's meant to be Terence Stamp in a future incarnation.)

I'm not worried about this. I like dogs, I've always been able to communicate with them, and this one is trained and being handled by no less a canine expert than Mrs Barbara Woodhouse.

She arrives on the set with a massive, slavering beast whose surname must be Baskerville. I look alarmed; she reassures me. My arm is tightly wrapped in a thick leather strip (already scarred with some nasty tooth gashes). The dog is looking at me suspiciously and drooling like the Niagara Falls. I am told to let my arm hang at a very particular angle, so the canine mummer knows which one to grab and won't need to tug it too hard once he gets a hold on it.

In rehearsal, the wedding guests are milling about in costume, grumbling about their agents. Barbara leads the dog onto the set. His ears prick as he smells my fear; I'm sweating so much most of the cast can smell it too.

She releases the dog. It makes straight for me in a couple of huge bounds, launches itself into the air like a rocket. And grabs the wrong arm.

After I've been sedated, cleaned up with TCP, injected against tetanus and, presumably, rabies, both my arms are wrapped in thick strips of leather and we do a single take – shit or bust – it doesn't matter which arm the beast grabs, so long as I drop the camera.

It works – why wouldn't it?

I leave the set in a state of advanced gloom that I should have spent the day as an elaborate prop to be ravaged by a mad dog.

I am an actor, after all.

📷 📷 📷 📷

As relief from the sporadic traumas of film-making, I was delighted to be able to flee to my friends William and Joybells O'Shei, who had recently bought a large Georgian mansion of considerable elegance, buried in the depths of deepest Devon. It was set in a vast and tranquil park which William was inclined to treat as a massive playground. I loved the place on sight and spent many happy weekends there, usually with Prue, over the next few years.

I was such a regular visitor to the local pub, the Bishop Lacey in Chudleigh, playing darts and generally telling the locals what was what, they thought that I, not William, was the squire of Whiteway. Prue and I spent several Christmases there; once, in order to stop me straying from the house so much, William created a complete pub of his own in the tackroom by the stables. This grounded me for a couple of days, though, in truth, there were always a lot of other distractions to keep me on the premises.

I guess it was William's unquenchable enthusiasm for new schemes, games and businesses, however implausible they may have appeared, that drew and endeared me to him. We were constantly hurtling about on motorbikes, in small aircraft or hot-air balloons, or teaching some new parrot how to blaspheme in French, while with the coming of each spring he would launch a new enterprise on the estate. His account of his experiences in rearing fowl always reminded me of Ukridge's in P. G. Wodehouse's wonderful *Love among the Chickens*.

Whiteway provided several joyful interludes in what was otherwise a somewhat turbulent time for me, although I still retained the capacity to extract as much fun out of life as I'd always done.

In the autumn of 1973, Gayle and I got back together for the première of *Scorpio*, a film she'd made with Michael Winner, and we resumed living together, at least partially. She had made up her mind to turn a blind eye to Prue, hoping despite her misgivings that the relationship would peter out in time. She felt that what she perceived as two aspects of my nature were constantly vying with each other and, in the end, the right half would win. It was, perhaps, always a forlorn hope, but she was correct in that part of me really would have liked it to work. In any event, we hung together, while Prue and I continued to see each other, at work and in her tiny flat in Paddington.

I wasn't made any happier by a sense that my career had entered a slightly stale patch. None of the projects in which I was involved did much to excite me and I was becoming increasingly bored by the business of acting – probably because I wasn't being offered any challenging parts. Nevertheless, with a pleasing manifestation of serendipity, the odd treat would sometimes turn up.

One morning in November 1973 I called round at Hemdale's offices, as I did from time to time to sort out odd residual matters with John Daly. There was, as always, a lot of rushing about. Hemdale had somehow got involved in the management of a couple of rock bands. From within the offices, Brian Lane was managing Yes and the Pat Meehans, Sr and Jr, were handling Black Sabbath. One of the people involved with these groups was Rick Wakeman, who, at the age of 25, had written what he described as a rock oratorio based on Jules Verne's *Journey to the Centre of the Earth*. It was to have its first public airing the following January at the Royal Festival Hall.

I walked into John's office to find Rick there with Brian Lane and a few others. From the tension in the room, it was clear that they had a crisis on their hands. I hadn't been to Hemdale much recently, so I didn't know what the state of play was with *Journey*; in fact, at that stage I knew very little about it at all. I didn't want to interfere.

I held my hands up. 'Sorry. Am I interrupting something?' I asked tactfully.

They all denied it.

'OK,' I asked. 'So what's going on?'

'We can't find a voice for the narration,' Rick said, with a shrug and a strong hint of frustration. 'We've thought of dozens who could do it, I suppose, but I don't think any of them are right.'

'Maybe Richard Harris?' John suggested, knowing I knew Richard well.

Rick shook his head. 'He's the only name on the list at the moment, but he's not right. He's just too Irish, and what we need is a voice that's 100 per cent, quintessentially English, with a real strong sense of story to it, if you know what I mean.'

At that moment, Rick was looking at me – and so was everyone else in the room. There was a sudden, charged moment before I knew I had to speak.

'Am I not good enough, then?'

'Christ!' Rick choked. 'Would you do it?'

'Sure, I'd love to – it'll be a great gig. I'd be delighted.'

And I was. I went to a lot of the rehearsals, often when I wasn't needed, simply to see how the piece was developing. It is a marvellous and sophisticated composition, and I loved the narrative I had to deliver. And naturally I loved the opportunity to work and drink with the musicians.

For the first performance of *Journey to the Centre of the Earth* on 18 January 1974, I sat in a vast wicker chair on stage at the Festival Hall and was very glad to be a part of it and the amazing reception it evoked. When Rick asked if I would also go to the studio to do the overdubs for the record, I needed no persuading. When it came to it, though, the process of putting my studio voice over the live music track took a lot of time, as matching up the levels was a tricky task. While we were sitting about for hours on end, I fought my regular battle with boredom by repeating my lines over and over again in every accent I could think of, until everyone in the studios was either pissing themselves with laughter or looking for somewhere to commit suicide. But it was done in the end and the album went on to sell over 15 million copies.

Rick also wanted me to join the subsequent tour, but I was already too committed elsewhere, which was a disappointment for me.

I did, though, have time to slip away with Prue for a quick respite from the public gaze, which had become particularly tiresome. I'd been told that the beautiful little island of Lamu, hidden just off the coast of Kenya, was a wonderful place to escape and was still pretty much off the tourist map. We decided to head there, without telling anyone where we were going. We had just settled into our seats for the first leg of our flight to Nairobi when the gossip columnist Nigel Dempster and his wife, Camilla, came bustling in. Although I liked Nigel, I couldn't think of anyone I wanted to see less, especially when he spotted me and his eyes lit up.

I begged him to pretend he hadn't seen me.

'That's all right,' he said. 'I'm on holiday. Of course I haven't seen you.'

I knew I'd have to wait a couple of weeks before I was back in England to see if he'd been true to his word. In the meantime, I could only hope and try to relax.

We reached Lamu and it was as heavenly as we'd been promised, and more. Tall, silent Arab men drifted in long white robes between sparkling white houses set between clusters of palms and the warm blue Indian Ocean. The peace was so intense you could almost feel it through your skin and I happily settled down to de-stress.

Not for long – of course. Within two days I felt myself being overcome by my habitual, incurable boredom. While Prue loafed on the white sand, I took to walking around the tucked-away corners of the town and small harbour, talking to anyone who spoke English or understood my sign language. I was fascinated by the history of the place – a small Arab land off the coast of Africa – and one of the former traditions that appealed to my imagination was a great dhow race which used to be held between the several islands dotted up and down the coast. Since the whole existence of the communities on this coast was a direct result of sailing dhows, it was not surprising that the skills involved should have been highly regarded and competed over. Since the sailing dhow had been replaced for trading purposes by bigger, faster, noisier and uglier forms of nautical transport, the race hadn't been held for many years. I was immediately inspired to resurrect the tradition. Enthused and excited, I managed to extend my holiday a little and set about persuading the various authorities and dhow owners to reinstate this great race.

Once I had undertaken to supply a substantial grand prize to the winner, all obstacles were removed and, before we left, the race was held. What's more, I'm told that the Hemmings Cup is still competed for around the islands.

When I returned to England, I was relieved to find that Dempster had kept his word and no mention of my holiday, or even the great dhow race, had leaked into the public consciousness.

Although there wasn't a good, hard job in hand, the usual backlog of work relating to projects that never get off the ground still had to be dealt with and, to add to that, before the 1974 election I found myself caught up in politics, whipped into activity by Honor Blackman and canvassing in London and Devon for Jeremy Thorpe and the Liberals. This was, of course, a few years before Norman Scott's infamous pillow-biting revelations and the inauguration of Auberon Waugh's dog-lovers' party. At that stage, the Liberal Party's main attraction for me was its championing of proportional representation, which has always seemed to me to be a better expression of parliamentary democracy than 'first past the post'. Now, of course, it's only available in the European Parliament, which seems to have the administrative clout of a toothless poodle compared with the unelected commission which makes the decisions!

The making of *Mr Quilp* that summer provided a welcome reprise of earlier times, working with David Warner, Jill Bennett, Michael Horden and Tony Newley, who'd written the music and words based on Dickens's *The Old Curiosity Shop*, with the whole show choreographed by the wonderful Gillian Lynne. But in July a crisis was reached in my marriage when Gayle turned up at Prue's flat in Star Street and almost caught us *in flag delict*. Once again, as in wartime air raids with my mother and in Michael Winner's room at the Grand Hotel, Torquay, I found myself cowering in a cupboard.

Gayle opened it, found me without many clothes on and almost dismembered me as she slammed the door shut. Perhaps my life would have been a great deal less complicated thereafter if she had succeeded.

When I went round to Bolton Gardens, I found that Aunt Hazel was staying – this had perhaps emboldened Gayle to provoke the crisis. When Gayle sensed she wasn't making it clear enough to me that our marriage was finally over, she decided she could make it clearer by flinging all my clothes out of the window into the Old Brompton Road beneath. (Bizarrely, as she did it I recalled P. G. Wodehouse saying that when he had lived there and had written a letter he couldn't be bothered to post, he'd simply fling it, stamped, out of the window, knowing that the next person who came along would pick it up and pop it into the pillar box on the corner. That was before the war, of course.) Gayle's final gesture, her *coup de grâce*, so to speak, was to take down from the wall a beautiful painting of our wedding – two lovers in a pink rose arbour before a Californian sunset – and hurl that out of the window to the pavement below, narrowly missing a policeman who was gazing up, surrounded by the scattered debris of my possessions. The picture survived, but the commotion was causing a pile-up of traffic on the Old Brompton Road.

When I arrived at ground level, by good chance two of my friends, the double-barrels Edward Millwood-Oliver and Anthony Greville Bell, turned up to help me sort out the mess and cart it all away.

On 23 July 1974, Gayle filed for divorce.

Now it had come to that, I realised bleakly that this wasn't what I wanted at all; I wanted to be married to Gayle and to go on seeing Prue. I saw nothing strange in wanting both of them. I knew Gayle didn't see it that way, but I was determined to win her back over a series of tearful reconciliations and almost instant bust-ups. I rather thrive on real-life drama, but it put a terrible strain on Gayle, who had been rehearsing the title role in a stage production of Zola's novel *Thérèse Raquin* at the Yvonne Arnaud Theatre in Guildford. In the end, she pulled out at the last minute, leaving the producers so high and dry they had to delay the opening for a couple of days while they replaced her. She fled to Leslie Bricusse's house in the South of France, where I followed.

There was, as often, a bit of a house party there and I was distracted from my purpose of patching things up with Gayle by the unmissable presence of Rex Harrison, who was keeping everyone on their toes – not to say driving them mad – by barking orders the whole time, wagging a finger and demanding attention. I thought it an interesting challenge to see what ways of keeping him quiet I could devise. Few worked, but on one occasion, while flying a kite near the top of a cliff, I persuaded him to hold on to it for me and left him there for nearly an hour.

This was a start, but not enough. After a visit to the Colombe d'Or restaurant, which thought a great deal of itself, in St Paul de Vence, a solution cropped up unplanned. A group of us went there for dinner, unbooked and led by Rex.

'We'd like a table for ten,' he said.

'Do you 'ave a reservation?' the maître d' asked politely enough.

'No,' Rex huffed in astonishment.

'Zen, I am afraid I cannot 'elp you, sir.'

Rex was flabbergasted. 'But I'm Rex Harrison!'

'I am so sorry,' the Frenchman said ambiguously, with a shrug to suggest the name meant nothing to him.

We went off and had dinner in a restaurant where Rex was recognised, but the lack of response at the Colombe d'Or continued to distress him.

The following day, I offered to go and pick up the Sunday newspapers, from Nice Airport and, for some reason, Rex told me he was coming too. The plane was late, and I suggested that we pop into the airport bar and swallow a few coffee-cognacs. He agreed and, to his profound delight, was instantly mobbed by English punters wanting his autograph.

This had the happy consequence that every time after that when he felt unappreciated – which was quite often – he would simply slip down to the airport bar and treat his ego to a little collective massage.

*

With Gayle, however, I fear that I failed once again in all my efforts to preserve our marriage. Back in London I knew she meant business when, for the first time, she was seen out and about dining *à deux* with various high-profile and outrageously eligible men, including Patrick Lichfield in San Frediano's and Marquess Douro in San Lorenzo's.

I caught up with her at a launch for a recipe book by Michael Parkinson at the Martini Terrace in the Haymarket. We talked, but then she said she was leaving and went out to get into her car. I had to go on bended knee to persuade her to let me in, which, in the end and after some eager nudging by fascinated passers-by, she did. Nothing, though, came of this meeting, and I had to leave for Rome the next day to carry on filming for Dario Argento. Prue, as normal, came with me, and of course we were spotted and snapped for the *Daily Mail*.

Gayle agreed to come with me to the royal première of *Juggernaut* at Leicester Square, but made a public statement that our marriage was over after that. On 19 December she was granted a decree nisi on the grounds of my adultery with Prudence de Casembroot. Gayle told the press that she was going off to Miami for a short visit but intended to carry on living in London. She had made a lot of her patronage of Yuki, the Japanese dress designer, and there were more rumours of her burgeoning relationship with Lord Douro. I finally had to face the fact that I now had two failed marriages behind me, and two children for whom I ought to have been responsible.

What I found impossible to explain to anyone, even to myself, was that I still loved Gayle and had warm memories of times we'd spent together and how I'd always enjoyed doing things to please her. When I was in Paris, I was reminded of the time we'd been there with our good friends Mark and Sandra Weinberg. Zoe Dominic, the photographer, had taken some wonderful shots of Gayle with her two Yorkshire terriers, Heathcliff and Cathy. I knew Gayle liked the photo, so I had it blown up into a poster and had several of them printed. Knowing that we would be passing that way later in the evening, I managed to persuade most of the shops in the rue des Beaux Arts to hang them in their windows, so when we were walking along the road to Castels that evening, there she was, lit up, on both sides of the street for fifty yards or so. It was a great joy to see how astonished and chuffed she was by what I'd done. And, of course, I'd loved the challenge of achieving it.

I knew she loved Van Gogh too, and when we'd been staying at the Plaza in New York for the première of *The Charge of the Light Brigade* one evening I brought back a beautiful Van Gogh drawing I said I'd acquired for her and showed her the item featured in an exhibition catalogue. Gayle was thrilled; she thought it a ravishing drawing.

For the next few years it hung in our flat above the harmonium (part of my now somewhat diminished collection of antique musical instruments) quite happily, pleasing Gayle, until, rather unfortunately, a Van Gogh exhibition arrived at the Hayward Gallery. Richard Attenborourgh had seen the Van Gogh I'd given Gayle and was surprised to find it in the show – only twice as big and in terracotta chalk. When I'd copied it from the black-and-white illustration in the catalogue, I'd been careless enough not to check the size and colour of the original, although I had taken the trouble to get old paper and the right ink for the period. It was only when the exhibition arrived in London that I had to own up to my fakery.

Gayle didn't mind at all. She loved the fact that I'd cared enough to do it, and she wasn't resentful that for years she'd really enjoyed thinking she had a genuine Van Gogh in the house. And she was able to reduce the insurance premiums a little.

She still has it. And the wedding picture that flew from the window of Bolton Gardens.

16

Bertie Wooster, Bowie and Berlin, 1975–1979

I've enjoyed reading P. G. Wodehouse since I first came across him as a boy and, like most fans, I still cannot accurately define that special, elusive quality that makes his style so impossible to reproduce. As Molesworth books coloured Benjamin Britten's speech, so Wodehouse's style and turn of phrase have permeated mine for years. While I admired his intricate and meticulously worked plots and the wacky idiosyncrasies of his dialogue, it was, in my view, his use of language, especially of metaphor, in the narrative of the books that made his writing unique.

For this reason, I'd always felt it was impossible to translate him satisfactorily to the stage or screens of either dimension. The only truly effective stage presentation of Wodehouse that I've seen was the late Edward Duke's one-man show, where he delivered the text as written with such skill as to create a riveting evening's entertainment.

I should, then, have been wary when people first approached me about a musical called *Jeeves*. But since these people were Andrew Lloyd Webber and Alan Ayckbourn, any doubts I felt were dispelled before I had them. The country's most successful writer of musical scores and the country's most successful popular playwright made a formidable combination. Neither of them had had a flop for years and if they thought they could make a Wodehouse musical work, then, by Jingo, so did I. I chose to overlook the fact that Prue's ex-boyfriend Tim Rice, who had worked with Andrew on all his projects up till then, was such a committed Wodehouse fan that he didn't think he could do justice to the master.

I was delighted to be offered the chance to act on the London stage again for the first time since *Adventures in the Skin Trade* in 1966, and in

February it was announced that I would play Bertie Wooster when *Jeeves* opened at Her Majesty's Theatre on 22 April. Michael Aldridge was to play Jeeves and Gabrielle Drake would play the female lead, Madeline Basset. Not only would I be acting, of course, but I also had half a dozen songs to deliver, giving me my first professional musical outing since *David Hemmings Happens*, which I assumed the producers of *Jeeves* had overlooked. I was nervous but excited, and with only eight weeks until we opened in London, I knew I was going to have to put a hell of a lot of work into the rehearsals and the previews in Bristol. This was probably not a good time to be launching a parallel business career as an art dealer, but we are seldom allowed the opportunity to choose our timing in these spheres.

Gayle had finally applied for a decree absolute and any remaining hopes I might have had that we would get back together again were now thoroughly dashed. Since she'd chucked me out, I'd been staying with Peter Bowles and his wife, Susan. Out of habit, we still liked to scour the antiques stalls and we'd gone one crisp, clear morning to Bermondsey market to look for a decent Georgian chest of drawers that Peter wanted. He soon spotted one and, expert as always, I was casting my eye over it with him, checking the construction of the drawers and that sort of thing, when I opened the bottom drawer and saw a stack of loose watercolours inside.

'I don't think we'll mention them,' I suggested out of the side of my mouth and hurriedly slid the drawer back.

A few minutes later we were driving away with the piece of furniture, bought at a good price from a lazy dealer who had underpriced it to make his job easier.

'I expect he intended to throw in those paintings,' Peter said.

'Quite,' I agreed. 'And they may be a pile of rubbish anyway.'

We hadn't dared slide the drawer out and take a look while we were within sight of the market, but as soon as we got back to Peter's house we unloaded the chest and feverishly slid out the bottom drawer. Inside was the most bizarre collection of watercolours I'd ever seen. Some were straight landscapes of English river scenes, while others were landscapes with extraordinary mystical scenes superimposed, together with fragments of all sorts of other decorative art works and scenes. In all my years of poking around markets, I'd never come across anything like them. Better still, they had the scent and aura of age about them and they were physically in good condition, although, of course, without frames or glass.

Peter and I spread them out and stared, frankly flabbergasted. There were nearly fifty of them, all utterly different, extraordinary and enchanting. We looked at each other.

'What do you think, old crumpet?' I asked in Wooster mode.

'I should say, old bean, that we've had it away.'

Further scrutiny and a little research soon revealed that the pictures had been painted between 1820 and 1859 by an obscure woman from Monmouthshire called Elizabeth Oakley. We were convinced that we had stumbled across and cleverly identified a little-known and virtually unrecorded talent. To amateur antiques hustlers like us, this was on a par with a punter hitting the jackpot on Gold Cup day at Cheltenham. We had acquired them for nothing and had only to invest a little in buying frames, which Charlotte Taylor, who had done up Grosvenor Crescent Mews for me, helped to fit. The game (and it was a game I loved) was then to have them seen and turned round fast, with a good profit.

In order to bring them to as wide a market as possible, on the day I was confirmed in the Bertie Wooster part we took over a shop called Fauve in Beauchamp Place, put the pictures up for sale and went about getting as much publicity for them as we could. The reaction was amazing. The public came in hordes, while the professional art world turned on us like a pack of dogs on a thieving rat and alerted the press. A reporter came into the gallery under cover and bought one picture, which he took round to experts at the British Museum and the V&A, who declared that it had been painted in the 20th century and must, by definition, be a fake. All the rubbish papers lapped it up. The *Sunday People*, locking on to my name and the publicity I'd had recently for *Jeeves*, ran a front-page story about the two actors who had been duped (being careful not to say we'd been doing the duping). In the meantime, we sold all the pictures.

I'd just found a new flat for myself in Chelsea and was meant to be keeping my head down while I tried desperately to learn the hundreds of lines I had in *Jeeves*. As Bertie is the narrator, I was going to be on stage for nearly the whole three and half hours that the early version of the show lasted. But when other news-rags accused us of deliberately misleading the public, Peter turned up to discuss what we should do.

By this time, some of the original experts had withdrawn their view that the pictures were fakes and said they could have been painted when we claimed and were almost certainly by Elizabeth Oakley, so I agreed a little reluctantly that we should sue the papers concerned. But while Peter was still with me, his wife rang and said that two of the most terrifying people she'd ever seen had called at their house looking for me. She hadn't told them where I was, but they seemed very keen to find me.

'For God's sake, H, what the hell's all this about?' Peter asked, suddenly very nervous.

I wasn't sure, though I had an inkling they might have something to do with the trader who'd sold us the chest and might well have recognised us. However, since they wouldn't know where I lived, I told him I hadn't a clue.

Twenty minutes later, while we were still discussing tactics for our claim, there was a heavy hammering on my front door. Prue, who'd been in the kitchen while we talked, answered the door and came into the drawing room to say that there were two men to see me, claiming to be friends of mine.

'What are they called?' I asked.

Prue went away and came back a moment later and told me their names.

I blanched. 'You'd better send them in,' I said, as if we had any choice.

Peter told me afterwards that, when they walked in, he felt a truly terrifying chill descend on the room.

The two men, about a generation apart although they looked similar, were not related. The features they had in common had been created rather than inherited. They both had broken noses, scarred cheeks and fists like small legs of lamb. I had no idea what was going to happen. I knew both men, certainly; I'd known them since my days at Toby's gym. They'd played at my roulette table then, and taken me to meet others of a similar profession in the Blind Beggar. If the business that these people were in could be described as a trade, then they were in the fear trade.

The older man spoke first. "Ello, David. We've been looking for you all over. 'Ow are yer, son?' He stepped forward. I tried not to flinch as he took me in his arms and crushed me in a massive hug. When he let me go, without looking at Peter, he asked, 'Who's the geezer?'

'It's OK.' I nodded, feeling that I probably wasn't in trouble. 'He's a friend of mine.'

'Can I talk in front of him? Is he orright?'

'Yes, you can.'

'Is 'e the other one who's in this picture deal wiv yer?'

I nodded again.

'Orright now, David, 'oo's stitched yer up?'

'Er, nobody,' I murmured, not entirely sure what he meant.

'David, son! Come on. Yer all over the fuckin' papers! 'Oo is it? Just tell us – that's all yer 'ave to do, son.'

I could see that Peter was still petrified, but I now knew they'd come here to help, in observance of the strange code of loyalty of their kind – the sort of loyalty that makes the friends of East End gangland murderers describe them as 'real gents and diamond geezers'.

I offered them a drink or a cup of tea. They declined.

'David, all yer gotta do is tell us 'oo stitched yer up. 'Oo's gone to the papers – 'oo's wrote all that terrible crap. And we'll sort 'em – orright?'

I shook my head. 'It's OK, I promise. It won't make things easier for us if anything happened to them. We've got a good legal case against the papers.'

''Ow come?'

'The pictures are right.'

They looked incredulous. 'Not Sextons?'

'No.'

The older one shook his head and asked to make a phone call.

''Ello, Mum. We've found him . . . No, he says he's orright, Mum. So we're coming 'ome.'

I didn't think it was his mum and I didn't know how they'd found out where I was. I was just incredibly relieved that they'd turned out to be on my side, and I was even more relieved when they nodded their misshapen heads in farewell and barged out of the flat.

'Jesus, H, who the hell were they?' Peter asked, still quivering a little.

I shrugged. I didn't really know how to explain what had just happened. 'It all goes back ten years or more, to when I was hanging around Toby's with John Daly. I got to know a lot of these people and got on well with them, and now I'm looked after. That's not the first time this has happened. In the old days, if I was in trouble and they got to hear, these people turned up. Not necessarily those two, it could be others, but in the East End they like me for some reason – I used to make them laugh, I suppose, and I didn't judge them. If I'd said who I think is behind this story, they'd have gone and done something quite serious.'

*

The truth was that pictures weren't fakes, but we had stirred up the unseemly side of the art business, where authentication is sought and paid for as a picture makes its way to a sale room. Peter went to a top lawyer and saw a barrister who cross-questioned him, knowing that the main paper was going to defend. Arraigned against us would be some leading experts who would be hard to discredit, even though others had changed their opinion. The lawyer asked if we were prepared to lose our houses, because a jury would know nothing about art and certain bigwigs, having said the pictures were fake, were going to stick to their guns. Whatever happened, it would cost money.

I was busy. This was the last thing I needed while I was trying to learn my part in *Jeeves*. When our lawyer dispatched a note to the paper's lawyer to say we were considering suing, a courier came back inside an hour with the message, 'Good. See you in court!'

From the paper's point of view, Peter and I were worth a good few column inches. Several distinguished people had bought the pictures and the case would have sold a lot of papers.

There was no point going on with an action. Nobody who'd bought the paintings had asked for their money back and the people close to us were entirely on our side, so we decided to get on with our lives, which in my case was soon weighed down with gloom over *Jeeves*.

It was obvious during rehearsals and the preview run in Bristol that the show was a mess. Ayckbourn looked defeated and despondent. He didn't enjoy writing with a committee; three-quarters of an hour of the 'drama' he'd written between the songs was cut. This was mainly because the show ran past the time of the last buses in Bristol, so every night a large proportion of the audience had to pile out before then, with a great clattering of seats, if they wanted to make it home. This did not augur well, and even I had to admit to myself that the songs I had to sing were instantly forgettable. It seemed incredible that Andrew Lloyd Webber should have a flop, but the reviews after our first night in London on 22 April confirmed that this was indeed the case.

Poor *Jeeves* was greeted with vitriolic derision by critics delighted to give the phenomenally successful Lloyd Webber a good kicking. Only the *Daily Express* – God bless them, I thought at the time – found it in their hearts to say something good about my part in this fiasco.

The show limped on towards an inevitable early death and for me the pain was relieved only by a successful showing at the end of

April of a BBC TV drama, *Private Affairs*, in which I appeared as F. Scott Fitzgerald.

It was also cheering, a few days later, when the *Observer* published a big feature in their colour supplement about Elizabeth Oakley, with a lot of illustrations which categorically confirmed the genuineness of our pictures and the greatness of the artist. Peter and I were totally and utterly vindicated.

By the middle of May, *Jeeves* had closed after a four-week run – about a month more than it deserved.

After that I took Prue away for a quick holiday to Jamaica, where the exotic, tropical Englishness appealed to me very much. When we came back it was not my intention to move in with her lock, stock and barrel, so to speak, but I did feel I should help her look for a better flat. We found one in South Kensington, and in August she started doing it up while I headed west, and west again, to Hawaii to make *Islands in the Stream*, with Frank Shafner and co-starring George C. Scott, Claire Bloom and Gilbert Roland.

When I arrived on the island of Kauai, to which I'd been summoned with great urgency, nobody seemed to be ready for us, with the result that George and I simply sat around for weeks in a tropical-paradise-style bar called the Beach House, drinking pina coladas under waving palm fronds – not so bad when you're being paid to do it. As ever, with time on my hands, my imagination ran riot and I was soon devising a series of initiatives for the development of the island's economy – rather as I had in the Seychelles a few years before.

There seems to be something about islands that has a tremendous appeal – perhaps it is that they represent a world, or at least a nation, in miniature, rather like a doll's house or a model village. Suddenly you feel that you are dealing with a society on a scale which is comprehensible and manageable. As a result of my interest, somewhere along the way I was made a minister of the Kauai Theological Ministry in Lihue. I can't recall the reason for it, or the perks, beyond the power to officiate at marriages, but I still have a chequebook specific to an account in the name of the Ministry, and I'm glad that, for a short time at least, I could legitimately be referred to as Reverend.

At the same time, over the months we were filming there, with me playing Eddie, Scott's boozing partner, I became great friends with George. He was one of the biggest, most expansive actors I've ever known, broad-shouldered and a great man, whom I admired to the extent that in October, when Prue announced rather to my surprise that she was pregnant, I resolved that if we had a boy (which we did) he would be called George (which he is).

I saw no reason why we should marry as a result of her pregnancy. Naturally, I got pestered by the press, who noted that I was looking a little stout and the hair was greying. It is one of their favourite ways of attacking an actor. I was quoted as saying that I didn't intend to marry because 'you can share a home and a baby without the benefit of clergy'.

In the same piece, they wrote that I had become a fanatical American football fan, which was true, and that I was taking bets on the football results from all the film crew (also true – I'd always rather be the bank than a punter). When asked about this and my other activities, I said, 'I find acting a very childish and frivolous occupation, and it can be excruciatingly boring, but it suits me – I have a very childish personality.'

A little like the ever-reluctant Bertie Wooster, though it might not have been my intention to move in with Prue or, ultimately, to marry her, these two scenarios were developing inexorably, kicked on by Gayle asking me if I could look after Nolan while she was away filming in Israel. He came and lived with Prue and me, which, of course, I loved, and there was no escaping the fact that we were already beginning to behave like a family. I was also persuaded to buy a bigger place nearby, a white three-storeyed house in Ensor Mews, just off Onslow Gardens, to accommodate our own imminent child.

On 19 March 1976, Prue and I were married at Chelsea Register Office, followed by a wedding supper of baked beans on toast and a honeymoon taken at Ensor Mews. Six weeks later, in the Westminster Hospital, Prue gave birth to George, a strapping little chap who weighed in at 8lb 1oz, and I was astonished to find how chuffed I was to be a father again.

When I was wearing my producer's cap at that time, I worked from an office in Curzon Street with an extraordinary man called James Mitchell. He was 28 going on 48, and had come to me claiming to be a whiz in US law – always an important aspect of movie-making. In fact, thanks to attractive tax shelters provided by the Canadian Treasury, like a lot of film producers I was keen to work on projects which could be made in Canada, and in this case with Canadian producer Garth Drabinsky on a picture called *The Disappearance*. Another Canadian, Stewart Cooper, was directing, and the film starred Donald Sutherland, John Hurt and Virginia McKenna.

I went back to Canada briefly the following year to act with Donald in a Claude Chabrol film called *Blood Relatives*. It was the only film I ever made with Claude, a most distinctive director. Aware that mine was a diversionary part, I asked him how he wanted me to play it. He shrugged, and a long caterpillar of white ash tumbled from the end of the cigarette which seemed permanently to dangle from his lips. 'You 'ave ze blue eyes. You are ze red 'erring,' he explained.

The Disappearance wasn't a bad (though not a great) picture, and was my third with a producer credit. At that stage I still felt, as I had since my days at the Arts Educational School, that my true destiny lay in producing films. I loved the creative side of production, sourcing properties, man and resource management, wheeler-dealing with distributors, negotiating with other people's agents. It seemed to me far more exciting than simply standing around like a prune, waiting to be told what to do.

Of course, marriage to Prue, unplanned as it was, had sharpened up my need for income. I don't know what it is about marriage that makes two married people cost twice as much to house and feed as two singletons – let alone the rusk-and-nappy factor of a newborn babe.

Nolan too was already a responsibility, and would be brought along to the office from time to time by Gayle. Often I took him home, where I would teach him how to ride his bike across the knobbly cobbles of the mews, or he would end up playing with my lovely sec/ass, Sally Derham-Reid's typewriter.

Sally was a good-looking, independent sort of bird whom I fancied continuously from the minute she walked into the office and whose attractions only grew stronger with every day that passed by without her allowing me to raid her drawers.

As usual, funding for my new project was still illusory, or, at least, theoretical rather than actual, and I had to scurry back and forth to Rome to make two pictures in quick succession, without spending too much time there. *La Via della Droga* (*The Dope Way*) and *Squadra Antitruffa* (*Swindle*) were not the most distinguished movies of my career, but they paid the bills for a while. These were closely followed

David Hemmings and
Gayle Hunnicutt on the
set of *Charge*, 1967.

David Hemmings working on his 'Free of
Charge' column and cartoon, *Ankara Daily
News*, Turkey, 1967.

Right: Gayle Hunnicutt and David
Hemmings: Wedding – 16 November 1968.

David Hemmings, Gayle Hunnicutt and Trevor Howard at the New York première of *The Charge of the Light Brigade*, 1968.

Left: David Hemmings with Nolan while directing *Running Scared*, 1971.

Below: Richard Attenborough and David Hemmings: *Only When I Larf*, 1967.

David Hemmings
playing two roles
in *The Best House in
London*, 1968.

Left: Anthony Newley,
David Hemmings and
Michael Horden: *Mr Quilp*,
1975.

Below: David Hemmings
with his mother Kathleen
Hemmings at the Elizabeth
Oakley Exhibition, 1975.

David Hemmings and Leslie Bricusse.

Top right: Donald Sutherland and David Hemmings: *Blood Relatives*, Canada, 1977.

Above: David Hemmings and his daughter Deborah.

Above right: Directing Tom Selleck – *Magnum PI Hawaii*, early 1980s.

Right: David Hemmings and Prue with Edward, William, Charlotte and George.

Top left: Robert Powell and David Hemmings with shoes at DH's exhibition of 'Eclectic Similarities', May 1977.

Above: David Hemmings' granddaughters, Esme and Molly Kemp.

Top right: Tessa Dahl and David Hemmings, 1992.

Below right: David Hemmings and Jimmy Webb at Richard Harris' Memorial, September 2003.

Above: John Daly and David Hemmings 'Eclectic Similarities'.

Right: Louisa Williams, David Hemmings' stepdaughter.

David Hemmings and
Oliver Reed: *Gladiator*
– Malta, 1999.

Inset: Joaquin
Phoenix, David
Hemmings and
Tommy Flanagan:
Malta, 1999.

David Hemmings,
Tom Courtenay,
Bob Hoskins,
Michael Caine
and Ray Winstone:
Last Orders, 2000.

Left: David
Hemmings, Ralph
Brown and Vinnie
Jones: *Mean
Machine*, 2001.

Leonardo DiCaprio, Daniel Day-Lewis, Martin Scorsese (centre) and David
Hemmings with members of the cast on the set of *Gangs of New York*,
Rome, 2000.

Staňa (David Hemmings'
dresser on *Gladiator*),
David and Lucy
Hemmings on the set
of *The League of
Extraordinary
Gentlemen*, Prague,
2002.

Right: David and Lucy
Hemmings.

by *The Squeeze*, which an old friend and Niv Jr's one-time sidekick, Linda Agran, had got me on to.

I enjoyed *The Squeeze*, which Michael Apted directed and which co-starred Stephen Boyd, Stacy Keach, James Fox and Carol White. It was a gritty little London thriller for which Leon Griffiths wrote a good, tight script. One memorable aspect of the production was the minder who'd been hired because stuff kept getting nicked. I thought it wonderful the way this taciturn character dressed for his part, as if he was actually appearing in the movie. He would turn up every day in wide checked suits with iridescent ties and spend much of the time checking the condition of his fingernails.

Bored as usual, I would take everybody's watches off and, by the end of the day I'd have a bucketful of them which no one had missed. I also thought I'd wind up the little gorilla a bit and told him subtly that Linda was mad about him. So he started putting on even snappier suits and ever more powerful aftershave – a kind of sweet-smelling napalm. Leon Griffiths was rather captivated by him too, and loved the minder situation, and it was from precisely this character that he and Linda developed the popular TV series *Minder*, with Denis Waterman and the incomparable George 'The World's Your Lobster' Cole, which she produced with her next company.

While I was trying to set up another production in Canada, *Power Play*, in which I also acted, I seemed to have a string of other parts and could almost have kidded myself that my acting career was firming up again. There was the Canadian thriller, *Blood Relatives*, *Murder by Decree* – a Sherlock Holmes – and a couple of big TV films – *Charlie Muffin*, produced by Linda Agran with Verity Lambert, and *Clouds of Glory – The Rime of the Ancient Mariner*, in which I played Samuel Taylor Coleridge in the Lake District, and experienced the delights of working with Ken Russell for the first time.

On the occasions when I managed to get back to the office in Curzon Street, Sally continued to present something of a challenge. The more firmly she kept her undergarments in place, the more I wanted to remove them. She said she was in love with a penniless young doctor, known to me as Rubber Gloves, who always seemed to be in the way. Often, on trips to Rome, I left her tickets to come with me, but she never would. I was reduced to leaving little notes on her typewriter with drawings of chickens: 'This is for you. Why didn't you pick up your ticket? Cluck cluck.'

In among this activity there was a string of meetings and discussions about the making of *The Prince and the Pauper* with Oliver Reed, though there was still plenty of time to lunch at Tiberio's or play darts at the Queen's Elm or snooker at the Chelsea Arts Club.

Domestic life was not all sugar and bliss. As a secretary Prue had been authoritarian and intolerant of any backsliding, which was fine; that's what you need – at least, it's what I need – in a secretary. However, once we married, I asked her to stop work – I wanted her at home in bare feet and diaphanous frocks, laughing and smiling, and doing skilful things with Mediterranean fish and exotic fresh vegetables. But bossy secretaries don't become submissive angels overnight.

She had enthusiastically taken up the task of teaching our young son to speak. She had decided the way to do it was, every time George looked at something and pointed, in that rather rude way babies have, to vigorously repeat the name of the object he was inspecting – 'Duck! Duck! Duck! Egg! Egg! Egg! Fish! Fish! Fish!'

I found that when I lurched into the house after a long day at the office or a bit of a sesh at the Chelsea Arts Club and poured myself a large restorative vodka, she would stare and point at it with an accusing finger, while I dutifully intoned, 'Drink! Drink! Drink!'

A number of poor George's goldfish suddenly found their small glass world hurtling through the air and shattering against a wall. We had to keep several spare bowls for emergency rehousing.

Prue did her best, though, to provide a stable home, which was largely an alien concept to me, and to some extent she succeeded. She had become pregnant again fairly soon after the birth of George and, on 29 September 1977, Edward was born. She was keen to see me as a hands-on father and encouraged me to spend more time with my mate Mike Leander, who had two boys, Luke and Rudi, more or less the same age as ours. Their mother, Penny, was a teenage friend of Prue's and Mike was a successful songwriter (if Gary Glitter's greatest hits can be categorised as 'songs') who had been musical director at MCA when Prue was working there. He was also the chairman of SODS (Society of Distinguished Songwriters) and, absolutely no slouch, had arranged and orchestrated 'She's Leaving Home' for the Beatles. As a result of my well-established affinity with musicians, I was quite happy when occasionally Mike and I were inveigled into taking our sons out together.

Mike, like a lot of my friends, was inclined to be very competitive. After a visit to the Round Pond in Kensington Gardens one Friday afternoon, over a drink in the Chelsea Arts Club we challenged each other to make model sailing boats from scratch and race them across the pond to establish a winner. We shot off to Hamleys, bought a brace of the most elaborate DIY model schooners on offer and rushed home. Neither of us would stop until our boat was complete and ready to launch.

We didn't sleep for 48 hours, and thus it was that after lunch on Sunday, with the park fairly well packed, two baggy-eyed, unshaven men of eau-de-Nil countenance met, with small reluctant sons, on the edge of the Bay of Cadiz – the side of the Round Pond with the least goose shit.

The mothers lurked in the background, tittering disloyally while the yachts were produced, shown off and admired for their beauty and fineness of construction before they were launched. It is seldom that I have won a challenge like this so quickly and so completely. Before Mike's yacht had reached the middle of the pond, it suddenly heeled over as if it had been pole-axed and sank with a speed James Cameron would have envied while making *Titanic*. Mike was apoplectic, Luke cried and the onlookers laughed, barely disguising their scorn.

Mike turned out to be a particularly loyal friend early the following year when it transpired that I had failed to settle an outstanding tax bill. I've never been good at tax and a serious backlog had been building up over a period of time. When two representatives of HM Collector of Taxes arrived at the front door asking for me, I told Prue to ring Mike and ask him if he could drive straight round and meet me very discreetly by the back entrance to our property. We couldn't ask a cab to do it and if I left on foot I would have to walk right past these humourless bloodsuckers (not, of course, that I had anything against them as individuals).

Penny Leander told me later that, after Prue's call, Mike lay in bed for a while, smoking a cigarette before he got up and went out to get his car – apparently he thought the wait would do me good – but he did turn up and, wrapped in a blanket, I scurried out of the back door, dived onto the floor of his car and we sped off.

This brought home to me rather starkly that I was in a serious mess financially and could be bankrupted if I didn't settle up or leave Blighty for a while, until I'd earned enough to deal with what I owed. I don't know what it is about tax demands, but they always turn up when you don't have any money in the bank. When you want a new car, there's money there; when you want to take your family on holiday, there are funds available; but the cupboard's always bare when the taxman calls. There is probably some little-known rule of economics that applies: Murphy's inverse sod-all-there-when-you-need-it Law.

As luck, or my old *amiga* Sister Serendipity, had it, there was a job all lined up waiting for me abroad, in the form of *Just a Gigolo*, which I was to direct. What was more, I had a lot of reasons to be very excited by the challenges this picture presented. It was being made in Berlin and was to star David Bowie and, in a speaking part for the first time in seventeen years, Marlene Dietrich.

The film is a heavily sardonic black comedy about a young, war-weary Prussian officer (played by Bowie) who comes back to Berlin after the First World War and can't recognise or settle into the new ways of the city. He drifts around until he becomes a gigolo, working for a baroness played by Marlene Dietrich.

Before Bowie confirmed that he would play the part, I had to go to Montreux, where he then lived, and convince him that he should. He was, as I had expected, hugely stimulating to deal with – clever, funny, original and with a very special natural elegance. He had a face that always looked beautiful on camera; he didn't have any bad angles, which, as it happened, posed a problem on this film. We went to a lot of trouble to make him look filthy and down-and-out, buying the scruffiest clothes we could find, but as soon as he put them on, they became an elegant new look. We laughed about it a lot – the 'Gardening Look', in wellies, baggy old cords, tatty sweater and a cloth cap. When I wore it, I looked like a gardener; when Bowie wore it, he looked like the front cover of *Vogue*.

Bowie, thank God, was fascinated by the character he had to play. He was anxious to delve into the persona of the gigolo, the male hetero-sexual hooker – a type he had always found somewhat inscrutable and difficult to get to know. And the role allowed him to show the sensual side of his nature, which hadn't been possible in his last film, *The Man Who Fell to Earth*, where his character didn't have any genitals!

I was going to play the part of a maniacal Hitler manqué figure whose hideout is a U-bahn station and the whole cast came in a variety of dialects: Kim Novak (Monterey), Curt Jürgens (Bavaria), Sydne Rome (Rome, natch, or Moose Droppings, Iowa), Hemmings (A3 corridor) and Bowie (Brixton).

I'd hardly seen Kim since our 'Brive Encounter' in the park on *The Eye of the Devil* and I'm not sure she even remembered the event – or perhaps it had never happened and I'd just dreamed it.

When it came to it, the business of actually making the film was not easy. There were ongoing tensions between the German and English crews, and not all the actresses were getting on with each other. Organisation on the producers' part was at best sketchy – and at worst positively Venezuelan.

However, I did enjoy working with Bowie and researching the cultural heirs of pre-war Berlin's seamy night life. I was encouraged in this by finding in the city the ever-lusty Kenneth More, who introduced me to several bizarre clubs. In one of them, we were not allowed through the door until we had taken off all our clothes, the first stage in what turned out to be a comprehensive fleecing, which was almost worth it, just for the memorable joy of seeing Kenny lolling naked on large cushions with three young *Fraüleins* in attendance and a sublimely happy grin on his face.

The greatest challenge on *Gigolo* was filming the 78-year-old Marlene Dietrich. She had refused, of course, to come to Germany, where she hadn't been since before the war. Instead we had to transport a complete set to Paris. Most of the shooting with the rest of the cast had been completed, but there were a few shots with Marlene and Bowie together. Marlene, though, was being a little coy about getting on with it – not to say a downright prima donna. At that stage even I hadn't seen her, but our producer, Josh Sinclair, had assured me, through gritted teeth, that she would perform.

In any case, we had shot most of Bowie's side of their encounter, which was just as well, as time ran out for him. He had other commitments and had to go, despite his expressed enthusiasm for working with the supreme diva.

In the end, Marlene was brought to the set by Josh Sinclair and her daughter, and I was surprised, not to say a little alarmed, to see how tense and nervous she was. Perhaps I shouldn't have been – she had not, after all, done the job for so long. I suggested my age-old and seldom-failed remedy for nervousness – a serious sharpener. I took one for each of us into her dressing room, where she dealt with hers in a few seconds. Before I had time to go and get a refill, she had unzipped a BOAC bag stuffed with airline miniatures that she must have thriftily accumulated over the years, and we had a couple more good, big drinks. After that, she smiled. 'All right. I am ready.' And she walked onto the set with all her composure and extraordinary charisma in place, like the star she'd been for over fifty years.

We shot her scenes in two days with a faultless performance, and she also came back the next day to record the title song for the movie. I had no complaints. She must have felt good about it too. Before she left the set, she stopped and talked to the German crew – in German, reportedly the first time she'd used the language in public for years.

This, however, was not enough to salvage what had turned into a disaster movie. Somehow, all the tensions during production seemed to show through in the picture. I cut and recut it to suit possible distributors (who were not easy to find) and, when the money ran out, I left and the whole thing was cut to ribbons in a way that lost all the humour and irony.

After the rigours of the Berlin shoot, Prue and I could not relax in London until my tax problems were sorted out, so we rented a house in Majorca, near Pollenca, where her father and the Leanders had villas. With two small boys and a couple of nannies to help out, it was a happy and peaceful interlude. It was marvellous for Prue to unwind from the tensions caused by the taxman and *Gigolo*.

Seeing the Leanders was also a great boost to the general sense of well-being that seemed to permeate that quiet and lovely northern end of the island, which even a brief encounter with the local *guardia civil* couldn't mar.

As it happens, that little bit of bother, like Bertie Wooster's legendary encounters with the constabulary on Boat Race day, came about entirely as a result of high spirits and, I suppose, large quantities of Majorcan plonk. In the Leanders' house was a cavernous fireplace, a little like the one at Oranmore Castle, and on the wall above it was a pair of crossed Majorcan sabres in their scabbards, which Mike had bought, no doubt, with a view to self-defence.

But that night, with a vast cream-coloured moon shimmering on a plonk-dark sea, seemed a night for scenes of heroic battles and ancient chivalry. We grabbed the swords off the wall and headed straight for the main old *plaza* in the middle of the balmy summer evening air of old Pollenca. In those days, the majority of the population were natives and that evening they were engaged in their *paseo*, an age-old summer custom in which the women stroll through the town gossiping their heads off while the men eye up all the young crumpet.

In the middle of the *plaza* was a small stage on which Mike and I leaped. We drew our weapons from their scabbards and proceeded to fight in the best English tradition of Errol Flynn. The *plaza* was packed and we drew an immediate audience, which only encouraged us as we parried and thrust. We were having a wonderful time and, when a small man wearing a strange shiny black saucepan on his head approached the stage and verbally challenged us, I assumed he wanted to join in the fun.

I spun round and pointed my sword at his chest. 'On guard,' I yelled cheerfully, and found myself instantly under arrest.

It took a long time and a lot of patient, halting explanation of the English sense of humour, but ultimately, thank God, with the help of a friend who turned up and spoke proper Spanish, we persuaded this zealous guardian of the people that we had not intended to insult him, his office or Spain and did not need to be arrested or detained. The audience, it seemed, enjoyed the arrest and subsequent passionate pleading and begging at least as much as the sword fight. In the end, we were released after a heavy reprimand, an on-the-spot fine and the confiscation of Mike's swords (which he got back a few weeks later).

The frivolous mood was somewhat dampened when David Bowie arrived to look at my version of *Gigolo* and a short documentary I'd made at his request around his last Earls Court show. He had incredibly specific expectations and he didn't like either of them. There wasn't a lot he could do about *Gigolo* but he binned the documentary, which, although not the end of the world, was very disheartening.

I couldn't help feeling that, for the time being and with a little encouragement from HM Collector of Taxes, my career in England had run out of steam, and I should broaden my horizons. Like a lot of Brits looking for a change, my sights turned back to America, and then, as a result of sudden, unexpected prompting, towards the Antipodes.

17

The Antipodean Years, 1979–1982

So, Prue and I had opted for Oz. It was far off and warm come winter, and, since neither of us had ever been there, it seemed the only logical destination. We arranged flights and hotels, when – explain this to me if you can – within minutes of booking our tickets, my agent was on the phone.

'Would you,' he asked with an edge of doubt, 'be interested in doing a film in Australia?'

'When?' I asked.

'Next week.'

Prudence and I packed our gear, cancelled the tickets we were about to pay for and prepared for an eight-week stint on a movie called *Thirst* – all expenses paid. What a wallop! The script was dreadful, but I didn't mind. Australia was exactly where we wanted to go and we all know that it isn't done to inspect the teeth of a gift horse.

And teeth were a factor. *Thirst* was a vampire movie also starring Chantal Cantouri and Henry Silva, who, in the last reel, I flung to his death from a helicopter. What I did to Chantal, don't ask. The film was produced by Anthony I. Ginnane, who, despite a reputation for extreme tightness, I found delightful.

Tony was leanly built and known locally as 'Gucci Ginnane', largely because he liked things that were labelled 'Rich'. He drove a drop-top red Mercedes with the number plate AIG 1. He always wore silk shirts, into which he sweated from the moment he put them on. He had a slight, tightly trimmed moustache that suggested he might have been in the stocking business in immediate post-war England, and he was funnier and sharper than Robin Williams on a good day. He carried vast office files in a suitcase – Gucci, naturally – that was so heavy you could believe it held his secretary. I carried it, just once, so I speak with authority.

The script of *Thirst* was by a first-time screenwriter called John Pinkney, a well-known journo and short-story writer. His protagonists were contemporary vampires – a group of businesspeople selling blood to other groups around the world (sort of international grocers). The secondary plot concerned a woman who was heir to the Queenship of the Vampires. She wouldn't accept it and it was my job as head of the group to convince her that she was, in fact, a vampire.

Tony had been looking for a foreign actor to play the lead character. He didn't concentrate much on where the story was set; anonymous big cities which could have been anywhere was the aim. Accents weren't a problem to him either, although a lot of other people didn't agree. In *Thirst*, a number of people were from different parts of the world and the mix of accents was appropriate, he said. Even the Australian actors sounded quite English.

Just before we started shooting, *Love at First Bite* was released and Tony had to decide whether to play our movie straight or camp it up a bit; he chose straight. He discussed all this with me very openly, deep into the night, and seemed to treat me almost as a co-producer, not just as a piece of celluloid flesh. He certainly knew my work, and it turned out that while he'd been doing a law degree at university, he'd had a job as a film critic. Before *Thirst* he'd made half a dozen small domestic pictures and now, at the age of 31, he thought he was ready to hit the international scene; and the best way to do it was with what he called generic product. Unfortunately, *Thirst* was not the one to make his name in international moviedom.

It wasn't much of a movie, but I'm grateful to *Thirst* for introducing me to Australia and to Tony. About three months later, John Barnett, a producer from New Zealand, asked Tony to put him in touch with me for a film he was doing there called *Beyond Reasonable Doubt*. As a result, I went to NZ to shoot the picture. I then picked up the threads with Tony when I passed through Australia on the way back; thanks to our previous experience, we had become firm friends.

Australia appealed to me and within a few months Prue, George, Edward and I, plus a nanny or two, were moving into a house rented from the distinguished film-maker Fred Schepisi, just across the way from Melbourne's long-fronted beach. The shore smelt of Brighton, the house itself of Victorian pine and, though there was no garden to speak of, you felt there was.

Tony's office was a short stroll away, around the corner and past the convenient pub, and it was from here that we prepared our next picture, *Harlequin*.

Harlequin was directed by Simon Wincer and the screenplay, by Everett De Roche, was much more elegant than *Thirst*. It was based loosely on the plethora of stories that have emerged about Rasputin at the imperial Russian court and the extraordinary influence he wielded over the royal family.

In production terms it was a hybrid film, which never helps. Although the story is set in the US, it was shot in Australia, which involved some unsatisfactory fiddling about and an attempt to reverse the frames to make the cars drive on the right. Most, though not all, accents were more or less American.

I was to play an American senator, and Tony had also secured Broderick Crawford, former American TV star and extreme drinker. We still needed the Rasputin character, the 'Harlequin'. I suggested to the producers that they get Robert Powell, whom I'd directed in *Running Scared* and who was not only a mate but also a fine actor. He was cast, along with Carmen Duncan. Carmen was a well-known Australian actress in TV and theatre who subsequently went to the States, where she became a successful soap star. She's a very good actress, a nice person and seriously beautiful. She was to play my wife, which she did with tremendous gusto. We fell into each other's charms like the villains that we were – cheeky, rude, outlandish even. Carmen lived in Rose Bay, Sydney, with her husband; I lived with Prue in Melbourne; but, as a result of production subsidies Tony had managed to squeeze out of Western Australia, *Harlequin* was to be made in Perth. This was deeply convenient for Carmen and me, and allowed us to have one of those very intense and exotic love affairs whose taste lingers for years.

Four or five weeks before shooting was due to start on *Harlequin* in autumn 1979, I was back in London for a short visit to set up some new deals when I got an urgent call from Tony. He had suddenly been let down for $50,000 of his funding. There was no leeway in his budget and he had to replace it. Did I have any ideas?

I thought for a moment. 'I wonder what would happen if I rang John Daly and asked him if he wanted to get involved,' I said.

'Are you sure you want to do that?'

'Maybe I can,' I said.

I still saw John from time to time, and I'd sensed that he felt a little bad about what had happened over Hemdale and wouldn't mind the opportunity to mend fences.

Tony sounded excited. 'Let me prime Larry Friedricks in LA.'

Larry, I knew, had started working for Hemdale in LA and was familiar with some of Tony's more successful projects.

'OK. Speak to him, then I'll call John.'

I rang John, who was more than happy to talk, got back to Tony and told him to work out the deal with John.

Tony flew to London and met John for the first time. As is often the way with John, Tony didn't come away with the best deal he'd ever done and John got a lot for his $50,000, although there was no doubt that it was a risk. So the project went ahead.

I have to take you to Perth, because it is one of my favourite places on the planet. It is the city that is furthest from any other city and to get to it is life-threatening. You can, of course, fly; that's about five hours from Sydney and NO SMOKING. You can take a bus; that's about five days. Or ride a train; around three days. Or drive; that's a week and counting. The big challenge is getting across the Nullarbor Plain, flat and endless, a place so arid it makes the Sahara look like Hobbiton. Even in Death Valley, up towards Los Vegas, there are yucca trees and cacti. On the Nullarbor there is nothing. Just the sight of it would make you want to drink a gallon of brake fluid.

I certainly considered it, driving in an old Mercury Station Wagon, staring at the temperature gauge, certain that every mile was my last. But at the end of the road, straight as an arrow, hugging the rail tracks from time to time, Perth emerged from the haze, and the first glimpse is of greenery and – a very welcome surprise – the Swan River meandering towards a city of immense charm.

Perth has been planned beautifully. On either side of the Swan is a quarter of a mile of parkland that has never been built on, so it is gloriously green, just as the river is dark blue and pollution-free. Only the Swan Brewery stands alongside the river, probably for the nearness of water, and it gives great beer. The river threads through the city like a glittering string of pearls around the neck of a princess. The planners loved their city and protected it. One could only wish that the planners of some of Britain's ancient towns and cities had had the same devotion.

Perth has high-rise buildings, for sure, but they sparkle with cleanliness, and the streets have never seen litter. The soft suburbs smell like winter moss, the sort of place where spotless kids drink milk and ride bicycles everywhere, as in a Spielberg movie.

I slunk into my parking space at the scrubbed and pristine Parmelia Hotel and hobbled grubbily up to the front desk to check in. There was a message from Alan Bond – an invitation to a party.

Needless to say, stinking of a week's desert dust and the weary tang of grease from the Mercury Marquis, I rang to accept, showered, shaved and taxied off. When Alan Bond had first come to Australia, he was a signwriter, and a very good one too, by all accounts. But in past years, here on the west coast he had, through various property deals, amassed an unspeakably large fortune and big chunks of Perth. His penthouse and his gargantuan appearance had swelled with profits, as had the rest of the city.

I was very happy at the prospect of spending time with Robert Powell again. It would be the first work we'd done together since I'd directed him ten years before. Although we'd been regularly in touch and saw each other when we could, none of the many projects we'd talked about had ever materialised – an aspect of the movie business I'd learned to accept.

In *Harlequin*, the US senator I play has a son who is a haemophiliac. Robert's Harlequin character is a strange magician who has come into their lives to help cure the boy and who exhibits some extraordinary powers, without ever letting the audience know for sure whether he's a con man or for real. The people backing the Senator deem that Harlequin has become far too powerful an influence and decide to kill him.

The political manipulator behind the scenes is played by Broderick Crawford. Tony admitted to me that he had cast Brod solely for what he judged to be his pulling power (such as it was) in the States. Tony felt that he was a force to be reckoned with: after all, we'd all grown up with *Highway Patrol* in which Broderick had starred, hearing his gravelly voice sign off each week with, 'Drive safely, and mind how you go,' or whatever it was. This was also a man who'd won an Oscar and given a great performance in *All the King's Men*.

However, time rolls by (don't I know it) and Brod had reached that stage in life where many things had become just too much trouble. He was content, on the whole, if his glass was kept topped up and he had a comfortable bed at night.

When we were shooting in a makeshift studio for a while, I was hanging around waiting to be called and I wandered to the back of the set, where Broderick was standing – leaning – against a pillar, huffing quietly to himself. I noticed that there was something odd and vaguely foreign-looking about his trousers. There were no flies.

I wondered what the costume department was up to. Surely it would be most unusual, if not outrageously unconventional, for a senior American political fixer to wear flush-fronted slacks. I gingerly sidled over to take a closer look without disturbing his reverie.

The camera was rolling and there was silence on set. I had to do everything I could to stifle the laughter trying to escape from me like steam from a tank engine. I was completely convulsed with mirth, writhing like some medieval halfwit having an attack of the vapours. I heard Simon Wincer, the director, snap.

'What the hell is that noise?'

I stuffed a fist in my throat.

Filming resumed. I looked at Broderick again, and the suppressed laughter was almost painful. My eyes were streaming. I couldn't help pumping out a few more squeals.

'What the fuck is that?' Simon bellowed. 'It sounds like a cat fucking. You guys, get back and kill it or something.'

A moment later some of the crew, followed closely by an ever-curious Robert Powell, found me standing with one hand over my mouth and tears streaming down my face, pointing at Broderick.

They all looked, and a second later they were also convulsed at the astonishing sight that met their gaze. They could see what I had, that there was no fly on the front of the trousers, but there was one at the back. It wasn't designed to be, so the only explanation was that Broderick had pulled his trousers on, found they were the wrong way round and, instead of dropping them and starting again like any other civilised member of the human race, thought, 'Oh, what the hell?' and reached behind his back to zip them up and clip the waistband. He was so far gone, he just didn't care.

In the end, *Harlequin* was a bizarre, surreal sort of picture that was only a moderate success, although, more pleasingly, it has become something of a cult. Anyway, the picture was finished and, the following spring, Tony and John organised a good première for it in London, with three days' press beforehand. Carmen came over too, which was nice, and the film got respectable reviews. Tony was very impressed when John Daly took him off to a gallery near his office and bought him a painting of a harlequin. John always liked to move in mysterious ways and went on to back a lot more of Tony's pictures.

On a social level, Perth was magnificent. The Perthians could not have been more friendly or done more to encourage our bad behaviour. While we were staying there, on Saturday nights Robert and I used to take over one of the bars in a nightclub called the Underground. How or why the management permitted it, I've no idea, but when I put it to them, they seemed to think it was a great idea, and it gave us something to amuse ourselves with after a slow day's shoot.

To provide a little originality, we decided that we would make and serve cocktails based exclusively on the colours people were wearing. I think maybe it was a first – drinks made to colour-coordinate with the punters. With a well-stocked bar, it's extraordinary what you can achieve with grenadine, green Chartreuse, blue curaçao, advocaat – even stripes, we found, when varying viscosities allowed – and we produced more fiery sunsets than Turner could have shaken a stick at.

Inevitably, there were more people ill after our sessions behind the bar than on any other nights, because we simply didn't care what we mixed with what, so long as the artistic results and the colours were right. Astonishingly enough, though, people kept coming back for more – would even swap clothes so as to experiment more widely with different drinks, and we never got out of there before dawn. Sadly, the only person who didn't appreciate our artistic achievements in the Underground was Prue, who, somewhat rashly, had decided to accompany me for a few weeks of the shoot. Robert was also a bit peeved at having to cover for me when I'd inadvertently lingered too long with Carmen. It was a tricky period, and my marriage to Prue came under a lot of pressure. In the end though, it survived, which was a relief.

We were still in Perth at the end of 1979, fuelled by a few drinks with Robert Powell one evening, when I suggested he should look at the possibility of doing more films in Australia, with its burgeoning film industry. At the time they were welcoming foreign actors with open arms. As Tony Ginnane seemed susceptible to any sound suggestions, we decided to set up another film with him which, this time, I would direct.

The script was based on a story by James Herbert, *The Survivor*, which is about an air disaster when a Boeing 747 crashes, killing 340 people and leaving only the pilot alive. It's a ghost story and a very powerful tale. I quickly got it converted into a script and, at the end of the day's shooting on *Harlequin*, we sat down in the bar of the Parmelia Hotel to have our first script meeting. For some reason I decided that Brandy Alexanders would be a frightfully good idea. Three hours later, after we'd finished this somewhat ad hoc script meeting, we asked for the bill. The barman told us it was just under $100. Robert and I must have raised our eyebrows and muttered a bit, but he was ready for it.

'I *knew* you weren't going to believe it, so I've kept all the glasses, and if you'd like to come my side of the bar, you can count them.'

Fascinated, we went round and there were indeed 24 empty glasses with traces of the offending drink. It was surprising, even for us, that we were still standing, although both of us shared the problem that we can take a lot of booze. Robert would admit, however, that he's only a second-division drinker, and tends to get knocked out in the third round of the drinking FA Cup. And even then he often cheated. He admitted to me that if he was on vodkas and tonic, every time he bought a round, he would get himself just tonic, surreptitiously cutting his intake by 50 per cent. Great actor, Robert; lousy drinker.

But that night in Perth he kept up, and from the session emerged the decision to make *Survivor*. Tony agreed with the casting: Robert Powell, who made sense from a marketing perspective; Jenny Agutter to play the lead female as the medium; and Joseph Cotten, Oscar-winner for *The Third Man*, in what would be his third- or fourth-last part; with me directing.

Tony was concerned about how John Daly and Larry Friedricks would react to my directing, since he intended to get back into bed with them for some of the finance. They raised no objections and, in spring 1980, we started filming.

When we had finished making it, I thought *Survivor* had some extraordinary qualities to it, marred a little by the fact that the version that Tony ultimately released was a straightforward horror film. We had originally decided we were making more of a psychological thriller, like *The Innocents* or *The Haunting*, where the horror was intellectual rather than axe in your face.

Tony's view was that this had turned out to be a big mistake. After seeing the director's cut he felt we had a film that was a little more

Antonioni than he wanted, when he'd sold it as being like *Harlequin*. He thought the film as I'd edited it was much too slow and we would need to cut a lot of material to try to pace it up. I could see Tony was worried and reluctantly went along with him to a certain extent, though Robert was much less keen – perhaps rightly, with hindsight.

Despite this, it won two or three awards at the Sitges Festival and the Paris Fantasy Film Festival, but the distributors were disappointed by it. It did less business than *Harlequin*, and it never had a theatrical release in the States. Naturally, I wouldn't attribute that to my directing or the material; rather, it was the result of an executive decision to cut.

The air crash itself was, I think, the best action scene I've ever made. It took a lot of devising – something that appealed very much to my love of magic and illusion. We were filming in Adelaide and, on the night of the big explosion, we had eight cameras running in a huge field in the middle of town. The South Australian emergency services were out in force. There were 24 fire engines standing by, with a dozen police cars and ambulances. When the time came, at nine in the evening, we produced a controlled explosion that was one of the biggest they've ever seen or heard in downtown Adelaide. I was thrilled with the scene – and, more than twenty years later, I still think it stands up pretty well.

In any event, the film solidified my relationship with Tony and didn't put any stress on it. We both saw what we had done and the mistakes we'd made, and it was during this process that we decided to go into business together. I still retained a strongly competitive edge, and I think I felt there was an opportunity with Tony to emulate on a smaller scale what had happened with Hemdale.

When we'd finished making *Survivor* in 1980, I joined Tony and, over the next few years, we went on to make many films together in almost every city in Australia. The incentive for making films in Australia at the time was a wonderful jam doughnut centre of tax legislation, called Division 10B. This allowed professionals to write off film investment, including losses, against their taxes. I had been in the tax-avoidance business since the Hemdale days, and Tony and I were able to spot a rich dentist with money to risk from across a Melbourne square.

Bill Fayman, our man at the money wellhead, had been Tony's partner for some time. Now it was the three of us, and we renamed the company, not very imaginatively, Fayman, Ginnane, Hemmings, or FGH, which was our logo. The principal aim was to fund films that could be shot in Australia and New Zealand (with me sometimes acting or directing), using Tony's production expertise, Bill's financial skills and my creative input and connections. It was also a way to maintain the relationship between Tony and me, which we both valued.

Although a few things were happening for me in Britain – *Charlie Muffin* had been successfully broadcast and I'd been cast by Jonathan Powell at the BBC to play the leads in *Jekyll & Hyde* (for which many people, especially my spouses and co-vivants, must have thought I was very well suited) – Prue and I now found we were in Australia to stay.

The first FGH project was called *Race for the Yankee Zephyr*. It was the biggest film that Tony had ever undertaken and he'd budgeted it at around $6 million. It was written by Everett De Roche and was going to be directed by Richard Franklyn in North Queensland. We hoped we might bring John Daly in as a co-producer, and if we did, he'd want a say in casting, which was going to be tricky. The actors' union was getting tough about bringing in foreign actors to work on Australian productions, but we knew to justify the budget we needed at least four significant foreign actors.

John Daly agreed, if we could get the cast I wanted, to put in between $1.5 million and $2 million through his associate company, Dawson and Johnson, including advances for rights.

Over the next few months, Tony and I went back and forth between Australia and the States, staying for long periods in LA, where we were running up huge hotel bills for four or five weeks at a time. In the end, we succeeded in getting together a cast that made sense of our budget: Ken Wahl, Lesley Ann Warren (who'd starred in *Victor/Victoria*), George Peppard and Donald Pleasence, with whom it would be a joy to work again. There then followed a lot more running around to fix up the rest of the finance. I didn't mind; I'd always loved travelling and a regular change of scenery.

By early 1981, *Yankee Zephyr* was ready, but Australian Equity abruptly announced that they wouldn't allow us to bring four foreign actors into Australia. We were faced with the option of stopping the movie – but we'd already spent a ton of cash trying to cast the thing – or doing it with three outsiders and one Australian, which would have been acceptable to our Australian backers but would cause Hemdale to reduce their contribution by a significant amount, thus making the movie undoable. In any case, Tony was absolutely determined not to give in to the union, so we decided to bring in John Barnett from New Zealand. A new tax regime had been instituted there which had allowed a banking group run by Michael Fay and David Richwhite to start up a tax-shelter scheme for film finance.

The original idea for the film was that a DC3 carrying a cargo of millions of dollar bills had crashed in a tropical rainforest, where the money was discovered with much glee by some locals who happened on it. We had the script rewritten so that the plane crashed in the snow in the New Zealand Alps and was found by deer hunters. It would work just as well, but Richard Franklyn announced that he wouldn't shoot it there.

Up until that point, I'd been involved only as co-producer. John Barnett, for whom I'd made *Beyond Reasonable Doubt*, was now on board as co-producer and raised no objections to our suggestion that I should direct as well. Tony seemed happy too, though he had slight reservations that I was more of what he called a 'visual and character painting director' than an action director, and this was unquestionably an action picture, an ambitious project and a very much bigger undertaking than *Survivor*. I was conscious even as I suggested the idea that I would be putting myself on the line and exposing myself to a lot of stress and all that goes with it.

Our locations were spread around Queenstown, a small, charming ski and summer resort at the bottom end of South Island, next stop McMurdo Sound. We were wonderfully looked after by the locals, in particular Don Spary, who supplied a good working Dakota DC3, so essential to the plot, and the helicopters for a lot of the action scenes. We became great friends with him and his wife, Jan, a Kiwi version of Bridget Bardot, and their tribe of children, whom I've carried on seeing for years.

The principals in the production were billeted in five houses scattered on the hillside above the town, with wonderful views across Lake Wakatipu to the aptly named Remarkable Range of mountains. Donald Pleasence, Tony, George Peppard, Lesley Ann Warren, Prue and I each had one. Due to the fact that once I'd seen Lesley Ann emerge from a water barrel with her shirt wet and her nipples standing to attention, I couldn't resist their inherent promise, there were times when the whole place must have looked like a scene from a French farce, with people rushing in and out of doors to places they shouldn't have been. Prue found out, of course, which only added to the stress and tension on the set.

I realised that I was drinking more heavily than was wise, which is a much worse handicap for a director than for an actor. The more conscious I was of this, the more stressed I became, and I wasn't helped by the fact that George Peppard was also a heavy drinker, as was Donald Pleasance, which meant that three out of four of the principals were confirmed boozers.

George did not give his greatest performance. He chose to put on a strange, camp accent, perhaps intended to be like Dirk Bogarde in *Modesty Blaise*, but because we had to fly our film back to Australia to get our rushes, we'd already shot three days before we realised how bizarre his delivery was, and it was too late to get him to change.

There were tense moments too when Peppard, never the most cooperative of actors, was required to spend a little time in Lake Wakatipu (a very chilly lake, it must be conceded) for one shot and suddenly decided that he wasn't prepared to do it after all. It happened when I was already under pressure from Tony and the other producers to speed the whole process up; at the same time I'd been up late, night after night, trying to rejig the script to give it the polish I thought it lacked. There was a nasty confrontation by the lakeside, which came to a head when I got tired of asking George politely to get into the water and just pushed him.

I thought he was excessively grumpy about it all, but at least we got our shot. A few years later, I was a little perturbed when I was asked to direct a string of episodes of *The A-Team*, which had shot George back to stardom, but the lake episode was all water under the mountain by then and we had a great time working together again.

On *Zephyr*, I found I was spending too much time setting up shots and worrying about the visuals. We were using a local crew who weren't experienced and we weren't getting enough material to make the film work as an action picture. It soon became pretty clear that we were going to run out of budget, but one of the problems for me was that, when I was wearing my directing hat, I took off my producing hat and hated to compromise. However, in order to pacify the money men, I accepted that I was going to need some help. Tony felt we had to make aggressive cuts to the script and drastically increase the rate of the shoot. It reached a point where I had to agree to approach the picture in a different way or the completion-bond company would have taken me off the movie. (A completion-bond company ensures that a picture gets finished if a film runs out of money. They will complete it so that investors at least get a finished product; once called in, they have the power to take over the film entirely.)

I knew that we would have to get someone else to run a second unit and film a whole lot of cutaway action scenes – jet boats, helicopters, deer hunting and so on – that simply weren't my forte (at least, not in those days). And it so happened that my old mate Brian Cook was working with us on the movie as production manager, and he was ready and willing to take on this second unit.

When I'd been planning *Survivor* the year before, I'd tried to get hold of Brian, who'd worked on *Alfred, Fragment of Fear* and *The 14*. Since then he'd worked on a string of very big films, a lot with Stanley Kubrick as assistant director. I'd tracked him down to a mud hut in an Indian Ocean beach resort near Durban in South Africa. I told him I was in Australia making a film and asked if he wanted to come and work on it.

'Australia?' he grunted. 'I don't know about that. It's a fucking long way.'

'But it's marvellous out here!' I urged.

'You always say everywhere's marvellous. Well, what's the film?'

I gave him an idea and told him about the jumbo jet crashing into a city.

'Who's directing it?'

'I am.'

'Oh, fucking hell! What's the budget?'

I told him – a million and a half dollars.

'What?' He gave a groaning laugh. 'You, directing a jumbo jet crashing into a city? With a million-and-a-half-dollar budget? I don't know, H. I don't think that's for me. You're just looking for someone to blame when it all cocks up.'

And, disappointingly, because I'd loved having Brian around on previous films, that was that, and he went off to make *Heaven's Gate* with Michael Cimino – talk about cock-ups!

When it came to *Yankee Zephyr*, I was more determined.

Tony and I found Brian in London this time, had dinner with him and overcame his doubts enough to persuade him to join us, helped by the simple fact that in Tramp the night before he'd met Greg Chappell, the Australian cricketer, who told him what a lovely place Queenstown was.

So he'd come down, to be joined later by his wife, Pat, and their tiny daughter, and once it was agreed he was going to start directing, he happily got stuck in to crashing our DC3 into Lake Wakatipu. We filmed up to two or three days before Christmas and Brian finished off his bit with an imported crew in four weeks in early 1981, when a tragedy occurred. One of the stunt guys on a jet boat was killed in the last week of filming and I found, as a director/producer confronted with this situation for the first time, that I felt a great deal of responsibility for it.

Once Brian was finished, I sat down and cut in all his stuff and had a final edit by May. I was fairly happy with it (no director is ever utterly happy with any picture he's made). It was never a great box-office hit but it's been played on TV incessantly for twenty years.

After *Zephyr*, over the next couple of years FGH made several more films in Australia and New Zealand in conjunction with Hemdale and various other financiers and producers. Brian Cook, despite his initial reluctance to come and work there, found that he enjoyed Australia so much he bought a house in Melbourne. He signed up to work with FGH for another two years and we made several more pictures together.

Dead Kids (please!) was made in Auckland, with John Barnett, who went on some twenty years later to produce a big hit in *Whale Rider*. As a result of our experiences on *Zephyr*, though, the director, Mike Loughram, brought in a lot of American crew he knew, which made a considerable difference to shooting times.

We followed that with another film which we produced in New Zealand with 100 per cent finance from 20th Century Fox, *Prisoners*, starring Tatum O'Neal, who played the daughter of a prison governor (me) who falls in love with one of the prisoners. Sadly, the finished film was never allowed to see the light of day.

Our next project was *Turkey Shoot*, filmed in Cairns with Carmen Duncan again. As well as producing, I worked on it as a second unit director, and once again I found it very hard to keep my hands off Carmen. It was this perhaps which pushed Prue into demanding that we leave the Antipodes for good.

I didn't want to move back to the UK, so Tony and I thought it might make sense for me to set up an office in LA to sell productions. At the same time, Bill Fayman had decided to move out of FGH to concentrate on his family property business and we renamed the company Film and General Holdings so as to retain the FGH logo.

Before I left, I visited the Cook Islands on the pretext of searching for a location and instantly, with my chronic weakness for islands, fell in love with a tiny, jungle-clad lump of coral called Aiutaki. It was the perfect setting for our next project, an updated version of the Adam and Eve story called *Second Time Lucky*, which Michael Anderson was going to direct. I returned thoroughly excited and John Barnett sent Brian Cook and David Copping, the production designer, over to have a look.

They came back in a very pissed-off state. There was only one plane a week, they said, and it had taken them less than an afternoon to discover there was only one twenty-room hotel on the island, which was anyway a short light-aircraft ride from the main island of Raratonga. The cost of shipping over all the animals required to establish the Garden of Eden would have used up about half our budget. The cast would have had to wear shoes while standing in the limpid waters, in order to avoid having their feet cut to shreds by the coral. It was, Brian swore quite noisily, a total non-starter, which was disappointing for me and marked the end of my direct involvement in Australian and New Zealand productions.

In the autumn of 1982, I opened an FGH office on the 41st floor of the Twin Towers in Century City, Los Angeles. Prue, the children and I moved into a house I'd been renting for the last year or so while I'd been back and forth, organising our Australian productions. It had never been intended as a family house and it was, frankly, a bit of a dump on Encino in Havenhurst, in the San Fernando Valley.

18

Malibu to the Mountains, 1982–1993

T he great master plan, devised by Tony Ginnane and more or less endorsed by me, was that the Film and General Holdings (FGH) office in LA would initially be funded by our Australian activities, bringing in enough production deals from the States over two or three years to a point where it would be self-supporting. At that stage the tax shelter offered by the Australian and New Zealand administrations meant that investors could claim back 150 per cent tax credit for their investment in film productions, only paying tax when a film they'd funded ran into profit – admittedly not a very regular occurrence in the movies for which we'd been responsible so far. To set up this company, Tony and I had pulled in an American partner, Mark Seiler, who was president of RKO for a while, and had recently made the Meg Ryan boxing film *Against the Ropes*. Mark was a very straight, smart chap and we were lucky to have him.

At first I loved the idea of sitting on black leather in swish offices on the 41st floor of the Twin Towers on Olympic Boulevard and Avenue of the Stars, no less, in Century City, looking out through large, squeaky-clean windows across the orange-khaki-smog-draped contours of Hollywood. I loved movies and the business of making them; I'd always told myself I wanted to be a producer. I found acting dull and, in the end, unrewarding and I'd never had much interest in stardom. Although none of the pictures made by FGH in Australia and New Zealand so far could be described as hits, it must only be a matter of time before we made one that was. This, I convinced myself, was my big chance.

It took only a few months, though, for the sheer drudgery and constant setbacks endemic in the movie industry to start getting me down. In hindsight, it seems to me that for film producers to succeed they must possess – above all other characteristics, including judge-ment – utter, dogged tenacity in the face of forces ranged against them, telling them their project is a complete waste of time and none of the elements involved will ever match, even if by a miracle some party makes a commitment to the funding and/or distribution, and then – the holy grail – follows it up with hard cash.

I was always competitive and I always loved a challenge, preferably completed as soon as possible. However, I did not have the tempera-ment, the stamina or, frankly, the stomach to fight for a deal against the odds for months – often years – on end. I found it much more enjoyable to meet my friends, to give and receive parties where we could talk about ideas for films, books, musicals, quiz shows, restaurants – any-thing vaguely answering to the description of art or entertainment – without any of the tedious hassle of having to produce synopses or flow charts or draft budgets. It was, I soon realised, the conceptualising, rather than the nuts and bolts of a project, that interested me. Thus it was that less and less of my time was being spent in the office, and more and more in bars and restaurants.

Of course, I could and naturally did justify this to myself with the simple defence that it is frequently in such circumstances that great creative ideas are born. But once born, ideas, like babies, need careful nurturing, guarding, feeding, scrubbing . . . you can run this metaphor as far as you want. And it is a matter of record that, while I love my children, I was never seriously hands-on in the baby department.

I took my lunching very seriously, though, especially on Fridays, when I always met up with a new friend, Anna Hall (or Sharples, as she was then). Anna was an English girl who had been introduced to me and Prue by my old sixties playmate David Niven Jr. Niv Sr, it turned out, had been a wartime friend of Anna's grandfather; of such tenuousness are many connections made.

When I first came across her, she was secretary to John Daly, who was now based most of the time in Hollywood. This wasn't in itself so coincidental, since the Brit expat community in LA is notoriously incestuous, and I would see her from time to time when I dropped into the Hemdale offices. But when she came to work in a more elevated job for HBO, she was housed on the 40th floor of the Twin Towers in Century City, right below me.

Anna in Hollywood was a wonderful anomaly. She was, on the face of it, quintessentially English. Her beautiful house was more English than trifle and she dressed, as it were, in Colefax and Fowler, with underwear in Liberty print. She spoke uncompromising, crisp upper-crust at a time when this highly identifiable Anglo-ness was very popular in Los Angeles, and she quite correctly made the most of it. But Anna also had a highly tuned nose for a good book or well-written piece of material. She slipped into the scene with great ease and developed some handsome projects for HBO and her subsequent employers, CBS, like taking Jeffrey Archer in hand and launching *Kane and Abel* onto the networks. But there was never enough to do and she became a little underemployed and easily distracted. I was finding the same – Malibu parties and a ton of tedious paperwork that amounted to nothing. And so the famous lunches became a weekly Friday fixture at the Four Seasons Restaurant or the Avenue Saloon opposite Harry's Bar in Century City, where we sipped the best white wine with cracked crab salad, caught up on the gossip and sparked off each other with what I fondly remember as electric wit. These lunches became known about and swelled in numbers, until there was always a crowd who also pencilled it in their Filofaxes as a weekly date.

Even dear old Uncle Stanley Wharf, when he came over for a visit with my mother, insisted on attending one of these famous 'Friday Lunches'.

Our first home in Los Angeles, the rented house in the San Fernando Valley, was spectacularly foul. It had been done up and decorated in the worst possible Hollywood taste, but Prue and the children soon settled into LA life – LA life is designed to be slipped into without effort – and I was finding new friends whom I enjoyed, whether we were co-writing musicals, playing bridge or fantasy football or simply drinking.

It's absurd how fantasy football can grab you, and for some reason I can't explain American football is more addictive than British soccer. The idea is that you put a team together of your choice of real players and progress according to their actual subsequent performance and statistics. You draw lots, pick your quarterbacks, kickers, running backs and so on in turn until you have a full team. I did it religiously for several years. We'd get together for the first draft of players, and occasionally for a redraft to make adjustments and pick up new players. From time to time we'd all go and watch a game together.

I played in the American Pye League, started by another Brit called Chris Pye, a successful independent producer of American TV shows like *America's Most Wanted* and *Unsolved Mysteries*. He and I were to spend a lot of time putting together and finally getting broadcast an early reality show called *Money Hunt: The Mystery of the Missing Link*, and Prue and I saw a lot of Chris and his wife, Frances, throughout our time in the States.

Another fantasy football player in our league was a writer called Jon Povill, whom I'd met when I'd been over in LA a year or so earlier, setting up *Prisoners* with Tatum O'Neal. He had finished working on *Star Trek: The Motion Picture* and, soured by dealing with studios, he was looking to do independent features. We met originally through Terri Dash, a finance organiser I was using to put together US money. I was looking for projects, and we thought John could find or produce ideas that would interest us.

In the early days ours was entirely a business relationship. We started to develop a project, shortly after *ET* had come out. It was an alien/earth-person love story for which we'd got a little development money from Manny Wolf. As ours wasn't a development company, we went with the treatment to Abco Embassy, and they liked the idea a lot. Pending the script, which John had yet to write, they would put up half the money, if we found the balance from New Zealand.

At some point, Abco Embassy got bought by Norman Learman and the new management didn't want to go forward with the idea, so Manny, John and I all began frantically looking for the other half of the money. While we were doing so, New Zealand changed their tax-shelter laws. That window had now closed, but we were still trying to pursue it in 1984, when *Starman* came out, which was the same sort of story. It often happens that two people come up with an original idea at the same time, and that finally killed off the project.

It was over the three frustrating years that we were trying to put it together that our friendship was built, because John and I both loved playing bridge. Later we played golf too and liked to be out as soon as the sun rose on the Roosevelt Golf Course, a nine-holer in the mountains, and be at the third hole by 6.45 a.m. at the latest.

He was a terrible golfer, though I was worse, and we had a lot of fun playing together. I also played golf with my new agent, Tim Stone and his partner, Scot Manners. Tim was charming and very good company too, as well as being a fine golfer. His father had been a powerful and popular agent, but, astonishing as it may seem, I was probably one of Tim's bigger clients. Tim also introduced me to an attorney called Burton Merrill, who over the years slowly took over the management of my financial affairs and legal problems. Burton and I became very good friends and in the end he handled a lot of deals for me where an agent wasn't strictly necessary.

A live list of active contacts is fundamental to a career in the movie industry and, distasteful though it might seem, one has to nurture and nurse along anything that looks as though it might yield one of the elusive parts of the jigsaw that makes a finished picture. Many new contacts may lead nowhere in themselves but offer paths to new territories that do. Some are just dead ends, providing a little amusement on the way.

My ex-sec, Sally Derham-Reid, she with the iron knicker elastic, called me from Australia, where she'd just moved, to say that an ex-boyfriend of hers was coming to LA and would I see him.

'My God! Not Rubber Gloves!'

'No, not Rubber Gloves. A man called Richard Northcote, who's very keen to spend lots of money making films.'

She still knew how to excite me. 'Ah! People like that are very popular here.'

This Northcote arrived, an affable chap, obviously with plenty of wonga and looking for fun. We spent a little time breaking him in. Regrettably, he was later unable to remember the first three days of his introduction to LA, but within a very short space of time he'd met up with a Brit producer (and son of a marquess), Anthony Rufus Isaacs, and against all the odds he found he had a hit on his hands, with the not very subtle but well-made $9\frac{1}{2}$ *Weeks*. Sadly, I never got my hands into that particular tub, and it was even rumoured that Northcote went back to England richer than when he'd arrived.

Prue and I soon got fed up with living in the Oriental Baroque horror of the Encino house. As the place wasn't ours, it wasn't worth spending money on it, so we moved to one of my favourite places on the coast, the Malibu Colony. Over the next couple of years we rented two or three houses there in succession, the first of which was small but right beside the sea and much more suitable, among other things, for keeping the massive Newfoundland dog we'd acquired in New Zealand when I was making *Zephyr*. This dog, along with a few others over the years, was always known as the BBD and was responsible for much slobber and a few alarming accidents. The boys and I used to love to walk her along the Pacific beach on an early, empty morning.

It was while we were here that my mother found a powerful second wind a few years after my father had died and came over from Pyrford.

She thoroughly enjoyed coming to see her grandchildren, but she was completely indifferent to the activities of the film world and the people who inhabited it. She was sitting on the white deck of our house one day when a lonely runner loped along the beach.

'You look hot,' she called.

'Yes,' he agreed genially, and trotted over to sit beside her.

'You should be careful in this heat. It comes up on you before you know it.'

'Yeah.' The runner nodded.

'Bounces off the sea. Haven't you got a hat?'

'Nope.'

'You'd better have some of this orange juice. It's nice and cold.'

'Thank you, I will.'

'Are you sure you don't want a hat? I bet my son's got one somewhere.'

'No, I'm fine, thanks.' The jogger settled back comfortably and sipped his juice.

My mother could be relentless with idle conversation. 'So, what do you do?'

She was answered with a wonderful smile and a pair of shining, pearly blue eyes. 'I'm an actor . . . well, some say. What about you?' There wasn't a hint of patronage in the soft voice.

'Me? I'm a mother with a very famous son. It's very difficult being famous, you know.'

Paul Newman nodded thoughtfully, and took my mother's hand in his. 'Thanks for the juice,' he said.

'It's my pleasure,' she said, taking the glass, then calling after him, 'You should have a hat, you know.'

But he was off down the beach, kicking up spurts of sand with his heels.

Having witnessed most of this exchange but not wanting to interrupt my mother's moment with Paul Newman, I now slipped down to join her as she walked out on to the beach. Her close-curled grey hair dithered carelessly in the Pacific breeze, while a floral-print frock played around her calves and her toes wriggled in the sand.

'What a nice young man,' she said. 'Warm smile. Honest eyes. He's an actor, you know.'

She had no idea whom she'd just met, but of course I told her. A few minutes later, Paul jogged lightly back along the beach and waved a tanned arm, grinning at my mum.

'You get a hat!' she cried out jokingly. 'Nice boy,' she added quietly to me.

At FGH, the money was beginning to dry up a little since none of my projects had yet started to attract the kind of funds they needed, but we were still leading a busy social life. Prue was a brilliant hostess and liked to put on massive lunch parties or barbecues most Sundays, to which a lot of the expat community and Americans in the industry came at one time or another. It was at one of these lunches that an old friend, Don Belisario, suggested I might think about directing some episodic television.

Frankly, I didn't need much pushing, particularly when the first idea was that I should direct a few episodes of *Magnum, P.I.* with Tom Selleck in Hawaii. A dose of Hawaii, of which I had very fond memories thanks to my time there with George C. Scott making *Islands in the Stream*, would go down very well. I took to the job at once.

Thus it was that while still partially employed trying to drum up business for FGH, I found myself launched into a new career as a television director which was to last almost a decade.

Although filming short action scenes had not been something I'd relished or, frankly, done well in feature movies, I found I enjoyed doing it within the shorter framework of a 45–50-minute television drama shoot. The immediate deadlines helped too; it must have been similar to the difference between being a novelist, with twelve months to finish the job, and a journalist, with just twelve hours. I needed that immediacy of pressure to get me going. There were a lot of chances too to test one's own ingenuity in devising shots. I loved drawing up my storyboards; I enjoyed doctoring the scripts. Directing the actors was comparatively easy, because they generally knew their characters, such as they were, backwards.

In the early days, I'd liked to tell producers that they could have two each of QUICK, CHEAP or GOOD, but not all three, and it was an approach they appreciated. In my episodic period, besides *Magnum, P.I.*, I directed dozens of episodes of *The A-Team* with my *Zephyr* adversary, George Peppard, *Airwolf*, *Murder She Wrote*, *Stingray*, *Werewolf*, *In the Heat of the Night*, *Quantum Leap*, *Hardball*, *Raven* and *Marker* – 200 or 300 hours in all, I estimate, and several pilots, which were always more demanding.

I developed techniques of my own that worked well, and would always try and produce quality where I could. Certainly by the time I was directing the *Quantum Leap* pilot in the late eighties, I was confident that I had acquired a distinctive and recognisable style, lots of smoke and back light, which to some extent was reflected in later series like *The X-Files*. I was able to start creating this 'look' of my own on *Airwolf*, where I had better budgets, and carried it on in *Stingray* and *Hardball*, where I'd tried to develop an artist's eye for composition and bring a sense of colour to a film.

On 16 February 1983, Prue gave birth to our daughter, Charlotte. Although I already had a daughter, Deborah, with my first wife, Jenny, I hadn't seen her since she was tiny and I was utterly delighted by the arrival of Charlotte. At the same time, it made me conscious of the deep regrets I had at not having seen Deborah. I felt, nevertheless, that I couldn't simply get in touch with her out of the blue, after I'd been so neglectful, albeit unintentionally.

Just fifteen months later, on 25 July 1984, our third son (and my fourth), William, was born. We were both very proud of our neat little family – four children under the age of nine. To help Prue we always had a brace of nannies in the house and whatever it took to keep the place running smoothly.

To accommodate them all we moved from the Malibu Colony into a bigger house a little further up the Pacific Coast Highway at Point Dume. It was not a pretty house, set in a wilderness yard with large areas of grassless waste ground full of tall weeds and all surrounded by a fifteen-foot chain-link fence with towering floodlights over the tennis court and electric gates. It looked like a concentration camp and quickly became known to us and our friends as Château Dachau. Ugly as the house was, Point Dume was, nevertheless, a wonderful stretch of coast and beach, and a great place to live. It was, though, slightly further from LA than Malibu, and a little harder to get home to after a long day and a busy evening. But on Sundays a large gang of friends usually made it up there to join us for lunch, music, swimming and tennis.

Some of my old friends from the *Camelot* days were still regulars, like the Bricusses, Samantha Eggar and Joan Collins, as well as all our new ones. Anna Hall came and John Daly, bringing Helen Mirren with him, though she and I had both forgotten about this when we met again on *Last Orders* seventeen years later.

There was also a fairly steady stream of visitors from London – John and Sarah Standing, Charles and Pandora Delevigne and Ned Ryan.

*

By 1985, Australia had changed its tax laws and FGH's LA office no longer made much sense. I was making more money directing television, so Tony Ginnane and I agreed to an amicable business split and he bought out my interest. I didn't go back to Australia again until 2002, to make *The Night We Called It a Day* with Dennis Hopper.

On the directorial front I was pleased to be offered my meatiest project since *The Yankee Zephyr* – a four-hour television drama, *The Key to Rebecca*, based on Ken Follett's book about Second World War code-breaking and set in Egypt. It was being produced by Taft Entertainment Television for a new syndication company called Operation Prime Time, at a period when syndication companies were becoming almost as powerful as the networks.

The leading role in the project was Alex Wolff, the son of a Bedouin father and a German mother, who was spying for Rommel. Our first choice for the part was former *Starsky & Hutch* and singing star David Soul. I didn't know him and I arranged to meet him over dinner at La Famiglia, one of my favourite LA hang-outs. He'd had massive exposure, both as Hutch and as a very successful singer ('Don't Give Up on Us Baby' was No. 1 in the US and Europe) and he had been fairly visible lately in a soap, *The Yellow Rose*, and playing Rick Blaine in a television series based on the original *Casablanca*, but I was sure there was more to David Soul than the public had so far been allowed to see. He had great presence and an interesting vulnerability, as well as a big fan base.

As I had expected, I liked him on sight; we found we had a lot in common. Over dinner, I told him about the role and for the next three or four hours we talked. By the end of that first encounter, I think we both already knew we were going to be good friends, and he agreed that night to take the part.

The film also starred Anthony Quayle, with his dusky moon face, and Cliff Robertson, neat, tidy and conscientious. We spent eight weeks in Tunisia, where we made the picture entirely on location, in Tunis, Sousse and the ruins of old Carthage.

Soul's character turns up in Cairo from the southern Sahara and adopts the guise of a charming party boy among the Allied forces stationed there. He gives them no hint of where he's come from, speaking English with a South African accent. But he is there to extract some papers from a susceptible English major, whom I play, and achieves this by taking him down to a seedy club, plying him with booze and setting him up with a tantalising belly dancer, who is also Wolff's lover. The belly dancer (played, curiously, by the wife of a Californian dentist) easily seduces my flawed character, allowing Wolff to nick the papers for Rommel, before sticking a knife in my stomach and stuffing me into a barrel of water.

I enjoyed making the picture and weekends sitting with David out by the Mediterranean in a flaky, green, ramshackle restaurant built on stilts over the sand. We would trade anecdotes, or I'd draw up storyboards for the next day's shoot, while the fishermen went out to sea to catch our dinner. At the end of one long, warm evening, as the sun dipped and was gone, I was feeling excruciatingly low; I just couldn't get the measure of the movie. All the crew were hanging around the bar and I needed to be on my own. I went down to the beach, beyond the lights on the waterfront, where I found an isolated spot and collapsed with the script in my hand, listening to the waves rippling up the sand, as the stars began to light a soft black velvet sky.

I hadn't been there long when one of the runners on the crew, a Yugoslavian and a terrific-looking girl, though so slender she'd have had to run around in the shower to get wet, came down to the beach and, without a word, gave me a tremendous Monica Lewinsky. That gets your attention a bit, makes you sit up and take notice. Inevitably after that, she and I became an item, and when she told me that what she wanted above all else was an American work permit, I had no option but to help, though it was unfortunate that we had become quite involved by the time my long-suffering wife arrived on the set.

I think David enjoyed working with me as much as I did with him. I certainly felt he produced a truly fine performance, perhaps as good as anything I'd ever seen him do. I had tried to provide the circumstances in which he could give what he had within him but had never been asked for. I sensed he was boosted by the fact that someone had recognised that he was a fine actor.

Our friendship burgeoned and, when we got back to the States, we kept closely in touch.

As it happened, around that time David was somewhat rootless. His last marriage had broken down irretrievably and he was skipping around between hotels and friends' houses. A couple of months after we'd got back, I told him I had a spare room and asked why he shouldn't come and live with us at Château Dachau.

He came; I even gave him car space in the garage to make him feel at home. Staying with us gave him a chance to regroup and sort out where he was going next. I was fascinated by what a different person he became when he was with Prue. He liked her and admired her for her strong-willed dominion over the Hemmings household. In the presence of Prue, whom he called 'the Baroness' when she wasn't listening, he was like a small boy in front of his best friend's bossy mum – all smiles and tongue-tied nods, with legs crossed in guilty embarrassment. I sometimes knew how he felt.

As soon I'd finished the edit on *Rebecca* I went on to direct a few more episodes of *Magnum, P.I.* in Hawaii. In a spirit of friendship, I'd asked my lovely Yugoslavian runner from *The Key to Rebecca* to come out, in order to speed up her green card application. That was all she wanted really – to get to the States.

But in the midst of prepping my job in Hawaii, I got a call from Tim Stone to say that my daughter Charlotte had been knocked into the pool at Château Dachau by one of the BBDs and had drowned; she'd been pronounced dead by the paramedics when they'd arrived at the house. In a state of total shock, I told my producer, Don Belisario, 'I've got to go home. Now!'

I grabbed the Yugo and told her we had to leave for LA that instant. At LAX I gave her some money and told her to find a hotel while I went back to Malibu. I didn't see her again for months, by which time she was hanging off the arm of a big-time producer – a man far more likely to be of help to her than me. She looked happy.

The drama over Charlotte had, mercifully, been somewhat over-stated. She hadn't died and was completely recovered by the time I found her in hospital. The doctor told me the water in our pool was so cold, it had somehow saved her. I thanked God, was suffused with relief, and she was soon back within the cosy ring of wire fencing at Point Dume, while we considered the fate of the BBD.

Our next drama was provided by David – or 'Daysoul', as my children called him.

David's brother, Daniel, was a Lutheran pastor who looked after a flock among the diverse communities around the steel works of Pittsburgh. For 150 years, West Virginian coal and the natural flow of the Pennsylvanian rivers had allowed a vast industry to develop and become the bedrock of US productivity, the war machine and the motor industry. But as each plant used up its tax credits and the motor makers did deals with the Japanese, the giant steel corporations were engaged in a programme of rapid closure, which would leave the workforce of some

250,000 people facing a very bleak future. The national leaders of the unions involved had made arrangements to secure their own positions, agreeing to nebulous retraining schemes which never really happened, and leaving the local membership to fend for themselves. A group of thirteen pastors of several denominations were left to lead the resistance with whatever non-violent demonstrations they could think of.

There was 'The Mellon Bank Policy Stinks' protest, when they placed fish in safety-deposit boxes on a Friday afternoon which, by Monday morning, had the vaults stinking so badly the bank had to drill into hundreds of boxes to find them, stumbling on large quantities of contraband in the process.

And there was 'The Mellon Bank Stick Up', when they brought in barrels of honey and emptied them all over the floor of the main banking hall.

Daniel had written to David asking him for help. David responded by going to Pittsburgh to make a documentary about the human tragedy that was unfolding there, along with an idea for a feature film – *The Death of Dorothy Six*, which was the name of one of the blast furnaces. He had seen men who'd worked these furnaces for thirty or forty years crying as the great structures were blown up and they saw their whole lives being wiped out.

Naturally, I was intrigued and sympathetic to his cause, and he was delighted when I asked if I could come along with him and see for myself.

The first time I went up, Daniel had arranged a protest at the Shadyside Presbyterian Church, where the bosses of the steel companies would dutifully be attending services during Holy Week. The plan was to go in and place boxes of rusting metal by the altar, as a symbol of the destruction these people had instigated.

David decided to use his undeniable pulling power to hold a press conference at the airport, which meant that when we got to the church, with David still behind a camera for his documentary, and me a little behind him, we were met by a phalanx of cops in front of the church.

At that point David made the mistake of coming out from behind his camera and was promptly arrested. He was thrown into jail for a couple of days, until the police and the prosecutors got so scared by the massive publicity this generated, they agreed to let him out on $50,000 bail.

David phoned his wife to tell her he was in jail and needed some money to get out, but it was left to me to put the bail together, which I did willingly.

It was sad that after all that David had a lot of trouble getting his documentary placed. One of the complications was that he had financed it himself, and a member of his own family was involved, which, technically, laid it open to a charge of bias. In the end he had to lose his producer credit and hand it on to someone else.

Back at Point Dume, David stayed for a while longer, cheerfully joining in the regular Sunday brunches, barbies, tennis tournaments and music sessions. I introduced him to Mahler, and we took rides up the coast to a Harley bikers' bar, where members of big bands still came to jam with old-fashioned spontaneity.

With the East European beanpole off the scene, my own family life ran a little smoother for a while, until one unfortunate and frankly silly piece of behaviour on my part.

Working late in LA, I had phoned Prue to say I was staying with one of my friends – Povill, maybe, or David Blake. In fact I'd met a well-bred English girl with a double-barrelled name and breasts of a shape and texture which I'd always found irresistible. We spent an exciting night together, including some very enjoyable and creative body-painting. We were getting on so well, I wanted her to come back home next day with a crowd of friends, one of whom agreed that he would pretend the girl was with him.

Prue, well versed in my habits, looked at her squiggly-eyed when she walked in, but in the end accepted that she was nothing to do with me. It was only when we decided to swim that the plan went wrong. We all stripped off, and it became immediately clear that the only two people who had recently been covering themselves with glitter body spray were me and the girl with big breasts and good breeding. Within minutes she was being ushered from the compound!

Throughout my professional life, starting with the *Surrey Advertiser* in 1954, I've had a mixed press. I never tended to keep press cuttings myself, or if I did they soon got lost in one of the innumerable moves I've made from house to house. However, my late Aunt Eileen, my mother's sister, did keep them up until the eighties, after which she passed them on to me. I haven't always handled the press with the greatest of discretion, and if one ever bothers to look back over one's cuttings, it can be a pretty salutary experience. I seem to have given dozens of interviews in which I try to lay out my philosophy as regards marriage, women, acting, drinking and life in general. But by the end of the seventies there is one consistent element, which was the regret I felt at never having had anything to do with my first daughter, Deborah. And as maturity crept on, so the urge to see her and, more important, to know her grew.

I would mention this in interviews, knowing that they would print it and hoping that she might see it, or be told about it. However, I still didn't feel it fair to make an approach myself.

Unbeknown to me, from the early eighties, Deborah had seen the pieces in the papers and her own curiosity and, I suppose, natural daughterly feelings had been aroused. At first she, like me, was nervous of making direct contact, but in 1986, when she was 24, she decided to write to me. She didn't know how to get hold of me, though, so through her uncle, Jonathan Ouvry, a solicitor like his father, she got my agent's address. I was ecstatic to hear from her, thrilled that at last my oblique pleas to her had been heard. I wrote back, and a regular, fulsome and revealing correspondence was started. Some telephone calls followed, and I was very happy when finally in 1988 she announced that she wanted to come over to California and meet me for the first time since she had been a tiny girl.

She flew in to LAX a few days after her 26th birthday. Much to my frustration and chagrin, I was in the middle of directing a TV show called *Down Delaware Road* and I couldn't be at the airport to meet her.

Remembering my own first introduction to the States, I sent a stretch limo, with a rose on the back seat to represent me, and she was driven to the set. I'd been working hard all day – it was an extraordinary and emotional reunion. I'd been reminded that Peter O'Toole, on meeting his son, whom he hadn't seen since birth, was confronted by a six-foot-six, Nordic young man, the result of his relationship with a Swedish beauty. They had met at an airport café, and found it unbearably stiff and awkward. I wanted above all to avoid that, but I'd already drunk too much to handle it properly, and kept diving in and out of bars, introducing her to everyone on the way home. It wasn't until next morning that we really sat down to talk over breakfast.

After that, Debs got on wonderfully with my four 'American' children, especially Charlotte. Prue, though, was wary about this hard evidence of a past which didn't include her, in the way that she'd always been a little nervous when Nolan came to see me. I took Debs off to dinner, just the two of us at the Beverly Hills Hotel, and we had a wonderful meal (apart from the oysters, which she'd never had before and couldn't handle – so I ate them).

I showed her around Hollywood, took her to parties and dinners, and introduced her to many of my eclectic gang of friends. She was a little overwhelmed by it all and admitted afterwards that she couldn't help feeling quite alien and conscious of the gulf between life in Fulham and life in California.

After that, every time I went to England to film or to see Edward and George at school in England at Wellesley House or Harrow, I always let her know and we would meet up. This prompted her then to look out for Nolan, whom she'd never met. After leaving school at Bryanston, Nolan had decided to follow me on to the stage and had caught the eye of a few directors. He had a part in a play at the Yvonne Arnaud Theatre in Guildford. Debs finally saw him by going to watch him there and sending a note back stage: 'If you want to meet your sister, I'm here in the audience.'

Over the years that followed, Debs and I became the greatest of friends. I'm sure that most people who divorce having had children feel responsible for the effect this might have on them. It's incredibly hard to achieve a balance between loving them and spoiling them, and I have by no means always got it right, especially when relations with their mother have been strained.

But although there were periods of deep, mutual suspicion between Prue and me, she knew how to handle my lows when she wanted to, and I was very conscious of all the effort she put into bringing up children with a father whose work kept him away from home from early dawn to late at night, with only Sundays free for contact, when the house would often be full of friends. There were times too when my exuberance and her competence and sense of humour were well balanced, positive and productive.

She could be very funny and perform when it mattered. On one occasion when I was directing an episode of *Hardball* and she was with me on the set, it was pissing with rain and we couldn't film. In any event, the shoot had not gone well for the last couple of days and everyone was feeling down and depressed. Prue said we ought to cheer them up and insisted that we step down from our trailer, with umbrellas and rain-coats, into the lane where the crew were huddled with their teeth chattering and looking miserable. We danced together a creditable version of Gene Kelly's famous routine from *Singin' in the Rain*, all the way up and down the lane, and one by one the crew sparked up, until they were all laughing and the mood of depression was broken.

At the end of the lane, the rain stopped, and I could turn to my cameraman and say, 'OK, boys! Over here on a fifty. Let's go – Bosh!'

In 1986, after a string of long, hard jobs, culminating in one of my many trips to Canada (where the tax shelter was sensibly effective) to make some episodes of *Stingray* in Calgary, I'd got enough money to buy an altogether superior house, not far from Château Dachau. On Point Dume, high up, with lovely views of the Pacific, it was a great deal prettier. It had plenty of space and a wonderful dining room with a massive fireplace at waist height which belted out the heat on a chilly January Sunday. We always knew it as 'the Pink House', and it was certainly one of the best I ever lived in.

The surrounding area was fairly star-studded, but one of my favourite neighbours was an affable and not overworked one-time cowboy extra called Ken Carpenter. Ken looked, growled and drank like a cowboy, though I don't think he'd ever roped a steer with his lariat. He was living in a trailer in the grounds of the house next door, acting, I think, as a sort of caretaker. I soon persuaded him on to the team as a general driver, runner, pool adversary, occasional extra and drinking companion. It was a very satisfactory symbiotic relationship and in due course we found ourselves developing his idea for a script, which I hope one day will get the glimpse of a producer's wallet it deserves.

When Nolan – 'Young H', as I liked to call him – was sixteen, Gayle rang to say she thought it would be a good idea if he came over from London to live with his father for a while. I agreed and, when he arrived, I was looking forward to a bit of paternal bonding. With that in mind, I soon put him to work as a runner on *The A-Team*. However late I'd been up the night before drawing storyboards, as director I liked to be first on set for a day's shoot and always started very early. Nolan would come down at five, bleary-eyed and bumbling as teenagers are.

'Morning, Pappa,' he'd grunt. 'How are you?'

'Not too shabby, Young H. In fact I'm excellently well. Ready for the fray?'

After coffee and a quick bite, he chauffeured me from the Pink House, over the mountains, through the twists and turns of the Canan Dume

Road to speed along the 101 Freeway to the studios in a lovely old white convertible Mercedes I'd acquired from Natalie Wood.

On the set he bounced around and made himself useful, thrilled to be in such close proximity to Face, Hannibal, Murdock and Mr T. He and I talked about everyone and everything as we cruised back and forth to LA, and we really did get to know each other better. For a while he worked as a runner for Scot Manners, my agent's partner, which introduced him early to a lot of the tricky ways and tricky people in the LA movie world.

He also got on well with his elder half-brothers, George and Edward, whom he'd known when they were very small in London, although even he would admit he wasn't necessarily the best influence on them – take the matter of the three-wheeled ATV, for instance. Before it was generally known how fundamentally lethal these vehicles were and everyone replaced them with four-wheelers, they were a big craze in California, and there's no question that they were fantastic fun on the beach, where if you did turn them over, it didn't hurt much. I bought one, ostensibly for the boys, though just as much for me, and we had a great time with it. The only thing I insisted on was that the boys bought their own fuel.

Poking around in the garage, Nolan found a rusty barrel full of petrol, which he reckoned would save a lot of time and money. He and George filled the ATV, started it up and roared off until after a few minutes the engine ground to a stop, seized solid. It turned out the fuel was massively contaminated with rust and water that had seeped in, and every tube and valve was choked.

I was absolutely livid that my new toy had been wrecked so fast and in such a crass way. I told the boys to strip the whole engine down, clean it and put it together. They weren't amused, but it taught them a lesson (though they never did put it all back together on their own).

There were a few more run-ins, but apart from these and a certain degree of hostility from Prue, Young H's stay went well. I was very sorry when he went back to England and urged him to come out to the States again as soon as he could. I felt he'd learned a lot, though, and had a feel for the industry – the good bits and the bad. Certainly, he had a good working knowledge of the geography of the more interesting bars and watering holes in southern California.

Although Prue was happy about the move to the Pink House, I think she must have been finding it quite a strain dealing with four very individual children, as well as a sometimes truculent Nolan. We always had a couple of nannies, but it seemed they created as much work as the children did, which was why we'd sent the two older boys to school in England. Penny Leander, with whom Prue had always kept in touch, had told her she was sending her boys, Luke and Rudi, to Wellesley House, a prep school in Kent, and on to Harrow, which had sown the seeds of Prue's decision to do the same.

In the meantime, the absolutely relentless pace of my work meant that quite often I worked too late to make it back to Malibu at night, especially if I had a six o'clock start the next morning. I had several friends who were prepared to put me up. Inevitably a few of them were women, and I couldn't help feeling, if they expressed any interest in sleeping with me, it was rather churlish not to. This chivalrous approach, as chivalry often can, did have its rewards.

It was late, and I had just put down a book by Gavin Maxwell – *A Ring of Bright Water*, extremely apposite as it turned out – and turned off the light when my svelte and lovely hostess crept into the room with an ice bucket. In the gloom, I surmised it contained more wine, but she was naked and slipped delicately between the sheets beside me; not a bottle to be seen, except in the cockney slang sense of the word.

'Do you mind?' she asked.

There was only one answer a normal, healthy chap could give. 'Of course not.'

'Have you ever done it with ice?' she murmured.

She plunged her hand into the bucket and popped in a couple of cubes. This was, I confess, new to me and I feel that I should pass it on.

Try it. You never know, it might have some physical benefits. I recall that Prue was very keen for me to dangle my tackle in iced water when she was desperate for a daughter, before Charlotte had arrived.

'How do you feel?' my hostess asked as I rolled out of bed at dawn.

'Well chilled, thanks!'

After that, I never mentioned this incident to her, though I saw her from time to time, and when she served Pimm's on a summer Sunday and the ice cubes clattered in the jug, I did find myself holding my ice up to the light, just to check its provenance!

For a few weeks later that year, I was kept on the path of righteousness when my Uncle Stanley came out for six weeks to see us in California.

Stanley Wharf is an upright sort of citizen, a Grand Moose and a stickler for good behaviour. Having been something hush-hush on the development of the bouncing bomb during the Second World War, he went into the motor trade when it was over and had always been a strong support to my mother as she tried to cope with my father's various eccentricities, as I may politely describe them. As always, he was keen to see whatever was going on, and he came with me to Canada for four days while we shot a few scenes from *Davy Crockett* with Johnny Cash, in which I was playing President Andrew Jackson, as well as directing. Stanley became a little incensed over some carelessness on my part while we were there. Some years before, I'd won an extraordinary necklace in a game of poker. It was a string of small solid gold nuggets and I loved it; I'd worn it for a long time and I was very proud of it. But on this occasion I must have given it to a wardrobe mistress to keep for me and completely forgotten to ask for it back. I didn't even think about it until we were halfway home. When I rang, no one on the set had seen it. I'm disinclined to be too worried about personal possessions, but losing that particular bizarre trinket did piss me off.

Back in California, now that Young H had gone, I recruited Uncle Stanley as my driver – partly at Prue's insistence, because, she said, whenever I drove I knackered all the hubcaps. At five-thirty each morning Stanley would be on parade and eat a hearty breakfast, while I settled for a vodka and an apple. Heading down the Ventura Freeway, we'd pull off and drop into a small bar on Hollywood Boulevard. By that stage, I simply couldn't go into the studio without a good helping of white wine to loosen me up. And I couldn't pretend any more that I didn't have some kind of a problem.

In June 1988, with encouragement and help from several of my better friends, I booked into a celebrated drying-out and habit-kicking establishment, the Betty Ford Clinic near Palm Springs. This was not the most enrapturing thing I've ever done, but the soul-searching and inward contemplation it encouraged, though uncomfortable, were no bad things if indulged in occasionally. For the first time I was urged to identify and confront my personal demons. I hadn't really thought I had any up till then, and was astonished how many there were, and they kept finding more, until I felt like a small corner of hell by the end of it.

Certainly, though, I had the opportunity to examine my relationship with my father. I was under no illusion that he had been a malign and destructive influence on me for as long as I could remember, but, because he was my father, I had thought that was what fathers were supposed to do and I'd accepted it. Even after some of his truly atrocious behaviour, I had kept wanting him to show his approval, although frankly, in the last few years of his life, knowing that he would never, ever admit to anything approaching admiration for anything I'd achieved or to affection for me, I had more or less ceased to care.

I was surprised to find how cathartic writing these things down could be, which is why, I guess, the Betty Ford folk encourage the inmates to do it. I still have my own handwritten appraisal of my relationship with my father which I produced for them, and the 'Teacher's Comment' scrawled along the top: 'Wow, what a job! I don't see long-term AA people doing this well. Keep it up. Now! Forgive, and move on.'

Even if it had not been too late to forgive him in person, I don't think I could possibly have followed that advice. I'd sort of tried in any case, and it seemed to me that forgiveness, like any kind of giving, is a two-way street.

I regret to say that, after John Daly had kindly picked me up after my sentence had been served, it wasn't long before I was back on the booze. But I felt – quite falsely, I dare say – that I had it under control to some degree. I was still trying to stick to the dreaded Kalibers ('All the alcohol taken out', sod it) when my old friends from the Seychelles and Whiteway days, William and Joy O'Shei, asked me to join them for a spell at their incredibly lovely and peaceful Strawberry House, in Lyford Cay, Bahamas, for a spot of what my children would call 'chilling'.

It was a wonderful interlude, when for the first time in an age I was able to get my watercolours out and spend long untroubled hours in front of the easel, and I've always liked the pictures I managed to produce there. I was also in a good frame of mind when I came back from a day's fishing on William's boat, *Sea Sleeve*, to find that Ken Russell's Brazilian producer had rung me from England.

This was rather intriguing, since Ken had asked me several months before if I could play Uncle Henry in his forthcoming production of D. H. Lawrence's *The Rainbow* and then been forced to withdraw the offer because his American distributors didn't want me.

There had since been a lot of talk about Ken's frankly eccentric decision to offer the part of Uncle Henry to Elton John. Such was Ken's reputation, though, that people assumed he could make it work, despite the fact that Elton, wonderful, precious songbird that he is, had never really acted in anything before.

But now Elton had got cold feet. There were, it seemed, issues over spectacles, wigs and acting lessons, and he asked to be excused. Alan Bates had been approached, and prevaricated for several days before saying no, and now Uncle Henry's scenes were to be shot in four days' time. I assumed they could now surmount the distributors' objections to me and that I was holding all the good cards.

As it happened, I'd have gone off tariff to work for Ken, because I'd loved playing Coleridge for him in *The Rime of the Ancient Mariner*. In fact I felt he was one of the few directors for whom I'd turned in decent work as an actor over the last dozen years. I hadn't seen him since 1984, when George and Edward had been ushers at his wedding to Vivian Jolly on the *Queen Mary* at Long Beach, and I was really bucked by the idea of working with him again. Nevertheless, chances are chances. They were desperate; I could do it. I upped the fee they'd offered last time, and got them to chuck in a couple of first-class air tickets. Four days later, kitted and coiffed, I was walking onto the set to deliver my first lines.

As usual on Ken's shoots, there was no shortage of drama or incident. Perhaps he feels a bit of tension is good for his actors' chemistry; perhaps he's right.

After a short, enjoyable piece of filming in the old country, with a director I admired, it was back to the television grind in LA, where I'd been relying on Burton Merrill almost entirely to handle the financial side of my directing work. He and I had become good friends, and I had to listen to him when he told me if I wanted to be at the top of the league, I had to let him turn stuff down on my behalf and I had to demand the highest fees. I'd always found this approach very tricky, being of a cast of mind that made me think I was damned lucky that anyone should want to pay me at all for what I enjoyed doing so much. However, I bowed to his experience and left him to negotiate in whatever way he saw fit. I also told him that I was looking for more challenging projects. A few weeks later, he invited me down to his place in Temecula, halfway to San Diego, to ride some of the cutting horses he owned. These horses were reared for the task of extracting individual beasts from a herd of cattle. They required specific training and characteristics, and the process has been turned, like so many everyday activities in America, into a competitive sport – a sort of grown-up version of an English gymkhana. As always, I was game for anything.

When I arrived, he told me the producer Juanita Bartlett wanted me to make the pilot for a new series, *In the Heat of the Night*, based on the original Sydney Poitier movie. Because they were the first episodes and vital to the launch of a new TV series, pilots were potentially more lucrative jobs for a director and could pay way over the standard DGA scale. I'd made several others successfully, but this was a bigger one.

The southernmost states of America are hard to describe, simply because they are their own masters. The difference between Maine and Louisiana can be best explained in the military colours of grey and blue. They even smell like opposites; their seasons reek of diversity. In the South, lynchings can still happen and the smell of sweat permeates every saloon; in the North, families sit in felt hats on fresh-mown lawns, with tea. You can walk into a bar in New Mexico and see the scars of bullets behind the stoop. In Martha's Vineyard there are gentle fishermen gathered at the edge of the harbour, worrying about cod.

I love the South. It makes me nervous, wanting a gun on my hip; after all, I did marry a Texan. And I loved New Orleans, where I'd been dispatched to direct the pilot for *In the Heat of the Night*, to star Carol O'Connnor and Howard Rollins, re-creating the roles so well crafted by Rod Steiger and Sidney Poitier in the original film.

Carol O'Connor had made his mark playing Alf Garnett in the US version of *Till Death Do Us Part*; Howard Rollins was black and deeply camp, with earrings to match. Though later he was to be damned for snorting his shag-pile carpet, he was funny, and a fine actor, and you can't be damned for that.

New Orleans is all that you might hope it to be. I would sit on the corner of Basin Street and Canal Street, out on the open pavement, and sooner or later trumpet, sax and the rest of a band would pass by. At night, the jazz clubs beckoned, Gumbo's or the Little Inn on Main Street, smelling, both, like elderly cigars or even older hookers. Or I would stroll along the canal itself, gas-lit in the evenings, and hunt down a mint julep alongside the cobblestones and the punts easing their way upriver with maidens looking for all the world as if they had just come from Henley. The Cajun patois drifted from half-open doorways where lovers might hide and, finally, I might find my way back to my hotel, the Grise, with wide windows and mosquito nets, and I would sleep to the sound of a sax echoing smoothly across St Stephen's Square.

There's something about the city, with its alleyways, its music and its food, where tabasco comes from, where chilli and alligators hide in the bayous, where songs are written and tales told. I just love New Orleans.

Carol O'Connor arrived first and we discussed the script. No big deal, just a conversation about plot and character, and we played out the role as it might be on the screen, and he seemed happy. We both drank lots of wine, and he seemed better than happy.

When I met Howard Rollins, a couple of days later, I took to him at once. He was a true actor and you could sense it. His charisma was enormous and his charm abiding. There were many events and epic moments during Howard's time in Livingstone, Louisiana. To start with, Livingstone is a cornerstone of the Ku Klux Klan. No shit. African-Americans are still called niggers, and rednecks are called by that name because that's the way a neck looks when it's been strung up from a local oak. If you think I'm bullshitting, let me take you to Livingstone. I'm a sheriff there, by the way, and entitled to tote a gun in that county.

Carol and I were invited to be inducted as sheriffs of Livingstone County, but black Howard was not. Both Carol and I protested that, in essence, we were all for one, one for all. So, with deep reluctance, the representatives of the local police relented and gave him his badge.

Another time, in a real southern saloon that we had requisitioned as a lunch parlour, the film caterers had done their bit and I had dismissed Howard early. He and his entourage had got their kit and made their way to the saloon, where tables had been laid and beers set out for a good southern lunch.

Howard, as usual, was wearing his earrings and his broad-brimmed hat, with a hint of lipstick shading his mouth a gentle pink. The bar had never seen a black man in a hundred years or so, and, leaning over the counter, there were cowboys with spurs even older than that. Shotguns hung on racks and a deeply off-colour blonde chewed gum and served shot glasses of dark gold bourbon, straight from the Mississippi mountain stills.

To loose Howard into these surroundings, straight from the set, was a touch thoughtless, but actually it was just bad luck. He walked in the door with his tray, his entourage around him, and there was that moment when the jukebox folds and all conversation comes to a halt. Every plug had been pulled, faces dropped like withered chins and jeans fade visibly. Howard smiled with teeth as brittle as gravestones, while the locals scowled and hit the spittoon with an angry 'thwack!' of soggy tobacco.

'Oh, shit,' Howard said huskily, as if all of his disasters had come at once. Here was a gay guy, dark of complexion, in Livingstone, Louisiana, with his lips on and his earrings clattering, carrying a tray of film feed and staring at a gang of unshaven heavies who looked like extras from *Once Upon a Time in the West.*

But, you know, it didn't turn out that bad. The buxom blonde behind the bar absolutely adored Howard; the jukebox went back on and the two of them danced the afternoon away. And the cowboys did too, often together, spurs clattering in a camp sort of way. I'm not sure how much real filming was completed that afternoon alongside the bayou, but it didn't seem to matter. Howard and the rest of them stayed on until the early hours and we picked up the pieces the following morning. He became incredibly popular among the locals, and never came close to being strung up. But work we did, and, like all pilots for television, the effort was gruelling, though the surroundings were spectacular.

I'd been dining with Leslie and Evie Bricusse in LA shortly before I left for the Deep South and I'd offered to take their son Adam with me. He was 23, fresh from English public school and Oxford. Eight weeks filming with Hemmings in the sweaty latitudes would make a wonderful change, we agreed, and put hairs on his chest. I'd known the lad since he was little more than an ankle biter; he had, after all, been ring boy at my wedding to Gayle. On the job, he was great to have around, but I felt it my duty to educate him; the easiest way to do that was by showing him as many sides of life he'd never seen before as I could.

'Now, young Adam,' I started to tell him, and watched his face drop. 'It's very important in life to experience everything, I mean everything, at least once. Of course you won't be offered opportunities to do everything, but any that you are, you must take. And tonight, my boy, we are going to a cockfight.'

Even I found the experience of the Louisiana cockfight pretty alarming. One of our local crew had suggested it and fixed it up. It was he who showed us the way, deep into a subtropical forest, where we found a very large ramshackle sort of timber theatre in the round. I guess in construction and general appointment it resembled a European cockpit of several centuries earlier. Within, crowded noisily on tiers of circular raked seating, were several hundred of the ugliest men I've ever seen. Not just ugly because chronically inbred, but sullen, dimwitted, vicious and, I had the impression, not very tolerant. All white, of course, though red of neck and no doubt not unfamiliar with white hooded garb.

The fight itself was vicious and beastly, and upset poor Adam not a little, but it was not as frightening as the audience's reaction as they bayed for their champion. The bloodthirsty glee was utterly terrifying to watch, and we cowered in our seats with feeble grins, pretending we were having a hell of a good time. We may not have been black, but I distinctly felt we'd have been lynchable if we'd put a toe out of line.

To make up for this, the next experience I devised for Adam, which, like the cockfight, he would remember for many years, was a backward banquet.

We started with large snifters of brandy, smelly cheeses, gooey puddings and continued through our reverse menu, until we were sipping preprandial cocktails. The only element we had been unable to reverse was the fact that we'd ended the meal, as it were, sober and started it properly pissed. I don't suppose my young protégé learned any particularly valuable lessons from that experience, but it was entertaining to devise and confused the locals no end.

We'd nearly finished and were filming outside Livingstone County Court with 200 extras scattered across the square. I looked at the happy scene and was struck that our two leading actors, Carol and Howard, now comfortable in their parts, had somehow come to understand each other in a way I had not expected, and I liked them both very much indeed for it. Carol was tough but wary; a bit of a bully but clever. Howard was a puppy dog. And *In the Heat of the Night* had been a wonderful experience for me.

By contrast, 1989 provided the next big watershed in the lives of the Hemmings family.

Work had been drying up a little. Fewer people were taking my calls. Old, loyal friends tried to hire me when they could, but, they said, although no one doubted my ability to make good television, producers were scared of my drinking. Some studios had reached a point where they went ape if anyone sneaked so much as a bottle of Chardonnay into the cutting room. There was a school of thought that felt I couldn't always be relied on, that I didn't follow through projects with the same vigour I'd brought to the job ten years before. That was probably true, but I had been exceptionally vigorous then. Frankly, after years of rising at five, working till late, every night, six days a week, making endless episodes of action shows, I was burned out. I was also deeply depressed by the fact that, however hard I worked, it seemed the family always needed more money.

The decision to move from California, with all its temptations for a man with a penchant for booze and philandering, was suggested by Prue, on the grounds that I was still working some of the time in Canada.

We looked, vaguely, at one of the islands off Vancouver before settling on Sun Valley, Idaho, which we already knew a little. My friends Denne and Wanda Petitclerc had a condominium where we'd stayed, and Denne had persuaded us to buy one ourselves, an ugly box of a place, as a holiday home and an investment. If you were to look on the map for Ketchum, Idaho, and observe the depth and crag of contour, you might think it looked a bit off the map, even for an unsociable grizzly. But you'd be overlooking the fact that Sun Valley has been Ski Resort to the Stars, or Hollywood-sous-Neige, since before the war.

It seethes with famous people getting away from it all, together. Perhaps that was why Prue favoured it. Perhaps that's why I did too. Not really a very good reason, and a decision I soon came to regret.

However, the beloved Pink House was sold – pretty well, as it happened – marching orders were issued, and I set off to drive to Ketchum with Nolan, Ken Carpenter and his two kids, Sadie and Jordan. The route took us through Nevada, via Las Vegas, then due north to Idaho. On the way, we stopped at the MGM Grand in Vegas. I hadn't planned for a gambling break, but it seemed silly to pass by an opportunity to defray our expenses on the way. To keep things under control, though, I felt we should restrict ourselves to losing only the cash we were actually carrying.

Outside the casino, I gathered my small squad.

'OK, what do we have in readies?'

We had a quick count-up.

'Right,' I said, feeling decisive. 'Let's triple it, and then we'll move on.'

We all went in. Ken wanted to play poker; I tried to talk him out of it. I knew how erratic his game could get if he passed a certain level of whisky consumption. He growled adamantly and slunk off, while the rest of us more cautiously settled for Black Jack and roulette.

An hour later, I'd lost all my stake money and so had the others, except Ken, who was nowhere to be found. We finally spotted him sitting at a corner table with four of the meanest-looking rednecks I ever saw. My guts lurched; I was amazed there was still a place for him at the table, until I saw the great stack of chips in front of him.

'OK, Ken, I think we're finished here.'

The rednecks glowered as I dragged him away.

Next day when we totted it up, our combined net wealth had increased by less than $200. I hoped I'd be able to find some directing work when we got to Ketchum.

Ketchum, a mile south-west of the town of Sun Valley, is also part of the resort. We had sunk our residual capital into a single-storey ranch-style house on the Warm Springs Road by the lower slopes of Bald Mountain.

It wasn't an obviously handsome house, but Prue was confident that she could do something with it and quickly set about getting the old asbestos pulled out and having a second storey and a garage tacked on. We changed the entrance from where it came off a busy road to come in round the side of the house. We also moved an outhouse, a twelve-by-ten timber playroom, known as 'the Shed', which became my studio, and the foundation of Stewart Hemmings Productions, acronymed to SHED Productions.

I'd decided that I'd reached a time in my life when I should flex my musical muscles once again and take the opportunity provided by a lull in directing to develop an idea which had been quietly germinating for some time. My partner in this venture was a brilliant musician called Chad Stewart, formerly half of a sixties folk duo with Jeremy Clyde. Chad was living in LA, but I persuaded him to move up to Sun Valley and together we settled down to create the musical *Hamelin*.

In August 1989, my mother, Kath, died. I was more devastated than I could have imagined, although it's clear to me now that she'd been my one consistent and unquestioning source of affection throughout my life. I always felt she'd had to double the strength of her feelings to make up for my father's total lack of them.

In her sweet, bumbling, innocent way, she had seen me through the extraordinary experiences of my young days in the English Opera Group. She had backed me up when my father had thrown me out at fourteen and I'd had to live in digs in London, when she would come up and drop me small sums of money which she could barely afford, to allow me the small indulgences she knew I craved.

In the few short years she had to herself, she crammed in everything that was possible. She travelled to see us in California as often as she could, even when cancer made that painful. Finally, sitting in her favourite spot in the porch at Pyrford, she collapsed into my aunt's arms. Eileen called me and I flew back to the UK to bid her farewell. We had a boy soprano sing 'Ave Maria' and 'Panis Angelicus', those melodies that she had listened to so often when I was singing as a child, and if I'd had the voice I would have sung for her again then; and do, in my heart, to this day.

I'm an old romantic, I know, and that is part of the reason why my mother peppers so much of the stock of my life. She allowed me, even as an adult, to retain the foolishness of childhood and we grew young together, particularly as her years advanced and we saw more of each other. Strange, that, isn't it? As her days tripped inevitably towards her final grasp on this world, she became brighter and wittier, light-headed and engaged, less responsible, showing the person she had always been but I had failed to notice, while at the same time and over the same number of years I was in a pretence of maturity that graduated from attempting to be elderly at fourteen to being stupidly happy at sixty.

Now she was gone, I was utterly remorseful that I hadn't seen more of her, although, to be sure, I had asked her over more often than she came.

When I went to England for her funeral, I was feeling very black and couldn't even bring myself to get in touch with Debs. I thought a father in the depths of gloom would be worse than no father at all just then. London seemed hostile and foreign to me, no one made me laugh, and I was almost glad to be going back to my mountain confinement.

George and Edward went back to school in England and I threw myself into writing *Hamelin*. Chad was doing most of the music and orchestration, using a little synthesizer, while around his music I was writing lyrics and a screenplay based on the folk story of the Pied Piper. What we had in mind was a full-blown musical – a book and at least a dozen good songs. I had visions of it being a stage show with a broad appeal and a useful application as a show which involved a large number of children for school productions, which, after all, was how Tim Rice and Andrew Lloyd Webber had got *Joseph* off the ground. At the same time, it was also something to sell to Disney as a musical movie.

It was a long, laborious though ultimately very satisfying process, laying down layer over layer of electronic instruments, effects and voices, and halfway through 1990 we were joined by a third collaborator.

I'd been coming back through the airport at Boise when I noticed an interesting-looking character picking up a keyboard. Always curious, if not downright nosy, I asked him about it and he told me he was collecting it for a friend with a small recording studio in Hailey, about eight miles down the road from Ketchum.

Chad and I were by then desperate for a more sophisticated range of equipment than we had and this seemed to me one of those serendipitous moments. I took the name and number of the owner of the studio, and as soon as I got home I rang him.

I could tell by the sound of his voice that we were going to get on and arranged to visit his studio to explain what we needed for our project.

Marcus Beresford turned out to be a young, thoughtful Englishman whose family had moved to Canada and then the States several years before. He was now a pilot who, in his spare time, had set up and operated a neat little studio which seemed ideally placed for us to put down the live instruments and voices we still needed.

Marcus felt this would be an unnecessary extravagance and said he had a good spare eight-track reel-to-reel recorder which he could lend and set up for us back at the Shed. The next thing we knew he was a very welcome addition to the project. Sadly, though, we seemed unable to get it beyond a certain point and the strain of working together on and off for a year was beginning to tell on my relationship with Chad. In the spring of 1991, when another idea I'd been nursing for a while came to fruition, the collaboration between us came to an end, though the *Hamelin* demo was eventually finished and is still available.

Dark Horse was a low-budget film which I was to direct. By then quite committed to my new surroundings, I fought hard to wrestle it away from its original location and convinced Steve Eiserhoff to have it set and filmed in Idaho. It was produced by Tab Hunter and starred Ed Buckley Jr and Mimi Rogers. Prue also worked on the film as art director, while SHED did most of the producing and Marcus was credited as 'assistant to Mr Hemmings'. It turned out well and ended up on the Disney Channel; people were pleased and my self-confidence was a little restored. The truth was that my marriage to Prue had been potentially unstable since my affair with Carmen Duncan in Australia.

Our relationship had come under pressure from the workload I'd been carrying for the last ten years and the steady increase in my drinking to compensate for it. With hindsight, there was no doubt that my confidence had taken a serious battering as a result.

The experience of making the picture reminded me what I could do, and how much I could enjoy it. I was determined somehow to raise myself from the lethargic negativity which until then seemed to have characterised my life in Idaho.

When I found I was in line to direct *Passport to Murder*, a 90-minute television movie for HBO being produced by Peter Katz and Tony Masucci, I did everything I could to make sure I got the job.

I felt like a new man as I flew to London in early 1992 to stay at the Athenaeum Hotel on Piccadilly, where I planned to cast some of the picture with English actors, preferably friends, as it was going to be shot in Budapest.

One of the first people I cast was Peter Bowles. It was really good to see him again. We hadn't completely lost touch, but we'd met only intermittently over the last dozen years and we'd last worked together on the Canadian film, *Blood Relatives*, in 1977. He had never been directed by me but if he had any misgivings about it, having accepted the part, he was, of course, polite enough not to say so.

The next old friend to turn up for casting was Mark Burns. I hadn't seen him for ages and, having given him a part too and dealt with the formalities, I suggested that we should pop round a corner to a pub to have a proper drink and catch up with each other's news.

But just before Mark had arrived, I'd had a completely unexpected phone call from Tessa Dahl. For a long time after our sporadic affair in the seventies I'd sent Tessa postcards from all over the world, just to let her know I hadn't forgotten her. She had pitched up once or twice in Malibu or at Château Dachau, but never for long and usually with a current lover. I wondered why she was ringing now and, naturally, I asked her round for a drink at the hotel later that evening.

My time-keeping was no more improved than it had been when I was a teenager staying out all night and, inevitably, Mark and I had gone on a bit and visited one or two more places before I arrived back at the Athenaeum a lot later than I'd arranged.

I'd invited the producers round for a drink too. They looked fairly squiggle-eyed when I walked in an hour late; they'd already made it clear that on the shoot I would be subject to a 'No Booze' clause in my contract. However, we hadn't started shooting yet, so that was all right, and Mark and I went up to my suite, where we found Tessa waiting rather impatiently. She looked amazing, as beautiful as the teenager I'd had an affair with some fifteen years before, but deeper and more, as it were, lived-in, knowing and experienced.

She had been let in by the woman who fronted at the Athenaeum and had helped herself from a bottle of wine she'd found open. She said she was in the midst of an illicit affair that was making her very unhappy, and she thought it was at a recent *This Is Your Life* for Gary Glitter that she'd seen someone who thought Prue and I had split up.

That day she'd been having lunch with Leslie Bricusse to discuss rights to *Willy Wonka* and he'd said rather mischievously, 'Guess who's in town.'

'I had to ring.' Tessa shrugged. 'I'd no choice. But, please, I didn't mind you standing me up when I was seventeen, but I do object to you doing it when I'm thirty something.'

I understood. I reassured her. It had been necessary to discuss the film with Mark; I'd been longing to get back and see her. And to prove it, I'd get rid of everyone else and we'd go off somewhere more intimate. We walked out and found a small bar where we settled down to talk and talk.

Tessa knew Prue. She'd come round to Ensor Mews in 1979, when Mike Leander had been there with Gary Glitter. At the time she was living with an actor, Hywel Bennett, who was a great drinker and Prue had given her a long lecture on why she absolutely should not marry him. 'She should know,' Tessa added.

Tessa's first novel, *Working for Love*, had come out a week or so before that visit. Prue had read it soon after and written to say how brilliant and brave she thought it was. She had started being a friend, and Tessa had asked us both to several parties. Prue had never had a clue about my earlier affair with Tessa; in fact she'd even confided in her a little when Tessa had come to Château Dachau a few years later.

So Tessa understood my predicament and my frustration over my deteriorating marriage. Besides, the attraction we felt when we'd first met and grappled with one another in Tramp didn't appear to have diminished at all. From the minute we'd seen each other that evening, there'd been a sense that this was the eve of a mighty occasion, that what there was between us was already so strong and so obvious, both of us knew we were on the verge of a second, more intense affair.

It was a wonderful evening which I've never forgotten and, as with so many affairs, the anticipation of it before it has happened (although in our case it had happened before) is in some ways the best bit, when all the potential is there and all the pitfalls and pratfalls are unimaginable. The evening was only slightly marred when Tessa, always a little prone to accidents, dropped a beautiful Fabergé egg, which she always kept on a chain around her neck, and lost it.

The shoot in Budapest and Paris was riddled with incident and powerful drama (unfortunately not much of it in the film itself).

With my customary inability to say no to a woman, for the first week or so in Budapest I was joined by Barbra Paskin, an English journalist based in LA who specialised in showbiz stories and went on to write the official biography of Dudley Moore. I'd met her five or six years before, when she'd arrived to interview me at a little restaurant on Sunset Boulevard where I was having lunch with Tim Stone, my agent. The first thing I'd noticed about her was an enormous and well-formed pair of breasts, from which I could not take my eyes for the rest of lunch. She did the interview, and when she'd finished I told her I just had to take her to dinner.

After that she became very hospitable and was always ready to put me up when I needed a bed in LA. She'd even gone to the trouble of organising a 50th birthday party for me, although she didn't come to it herself as she was concerned that Prue might make a scene. (In the event, Prue didn't come either.)

But now she was in Budapest, where I'd also asked Tessa to join me. For some reason of her own, she left and they did not, thank God, quite overlap, though it was touch and go. During the few days I'd been in London, casting and setting up the shoot, I'd spent every spare minute with Tessa. We pushed all the buttons we had when we'd first met in Tramp in the seventies, and they still worked. There was a magnetism between us too strong for either of us to withstand, and she'd instantly agreed when I asked her to join me for what promised to be a fairly tough shoot.

When Tessa turned up, she had brought her children and Maureen, her nanny, with her. Having settled her own movable household, she soon found that, although Barbra had gone, she'd left plenty of spore – a huge bright-pink bra and tiny pink knickers were tucked down the sides of chairs – to let Tessa know she'd been there and to mark her territory. More bizarrely, when Tessa had rung to speak to me, Barbra had answered the phone saying she was my secretary and was perfectly friendly towards her. This was all soon forgotten, though, and Tessa and I were able to get on with our affair, which in the early stages was every bit as wondrous as I'd hoped it would be.

There were complications in trying to film with a 'No Booze' clause. In the bar it was easy enough after I'd bribed the barman, when I ordered 'the usual', to serve me discreetly with a Coke and whisky. Otherwise it was tricky, and Tessa had to help me out. She would order all the wine I wanted as if for her own consumption, mostly filthy white Hungarian stuff for which I'd developed rather a liking. The waiters must have thought it a miracle she survived her month there. She would also smuggle all the bottles from the minibar to the set – vodka, crème de menthe, kümmel, Warnincks advocaat, anything.

I'd say, 'What are you drinking, Fred?' – which I always called her.
'I'm having coffee.'
'Great!' I'd reply. 'Can I have one too?'
She made sure the cup wasn't too full and I'd slip into the bushes, or bend down to tie a shoelace, and tip one of the bottles into the coffee.

Inevitably Tessa, being of strong character, developed a touch of righteous indignation at my behaviour and rebelled a little. Once – out of desperation, she said – she locked me into our hotel room and took all the phones and the contents of the minibar out in a big bag. I'd had a bad night detoxing and she thought I'd have a drink while she was gone. I couldn't get out or ring anyone to come and release me and, naturally, I was a bit cross when she got back.

She said she felt I was pushing it too far. I tried to explain that I enjoyed playing cat and mouse with the producers; and astonishingly enough, Tony Masucci and Peter Katz never caught me red-handed with a drink. However, they were concerned that I was concentrating more on the women than the film, which wasn't really my fault, or true. In addition to this, the filming had met with a few obstacles and money was getting tight, which prompted a crisis over one of Peter Bowles's scenes.

Peter was playing a chief of police who had to question the two American stars. There was a big scene after he'd arrested them with lots of fighting, followed by a very good scene in the chief of police's office.

We'd done all the fights, no problem, and the next day we were shooting the office scene.

That evening I was told that we'd run out of budget for the chief of police's office and we'd have to shoot the scene in a corridor. I said that I didn't feel this was a good idea. Too bad, there was no more money. Period.

With some trepidation, I dispatched an assistant to tell Peter. Knowing him as well as I did, I was aware that he was a highly experienced actor with a sharp eye for quality and he wouldn't be at all happy about the change.

He didn't take long to find me.

'Look, H,' he said calmly enough. 'Chiefs of police don't do this sort of thing in corridors. I can't do it. You've got to shoot the scene in an office.'

'Sorry, Peter, they can't afford an office,' I said.

'In which case, I'm not going to do it,' he came back, still very calm.

'You're not being serious!'

'Yes, I am. But I've got another idea.'

'What the hell is that, then?'

'I'm going to tell them to replace me, and I'll pay for them to reshoot all my scenes.'

I didn't need to ask him to know exactly what he was up to, and I liked the sound of it. I agreed and we went straight off to find the producers.

'Mr Bowles has a proposition to put to you regarding this scene,' I said.

I was enjoying myself. I knew Peter was pulling exactly the sort of stroke I'd encouraged him to 25 years before – a bit of out-and-out brinkmanship, and I knew he'd do it well.

The two men, hard-nosed and steely-eyed, looked at him, never quite certain of how to deal with what they considered old-fashioned British-gent actors.

'OK, what's your proposition?'

'I cannot do this scene in a corridor,' Peter said with quiet firmness. 'If I'm to convince as a chief of police, I have to do it in an office. That is the situation. Now, I quite understand that you can't afford it – these things happen making movies – so what I propose is that you recast and reshoot all my scenes, and I'll pay, whatever it is – £100,000, £200,000 – I'll pay.'

I knew that there was no way Peter would – or could – pay. It was pure bollocks, delivered with true aplomb.

But because no one had ever spoken to them like this, these fellows were so impressed they just said, 'OK, OK. You got the office.'

Blow-Up

Once I'd finished in Budapest, I had a little more shooting to do in Paris before going on to England with Tessa for a week or so. We stayed in her house in Henning Street, Battersea, and she took me down to see her family house at Great Missenden, where her father was buried, and we went to the witch's tree – three trees entwined in the middle – where Roald Dahl used to sit with Tessa and where he wrote *Fantastic Mr Fox*.

Passport to Murder had ceased to inspire me, but I still had to get back to LA to edit it. Tessa came with me again, and we found we'd been booked into a rat house of a hotel. This didn't suit our current highly charged and romantic frame of mind one bit. By now, almost certainly not in the most sociable condition we'd ever known, we descended on Chris and Frances Pye, who took one look at us and realised they had no choice but to ask us in. We stayed there for a night, both of us feeling as if we'd been cut loose and left to float, weightless and rudderless, like in a surreal dream. Tessa demanded that Frances ring her mother and talk to her, about what she wouldn't specify, and she produced a battered handwritten book, her father's personal thesaurus, which she carried everywhere with her and which obviously represented some kind of anchor in her life.

In the morning, I'd come down enough to know we couldn't stay or impose ourselves on anyone else and I booked us into the lovely Hotel Bel-Air, where we stayed for a month.

Although I insisted that we book in as 'Mr and Mrs Wharf', there was nothing particularly discreet about our stay there. Prue knew we were there and we kept changing rooms because I was sure she was going to come and find us.

Prue and the children were staying in LA with her friend Belinda, and the children even came over to play at the Bel-Air. Inevitably, this sparked a few noisy scenes and rowdy phone calls from Prue. 'How dare Tessa tell one of my children she loves them! They're my children. How could she possibly tell Charlotte she loves her?'

She knew I loved my children enormously but she seemed to want to involve them in all the misery of our separation by getting them to ring me. Or she'd ring the Bel-Air herself and tell Tessa that William was desperately ill. Once she rang, insisting that I come and see them, and sent a girlfriend to pick me up.

When I arrived she opened up her shirt, put my hand on her breast and said, 'Doesn't that remind you how great it was?' and tried to make me promise that I would pack and leave the hotel the next day.

Tessa and I had invited Harry Nilsson and Nolan over that evening, but I couldn't get away from Prue. When Nolan rang to find out what was going on, Prue wouldn't let him talk to me.

But I decided I couldn't stay with Prue and went back to the Bel-Air next day. For the rest of our stay there the phone kept ringing and messages kept being delivered and slid under the door. 'Willie Wombat is still very ill'; 'Charlotte needs you'; 'Mrs Hemmings will be coming to pick up Mr Hemmings at ten o'clock . . .'

When she turned up we hid in the room, knowing she was in the car park, until we could sneak out of the back to go to Chris Pye's place.

John Daly came over to the Bel-Air all the time. Despite the erratic history of our friendship, there was still a tremendous bond between us and we could reminisce for hours about south London days and Toby's gym, and how I'd always been known as 'Itwasn'tme'; but we avoided talking about films.

Of course, Nolan and a lot of other friends turned up while we were at the Bel-Air and there was a great coming together of most of my old LA friends, who all got on with Tessa, although a few had decided that they were going to place themselves in the Prue camp in what had now become a rather public disintegration of our marriage.

I hated it. I hated all the bitterness and the recriminations. I hated seeing my children upset and could only hope that one day they would give me a chance and judge me outside the context of my relationship with their mother.

We left the Bel-Air having run up a huge tab of around $80,000, which seemed to follow me around for years, but I still think it was worth it.

Tessa and I went up to Idaho for the première of *Dark Horse*. I was relieved that Prue had decided to stay with the children in LA for a little longer, though it seemed we couldn't escape her completely. The second night in Ketchum we were in a restaurant when a small, ill-mannered child sidled up to Tessa and pointed at her offensively. 'You're not Prue,' she whined.

The next day, I picked up some of my stuff from the house and went to see my local bank manager. I tried to convince him that somewhere in the Cayman Islands I had a deposit of over a million dollars, if only I could find it. I don't think he believed me. And then I got drunk.

Dark Horse was being premièred that night and I was very keen to go, but we'd gone back to see Marcus Beresford in his trailer and there, rather inconveniently, I passed out. When I came too, Tessa was looking very shirty.

'What's the trouble, Fred?' I asked solicitously.

She sucked noisily through narrowed nostrils. 'I'll tell you. There's a fish tank there that's been going glob, glob, glob for the last three hours, two very smelly ferrets have been sniffing up my trouser leg, you've been snoring like a sea lion with sinusitis, and I can't get away because I'm locked into a fucking trailer in Idaho!'

'But why? Why are we locked in?' I asked, feeling all Kafka-esque again.

'Presumably because Marcus didn't want you turning up at your precious bloody première pissed out of your tree.'

In June, we flew to London. I had made up my mind that this was the moment to call it a day with Prue. Of course, I didn't kid myself that I wasn't as responsible for what had gone wrong as she was, but somehow she had done so much to lower my self-esteem when I was with her that I didn't see how, together, we could ever crawl out of the pit we had dug for ourselves. Besides, I found Tessa incredibly stimulating and I loved being with her. She was self-willed, certainly, but she was honest. I asked her to marry me. She said she would, and I promised to try to sort things out amicably with Prue.

We even fixed a date, 12 September, and a church, St Mary's, Battersea, not far from Tessa's house, into which I now moved with a small pile of my belongings.

For a while, it was heaven. I loved living in London again, and started to pick up a few threads from my old life here. Edward was still at school in England, and now I had an opportunity to see something of him away from my unravelling marriage. Tessa would come with me to Harrow to take him out and watch him play cricket.

I could see Debs too, and Nolan. Debs was teaching drama now, and enjoying life with Mark, her boyfriend, whom she told me she loved and trusted. She liked Tessa's three children – Sophie, who was then fourteen, Clover and Luke. I was building a relationship with them too, teaching them to paint, and I hoped Tessa might be able to do the same some time with Charlotte and William.

Although all this was good, it wasn't made easy by the fact that I'd been able to bring very little money with me to London. I'd had to make sure that Prue had enough to run the house, feed the children and pay the school fees. At the same time, she was dragging her heels over our divorce. She was also very angry about a largish spread on Tessa and me which had appeared in *Hello!* magazine.

I genuinely did think that as a result of a deal I'd done some years before that a sizeable sum of money, though admittedly not a million dollars, had been deposited in a Cayman Islands bank account for me. I spent a lot of time trying to track down the other parties involved, but drew a complete blank. In frustration, I told Tessa that I would have to go back to the States, simply to make some money. She agreed and suggested we went via Massachusetts to stay with her mother, Patricia Neal, who was living at Martha's Vineyard.

I'd always liked Pat Neal, but I couldn't pretend that she was impressed when I drank everything in her house, including the cough medicine. I guess I was dreading the next confrontation I knew I would have to have with Prue. I was tired of all the yelling and shouting; I'd had enough of souring the children by hurling accusations back and forth. I hated them seeing me like that and I just wished there were some way it could all be resolved peacefully and sensibly. But I knew there wasn't.

When Tessa followed me into town one day when I'd gone to find some drink, she told me how worried she was about it all and said she really wanted to help. A few days later, she told me we were going to pick up Nolan from a hotel in Boston. I thought there was something mysterious going on when she took me up to a room. When I walked in with her I found not just Nolan and Tessa's daughter Sophie, but a whole goon squad – Jon Povill, Tim Stone, Chris Pye and Burton Merrill.

'Ah,' I said, immediately recognising what this was. 'An intervention.'

An intervention is a process recommended by AA in the States by which someone who is perceived as having a problem is encouraged by their friends to look for help.

These people in the room, all gathered there by Tessa, with John Daly on the line from LA on a speaker phone, were all concerned enough to have come to tell me that they cared, that they were truly worried about the damage I might be doing to myself.

'Please,' they said, 'as a favour to your friends and all the people who love you, you've got to stop doing this to yourself.'

I was shocked, and very moved.

Although I knew my condition wasn't as bad as they thought and had probably, with the very best of intentions, been a tad overdramatised by Tessa, I could only go along with their suggestion that I should book into a clinic again.

Blow-Up

I agreed to check into the well-respected Hazelden Clinic in Minnesota, if Tessa was prepared to come too, and within the week, I was there.

A month or so later, before my course was through, I was back in Idaho with Prue.

I don't know why Hazelden didn't work out. I don't know why my affair with Tessa came to an end. Like an extravagant, magnificent firework or a lovely big, iridescent bubble drifting along on a summer breeze, it had simply, suddenly burst, and now I can look back on that interlude, which lasted no more than four or five months, with warmth, affection and admiration.

Prue, also brimming with good intentions undoubtedly, was encouraging me to stay dry, and for a long time I was an attendee at the local AA (which did remarkably good business among the escapers of Sun Valley) and a regular consumer of AntAbuse tablets, whose function is to make you really quite ill if, inadvertently, you do take a drink.

Naturally, although Prue liked to stand over me while I took the horrible little pills, I tucked them under my tongue and never swallowed them. But there was no booze in the house either.

To begin with, I got round this by buying miniature bottles of vodka from the store where I collected the papers each morning. Driving back, I'd tip the contents of several of them, one after the other, down my throat and, it being winter by now, with a thick covering of snow all around, hurl the bottles out of the window as I came up the drive. This was fine and reasonably undetected, until a flash thaw one morning revealed a sea of little bottles up the side of the drive.

After that I thought it wiser not to drive any more, and I had to conjure up another way of maintaining a convenient but covert supply of booze on the premises, and when Prue and the children had flown down to LA for a little shopping, I brought up dozens of bottles of vodka and fifty yards of garden hosepipe on a roll. With the help of a large plastic funnel I poured all the vodka mixed with water into the hose and that served me very well. As it was winter, the diluted vodka froze. I'd have to break off a piece of the ice and squeeze it along the pipe to get it out. And the children soon got used to the sight of me poring over my keyboard in the shed, sucking an icicle.

Prue also insisted, not unreasonably in view of what had nearly happened between Tessa and me, that she had to know she would always be able to provide for the four children, who were then between eight and sixteen. My other two children were grown up now and not directly dependent on me, so she wanted me to sign a pretty stiff post-marital agreement.

In the event that we did split up permanently, I thought I would always be able to make a living for myself, though preferably not as an actor or director; rather as a painter or writer. For the time being, though, I agreed to stay, and set about drumming up some new projects. I sort of numbed myself to my circumstances to help me through it.

This wasn't going too badly when Nolan drove up from LA to spend Christmas with us. I still loved Christmas, wherever I was, and I wanted to make it as good as I could for all the children. They responded well enough, deciding for the moment to overlook my erratic behaviour, and someone gave me a lovely bright-red Santa Claus sweater.

📷 📷 📷 📷

I'm still wearing my Santa Claus sweater on Boxing Day, when I find myself alone in the house. From a well-hidden stash, I pull out a bottle of superior Scotch and pour myself a goodish nip. I'm just thinking about another when the phone rings. It's Charlotte, who has been on the lower slopes of the mountain with William and now wants to come home. It's a long walk but only a five-minute drive.

I tend not to drive these days. There have been so many prangs and, due to my particular lifestyle, I'm seldom under the permitted alcohol limit. However, I don't want to leave little Char and Young Wills staggering about in the cold, and I know that Nolan's old Ford Bronco truck, which he uses to cart his snowboards around, is standing outside and facing down the drive.

Nolan and George are supposed to be on their way back from town, but there's no sign of them. Thinking of the little kids freezing, I go outside, clamber into the cab of the truck and look around at the controls. I've never driven one of these before and there are a couple of gear levers, which doesn't look right. But the key's in the ignition and I guess the principle's the same as any other vehicle, once you've sorted out what's where.

I start it and, pleased with myself, set off – a little jerkily, it has to be said. I reach our gate and stop. I make the mistake of fiddling around with the stick shift again, but in time I find a forward gear and move off. I turn into the road, with the traffic, though I know for sure there's something wrong with these gears. I'm stabbing at the clutch pedal, missing sometimes, until I've completely lost it. Abruptly, I realise the Previa people carrier in front of me isn't moving. I've got nowhere to go, and zero braking distance.

Nolan has decorated the front of his truck with a completely pointless and massive bull bar which effortlessly buries itself into the back half of the people carrier, which is empty. My engine stalls; I open the door, slither out and stagger round to inspect the damage. Nolan's truck is fine – that's good – but the other party's vehicle is, frankly, destroyed. It has been shortened like a can in a crusher.

I am undoubtedly over whatever limit of alcohol in the blood the state of Idaho imposes. There's no driver in the other vehicle on whom I can offload the blame. Whichever way you look at it, my position isn't good.

Bowing my head to avoid eye contact with any witnesses there may be, I turn and trot back up the road until I'm out of sight and can duck back into my own place.

It isn't the best solution, but right now it's all I've got. I'm still pondering my next move when Nolan and George arrive back at the house.

'Pappa, where's my car?'

'Agh.' I search for the right words. 'There's been an incident . . . well an accident, really. It's down the road.'

'What's it doing down the road?'

'Well, I went to get the two little ones. And this car was stopped . . . in front of me.'

'We'll go and deal with it,' Nolan says, looking pale.

They go. I have another swift pull on the Scotch.

This is what happens . . .

Nolan and George arrive at his truck and the wrecked people carrier. The police are there. So is the owner of the Previa. He looks nervous and scared. Why?

He's saying, 'It's OK. It's cool. The insurance'll pay up. I don't want to file a complaint . . . I'm busy.'

It turns out later he's been dealing a good weight of coke in the house opposite. There may be more stock in the car. He's not travelling under his own name. He needs the hassle of the police like a rocket up his arse.

The police ask Nolan, 'Is this your car?'

He agrees it is. 'It was taken by a joyrider, just now, from our place.'

'Yes, yes,' says a witness. 'I saw him. A short sort of guy, with a lot of grey hair and a Santa Claus sweater. He ran that way.' The witness points back along the road towards our place.

'Well, too bad,' Nolan says. 'He'll be long gone by now.'

'No!' says the witness. 'There he is. That's him, walking back towards us now!'

Everybody except Nolan and George turn and stare at me walking back down the street. Nolan is wincing painfully. This isn't going to be easy.

After another quick Scotch, I have decided the best thing is to go out and be honest. Truth is the best defence, truth and tact. I assume a self-effacing smile as I approach the little group around the truck and the wreck. I notice the owner of the Previa, who looks like he wants to sink through the road.

Nolan is groaning and shaking his head.

'OK,' says the cop. 'Here's your joyrider. D'you recognise him?'

'No,' says Nolan, shaking his head and glaring at me.

The cop turns to me. 'Do you know these guys?'

'Yes, of course,' I say. 'They are my sons.'

'Ughugh! And were you driving this vehicle?'

'I was,' I nod.

Nolan is nearly weeping with frustration by now. But honesty is my policy for dealing with this crisis.

The second cop has produced his handcuffs which he clicks around my wrist. 'OK, buddy, you're coming with us.'

It was all right at the police station. Some of them knew me; I'd played pool against one. The man with the Previa hadn't wanted to know.

'I am a sheriff, by the way,' I told them, hoping this might soften their approach. I pulled the deputy sheriff's badge I'd had presented to me in Livingstone County from my pocket and showed it to them. I also showed them a few of my magic tricks.

They gave me a warning and let me go. I vowed never to drive a car again.

The following June, Deborah was due to have her first baby and my first grandchild. I was determined to be there. I was in touch with my old friend and one-time collaborator Chris Pye, who was now working in England. I rang him and told him I was coming and arranged to meet him to talk about a couple of ideas. He also wanted me to talk to British production companies about American methods of making episodic television. In the States, for an hour's programme, we'd prep for a week and shoot for a week. The same process in England seemed to take months. He felt as an Englishman with a mass of experience in the US, I was well placed to pass it on. Once my trip had been fixed, I couldn't wait to get there.

Idaho felt chilly and faintly hostile, while California had long ceased to be friendly towards me, and the feeling was entirely mutual. Most of the people I knew were heading away from the traditional haunts of Malibu, Bel-Air and the Hollywood Hills.

To be sure, fashionable restaurants were still there and heads still turned where celebrities dressed the tables at Ma Maison on Beverly Drive, or Michael's in Santa Monica, or, for the fervently British, at Le Dome on Sunset. There were still breakfasts being served in the Polo Lounge Garden, of course, where, as ever, deep-red bougainvillea clashed noisily with pink tablecloths. But Nilsson, round and red, with wonderful brandy in hand, would no longer be found at the Hotel Bel-Air bar.

New places, like new fashions, would appear, and new faces too, that would soon be deep-fried like Caprizzio's calamari in the batter that is Hollywood, wrapped and curled with care for a minute or two.

Andy Warhol's infamous fifteen minutes of fame for all does not apply under the Hollywood sign. Everyone is famous for only a nano-second, for the flash of optimism in their head the moment they get off the bus, before they work their way through doubt and disappointment to being producers or writers or development dealers, taking endless meetings about projects that will never happen but, right then, will pay for a hamburger.

There are exceptions of course – the truly great, who deserve their fame and have earned the respect of audiences who flock to their films – to whom the movie world clings like a ticket for a guaranteed seat on the bus to Greatwealth, Ca.

For me, the bus had gone, and London was the only answer. Back to roots. Regroup. Find old friends who'd fallen from my Filofax far too long ago.

Anna Hall, now living in London too, and about to get married to a property developer, offered me a room in her house in Redcliffe Mews near the Fulham Road.

The familiar city felt like your favourite pair of slippers after a winter in Idaho. I had to work hard, though, to establish that reports of my death had, as they say, been exaggerated. I had returned from exile, I announced. I was available.

One Sunday evening at Anna's, after a day spent with Debs and Mark, she asked me to join her for dinner at Glaister's in Hollywood Road (London SW10, that is; not Beverly Hills). We were to meet an old school friend of hers who was thinking of taking on a new boyfriend, who for some reason was known as Bagel – and the nickname had stuck. This Bagel, I was told, liked to have a fair woman on his arm and his position as official 'greeter' at the right sort of club had done him fairly proud in this respect. Anna, with her chap and me as independent observers, ready to hold up numbered cards above our heads like judges at a ballroom-dancing contest, were there to vet him on behalf of her friend, a reportedly shy young lady of elegant stock, whom the Bagel was vigorously courting, called Lucy.

"Easily, Henley Regatta', (Watercolour).

19

Return to London, 1993–1998

There were five of us at dinner in Mr Glaister's crowded eating house – Anna and her fiancé, Nicholas Barley, Lucy and Bagel, and me.

Bagel gangled, with a manic fire in his eye and the long fingers of an arthritic cellist, which he prodded at the menu to order champagne. I generally don't like champagne; unless it's the very best and very old, it leads to dyspepsia and flatulence, both embarrassing in a crowded restaurant with an interesting, slightly timid creature perched on the chair beside one. I hid quietly behind a beaker of Californian Chardonnay, my comfortable staple, and observed the Bagel. He wasn't so bad, I thought, but Lucy, his putative target, didn't seem at ease. Her eyes darted from side to side, as if searching for a dark corner in which to hide, and she didn't converse much at all, particularly as Bagel was making all the running, with lengthy anecdotes where he always came out on top, told with an extravagant waving of the arms.

In time, apparently seeking a wider public, he started to table-hop and embraced into his audience our neighbours, a nubile group hosted by an attractive teenager in a braless chemise. A few glasses of wine had got hold of their group and shaken out all inhibition, and our consideration of Bagel was henceforth marred by the two tables merging into one, with all the hubbub and maelstrom of inefficiency to which this leads.

I engaged Lucy's eye and we sought to rescue each other from this babbling chaos, while Anna and Mr Barley gazed longingly through each other, as lovers will, perhaps at half-glimpsed futures.

Bagel, eschewing subtlety in his approach, was trying to pull the next table's hostess, making my metaphorical number cards redundant. My only recommendation could be that Lucy should cancel forthwith her membership of the club about whose portals Bagel lurked.

Though she looked dismally alone that evening, I found her shyness and quiet good manners utterly charming.

*

Since, for me, divorce lurked in the wings like a prowling wolf and I was still feeling a little alone in London, when I saw Anna next morning I suggested that, when Lucy called for a report, I might invite her to dinner on my own one evening.

On such small and gentle decisions are worlds turned and great landscapes crafted.

With Anna acting as careful if slightly unwilling intermediary, Lucy agreed and we settled on the following evening. I opted for a quiet Italian restaurant tucked down a small mews at the back end of Fulham, where still could be found the red gingham and wax-encrusted Chianti bottles that recalled old London for me. The proprietor and general *uovo buono*, a generously built man with a lot of pasta belly going on and a rococo moustache, looked undeniably Italian, though his name was Michael Halifax. I'd known him for years, first as an actor – a good one – and had stumbled across him later in Adelaide, where I was filming; he was mine host at a stunningly filthy though hugely enjoyable pub just off the Maralinga Highway, the last watering hole going west before you reach the parched and endless Nullarbor Plain. He had married a stern *Torinesa* who had firmly set him before a chopping block and I'd kept a bit in touch. When I'd heard he'd opened in London, I'd flown there, and returned whenever the chance arose.

I always believed in taking new ladies to a restaurant I knew and where I was known. To do otherwise could lead to gastronomic and romantic suicide, as well as being hell on the bladder if, like me, you hate to ask the way to the loos.

Lucy was relaxed and, it seemed, in fine form – a different person from the one I'd met at the Bagel fiasco, and we chatted like old chums for hours. Mike, discreet host and donor of brandy at the end of dinner, joined us for coffee and a fag. He introduced us to his wife, Katrina, who wagged a disapproving digit at the cigarette, then he left us in peace to talk on.

In the end, it was getting late for Lucy (never for me) and, with a vague suggestion that we would meet again, we parted, she to her house in Battersea, while I went back to Anna's with a strong feeling that there was going to be more to me and Lucy than a couple of dinners.

In the meantime, my daughter Debs and her partner, Mark Kemp, were excited, with a little trepidation, about the very imminent arrival of their baby. I went to see them in their place in Tooting, and took Debs back with me to Peter Jones in Sloane Square to indulge in some grandfatherly spending. We bought every bit of kit we thought the baby might need – cots, sheets, grow-bags, bibs, bonnets, small furry beasts, woollen booties that you could just about get your thumb in. Debs was very grateful but extremely reluctant to set up the cot or unpack anything until the baby was safely born, which Esme was, on 21 June 1993.

It was a wonderful moment for all of us, and for Debs made even more poignant by the fact that Jenny, her mother (and my earliest big love), and I were reunited, briefly as it was, on either side of her bed. It was the first time the three of us had been together for nearly thirty years.

Before Debs and Esme left hospital with Mark, we remembered that the cot hadn't been put up yet.

'I'll do it,' I offered gallantly.

Debs looked doubtful. 'It's not really your sort of thing, though, is it?'

'Of course it is,' I lied, and scooted off to Tooting. I knew where they lived, of course, but the door was locked and I hadn't brought a key. No matter; there was a sort of conservatory over the back and a window open above it. More agile then than now, I scrambled up and climbed in through a kitchen window and made my way though a couple of rooms. In one of them, lying on a sofa, was a guitar.

I am compulsively incapable of passing a guitar without picking it up and playing it. I sat down and strummed for a few moments until I heard someone opening the front door down below. It must be Mark, I thought, and I hadn't even started on the cot. I leaped up and ran down as he came.

He looked surprised. 'How did you get in?'

'No problem. I shinned up over the conservatory and let myself in through the kitchen window. I'm sorry I got waylaid, though. I've been playing the guitar upstairs.'

'But there isn't an upstairs,' Mark said.

'Yes, there is, that's how I came in, and where I've just come from.'

'But we've only got the ground floor. There's another flat upstairs, nothing to do with us.'

I let Mark do the cot.

The summer season so beloved by Anglo-Saxons was in full swing. In my previous life in England, I was always running so fast that events like the Chelsea Flower Show, Royal Ascot, Henley Royal Regatta,

Wimbledon, May Balls, even David Frost's annual summer party had passed by me more or less unnoticed. But these things were, it seemed, fixed markers in the passing of each year for Lucy, for reasons both personal and professional.

Having grown up amidst the riparian meadowland where the Thames glides serenely between Ox and Bucks, at the end of each June she had watched the family home fill to overflowing with bright-blazered rowers of elegant eights, there to cross oars in combat, between the marquees and picnics among the traditional charm of the regatta.

As long-time ADC to hat-designer extraordinaire David Shilling, Lucy was also aware of the importance of Royal Ascot in her working life. I saw how these social events could impose a measured rhythm and reassuring structure to life which had been absent in the ad hoc sort of existence I'd always led.

I was made aware of these fixed interventions when I tried to arrange another dinner with Lucy. In the end it was only after Royal Ascot that we could meet again, this time with the Pyes, Anna and her man.

One topic of conversation that inevitably popped up was the official verdict on Bagel, which was pretty much *nul point*. But how to get rid of greeter? We debated the options:

- The Honest Approach – Look, frankly, I don't fancy you. Sorry.
- The Gentle Approach – Listen, I think you're really super, but I don't think I'm quite ready.
- The Physical Approach – Oops, mind that bus . . . Oh dear.
- The Fear Approach – The rest of my family are in Broadmoor.
- The Psychological Approach – Have you considered that you're only interested in me because you're running away from yourself and I represent your antithesis?

Lucy, of course, chose B, and Bagel was struck from the agenda.

The threads I'd been hoping to pick up in London were beginning to come to hand. Old friends, old faces started to reappear and the idea of London, where I hadn't lived for over fifteen years, was growing more attractive by the day. I hadn't been back long when I found myself arranging dinner at the Ivy with Joan Collins and her then beau, Robin Hurlstone. By the time I'd got it sorted out, there were still too many men. I rang Lucy and asked her if she would like to join us. The poor girl sounded terrified by the prospect. I assured her that Joan didn't bite and she agreed to come.

On the night, she sat next to Robin, who relaxed her with great charm. Joan was in warm cuddly mode and, as far as I recall, everything went off OK – just another dinner at the Ivy really. I escorted Lucy back to her house in Cupar Road, Battersea, where we were waylaid before going into the house by a bizarre singles party to which Lucy had been invited at the last minute (and passed up to have dinner with me). The host had told her it was a Eurotrash party; I have never, then or since, really worked out who is or isn't Eurotrash. I was no wiser when a man with a strong Greek accent staggered out clutching his face which, it turned out, had just been severely slapped, presumably – though this wasn't confirmed – by a woman. There was a lot of the kind of noise I like spilling out into the street, and I was still in a party mood. 'Let's crash it,' I suggested, and in we went.

Lucy talked me into giving a demonstration of my magic, which although I wasn't entirely sober seemed to satisfy the punters, along with a couple of quick stories. I was having fun; Lucy was having fun. It seemed to me that this was something we should push along.

Later I said to her, 'Shall I let the driver go?'

She looked back at me with a show of coyness that I loved, and nodded.

Anna Hall was a bit grumpy about my seeing Lucy. Lucy, it seemed, was the old school friend she kept for cosy chats, small confidences and reminiscences about teenage adventures, not for succumbing to the wiles of old roués from her former life of films and frolics.

'Too bad,' I huffed, and there was a slight falling out.

Lucy went to Henley Regatta; I went to Tooting, to stay with Mark and Debs – on the ground floor.

While I'd been in London, letting people know I was back, Prue had been calling to ask when they were going to see me in Idaho again. I hadn't yet had the heart to say 'never' – for one thing because I dreaded losing touch with my children there, especially as the two older boys had now left Harrow to finish their education in the States. However, the need for a decision was deferred when an unexpected deal materialised. I was asked by a Welsh producer, Carol Byrne Jones, to direct *Gypsy Fires*, a film for television for S4C and Saban, a US company. It was to be made simultaneously in Welsh and English, with the American version being topped and tailed as a Christmas story, with the venerable James Coburn appearing as Santa Claus.

I jumped at it – a wonderful excuse to spend more time in Britain, where Lucy lived. And I hadn't been to Wales, as far as I could remember, since making *Unman, Wittering and Zigo*, when Nolan was born.

A journey to Cardiff to meet the producers gave me first sight of the script, based on *Fire on the Common*, a fine children's story by T. Llew Jones. Unfortunately the script lacked the magic of the book and I knew at once I'd have to rewrite the whole thing, on the hoof, as it were, which would only add to the customary freneticism of film-making. Air tickets for Prue, in an art director capacity, were thrown into the equation.

In mid-July, for the first few weeks, staying up near the world coracle-making centre of Newcastle Emlyn, Lucy joined me on the preparation for the shoot and helped me hugely with the script. She'd never had anything to do with movies before but she was soon cutting and pasting away like a hardened old blackmail-note writer and giving me massive support, laughing a lot and refusing to let me get fazed, though we'd be up all night sometimes, trying to finish the ruddy script. In fact, it got so absurd that the producers came and took my computer away to make sure I got a little sleep.

Making a bilingual film has special problems of its own, in that, for instance, someone had to hold up idiot boards with the phonetic pronunciation for non-Welsh-speaking actors, like Edward Woodward (whom I hadn't seen since we'd worked together on *The Equalizer*). Or sometimes we would shoot a scene in Welsh, then do the same scene in English, after which the producers might complain that the second version had worked better than the Welsh and would want to reshoot.

For the early period of filming, we had been staying at the Emlyn Arms, near the centre of the small town, but as there were several weeks to go, I asked the producers if they would rent a house for me. They came up with a grim, grey farmhouse a few miles away, but even that was better than being holed up in a small hotel bedroom. They also supplied me with a rented car of innocuous specification.

I had not driven at all since the embarrassing incident in Ketchum the previous winter, but it was a harmless-looking car with recognisable gear arrangements and I was reluctant to own up to my ineptitude. I transported Lucy and our luggage from the hotel to the farmhouse. I took particular care to drive slowly, seldom moving up from second gear, and it seemed to me that the journey passed in remarkably safety, but every time I glanced at her, I observed that her jaws were clenched and there was a look of thinly disguised terror in her eyes. Her fear was quite unfounded; we reached the house without incident and moved in. My confidence in my ability to drive was sufficiently restored that I decided to leave Lucy sleeping and drive myself to the shoot next morning, soon after daybreak. Lucy was going to get back into the town and pick up her car before joining me later at the location.

By the end of the day, I was knackered and had taken in a few brandies. It was thought advisable that I shouldn't try to drive back to the farm, so we went in Lucy's car. I had parked the rented car on a road that pointed downhill into the valley towards the town and the River Teifi.

It was only the following morning that I realised I'd left the keys in the hire car, but, in a small town in a distant corner of west Wales, nothing would have happened, I thought.

I was wrong. Some kids, finding the car open with the keys in the ignition, hadn't been able to resist jumping in – I would have done exactly the same at their age. It transpired, though, when they were questioned by the police, that as soon as they got in and took the handbrake off, it had started rolling down the hill. They had panicked and jumped out to save their skins. The car had rolled on, ignoring the sharp curve in the road that led down to the town and the river, to launch itself off a sheer cliff into a gorge below. It was a total write-off.

I was severely shaken. Although I wasn't directly responsible and hadn't even been in the vehicle at the time, yet again I vowed that I would never get involved with driving cars; I seemed fated to send them to their deaths.

Adding to the tensions this and the filming created were Lucy's departure and Prue's arrival, with her mother, the two younger children, a nanny and a girlfriend who all wanted to be put up in the farmhouse. Prue soon shipped William and Charlotte off somewhere, then disappeared herself. As always when I was on a film, I was too wrapped up in it to notice what was going on – thank God.

When Prue and her entourage had finally regrouped and moved on, Lucy joined me again for the last leg of the six-week shoot, finishing in Cardiff to do James Coburn's bit. When we went back to Newcastle Emlyn to do the edit, I could afford a little light relief when my soul brother Mike Leander turned up on the pretext of talking to me about the still unfinished *Hamelin* project.

Somewhere along the way, I found that I'd bought the wonderful gypsy caravan that had been made for the production. I don't know why. I didn't need a gypsy caravan; I had nowhere to keep it and I didn't have a horse to pull it. I suppose, like a lot of romantic fools, the idea of roaming around without ties or responsibilities, communing with nature, cooking over a wood fire, had its appeal for me too. Anyway, the caravan's gone now.

By the end of August, I thought I'd finally made up my mind that I wouldn't be going back to Idaho, especially after Lucy had invited me to stay in Scotland, where her mother, Anne Chenevix-Trench, had a house. Although the original Georgian house had been greatly enlarged in Victoria's reign, with all that that implies, I immediately fell in love with the place.

I started writing a letter to my son George . . .

📷 📷 📷 📷

Knockbrex, near Borgue, stands on the coast of Galloway, where Scotland thrusts long fingers south into the Irish Sea. It tumbles into the gentle swell of Wigtown Bay – grey-blue, Gulfstream-warm and very swimmable.

As the tide flows, the rocks, rubbed round, like an army of Henry Moore's, lie still and limpet-crusted, drawing in the Atlantic waves from far across the Solway Firth to cover and to sculpt them a little more. These are great rocks to gaze on and splendid to paint; many a study I've done of them, for the moment, quick watercolours, seeds of paintings to come.

There is a tiny harbour at Knockbrex where men pulled contra-band – 'Fair Trade' – from Ardwall Island across the strand, away from the eyes of the customs men. Grey stone phalli placed by men still stubbornly project from the rocky seabed to guide the smugglers' boats up the stone-strewn inlet to the haven. When the tide's up we can see them from the kitchen window, sticking out of the water like great grey thumbs.

A burn that rushes by the house, through a rambling rock water garden with high granite walls and corners of light and dark, burbles into a long narrow freshwater loch, which glitters silver in the early light around a small bracken island. The loch is edged with bulrushes where coots, moorhen and duck hide with their infants. A couple of hundred yards further, the burn trickles out and skips and jumps down to the sea beside the harbour wall and joins the Wigtown Bay.

A castellated greystone boathouse stands beside the harbour, a hundred years old and so low-ceilinged you must crouch through the door to find, where once pretty boats were kept, the remnants of fires laid by trespassers to warm themselves as they fling their picnic litter and empty bottles into the gloomy corners for us to clear.

At 5 a.m. I take my shepherd's crook and walk up over the ridge to a long sandy beach on the far side to see Barlocco Island, near and friendly. You can reach it at low tide, if you've a taste for scraped feet and scratched knees; I don't. I walk on, among sheep that roam and graze between the house and the sea. They bleat a little, in mild protest at the old pied sheepdog, who sees no need to nip their legs or lie in hawk-eyed wait to guide them. They know where they're going and he trots along beside them, on their lazy way to Bethlehem.

In this serene and peaceful isolation, the coastal landscape changes with every small shift in the weather and movement of the tide. The low knolls behind the far beach are draped in pale-green table linen and billiard-table baize as they swoop gently down to the beach house, castellated too, where, from inside, a large arch frames an elderly pier that stretches into the bay.

On the way back to the house a dark cavern takes me back to Enid Blyton stories, lingered over in lonely Tolworth boyhood, of smugglers and adventure. The bats hang from damp rock ceilings above a slippery floor where once the liquor barrels were stored.

Climbing up the hill once more, both big islands come into view, surrounded by a cluster of lesser ones, like pebbles, some no more than rocks above the high-tide line. On a crisp, clear morning, the Isle of Man shimmers in the Irish Sea and the spit of Therins sprawls along the western horizon like a long, thin snake with the Mull of Galloway for its nose.

A whiff of sea and kelp gusts up the hill to clear a clouded head, and lifts the giant gulls cruising along the coast. The uncertain Scottish sun rises fitfully, for a moment veiled by cloud, reappearing to a faint rattle of thunder in the west, and splashing like a follow-spot on the 2,000-foot slope of Cairnsmoor, as I drop down to the house, and coffee and kippers for breakfast.

This peaceful pace felt like another world, a million miles at least from the rambunctious movie world of Los Angeles. It worked on me like a miracle charm. Being here with Lucy, leaving all the hassles of the past year behind, was giving me the strength to deal with the decisions I had to make, that I'd already made but had to see through, no matter how torn I was by thoughts of letting down my children back in Idaho. I thought of them. I started letters to them; finished some, posted one or two. It seemed almost unfair that I should be so far away, as if my country were at war, while I was on holiday in a distant land.

After the rigours and strains of the Welsh shoot, it couldn't have been more perfect. And I found being with Lucy relaxing, undemanding and devoid of the constant showdowns with Prue that seemed to have characterised a large part of our marriage.

While I must accept that the cause of these battles was often my own idiosyncratic behaviour, in my defence I would say that Prue, having been my secretary for several years, knew all about me and the way I lived long before we were married. It still puzzles me how some women, in astonishing displays of hope overwhelming logic, or the evidence, think they can change the men they marry. I don't dispute that I was probably in serious need of changing, but that's not the point.

After Scotland, we returned to London and I moved in to Battersea, fervently hoping that enough people knew I was back and more work would come my way in England.

Anna had rung to say that she was going to get married in November at St Mary, the Boltons. I was deputed to look after Joan Collins, who was an old friend of Anna's, and organise picking her up from where she was having lunch in Jermyn Street and taking her to the church. I really couldn't imagine Joan in the back of one of the characterful but not very elegant minicabs we used in Battersea, so I hired a Daimler limo for the day. That was all fine. Lucy and I scooped her up and got her to the wedding, and then to the reception at the Franklin Hotel.

Outside, a snapper was waiting to get a shot, not of Joan, as one might have expected, but of Lucy and me. He tried to follow us into the hotel, asking impertinent questions. We managed to escape, but when a story appeared next morning in the gossip page of the *Daily Bogroll*, unflattering in content and stuffed with pithy quotes from Prue, it was obvious that she was involved.

But no real damage had been done and we got over it, until Anna arrived back from her honeymoon, outraged that we had, as she thought, used her wedding to publicise our own activities. Lucy pointed out to her that it was hardly an image-enhancing piece for us, and it had obviously been written with Prue's co-operation, and Anna did agree.

Soon after that Prue rang to have a quick shout at Lucy, and to tell me she had filed for a divorce in Idaho (for the third time, as it happened).

Reluctantly, I flew back to America in December 1993, promising to sort it out once and for all. I would, I said, be divorced in a week and back by Christmas.

The following March, I was still in Idaho. Prue had persuaded me to stay, convincing me that to leave now would greatly upset William and Charlotte. She was right, of course, and I thought that their emotional health was more vulnerable and important than mine.

So I stayed, but money was tighter than ever. There were no serious jobs in the offing until John Ashley, loyal friend, booked me for a few days' filming in Dallas on a Chuck Norris straight-to-video sort of movie. I'd been phoning Lucy regularly, and now I suggested she came out and joined me in Dallas.

She did, and it was wonderful to see her, but I was in bad shape, emotionally raddled by trying to handle what was going on at home and indulging in a little too much comfort bingeing. We checked into one of those big, anonymous Hilton-style hotels three days before filming started. Prue had the number there and rang every night, convinced that I had Barbra Paskin with me – as if!

There were a lot of dramas going on up in the mountains, it seemed. I understood that Prue felt very insecure, but this wasn't going to help.

Lucy calmly did her best to straighten me up a little and help me with my lines, but the production unit kept me hanging around for so long, all made up and in the full kit and caboodle, that when it came to it, frankly – I blew it.

I was told I wouldn't be needed again and slunk back to Idaho with my tail between my legs, while Lucy flew back to London.

For the next few months I did a little more work on *Hamelin*, although I'd lost much of my enthusiasm for the project after Chad Stewart and I had bust up over it. To stop myself from going mad with frustration, I tinkered around with a few plays at the local theatre – where I was cast as Polonius in *Hamlet* – and I directed a hard-hitting, Aids-related stage play called *Lonely Planet*.

I spoke to Lucy on the phone as often as I could, which cheered me but made me feel a total fraud – both to her and to Prue – and useless for not just packing up, going over to England and taking my chances. However, in early autumn, Chris Pye came to the rescue again when he rang and offered me a small part in a P. D. James miniseries called *Murder in Mind* being made for Anglia in England. To pacify Prue, I said I'd stay with William and Joybells O'Shei, who were now living in London. She certainly wasn't going to trust me again at Anna's after what had happened last time.

Naturally, as soon as I arrived, I went straight off to see Lucy.

The following day, I rang Brian Six-One (as we knew him from his call number), a driver whom I'd used last time I was in London and who had become a friend. I asked him to take me out to the *Murder in Mind* shoot near Ipswich. We left Battersea at three in order to arrive at five, in plenty of time to have a chat with Chris and the crew before filming started next day.

Exactly how this simple journey went wrong, I can't remember, but something happened that turned it into a pub crawl that would have challenged Jason and the Argonauts. I guess I'd asked Brian to stop for a quick one as we passed some attractive Essex roadhouse, and because I'd been away from England for nearly a year, I couldn't resist sticking my nose into a pub again, just for a few minutes. We had time to spare, after all.

Over the next few hours I couldn't say how many PoGs I quaffed or how hard I'd chased them, but we met an astonishing number of affable, warm and witty people, as each pub we passed looked more attractive than the last. I'm sure Brian wasn't drinking, but he was certainly enjoying himself. I allowed him and various other new chums I'd made to beat me at pool, darts, shut the box and that game where you try to sling a sort of rubber band over an upright nail.

We reached the hotel at two, just in time to avert a search party, apparently, and with a string of anxious messages from Lucy waiting for me. She understood when I explained – I knew it was a silly time to go pub-crawling but I'd really needed it and I'd forgotten just how enjoyable an English pub can be. She also understood that I certainly hadn't been tempted to philander anywhere, although next morning I found my pockets stuffed with bits torn-off fag packets and beer mats with women's names and phone numbers scrawled on them, and not in my writing.

I had a quick cameo part to play in Canada the following week, but, feeling I must follow my instincts and knowing that I felt so much more alive when I was around Lucy, I came straight back to England and had a wonderful ten days with her. An old friend, Michael Mondini, who for entrepreneurial reasons now lived in St Petersburg, had also come to stay at Cupar Road, bringing with him a beautiful little Russian girl of tender years – his new fiancée, apparently. Michael was a Sicilian- Irish-Texan of flamboyant mien who had worked with me in Santa Monica while I was developing a scriptwriting software program called Final Draft. To keep him – and me – amused, we decided to have a few people round for drinks, which gave me the chance to get back in touch with Robert Powell and his wife, Babs, and indulge in some familiar and comfortable yarn-spinning.

It was, I thought, great to be back in London, but almost as soon as I felt I'd settled in again, I had to go. John Ashley had asked me to do another round of episodes for a TV show called *Marker*, starting around Christmas 1994 and filming in Hawaii, one of my favourite locations. William O'Shei and a couple of business colleagues were going to the States and I told Prue I would come over with them and that they would stop off and ski in Ketchum for a few days.

I tentatively suggested to John Ashley that it would be good for me to have Lucy out in Hawaii with me, but he didn't know Lucy, and he did know that Prue intended to come out too. Foreseeing, quite wrongly, serious distractions, he wouldn't agree to it.

I got on with the job, but did all I could to keep contact with Lucy alive and active by phoning her and faxing to ask her to do various things for me as I tried to lay the foundations of some kind of new career in the UK, for when I finally got back there.

Marker kept me busy until the end of March, when I returned once more to Ketchum to try and sort out the best way to deal with the absurd situation I'd got myself into. Around then, Ken Carpenter got in touch with me from LA. He had been working for some time on a project with the working title *Wild*, a nice script based on a children's story about a young native American boy and his relationship with a herd of wild mustangs. He was anxious for me to go down to LA to give it a last bit of polish and sell it. As there was no firm deal in the offing,

I knew that Prue would try to stop me going and I didn't think it merited yet another battle. Instead, I told Ken to ring Lucy and talk to her about it. Of course, she didn't know anything about film scripts or pitching them to studios, but she had masses of common sense and was bound to have a few constructive and positive ideas. Besides, I just wanted to share things with her, even long distance.

She had an idea, all right, and it was brilliant.

In early June, nearly two years after I'd first met her and a few weeks since I'd put Ken in touch with her, she rang.

'David, I've spoken to Ken and we've decided that if you want to sit halfway up a mountain in Idaho for the rest of your life, that's fine, but I'm about to go to the airport and fly to California to stay with him. If you want to see me, that's where I'll be, and he wants to see you too – he's got as far as he can go on *Wild* without you.'

'I'll be there,' I agreed without hesitation. The idea of Lucy and Ken alone together in his current dwelling, the Outlaw Den, up a canyon in the hills behind Malibu in the middle of nowhere, was unthinkable.

I was already planning my flight and my excuses for going when Lucy went on. 'If you come to Ken's, when you've finished whatever you have to do with him, I expect you to come back to London with me, because I've had enough faffing about. There's a limit to how much a girl can take.'

There was an unmistakably determined edge to her voice, and I realised that this, finally, was it – no more shilly-shally; make or break; CRUNCH TIME.

'I'll see you at LAX,' I said warmly. 'Have a great flight.'

I took the little plane from Hailey to Boise, and hung around until the next flight to Los Angeles. My plane landed there about an hour after Lucy's, and Ken was there to meet us in a pickup that looked like it had been buried in a bog for the last hundred years. Ken is a good friend and I'm reluctant to carp about the conditions in which Lucy and I stayed with him, but the Outlaw Den was a sort of unfinished shack that wouldn't have looked out of place in a Rio shanty town. All around it, like Steptoe's yard, metal objects that had once been something rusted, as weeds grew through them. The insect life, in and out of the house, was extravagant to say the least. There were even fleas hopping in the grass outside. Cats with their kittens lived under our bed. A massive black tomcat called Trigger would pounce from a gap at the top of the walls, straight on to the bed when we were in it, so we ended up spending half the night waiting for it.

But although it may not have been up to the standards of the Hotel Bel-Air, it was wonderful to be with Lucy again. I had to admire her for having the sheer grit to get out here and put me on the line like this. I adored her high-spirited adaptability, which allowed her to laugh through thick and thin.

For the first few days we just relaxed. Ken, wearing his cowboy persona out here in the hills, liked to behave like an *hombre* in a Sergio Leone movie. One evening, to demonstrate his prowess with a handgun, he lined up a whole lot of beer cans on a wall and, sitting back in his chair with his wide-brim hat over his eyes, he fired off half a dozen rounds at them, and missed the lot.

Incurably competitive, I stood up to shoot, and hit a couple of them. I was teasing the cowboy for missing all his when Lucy interrupted.

'Excuse me, can I have a go?'

We both looked doubtfully at this diminutive English former debutante.

Ken raised an idle brow. 'Ever done it before?'

'No, never,' she said. 'At least, not with a handgun.'

'Let her,' I urged, pleased for her to join in.

Ken loaded the gun and Lucy took it. She crouched and leaned forward, clutching the gun with two hands. Squinting through one open eye, she fired.

A can spun away into the dusty brushwood.

'Wey-hey,' we laughed. 'Beginner's luck!'

Lucy gritted her teeth, crouched again and fired.

Another can bounced up towards the setting sun.

Followed by four more.

Ken gazed at her, shaking his head in frank admiration.

I was fairly flabbergasted myself. I knew Lucy possessed a lot of useful qualities, but I had no idea she was dead-eye shot, and I wasn't really sure how useful a quality this was. Above all, though, it demonstrated to me the wonderful quiet determination she possessed, and not in a way that required her to impose it on everyone around her. If I'd still had any doubts about leaving the States and going back to England with her, they were all gone once I'd seen the way she'd coped with the extraordinary and utterly unfamiliar circumstances she was in now.

Ken and I did a little more work on *Wild* and then I thought it was time Lucy and I started making plans. I'd brought with me from Idaho all the things I'd need in England. Lucy laughed when she saw I'd included my riding boots, but they sort of reflected how I saw life back in the old country.

After a couple of weeks at the Outlaw Den, we told Ken we had to go back to England, but first we went into LA, where we said goodbye to Nolan, who was living there and had been up to see us at Ken's a couple of times. We also visited Burton Merrill's office in Marina del Rey to discuss the gloomy business of divorce.

So it was that two years after I'd first met and fallen for Lucy in a London restaurant, I was flying back to London with her, with the intention of marrying her as soon as I was free to.

In London, living in her Battersea house, I truly sensed I'd come home at last, and Lucy did everything she could make me welcome. I made my way back to some of my old haunts, in particular the Chelsea Arts Club, where I soon immersed myself in the timeless ether of the place. It was a fantastic relief after all the tensions and drama of the last half-dozen years. Of course, I missed my children. In some ways I missed Prue; after all, I had spent over twenty years with her and they had by no means been all bad. It was a terrible shame that so much acrimony had crept into the later years, and that this kind of souring is almost impossible to reverse without incredible determination and tolerance from both parties.

But now I could reflect and, of course, I could see more of Deborah and my granddaughter, Esme.

Falling into step with the tempo of an English summer was tremendously reassuring for me. Lucy had probably never missed a Henley Royal Regatta since she was first out of nappies; I, on the other hand, had never been. Lucy said it was something I would either love or loathe and we decided that I should give it a try.

All togged out in pristine Panama, plain navy blazer and white flannels creased with the razor edges I'd so admired among habitués of the Hillcrest Country Club when I'd lunched there with Abe Lastfogel, I entered Lucy's world with some trepidation. As soon as I'd sat down and read up on the whole business and worked out precisely what was going on, I absolutely loved it – the absurd, shameless display of colour, rank and personal history in the blazers that are worn; the quintessential Englishness of elegant picnics in the car park; the military band and razzmatazz; the strawberries and Pimm's, while gangs of large, fit and usually young men flog up against the strongly flowing stream of the glittering river, with only their doggedness and the yells of the coxes to drive them on. I was hooked; I had my sketch-book out from the start. It was the beginning of a long relationship between Henley, me and my painting.

The following month, I went with Lucy for the second time on her annual visit to Scotland, where Debs, Mark and Esme joined us for a week of a wondrous, belting-hot month. For the first time in years I was relaxed enough to sit down with my paints and easel, and it was then that I really got to know Lucy's fifteen-year-old daughter, Louisa, whom I already thought of as a daughter too. I wanted to teach her how to paint; I suggested we take water, paints and sketchpads out onto the hillside and find some windless nook from which to practise. She seemed keen; I was flattered, until I discovered she wanted simply to lie on her back on the grass, in the gentle sunshine and smoke where her mother couldn't see her.

She'd already sussed that some of my water jars contained, like the amphorae at the marriage feast in Cana, wine not water. She considered our mutual discretion a fair swap. I nevertheless persuaded her to paint a little, to sustain the modest illusion, and we passed many happy hours in the process.

We became great friends from there on, and I was as involved on visits to her school at Westonbirt and holiday trips as if she'd been my own. And she repaid the warmth I felt many times over, to the extent that she is the only person I've ever allowed to call me Davey – a major concession, I have to say.

In September we returned to London and I knew I now had to get on with the business of living. I decided first to contact Duncan Heath of ICM to see if he was prepared to act as my agent. I went to see him in his wonderfully shambolic offices. He seemed to think I wanted to relaunch my acting career in Hollywood, which was precisely what I was trying to get away from. Time passed with a couple more meetings, the arrangement sort of petered out and with growing disappointment I had to accept that there was no work forthcoming from this source.

I also visited a few firms of lawyers to talk about my divorce, but all they could guarantee was a steady stream of massive bills, for which I had no money to pay, while Prue sat up in the mountains sheltering behind Idaho state law. From time to time I consulted other lawyers and was given the impression that it was going to be very tricky to sort it out from England, and I had no wish just then to go back to the US.

If I hadn't had Lucy, the future might have looked fairly bleak, but I did, and I knew we'd muddle through somehow. I was also enjoying the process of rediscovering people and places from my earlier frenetic life in London, which I was able to view now in a more circumspect, less haphazard way. Lucy and I could entertain friends privately at home, without having always to rely on meeting in bars and hotels.

When I saw that Peter Bowles was appearing in a play, *Gangster No. 1*, at the Almeida, Lucy and I went up to see it at the first opportunity (also almost the last, as it finished its run the next night). It was a strange feeling to be in a small London theatre again, so many years after my time at the Hampstead Theatre Club. Although Peter and I had been very close friends in the sixties and seventies, apart from the strange shoot in Budapest, I'd seen little of him since my migration to Australia and the States, and he had no idea I was coming to see the play. I don't suppose he even knew I was in England.

When we got to Islington, I asked in the pub nearest to the Almeida if the cast came in after the show and was told that they usually did, including Peter. We went in and enjoyed the play, and when it was over, rather than giving Peter a frightful turn by appearing backstage like Marley's ghost, we went to the pub and waited until he came in. When he did, once he'd recovered from the shock, we were both immensely pleased to see each other again and he immediately asked us for lunch the following Sunday with him and his wife, Susan, at their house in Barnes.

On the way there I took the opportunity to show Lucy the site of my early singing solos as a chorister at the Chapel Royal in Hampton Court. It felt very strange to be back there beneath the ancient arches, where Anne Boleyn's Gate still made my spine quiver. We went to matins, which had changed hardly a jot in form and content in the forty years since I had sung them. And at lunch it was wonderful to engage again in a little competitive English raconteuring and to swap with Peter stories as embroidered as the Bayeux Tapestry.

The day before, it was lovely to see Evie Bricusse again, along with Joan Collins, among a gathering of old friends to celebrate the wedding of my old friend from *Charge*, Mark Burns, to Pauline Stone. Pauline was one of Bailey's former models, a great fashion icon of the sixties and widow of Laurence Harvey.

Blow-Up

*

After the success and pleasure of seeing Peter Bowles in his play, in late October, Lucy, Louisa and I followed it up with a similar trip to the Cafe Royal, to see David Soul, who was appearing in concert there. It was wonderful to see and hear him still in great form and oozing charisma in front of an audience that looked like a block booking from Saga. We hadn't told him we were coming, but this time we went backstage to see him for an emotional reunion, and met his girlfriend, Alexa Hamilton. We went to see them soon after that in Little Venice, where they lived in a lovely narrowboat, which brought back a host of memories of my own boat at Chiswick Mall and the canals around Braunston which I'd got to know so well when I was making *Running Scared*, a quarter of a century before, with Robert Powell and Gayle.

We were able to return some of the hospitality we'd enjoyed. For my 54th birthday, Lucy excelled herself. She gave me a wonderful dinner party at Cupar Road and invited some of my closest friends – a real team of supporters who had welcomed me back and renewed a sense of identity which seemed to have atrophied in me over the last few years in Idaho. Robert and Babs Powell came, along with the O'Sheis and the Bowleses, and David Soul and Alexa (and their large dog).

At the end of November we were asked to Babs Powell's 50th birthday party, to be held in a far-flung corner of a foreign field in north-west British Highgate. Babs, best known for her career as a leading member of Pan's People, was bound to have a great party, so we renewed our passports and set of for N6. We weren't disappointed. I bumped into dozens of one-time friends and colleagues who expressed surprise and, for the most part, a modicum of pleasure that I was still in the world of the living. Which goes to show what I'd always thought – that far fewer people read the gossip columns than most people think.

Andrew Lloyd Webber told me he was still thinking about reviving *Jeeves*, although he didn't suggest that I might revive my performance as Bertie Wooster – an unlikely prospect, given the passage of time, but one can always hope.

Tessa Dahl was there too. Since our crazy, frantic affair in 1992 had ended at the gates of Hazelden Clinic in Minnesota, I'd seen her once, a month or so earlier, when I'd taken Nolan with me to lunch at a restaurant in Battersea for him to catch up with Sophie, and for me finally to pick up a few bits and pieces I'd left with Tessa three years before. Now she was as quick as ever, bright-eyed and looking great as she gazed around the gathering.

'Isn't this wonderful? I should have brought my autograph book,' she sighed.

What happened the following week must, I suppose, say something about my priorities. It was just before Christmas and someone – I don't remember who, but they must have been pretty desperate – had sent me a script to look at. It arrived in a rather battered Harrods bag which had obviously been passed around quite a few hands and made several journeys under the seats of buses and other forms of public transport. The script itself, had it been given the chance, might have had a more interesting tale to tell of its travels than the text it contained – but that is conjecture.

What is certain is that it wasn't a good script. My first instincts were that it was a thoroughly rotten script of the type which is churned out by the thousand by people who ought to know better, who then spend the next ten years shuffling it around acquaintances of the remotest connection in the hope that somehow it will transmogrify into something by Stoppard or Hare.

However, such is my modesty that I thought I should get a second opinion and I lumbered Peter Bowles with the offensive object.

Peter isn't in the habit of mincing words. He rang me and told me shortly what he thought of it, best expressed in the single word, 'Rubbish!'

I agreed to pick it up when we met for lunch and was taking it home in the dark afternoon, having thriftily come back on a bus (almost the first I'd ridden since I'd left the Arts Educational School). Strolling along the parkside thoroughfare of Prince of Wales Drive, with the offending typescript dangling from my hand in its grimy Harrods bag, I noticed a woman ahead of me, toting a great collection of Harvey Nichols bags. It occurred to me vaguely that she looked a bit of a target for one of these muggers I'd heard about but never encountered at first hand, and I grew a little wary when I heard footsteps catching up on the pavement behind us.

If this woman was going to be attacked, I thought, I'd have to think about what I could do to help, bearing in mind that even in the days of Toby's gym, although I'd been fit, I was never, ever going to be a boxer.

I thought I might best defer the mugger by slowing down and stopping.

My suspicions were confirmed when the footsteps behind me also slowed and stopped.

I carried on; the footsteps carried on.

I stopped; they stopped.

By now the woman with the big shopping was well ahead. I prided myself on averting her attack, but suddenly the footsteps were running up behind me. I just had time to switch the bag to my left hand and wrap the handles around my fist to hang on to it. The very next moment, a young man of no great stature and somewhat foetid breath lunged round in front of me and tried to grab the bag. As he leaned past me, I used my free hand to give him a whack in the chops – an action in which I have absolutely no experience – and, as my hand made contact with his teeth, I felt a searing pain across the back of it.

But, caught off balance, he went down. With less than lightning reactions, but fast enough, I stomped on his chest to wind him so he wouldn't be able to chase me and legged it as fast as I could the few dozen yards back to my front door in Cupar Road.

As I opened it and staggered in, to be met by Lucy's horrified gaze at the blood oozing from my hand, I realised I'd undergone all this danger, exertion and pain for the sake of a script of such deadly crappiness that I couldn't have given the thing away.

But there it is. I love words, I suppose, like dogs, and I know that, like the lowest mongrel, even the lousiest of scripts, perhaps representing someone's supreme personal achievement, should be treated with respect.

Lucy thought I was mad, and I vowed never again to carry a Harrods bag in the open street after dark.

Half an hour after this incident, in bizarre contrast, we set off to see a concert with our friends Mike and Penny Leander. It was, as it happened, one of the last to be given by the former record company office boy Paul Gadd, transformed as he had been into Gary Glitter and launched on the back of the songs Mike had written for him.

With my weakness for dressing up, I got into the mood, wearing a glitter wig and T-shirt, and it was a great concert, enjoyable perhaps for the utter familiarity of the songs – 'D'You Wanna Be In My Gang?' – rather than their subtlety. We went to see the performer afterwards, but he seemed rather gloomy, with other things on his mind. It was sad too that this was to be the last time we spent an evening out with Mike – the last of dozens over the years. The following spring, the cancer which he'd been battling for several months finally overcame him. I missed him a great deal.

While my movie career, both as actor or director, seemed to have ground to a halt, I was launched almost imperceptibly and without warning into another career, and one after which I'd always secretly hankered. We decided that we should use one of the paintings I'd done at Knockbrex as a Christmas card.

We had sent one to a friend of Lucy's, who asked us to a drinks party just before Christmas. To my great pleasure, she told me how much she liked the painting on the card and introduced me to her cousin, Geoffrey Hughes, who ran the Osborne Studio Gallery in Motcomb Street.

He asked who exhibited my work in London.

'Well,' I said modestly, 'nobody, at the moment.'

'Would you consider showing at our gallery?'

That was it. Now I was an artist – official – and I needn't feel a fraud any more every time I went into the Chelsea Arts Club. Of course, I'd been painting for years, ever since Sam Hinchcliffe at my grandmother's house in Woking had patiently shown me how, but I'd never put myself up as a saleable, showing artist, and I was thrilled at the prospect, especially at a time when all other doors seemed closed.

After Christmas, Geoffrey got in touch and asked if I would take part in a mixed exhibition the following July. I set about preparing for the show, because although he'd asked for only eight or ten pieces, I wanted to give him a decent selection so he'd have the best to offer.

📷 📷 📷 📷

Valentine's Day 1996.

In my time, I've been described as a philanderer and even, sometimes, as a Lothario – usually by idle journos who probably don't know what either is. In any case, both are inaccurate. A better definition would be 'enthusiastic romantic', which has often led me into unforeseen trouble . Thus, while I won't generally do 'Romance' to order, I'm prepared to fall in with tradition and treat 14 February as a day for special activity with the one you love. This year is my first chance to show Lucy.

What to do? Dinner, of course. Red-gingham tablecloths and guttering candles, of course, like our first dinner *à deux* at Mike Halifax's in the back end of Fulham. Chuck in a few obsequious waiters, trained to lurk silently while we cluck and coo.

But where this time? I think, Perhaps, they do these things better in France – a train journey to the coast, a short boat ride across La Manche.

To find out ferry times, I ring Victoria Station, where I am put on hold for an hour with music from *Come Dancing*. I give up. We will just take the train to Dover and see what happens – an adventure.

The brain-dead receptionist at Victoria, half strangled by his Sea Link tie, fails to inform us that BR now insist that no one smokes. By Faversham we can take no more, and seek out our own, private *carriage fumeur*, which we share with a bicycle and a wheelchair; there are no seats, but our personal attendant, the conductor, looks after us well and we consider the luggage compartment an excellent compromise. Here smoking is not an antisocial act, merely a negligible fire risk.

In Dover, it's rush, scramble and small fibs about the desperate need to reach Calais before we are allowed to nip, unbooked, on to the next P&O. 'Nip' is an exaggeration; it suggests speed and agility, which can't be done with Lucy's bag. She and I share many things but not the same conception of what it is to travel 'light'.

'Light' to me is a slim volume of the works of Polish poets, a newspaper and a Mars bar. To Lucy, it means taking the bath, 'just in case'. With my arms feeling like an orang-utan's, my heart under severe pressure, we stow the bag and urgently seek out the bar.

Refreshed, and braced by the February blow, we stand on deck while the boat shudders out of port and I deliver a short burst of Vera Lynn to the White Cliffs.

When I used to drive the drop-head Roller through Calais in the sixties, it was a French place. The odour of garlic hung in the air, men wore berets, young girls rode *mobilettes*, women covered their heads in squares of chintz, the radio played accordions and Johnny Hallyday; it was, I remember, distinctly foreign. Now it is just an extension of Kent, with cheap beer and tricolours. Everyone seems to be English; most of the signs are in English. This is disappointing.

French is romantic; English is not. This is not a logical statement; it is an emotional reaction. And if we wanted to dine among hordes of Brits, we'd go back to Fulham.

However, laughing and undaunted, we seek out a taxi and pray for a driver who is honest, *sympathique* and, above all, French. We tell our man what we want, and he takes us out into the country of the Pas de Calais, where he delivers us to a small auberge, thatched and timber-framed, like something from the set of Jack and the Beanstalk – even down to the AstroTurf that surrounds it, which isn't even AstroTurf, just green carpet. Our driver doesn't say that the place belongs to his cousin/wife's uncle/grandfather's mistress, although it probably does. But it's getting late and, ignoring a tariff that can only reflect the rambling fantasies of a maniac proprietor, I book a room and say we will dine.

The tablecloths are not red gingham; there are no *bougies* stuffed in bottles, until we plead. No waiter lurks with silent obsequiousness but, as planned, we cluck and coo, and I eliminate any thoughts of tariff from my consciousness – another triumph of romance over reality, thank God, and this time it doesn't get me into trouble.

[◎] [◎] [◎] [◎]

After this interlude, surprisingly magical as it turned out to be, I was severely distracted in the early spring when I had to go back to Los Angeles with Lucy to organise my green card. I didn't need an American work permit for myself, since I had no intention of working in the States again, but the form was that if I had one, all my dependants who hadn't been born in the US would get one automatically, which was why Prue had asked and I had promised to do it before we took divorce proceedings any further.

This meant going for a series of searching interviews and putting on a front that suggested Prue and I and the children were all one big happy family and not about to be sundered by divorce.

As we'd declined Ken's kind offer to put us up at the Outlaw Den, he'd booked us into an out-of-the-way hotel called the Malibu Inn, and we didn't tell anyone else we were there. Prue had rung me in England when we were fixing the arrangements and told me how she'd bought a new designer outfit that she knew I'd love, so she'd look pretty for me. This had made me worried that, despite everything she'd said and all that had happened, she still had in mind to inveigle me back up the mountain, as she had so often before. Lucy and I decided to get over there a few days early and lie low, so I would only see Prue for the interviews at the immigration office.

We couldn't really relax and we scarcely left our rooms. I went for the family interview and did everything I could to avoid conflict with Prue.

Blow-Up

There was no objection to the granting of the green cards, and Prue agreed to my taking all the children out to lunch, along with Nolan, who was still living in LA. Ken, who had been helping out as driver and general minder, joined us with his girlfriend, Devra, and his son, Jordan. I asked Lucy to come too, as she had never met the 'American' children. Although she was apprehensive, she agreed that it was good opportunity to meet them all.

We went to Gladstones 4 Fish in Malibu and I was thrilled at the chance to see them all again, but inevitably, like the rest of the trip, it was a fairly tense affair, and we were conscious all the time that something might happen to make things suddenly more difficult, just when they seemed to be getting manageable.

The day we were due to leave, we were in Burton Merrill's office and he was begging us not to take the flight we'd booked out of LA. Better, he insisted, to go from San Francisco or anywhere back to London, because he was sure that if Prue knew what flight we were taking back, now she had her green card, she would try to get divorce papers served on me.

I didn't think so, though. Burton had told me I mustn't get them served in the US and I'd told Prue that if I came over to deal with the green cards, she was not to let that happen – and she'd promised it wouldn't. Besides, we had paid for the air tickets, they were non-refundable and we simply couldn't afford to change them.

As we shuffled our bags up towards the check-in for our return flight, a small, nondescript female in an ill-fitting outfit sidled up to me and said, 'Mr Hemmings?'

'Yes,' I answered, reaching for my pen.

Before I'd realised she wasn't asking for an autograph, she had laid the divorce papers on me and walked away, leaving me clutching them, staring at them in bewildered horror.

The next thing we knew, Virgin had overbooked the flight. We had to accept an upgrade to upper class. Lucy suddenly perked up and looked more sanguine.

'At least,' she said, 'something's happened at last, and we can get on with our lives.'

Soon after we got back we went and spent a day with David Soul and Alexa in their floating home for the blessing of the narrowboats in Paddington Basin by our friend Father Gary Bradley, vicar of Little Venice. Needless to say, I had made great friends with Alexa's dog (trying to forget that Joybells O'Shei always called it the 'Poodle') and still rather missed the various animals I'd had in America. However, it had been decreed that the house in Battersea did not lend itself to dog-keeping and, frankly, after picking my way through an obstacle course of dog turds in the otherwise charming purlieus of Battersea Park, I can't see much of a case for keeping a dog in London at all.

Other memories of dogs were revived when Brian Cook, much-loved colleague on *Alfred*, *The 14* and half a dozen Antipodean disaster movies, pitched up in London, announcing that he, like me, had come home and was here to stay. He'd spent years in Australia and then the States, working all over the world on some of the biggest studio pictures around. It was wonderfully reassuring to hear the old sardonic, myth-defying laughter again and the iconoclastic irreverence (although he still wouldn't hear a word said against his own personal maestro, the Great Kubrick). And he, like me, hadn't lost his interest in dogs, although, rather than Rory, King Alfred's wolfhound of Oranmore, he still favoured very thin ones, wearing waistcoats with numbers on the side.

An evening with Brian at the Walthamstow greyhound track had always been a bit hairy, and it still was. But then, Lucy had taken me to the Royal Regatta; I thought it only right that I should take her to the dogs. It was fascinating to see it all again, to relive the adrenalin rush as the Six dog you've backed gets pipped. It was fun – any student of social anthropology would have mined the experience greedily – but it was not profitable. Despite a highly developed sense of cynical pragmatism, Brian still possessed that extraordinary, myopic optimism that clouds the judgement of most owners of racing animals – horses, dogs, ferrets and pigeons too, I dare say – and makes them believe theirs is the one just waiting for the moment. Of course, Brian owned more than greyhounds now. It seemed that all over the globe horses were munching their way through bale upon bale of specially grown organic alfalfa in mangers in training yards, all at his expense.

I wondered if it would have been helpful to have him by my side the following month when I attended my first (yes, it really was) Royal Ascot. If only I had recouped the cost of the black top hat I'd bought for the occasion and have never worn to anything else, I would have been happy – happier, I should say. It was wonderful to be there, a million miles from racing at Santa Anita in Los Angeles, where once I sat next to a man who put a cigar in his mouth at the beginning of the meeting and, by the end, was left with a short stub sticking from between his masticating jaws, and he still hadn't lit it. I may have few reprehensible habits, I thought, but at least I don't eat my Havanas.

Waiting for the 'off' at Walthamstow dogs had provided a few tense moments, but they came nowhere near waiting for the opening of the *Living London* exhibition at the Osborne Studio Gallery in July.

I was far more nervous about it than I'd been for the first nights of the stage plays I'd done as a youth, back in the early sixties. People had heard about the show and were asking each other what the hell was I up to now. To put more pressure on me, Geoffrey had decided to put my watercolour of Battersea Power Station on the front of the invitation.

In the end, I was incredibly relieved when my ten pictures were sold, and it was a bonus that my friends from Queenstown, NZ, Don Spary, who had flown the choppers so scarily, and Jan, his wife, were in London. Jan came to the show and bought my Battersea Power Station, which will give them a bit of a change from gazing endlessly at the Remarkable Mountains outside their window.

An unexpected blast from a very distant past came about as a result of the show. One of the gallery's invitees who came and saw my work told me that he was a friend of Peter Goodchild, with whom I'd lost contact, I suppose, even before my marriage to Jenny was over. Once he'd gone off to Liverpool University, I'd never seen him again. Now with a phone number in hand, I jumped at the chance of seeing him. Apart from Uncle Stanley, I had not a single other contact from my early days in Woking. We met for a drink at the Arts Club and took a long meander down memory lane. Both as competitive as ever, I challenged him to a game on the snooker table in the bar. Sadly, however, the club rules preclude non-members from playing at all, and we were never able to see it through. I think he might have beaten me, though, if we had played. He always did when we were kids.

Shortly after my launch as a working artist onto a wary public, Andrew Lloyd Webber asked us to the opening of a new production of *Jeeves*, in which, you may recall from about two hundred pages ago, I played Bertie Wooster in the original. This new production was only due for a short summer run, and had been cleverly improved, most strikingly by staging it in a far lighter set. It had always struck me that the first production had felt as if were playing in the dark, which can never really work with comedy. We enjoyed the show and I admired Andrew's commitment to a long-held enthusiasm.

Feeling that I had at last, in some degree, achieved my aim of being an artist, we decided that I should move all my paints and easels and empty Guinness bottles out of our dining room into the attic, which, after the introduction of light and a flight of stairs, would become my own personal garret. This symbolic recognition of my new career received a bit of a jolt when, more or less out of the blue, I was given a part in another television drama, the first since I'd done *A Mind to Murder* with Chris Pye a couple of years before.

Linda Agran, a great old mate who'd always made me laugh and had actually employed me in a few films (I think the last had been *The Squeeze*, when *Minder* had come into her life), was producing a pilot for a show called *The Vanishing Man*, an update of *The Invisible Man*, in which Neil Morrissey 'morphed' into water, and thus invisibility.

It was lot of fun to be on set with Linda again, and there was a good crowd of young actors to work with. Even younger, by the look of them, were the special-effects boys, computer wizards from a company called The Mill, whom Linda couldn't resist asking, 'Does your mother know you're out so late?'

They may have been young, but what the chaps from The Mill could do was truly astonishing and I was delighted when I came across them again on a much bigger production a couple of years later.

Mine was a character part and not too demanding. But where I would never have been nervous about lines when I was younger, now I was finding that sheer age made learning lines a lot more difficult than it used to be. However, one develops strategies to deal with these things. I tried to relax, and I hope I turned in a good job.

The year 1996 drew to a close with a flurry of lawyers' letters and interminable telephone calls to the States at difficult times of night, none of them producing the quiet, uncombative divorce settlement that I had very much hoped for. The expense of it, as always, was hideous. Are lawyers the only purveyors of goods or services who tell their punters how much they need? You know how many pounds of potatoes you want when you go to the greengrocer. But it's the lawyer who tells you how much law you need – probably just enough to keep their order book full, and growing.

Blow-Up

One thing I achieved was an agreement that Prue would ship over some of my personal possessions. And, in December, I received notification that a decree nisi had been granted.

My son Nolan was living back in England now and, never having had any formal drama training, had decided to book himself into the Webber Douglas School. I enjoyed having him around, and we were able to meet up regularly for a game of snooker or darts, like a couple of mates. I loved that, and loved it too when he turned up after Christmas with a new easel for me to put in my now-refurbished garret. Debs came round too with Esme and a bulge that announced the imminent arrival of a sibling.

Now the painful business of unravelling my life with Prue was over, I did feel an entirely different person from the confused and aimless individual I had been through the first half of the nineties. I was leading – at last, and, in truth, for the first time in my life – what I could call a proper life, and I was in no doubt whom I had to thank for that.

I wanted Lucy to look her absolute loveliest for dinner with my old and dear friend Jack Hemingway and his wife, Angela. Jack, son of Ernest and father of Muffet, Margaux and Mariel, was in his seventies now, and lived some of the time in Ketchum. He had a marvellous and generous mind and he had become one of my most solid friends there. He and I spent many pleasurable and stimulating hours talking ideas and philosophy as we took an occasional sip of whisky and gazed out at the mountains.

He came to England every year to shoot, usually spending a few days in London, and he had rung to see if we could meet. I was only slightly concerned that reports of our getting together in London would perhaps seep into the ether of Ketchum gossip, but if reports were going to seep, I wanted them to be as good as possible.

Lucy was quite nervous on our way to the Stafford, where the Hemingways were staying and we'd arranged to meet for drinks. She need not have been. Jack approved on sight, and Angela was confiding in her before we'd even set out for dinner, along with the Bowleses and the O'Sheis, at Carafini in Lower Sloane Street, run by a favourite restaurateur, Paulo, who had Como Lario round the corner for years. It was an evening so enjoyable I almost missed Ketchum by the end of it.

Perhaps a little less so when the decree absolute for my divorce arrived the following week.

Lucy, who has an eye for a bargain, spotted an advertisement for a last-minute-priced holiday, which we both needed, and I was looking for a writing project into which I could sink my teeth. This seemed like a good opportunity. We booked our tickets and before March came in, roaring like a lion, we were on the wing to Africa.

An island called Charlie didn't readily fire up the wanderlust. Charlie Paradise sounded even more suspect. Things were not quite what they seemed, however. Chalé, pronounced 'Charlie', was a Kenyan island, just off the coast, not far from the Tanzanian border.

'Charlie Paradise' had a kind of Damon Runyon ring to it, but this was about as far from the bars of Broadway as you'd get. And while 'Paradise' was a tag much abused by brochure writers, we were assured the island had good claim to the title.

Chalé was considered 'holy ground' by the local elders who protected it, a view keenly endorsed by Joe Bruenlander, who owned the island. In order to be given access to the small area of ground which accommodates the Chalé resort, he'd had to attend a tribal ceremony demonstrating just what a responsibility he would be taking on. He had witnessed, he told us, the incredible power of the place. Among the holy stones that abound on the island, he watched the levitation of three small boys, raised up for a few moments and set down gently in a clearing. I later searched this same clearing for a lurking Paul Daniels but drew a blank, so I had to assume this was a very special spot.

As we slipped alongside the pier on the island, porters raced around with luggage on their heads, leading me to expect Stewart Granger to step from behind a bush with a strip of leopard round his broad-brimmed hat; or, failing him, George Hamilton in his impeccably pressed safari suit, with a coral snake for his hatband.

The entrance to Chalé lay beneath two tusks that you might have thought had been taken from some massive woolly mammoth of the ice age, until you realised they're made of plaster. The brochure had told us that we would be housed in thatched tents, evoking an unhappy image of something between Baden-Powell and a Wiltshire cottage. Along a quiet path, past whitewashed stones and bougainvillea, we came to a group of tents which Dr Livingstone himself would have commended. Canvas, certainly, and thatched, but even the good doctor wouldn't have expected a full mosquito net covering a four-poster bed, with an en suite – albeit open-fronted – shower room.

To welcome us, our names had been spelt in petals in the bed. We never heard so much as a faint buzz of a mosquito or suffered from their busy mandibles; however, our tent was visited by some other living creature during the night which munched our soap, leaving great teeth marks – mongeese, or mongooses, depending on your etymological preference, we were told, suffering from lanoline addiction, perhaps, or serious halitosis.

Stewards padded round looking after us like pukka sahibs and we had candles lit on the table at our tent as we dined looking out across the beach to the quietly lapping Indian Ocean, which reminded me of Lamu, 200 miles up the coast, where two decades before I'd helped to resurrect the dhow race, and all the other islands I've known and loved. We went out to sea too and fished a little, and were offered Lucy's catch for dinner that night, and we sat around drinking Naivasha wine (best served very chilled) or French (best paid for under anaesthetic), forming new acquaintances in the way one does away from familiar ground.

Chalé gave us the most fantastic break, and would have been well worth it even if I had not managed to persuade a Sunday newspaper to buy my written account of our holiday, which went a little way towards recouping the cost of the tickets (though it barely made a dent in the bar bill, I'm afraid).

We arrived back in England on the Irish feast day of St Patrick, in time to celebrate the arrival of my second granddaughter, Molly, on 29 March.

After that I had to kick bollock and scramble to produce another collection of paintings. I'd been asked to exhibit again at the Osborne Studio Gallery, a one-man show opening on 21 May. Entitled *Eclectic Similarities*, to suggest the 'diversity of my styles', I was expected to show around sixty paintings, and this time I was determined to include at least one piece of sculpture, which I wanted to reflect my interest in racing.

The finished sculpture, of which two were cast in bronze, was a colossal trial. I called it *Seventh Heaven* and it depicted Frankie Dettori (lovely little fella) leaping off his horse at Ascot after the famous seven winning rides. I suppose a critic would call the piece naïve, if he was feeling generous, but I feel it expresses the exuberance of the moment, even though, if you saw the horse at a sale, you would want to give it a very wide berth.

The show went better than I could have hoped. A lot of old friends made the effort to come and I was delighted that so many chose to buy paintings. As is often the case at these things, there were pleasing spin-offs. Gayle, my lovely second wife, came with her friend Yuki, the dress designer. Although we had always been in regular touch, especially over Nolan, I hadn't seen her for a while, and she met Lucy for the first time. I was pleased to see how well they got on, and they always have since.

One of the more absurd exhibits was quite a success. A few weeks before, Christopher Middleton, doing a bizarre series for the *Sunday Telegraph*, had wanted to discuss my favourite shoes with me, and then photograph them. I didn't know so many shoe fetishists read the *Telegraph*, but naturally I agreed to do it. One of the pairs I offered him, since I had an exhibition to publicise, I described as my 'painting shoes', which were in fact a perfectly ordinary pair of canvas gym shoe-type things I'd bought in a fisherman's shop in Kirkcudbright and then splattered vigorously and randomly with paint.

The shoes I'd sent were returned to the gallery, and when Geoffrey Hughes saw the 'painting shoes', he couldn't resist hanging them on the wall as an exhibit labelled, 'Shoes', with a red dot beside them as a joke. But Babs Powell loved them and asked if she could buy them for Robert as a surprise birthday present. Naturally I agreed, and had them mounted on a canvas, which I also splattered. I think they might have been the most original items in the show, but in any event everything else sold too, which was just as well, since my agents had produced no hint of film or acting work since Linda Agran had wanted me for *Vanishing Man*.

Another agreeable outcome of the show was that as a result of seeing Gayle again, she put me in touch with Charlotte Taylor, now Lady St Johnston, who rang and asked us to drinks. It was wonderful to see her for the first time in so many years, and we picked up just where we'd left off. When I met her husband, Kerry, we found an immediate rapport and mutual interest in horse-racing, and we've all stayed in very regular contact since.

Just at the time we'd been preparing to open the exhibition, Prue had rung from Idaho to ask me if I could have our daughter in England for a while. She had in mind that Charlotte might come to school here for a year.

I was frankly concerned that Charlotte, still only fourteen, might be seriously disrupted by spending a whole year away from familiar surroundings and all her friends, and suggested she come for the summer holidays. Prue was sure Charlotte would cope with a year, so, soon after the exhibition ended, we picked her up from Gatwick, after which we had to go straight on to another exhibition and charity auction of paintings (including one of mine) which I had been asked to open at the Yvonne Arnaud Theatre in Guildford.

It was lovely to see Charlotte again, looking as pretty as ever and demonstrating plenty of character. But getting back to Battersea with a jet-lagged young teenage girl, we realised that it was going to be hard to find a school for her, as Prue had hoped. We'd already done some research and found that the local state schools wouldn't take a child for just a year – the first year of the two-year GCSE courses. We showed her Westonbirt, where Louisa was, and took her to see a production of *Godspell* at the Arts Educational School in its most recent Chiswick premises, where Dorothy Ind, now a governor, cast a kindly eye over her. On my current earnings, I didn't know how I was going to afford the fees, but I guessed I'd be able to sort something out. Anyway, it turned out that Charlotte wasn't at all keen to go to school in England, as we'd rather expected, so we opted for showing her as much of London and England was we could. Luckily, Brian Cook's son, Toby, was over from Australia, where he lived with his mother, and, about the same age as Charlotte, he took her round and showed her London from his perspective. She also spent a few days with Prue's mother in Kent and with her grandfather in France. In the end, she wanted to go back to where her friends were, and I didn't blame her, though I hoped it wouldn't be too long before she came over again. And I was disappointed that she hadn't been able to get more out of the trip.

Charlotte's visit left us feeling that if I wanted to accommodate wandering members of my numerous family, it was time to move somewhere bigger, and we felt we were also ready to move out of London. We started looking around, and told Lucy's mother, Anne, who lived a couple of hours west of London, which was where we wanted to be. Within days she had identified what she considered a place that answered all our criteria – a former mill in the middle of the historic town of Calne in Wiltshire.

We went down and looked at it. It was a fine old stone building with lots of space. Inside it was a complete wreck, and it needed all of our practical imagination and experience to decide what we could do to the place, but we left feeling that this was it – and in the end, it was, but it was another eighteen months before we had fully moved in.

Although I wanted, if possible, to make a living without recourse to my skills and experience in the movie industry, by now I felt I owed it to Lucy to make use of them, if there was a market. It occurred to me that doing voice-over work would be one way without taking up a lot of time or intruding too much on my painting. I got in touch with a number of agents, and one of them, Kate Plumpton from Conway Van Gelder, replied enthusiastically and invited me to come in and see her.

While I was there, Jeremy Conway came into the meeting to ask if I had representation for film work.

'Apparently not,' I answered.

(I was thinking of my last conversation with Duncan Heath. 'Hello, David, how are you? Great to hear from you. Who's representing you these days?')

'Well,' Jeremy said, 'we'd love to.'

This was encouraging, though nothing came of it immediately.

However, there were activities on the horizon. Among other things, I'd been asked by the Minister of Tourism, Mina Gabor (ever after known as ZaZa), to go with Lucy to the Philippines in early 1998 to take part in the opening of the Far Eastern equivalent of the Chelsea Flower Show, the Florikultura in Manila – one week for the ceremonies and generally being around and a week on Pearl Farm, a holiday island, to relax afterwards.

Neither of us had been there before, and I remembered that my great love from my Arts Educational years, Ann Thorn, lived somewhere in Manila. 'We'll find her,' I told Lucy, 'and she'll show us the real place.'

A great idea, on paper, until you realise you don't know where to start looking for an individual in a city of 15 million when you don't know her married name. We didn't find her but the organisers looked after us well, and we both came home with a barong – a heavily embroidered white top of woven pineapple fibre, the national costume, which we'd worn for the opening ceremony – and an invitation to hold an exhibition of paintings with a Philippine theme at the embassy in Kensington Palace Gardens the following May.

The rest of spring 1998 was taken up preparing for a mixed show in which I'd been asked to participate, *Cities of the World*, once again at the Osborne, being held in July.

At the same time, we started the long-drawn-out move into the Mill, where we camped among the rubble – and loved almost every minute of it. A shared period of nest-building can be either disruptive to a relationship or seriously bonding. We were lucky: the next few months flew by in a haze of harmonious planning until December, when I got a call from my old mates Brian Cook and Terry Needham, who were working with Ridley Scott on his new picture.

'Hello, H,' Brian said. 'We've got a job for you. You're going to be Cassius, Master of the Games, in *Gladiator*.'

'GLADIATOR' MALTA 1999.

20

New Beginnings,
1999–2003

We'd spent our first Christmas at the Mill, and I hadn't stopped buzzing since I'd heard from Brian Cook. I couldn't pretend to myself that I wasn't exceedingly chuffed at the thought of working again – and in a full-scale studio production.

When I'd left Idaho, almost four years before, I'd wanted to walk away from the world I'd been in for so long, and I'd enjoyed branching out in other directions, but when this job was placed in front of me, a good cameo role with a respectable wage attached, I suddenly remembered how it had felt all those years ago, only this time, without the confidence and ignorance of youth that cynically discount the good fortune that got you there. I was all aglow with anticipation and just a hint of trepidation at the thought that I might not be able to pull it off. But then, I'd always suffered from this kind of doubt.

I loved spending Christmas out of London, trickling along the local lanes to dinners and parties. At one such event in a Wiltshire village, where the Music of Time plays as strongly as anywhere, the hostess turned out to be the sister of Prunella Ransome, my co-star in *Alfred the Great*. Prunella was there too, and I hadn't seen her for over thirty years. Since then, I'd always felt a little guilty about my ungracious handling of her reluctance to engage in my method acting over the matter of clinches and kissing. I recognised her immediately and she looked terrific. I was delighted to be able to tell her at last how sorry I was that I'd been was so boorish back then on *Alfred*.

Early in the new year, Jeremy Conway rang to confirm all the details and dates for my part in *Gladiator*, Cassius, who could be described as the 'Don King' of the Colosseum. I wasn't needed for the earlier battle scenes in Germania, which were being filmed in woodland near Farnham in Surrey, but I would be needed on the Colosseum set in Malta during April and May.

I enjoyed the build-up to it all, the meeting of old friends in the cast and crew, and the inevitable dramas that arose. Not surprisingly, one of the earliest of these involved Oliver Reed, who had come over from his home in Ireland for a fitting and had got so drunk and abusive at Heathrow on the way home that he wasn't allowed on the plane. People were beginning to wonder if Ridley Scott might not have been a little rash in employing three of the most notoriously overindulging actors in Britain, Oliver Reed, Richard Harris and D. Hemmings. (In fairness to Harris, he had put his boozing days behind him, though he still enjoyed a good shout.)

I had a lot of the usual preparation – visits to Angels for fittings of wigs (bright orange, for heaven's sake, evoking the affectionate nickname 'Dame Edna' from Brian Cook) and a set of togas and sexy gilt-thonged calf sandals. I also visited Ridley Scott at the set in Farnham, which gave me my only chance to see Richard Harris. Richard was filming here as Marcus Aurelius, who dies in the film, and would not therefore be required in Malta.

He was sitting in a tent near the action, intently watching the monitors and, as a friend of long standing and shared experience, I allowed myself to sidle up beside him. He sat back with a quick double take and gave me a warm, Guinness grin and a corn-husk laugh. The film industry and the theatre weave eternal brotherhood into an uneasy tapestry of reminiscence and confrontational warmth. While we look back, we love one another; should we look forward, we are duellists. But Richard was too old, too rich and too splendid to succumb to any petty rivalries. He was a friend.

'You know, Hemmings,' he said, not looking at me, 'they think both of us are dead! They do!' He turned to me, as if we'd not been apart for more than a moment; the flip of a postcard. 'You know . . .' He scruffled his beard. 'He told me – Peter O'Toole told me – last week, it was. Well . . . I t-t-think it was.' He reflected a moment. 'Isn't that great, to be alive while everyone else thinks you've clogged it? And you still here, like me. You are a little bastard, you are!'

He twinkled as only Richard could – a sly grin becomes a full smile that changes the face you thought you knew into the one that lies beneath. Then, like an ad for toothpaste, his eyes 'ping' and he's in naughty mode – a giggling youth shrugged into the mantle of a man. 'You shouldn't be alive . . . I shouldn't be anywhere near alive, and there's O'Toole, the phoney Irishman. I thought *he* was dead!' There was a reflective pause and a slight Harris stammer. 'W-well, I had heard that he'd given up drinking. That amounts to the same thing.' He stood up and hugged me – a rib-crunching experience, in much the same way he was said to have hugged Jack Warner when 'the little leprechaun' had given him the part of Arthur in *Camelot*.

After Farnham, the production moved to Morocco for the scenes in Ollie's gladiatorial academy, and in early April, Lucy and I flew to Malta.

We are in Rome!

No, we are in Malta. The casual traveller, however, could be forgiven confusion, for the vast Colosseum of Rome, with sweeping arches and tumbling terraces, hunches around an ancient Maltese fort like a giant's embrace. Built just across the water from the capital, Valetta, but created only for our film, Rome has come to Malta – all made of scaffolding, plaster and plywood, of course, but to the visual senses the original. Any visitor could not but declare this a vision of the past, a step back in history.

Gladiator is a tale of bravery and deception, intrigue and revenge – a traditional epic movie, the like of which has not been seen for decades. It is a film in the tradition of *El Cid*, *Cleopatra*, *Spartacus* or *Ben Hur*. Cecil B. De Mille, eat your heart out!

Ridley Scott and art director Arthur Max have transformed the shell-pocked old biscuit stones that were once part of the Maltese military defences into the majestic amphitheatre of ancient Rome. We gasp. We really do, with mouths agape. It is a testament to what movie ingenuity can achieve. It is a stunning re-creation. Domitian, who completed the original, will be smiling benignly from his tomb. Only the sharp crackle of walkie-talkies would disturb his peace and contentment with the result.

The Colosseum's three tiers will house more than two thousand spectators and, with the addition of computer graphics, it will extend to six lofted galleries, crammed with roaring crowds. Chariots will thunder around the sanded floor as tigers leap from the hidden passages below to threaten all but the fiercest gladiator in arena combat.

Outside, the market merchants will spill like loose change from every stall. Close to the walls are wide café tables under seedy arches, covered by striped cotton awnings, plum and orange, brown and pink, colours faded by the sun. Here the men are loud, combative and placing heavy bets on the games inside. The extras, the crew, the stray dogs even, wandering around to pick up scraps from the catering trucks, fall asleep in the shadow of the statue of Jupiter (or some other Roman deity), and they all contribute to an atmosphere that even feels like Rome.

I feel very fortunate to be part of it all, finding myself in the daunting shadow of this immense construction, on my first day, muttering, under my breath, a mild expletive of wonder. As actors, for a few months, Russell Crowe, Joaquin Phoenix, Derek Jacobi, Connie Nielsen, Ollie Reed, along with the rest of the cast and crew, will share themselves with Malta, an island renamed by us 'Hard Rock Café of the Mediterranean', it has survived so many invasion attempts. Most of us are crammed into the Meridian Phoenicia, once the most lavish and elegant of all hotels on the island, now, sadly, a rusty remnant of its past. It is helped along, though, by an enthusiastic staff who seem to work endless shifts. You might have a chambermaid serve you breakfast, pass you towels at the pool, serve you a beer at the bar and then drive you to the airport – all in different liveried outfits.

The Phoenicia's south-facing rooms also enjoy the benefits of the bus station next to the town gates. There are no timetables, it seems, and their function is met by a little man calling out when and where the buses are going through wildly over-amplified speakers, just below our balconies, starting at about five-thirty. Fortunately for most of us, it's an early-morning wake-up/make-up call. Activity starts on the set earlier, at about four, with extras to be costumed, prosthetic limbs to be scattered, tigers to be wrestled out of puppy sleep – all early-morning mayhem that making epic films demands.

On a morning off, with time to look about you, it's depressing to note that the gardens of the hotel grow soft and dusty from lack of attention and, strolling down to the pool, you observe that mini-golf has taken over what were once immaculately manicured lawns. Yet to all this there is a kindly rakish charm, a sort of 'shabby-chic' feel. It makes you want it to be the Singapore 'Raffles' of Malta. But it isn't.

What the Phoenicia has become is a prime location for weddings – very loud weddings, in the Maltese tradition. So much that, denied access to the lounge and the bar on a Sunday afternoon, Oliver Reed, never one of the quietest voices himself, peers into a tremendously loud and ebullient nuptial party that is taking place and bellows, 'Shut up! Or I'll come in and join you!'

📷 📷 📷 📷

I had known Oliver for forty years, but hadn't seen him in a decade or so. We had trampled many paths together, films and friends. We had even learned to love Michael Winner together! When Oliver walked into the Phoenicia bar, ordering orange juice, he looked forever the gentleman that he sometimes could be. With grey flowing hair, a silver beard and a white linen jacket, he looked the quintessential expatriate, at home in Malta, swirling an arm at the assembled company, as if he were Her Majesty's representative, bestowing pleasure at the drop of his white Fedora.

He grinned at me, laughed in recognition, and we lapsed into tales of old, of lovers we'd shared and, in particular, *The Prince and the Pauper*, when he'd beaten me to a pulp in a horse-drawn carriage on the pretext of making it look 'real'. And where Raquel Welch, smitten by Ollie's mischievous eyes and aggressive wit, had to be rescued from despair on the edge of the Danube.

The Phoenicia Hotel, then, had become home, and all of us accepted its shortcomings with good grace. Derek Jacobi sat in the lounge with his hands clasped around his knees and a small glass of wine in front of him, hardly touched. He had to spend many days staring into the middle distance, a victim of the 'hurry up and wait' syndrome. He had been one of the first arrivals in Malta, and a pioneer, striking out at once to take in the 'Maltese Experience', an audio-visual presentation at the Mediterranean Congress Centre.

Although Derek didn't know Malta at all, as he watched the history of this brave little island unfold, an uncomfortable feeling of *déja vu* came over him. He felt sure he had been here before – perhaps in some other incarnation? It wasn't until he'd left the building and settled on a bench, guidebook in hand, that he realised that it was the voice of the narrator that had been familiar. It should have been. It was his own.

Sir Derek, by the way, is one of those rare characters to whom one can genuinely apply the term 'gentleman'. Patient, thoughtful, a listener, a thinker. Where have they all gone? He sat for many days, waiting in the hot sun of the Colosseum in toga and blistering sandals, longing to get on with it. To act. To do the job. But he waited with just the same dignified patience I had seen in Sir John Gielgud on the Anatolian plain in Turkey while making *The Charge of the Light Brigade*.

While Derek never really took to Malta as a holiday resort, Joaquin Phoenix slipped it on like a glove. Joaquin ('Whakeen', by the way, and as a baby he was named 'Leaf') was manic, dedicated, funny and neurotic, and one of the best friends or brothers you could ever find. He, along with Tommy Flanagan, a fine actor with a totally unintelligible Glaswegian accent to all but those who love him, called me 'Dad', a compliment that I enjoyed and that put my waistline into perspective.

Those who had said that the combination of Harris, Reed and Hemmings was fraught with imponderables hadn't reckoned with Joaquin and Tommy.

Tommy had a face that closely resembled the cutting edge of a chain saw, having stood up for his brother a few years before in an uncompromising Glasgow pub brawl. His humour always made it clear that he would rather laugh than fight, but his face could empty a bar in seconds. Joaquin was the more circumspect of the two, a backgammon player of considerable enthusiasm and skill; also an arm-wrestler of 'not much repute' – or so said O. Reed after one engagement. Joaquin and Tommy decided that they were going to take a trip to Glasgow over a long weekend; Joaquin had never been to Scotland and I thought I'd never see them again. We felt it unlikely that a vegan and haggis would find a meeting point in the lively society north of the border. But they did return and commandeered Peppino's, an Italian restaurant in Spinola Bay, for a surprise birthday party for John Shrapnel, who was playing one of the noble senators with Derek Jacobi.

Shortly after, two friends of Derek's, actors Richard Clifford and the utterly outrageous Frances Barber, arrived. There comes a time when film-making demands fresh blood, and Richard and Frances were the transfusion we needed. Frances can't speak except in a gabble of outrageous political incorrectness, balanced with a humorous tilt slightly to the left of Ken Livingstone. Richard's luggage had been sent to Frankfurt, always a reliable topic for entertaining small talk.

At weekends, while the tigers, the elephants and the horses slumbered and the clean-up crew wrestled the Colosseum dust bowl into some measure of cleanliness in preparation for the Monday morning onslaught, the actors rested.

On a Sunday morning, Ridley liked Marsaxlokk harbour, where Napoleon took the surrender of the Knights from this small community in 1798. Now it is a fishing village and here is the only real market on the island, with fresh fish, Maltese lace, some tripper trash – a lively mixture that took me back to days of trading in Petticoat Lane, and a hint of guilt at the shameless way in which we'd sold rubbish to gullible punters. From then to swanning around the Colosseum in a top-of-the-range toga – it sometimes seemed unbelievable.

The restaurants alongside the harbour offer a fresh catch, though service is never speedy, for Sundays are also for church bells and small children dressed in white-embroidered finery, muttering along behind best-black-frocked mothers and sober-suited fathers. By midday the market is closing, and the pavement cafés are bustling with church-comers and visitors.

Ridley settled in at Rizzu, on the corner of the harbour by the tie salesman, while Oliver's Sunday choice was a sailors' pub in Valetta. He was being a good boy, though, for the moment, giving the performance of his life without the benefit of booze – a tipple or two, maybe, but good, responsible and at the top of his form.

Russell Crowe had a villa overshadowing a Mexican restaurant. He was generous to a fault and invited all for supper. He worked hard, always demanding, always questioning. He knew that the role and the movie were on his shoulders, and like the gladiator himself, he bore responsibility for the outcome. He and Ridley Scott defined and refined, a gesture here, a nuance there. Russell was a competitor at heart, fighting for his right to be right. Ridley was a visionary who saw an image, grasped it like a painting, a canvas spread and pinned, and his was the final view.

One Sunday, Russell organised a football match in which he played, while the producers watched, paralysed with fear because they had not insured him for sporting injuries. This was followed by a cricket match which he'd arranged against a local team.

I had, with quiet pragmatism, excused myself from active partici-pation. I was equipped with a perfectly good Panama, from beneath whose broad brim I was prepared to spectate with torpid curiosity. I was, in any case, already quite knackered from watching the footie. But Ollie, who was supposed to be playing, could not be found, and I was press-ganged into taking his place, although I had no suitable shoes, no cricket trousers and, Lord help me, no box.

I was appalled to learn that we were going out to meet the opposing team at McDonald's next to the airport – by far the ugliest, most culturally unrepresentative and least romantic spot on the island – which was a pity. From there they led us to the cricket ground.

The sight of the other side – fit, young and terracotta – didn't augur well for our chances. This impression was confirmed when Russell was quickly bowled out by a small boy and was rather upset – or so it seemed, unless, perhaps, he'd seen a wasp on the ground and was trying to hit it by throwing his bat and pads at it.

However, as we were still short of players, he was going to bat again at No. 10, while I went in at No. 9, and quickly lost my first partner, to have him replaced by Russell. Although I was suffering from seriously wobbly knees on account of my lack of protector (though, God knows, I don't really need any more children) and the rate these Maltese were hurling the ball at us, I managed by some incredible fluke to hit the ball straight past the facing wicket, where it gamely trickled on towards long stop. To my horror, Russell was galloping towards me in an unstoppable way, yelling, 'Yes!'

I simply didn't have time to explain to him that I was pretty sure it was my call – which would have been 'No!' – and set off obediently towards the other end, seeing the wicketkeeper knock the bails off the stumps as I reached the halfway point, hobbling badly in leather-soled shoes.

The umpire's finger went up and I walked. I didn't throw my bat down, though, I must confess, I was rather relieved Russell had run me out.

I was less pleased to find Ollie back at the bar of the Phoenicia, all dressed up in his whites, with a bag full of pads, jockstrap, box and bat, and well beyond the danger level on his inebriation scale, demanding that someone take him to the game. When it was clear that no one was going to, I went off to find his lovely wife, Josephine – one of the few people who could handle him – and left Lucy with Ollie, who was beginning to crash about and breathe fire.

The barman was studiously ignoring his requests for more drink.

'Come here, you monkey!' yelled Ollie, well practised in the art of catching the attention of reluctant barmen.

I came back with Oliver's supremely patient wife to find that he now wanted to fight the barman, and was still droning on about playing cricket. We told him it wasn't happening, but he wouldn't leave the bar and soon wanted to fight with anyone, upsetting all the old greys and the other people on the film who were beginning to fill the place.

The hotel management were moving in with ugly looks on their faces. I told them, knowing Ollie of old, that if they tried to get him out now there'd be real trouble.

I thought of myself being dangled by the ankles by Oliver outside the sixth-floor window of the Torquay Grand, forty years before, the grinning, simian face and warm beer that trickled onto my naked buttocks. But despite these memories and all the bullying I'd seen and received from him over the years, he was part of my tribe and I owed him loyalty.

'Let me give him a drink,' I said. 'Then I'll calm him down and get him upstairs without a scene.' And, astonishingly, I did, without further trouble.

However, the management thenceforth banned him from all public parts of the hotel, except the pool.

The week after the cricket, a card was slipped under our door by Josephine, asking us if we could have dinner with Ollie and her the following Saturday, just the four of us. When we met them in the hotel lobby, Ollie was utterly sober, which was a great relief for Lucy, and we took a taxi to Marsaskala, known as the best place on the island for fish. Gabriel's was a restaurant at the bay's edge which had been recommended and the sight of Robin Demetriou, the superb catering boss on the *Gladiator* set, already there with his wife, was more than reassuring. We all accepted the 'catch of the day', as we'd been advised. And, in any case, it was clear that Gabriel didn't ask his punters what they wanted; he just told them.

In our younger days Oliver and I would have considered 'catch of the day' an altogether different proposition, but now dinner was a quieter, even *sotto voce* affair – a single bottle of wine drunk between the four of us. Ollie was reflective, Josephine happiest to talk about life in Ireland and their horses. There was no reference to or hint of the scene that had taken place a week before, and we headed back early to the hotel, where, because Ollie was sober, we were allowed in a corner of the bar. We drank coffee there, chatting quietly for a while, until Ollie announced that he was tired, and he and Josephine went to bed. He looked tired, too, I thought, and worn out in a way I'd never seen him.

In the morning, Lucy and I set off early to catch the ferry to Gozo, to check out hotels for the short break we planned to take there as soon as filming was over. We arrived back at the Phoenicia in the early evening and, as we walked in, we saw Ridley Scott with his producer and Rob Harris, the publicity man, in a huddle.

I didn't like the look of that; there was something ominous about it.

Lucy went on up and I walked over to the bar, to buy a drink and to discover what had happened. Rob Harris caught my eye and came over to tell me himself.

Ollie and Josephine had been in a bar together at lunchtime, where Ollie had said he felt tired and had lain down for a quick zizz. Seeing that he hadn't moved for a while, Josephine went to wake him, finding to her great distress that she could not. It transpired that he had suffered a major heart attack, and had died.

It was an appalling shock to me – that this massive character, this man who had always dominated every room he had been in, every event he had attended and who had entered and re-entered my own life so often over the last four decades, should suddenly have ceased to be. As I rushed to the lifts to go up and find Lucy, tears filled my eyes and I could barely tell her what had happened. When she had calmed me down, we went off to see if we could do anything for Josephine.

Poor Ollie, his was such an abrupt end, though perhaps that was inevitable, even preferable, in one who had lived his life so much at full throttle.

Ollie's untimely death cost only a single scene in *Gladiator*, which was in any case very close to completion.

Lucy and I returned to England in the middle of May, exhausted but exhilarated with what had been achieved, and a strong sense that the film was going to succeed, perhaps even have the impact of illustrious forerunners like *Ben Hur* or *Spartacus*.

But I had other work to do. I'd been asked to exhibit at Henley Regatta, in the Stewards' Enclosure, with the brief: not too many, not too big and not too expensive, and connected with either rowing or the river. In the end I gave them eight, based on the social activity in the bars and the picnics and the wonderful, kaleidoscope of colour that abounds.

I was also preparing for another one-man show, *Pimm's and Picnics*, which was scheduled for September at Geoffrey Hughes's gallery.

Now that Cupar Road had been sold, we were camping among the muddle of the Mill, while I was perched in an empty spare room, with Lucy standing over me to make sure I didn't tear up too many pictures in my frustration or work away interminably revising already finished pieces. And, as always, deadline junkie that I am, I didn't feel the pressure until the week before they were all meant to be finished; as usual, most were framed still wet.

A lot of old friends, and new ones from *Gladiator*, were loyal enough to come along to the *Pimm's and Picnics* opening on 27 September. Joaquin Phoenix, who was in London, making *Quills* with Kate Winslet and Michael Caine, arrived with Tommy Flanagan. Derek Jacobi came too, with David Schofield and John Shrapnel, whose wife, Frankie, was Deborah Kerr's daughter, taking me back to the Laplander incident at the Connaught and *The Eye of the Devil*. It was a great night, and resulted in a severe attack of measles – a rash of red spots.

In the last week of the exhibition, my oldest son, George, announced that he was coming over to London to live, which was great news, although a little alarming as he hadn't finished his university course in the States. We met him at the airport and took him down to Chichester, where Nolan was appearing at the Festival Theatre in *An Unexpected Guest*. Once the two of them had got together again, George moved into Nolan's flat in London, which meant he couldn't get down to see us very often, which was a pity.

The Mill, in any case, was still a complete shambles, which was added to when Lucy's mother, Anne, sadly sold Knockbrex, her house in Scotland. We went up to help her close down the place in a state of great gloom. I had become very fond of it; though it was a pleasing consolation when some of the furniture arrived in Calne two days before Christmas.

After the new millennium had opened, work proper started on the Mill. I became site foreman, a job for which I am pathologically unsuited, and which undoubtedly held up the builders, while Lucy dashed around like a bee in a meadow, collecting up obscure Farrow and Ball paints and discontinued lines of tiles, haggling with purveyors of curtain material and searching in dusty warehouses for hidden bargains. The aim was that, by the end of the year, we would be properly moved in and civilised.

*

In April, there was a screening of *Gladiator* at the Empire Leicester Square for some of the cast and crew – mostly crew – to which I took Lucy, Nolan, George and Louisa. I was astounded to see the final results of the computer graphics which had been achieved by the *wunderkinds* from The Mill, the company who had so cleverly made Neil Morrissey disappear for Linda Agran, and there was a lot of noisy cheering when their names came up on the credits.

I'd been nervous about how my part would turn out. But although it felt strange, it was undoubtedly elating to be part of a big picture again. I was truly amazed at the finished result: Ridley's direction and cut had made wonderful use of the material. As I'd privately hoped, it triggered responses from several other sources, people for the most part who, as Richard Harris had suggested, had no idea I was still alive until they'd seen me, like a twenty-year-old ghost, appearing in this movie with a pair of flaring eyebrows they'd never seen before.

Perhaps the eyebrows were a bit of a statement, an acknowledgement that I was no longer (if I had ever been) an actor who relied on pretty-boy looks to get his parts, as it were. Besides, Lucy defended them fiercely and when I caught make-up girls sneaking up on me when I was dozing, with scissors poised to cut my horns, I told them they'd have Lucy to answer to if they did it.

Shortly after *Gladiator* opened officially, George decided to go back to Idaho. I'd been looking forward to seeing more of him, but he'd come to the conclusion that it was wiser to return to college. In the meantime, at the Mill we had a wonderful pair of decorators who came to plough their way through the long job of finishing off the inside of the house. They stayed with us and, besides being top-of-the-range painters, they were also a supremely polished drag act, so kept us permanently entertained. It was absurdly funny at times, and with the right sound-track would have made a great camp version of *CarWash*.

I was painting fairly vigorously myself, once again for the exhibition at Henley Royal Regatta, and about a week before this was due to open, I was invited to a meeting with some people from Miramax to discuss a part in Martin Scorsese's pet project, the 19th-century histopic, *Gangs of New York*.

In July, while I was at the regatta, the super-efficient Liz Nelson from Conway Van Gelder rang me. With her customary wit and chutzpah, she told me my part in *Gangs of New York* had been confirmed. I was thrilled that I would be working with Martin Scorcese, a director I admired hugely, and this added an undeniable fizz to the picnic lunch I was having at the time. This was, I suppose, the start of the *Gladiator* spin-off which a number of people had told me – and I hadn't dared – to expect, since later that month Elizabeth Robinson and Fred Schepisi also got in touch to discuss a film he was making of Graham Swift's 1996 Booker Prize-winner, *Last Orders.*

The part of Lenny was a bigger and more challenging role than Cassius had been, or the 'Rich Man' from New York in *Gangs* would be. With Michael Caine playing the lead (albeit some of the time in a small urn), the lines were fairly evenly distributed between Bob Hoskins, Tom Courtenay, Ray Winstone, Helen Mirren and me. What promised to give the film a special poignancy for me was the fact that Nolan was going to appear as young Lenny in a series of wartime flashbacks, capitalising on the strong resemblance there is between us.

By now, I was beginning to feel a little as I had in the late sixties, when producers were phoning up with parts every few days. Obviously they weren't coming quite so thick and fast, but after such a long fallow period, it felt like it. I can only assume that now I'd been, as it were, 'rediscovered' in a strange kind of way, I offered what was effectively a new face, but with a bit of a name and a lot of experience. In any event, hot on the heels of the confirmation that I'd got Lenny (and Nolan had got Young Lenny) in August, I had a meeting with Lucinda Syson, who was casting director on *Spy Game*, which was going to be directed by Tony Scott (Ridley's brother). This yielded another small character part, and my diary was beginning to look pleasingly well filled.

By mid-August, Lucy declared the Mill finished to her complete satisfaction, and she had indeed, from a very rough skeleton, produced a wonderful and elegant functioning home. We hardly had time to sit down and enjoy it, though, before we had to fly to Rome for a fortnight of costume fittings and first scenes for my part in *Gangs*.

The Empire Palace Hotel, in which we were billeted, was OK but not very exciting and not in a part of Rome I knew, so I took Lucy off to show her all the little places I used to love around the Piazza Navona when I'd been making movies for all the budding young Federico Fellinis of the seventies.

The whole area, like me, had changed since then, but where I had become more baggy and wrinkled, it had been renovated and spruced, to a point where it had almost lost its charm – an inescapable consequence of rampant tourism. The little hotels and open cafés I'd loved were now full of loud, bulky Americans.

But close to the Empire was a wonderful restaurant fairly devoid of tourists and packed with natives, which became a bit of a haunt. The owner we called Nero, from a photo on the wall of him in total toga and wearing a laurel wreath. Besides his, the walls were covered with photographs of film stars (mostly female). He claimed that while Liz Taylor was making *Cleopatra* she'd come to his restaurant for dinner. It was at the height of her much-vaunted seesaw affair with the great Welsh Rarebit; the paparazzi had caught on that she was there and she had to make a speedy exit. In the scuffle to leave the restaurant, one of her shoes, like Cinderella's, had fallen off and was left behind.

Nero, fighting temptation (or so he said), decided next day to take it back to her, but she declared that he should keep it, and there it was on the wall, in a frame, Liz Taylor's running-away shoe – possibly not as original as my 'Painting Shoes', but a piece of historical trivia none the less.

We were, on the whole, an exuberant crowd at the hotel and did our best to wake the place up a bit, with a great deal of singing, dancing and encouragement to the otherwise more or less totally ignored pianist who tinkled away for most of the evening in an empty bar.

Filming on the vast and wonderful set at Cinecittà – the Five Points in 19th-century New York – was a great experience, like entering another world, it was so staggeringly real. As I nearly always have done, I enjoyed being on set and the comradeship of the other members of the cast. One slightly irksome incident occurred when Martin Scorsese, Daniel Day-Lewis, Cameron Diaz and I were sitting in a tent on the set during a lull in filming. A runner came in and picked up Leonardo DiCaprio's chair to carry it off to another corner of the set; it seemed the young superstar thought he was too grand to mix with the director and other members of the cast.

I was surprised at what I took to be an offensive display of bumptious self-regard. It was the first time I'd ever come across this sort of behaviour in a long time of film-making. The camaraderie of the set not only made life more enjoyable, it made the whole process a great deal more efficient. For me it had always been a golden rule that one treats every single other person on the set – cast and crew – with the same degree of respect. I remembered how I'd been at Leo's age, and the position I'd been in then, when I loathed the idea of pulling rank.

Foolishly, I referred to this minor event, more or less *en passant*, in an interview I gave soon afterwards. I should have known that it was exactly the sort of trivial non-story onto which showbiz journalists leap like scavenging wolves. Quotes were conjured out of thin air and attributed to me. I don't suppose they distressed Leo all that much, but I was embarrassed that this tiny event had got so blown out of proportion. However, the incident itself, small as it was, was undoubtedly an exception to the good feeling which prevailed throughout the picture.

Some of the fringe consultants on the film were especially intriguing. One of them was billed on the call sheet as 'magician', which obviously caught my eye, and turned out to be something of a euphemism.

Cameron Diaz's character had to pick my pocket and this chap was, we gathered, one of the best pickpockets in Rome, and frightfully smart and prosperous-looking in a way I can't imagine any London 'dip' could be. He was known for orchestrating very elaborate systems for robbing passengers on the underground undetected and with large teams to pass the booty on and away in seconds, and this expert had been engaged to teach Cameron how to do it properly.

As a result of a mismatch in the weather and availability of actors, which created continuity problems, after I'd done most of my scenes, I knew I would have to go back at various times in the future to complete several unfinished sequences.

In the meantime, by early October I was back in England to start rehearsals on *Last Orders*.

Nolan and I turned up for the first read-through and met up with the gang I was to spend the next few months with. Most of us knew each other, and some had worked together before. I hadn't met Ray Winstone, though I knew his work and propensity for playing uncompromising hard men of an East End persuasion. During a break in the proceedings I went out on to a balcony for a quick gasper with Nolan, where we remarked on the positive qualities of one of the girls there. Ray, joining us, took me to task.

''Ere, that's my daughter you're talking about,' he said with inescapable menace. 'You want to be careful what you say about her.'

I laughed at what was obviously a jest.

'No, I'm not joking. That is my daughter.'

I realised I'd committed a small faux-pas and hoped Ray hadn't taken it too seriously. Although, of course, when he was being one of his hard men, he was acting, in the flesh at first sight it was easy to think that was the way he really was, and I must own up to a little nervousness.

But once we'd started working together, I found he was a pussycat and we soon bonded. I think he came to the conclusion that I wasn't quite the stuffy, portly old actor I might have seemed. We discovered we had the same sense of humour and outlook on several things. There was a critical scene in the film where Ray was supposed to give me a clump and push me to the ground.

Ray was of the view that in an east or south London family, respect for the elder members is so strongly a part of the culture that a young man would not have raised a hand to his elder. From my early experiences in Toby's gym and around the East End, I entirely agreed, and between us we reworked the scene so that I attack him and he accidentally pushes me to the ground. We felt that this would produce a sadder and more poignant scene and give greater depth to my character; and that was how we played it. Ray and I grew closer and have remained good friends.

For me, the whole process of making *Last Orders* was a delight. It's based on a beautifully observed novel, and Schepisi was a serious, grown-up director. But, above all, I was working with people I knew, respected and liked very much. The final piece of filming – the interior of the car on the journey from London to Margate to scatter the ashes of our dead friend – was a green screen sequence made at Pinewood with Ray Winstone, Bob Hoskins, Tom Courtenay and me. This kind of filming can be fairly tiresome, especially among people who aren't particularly simpatico, but we sat there happily for several days of laughter and Bob's dry humour. I adored this camaraderie, and the opportunity to play a few pranks.

At the end of it, just before Christmas, we decided to have a farewell lunch at the restaurant in Pinewood. When Tom arrived there was a bottle of champagne with a card leaning against it with the words 'Happy Birthday, Tom' inscribed on it.

'B-but it's not my birthday . . .'

'Don't worry, don't worry,' I said. 'I had to tell them it was. You only get a bottle of champagne if it's somebody's birthday. And we chose you.'

Towards the end of lunch, Tom had a shock when he was tapped on the shoulder and spun round to find a lady, noticeably past the first flush of youth, standing behind him wearing a voluminous coat.

'I hear it's your birthday and you haven't been feeling very well. I've come to cheer you up.' With which she took off her coat to reveal a pair of large, somewhat pendulous naked breasts covered in glitter. Before Tom had a chance to react, she leaned over him and proceeded to rub them in his face.

'The make-up girl's not going to like this one little bit,' I heard Tom murmur faintly.

Although I'd known Tom for years – in fact he'd been at one of my epic parties at Limpsfield Court about forty years before – we neither of us could recollect having worked together, and it was a great opportunity to renew an old friendship. Tom also had a beautiful English pointer, called Gus, whom I took a lot of interest in, and felt rather jealous about. Although the house was finished, I hadn't yet been able to introduce a canine factor into our lives in Calne, as we were travelling around and staying away so much.

This roller-coaster was still going on. Between sessions of filming *Last Orders* we took a quick trip to Berlin for two days' filming there for Brian Cook, followed by a quick trip to Rome to try and redo the missing scene, but the weather still didn't come right, which meant a lot of sitting around in a state of thick whiskeriness and several more dinners at Nero's.

Early in the new year, I grew increasingly excited at the thought that my short scene in *Spy Game* was scripted to take place in Hong Kong, which might afford a slight diversion on the way home, via Australia and New Zealand, to show Lucy some of my old stamping ground.

Disappointingly, at the crack of dawn on a raw February Sunday, we were met by Tony Scott, in shorts, to film my scene in the Lloyd's Building – posing as Hong Kong – in a deserted City of London. What can one say? No jet lag, of course, but no refreshing views of the Remarkable Mountains from Queenstown, NZ, either. I did, however, have the pleasure of one more trip to Rome, now at last the weather was right and everyone was available, to make the final missing scenes on *Gangs*.

Another good role as the prison governor in *Mean Machine* a couple of months later was an interesting experience, allowing me the chance to pass on a few tips on filming to the redoubtable Mr Vincent Jones. I showed him the importance of underplaying, like delivering a ballad *au* Sinatra and letting the melody fall off the back of the beat. The picture was being produced by Matthew Vaughn, whom I'd seen with Guy

Ritchie a year or so before to discuss a part in *Lock, Stock and Two Smoking Barrels* that might have (but didn't) suddenly become vacant due to the incumbent's line-learning problems.

Curiously enough, while I was in the middle of making my few scenes in *MM*, I was called for jury service in Swindon, which, to my great disappointment (yes, I mean it), I couldn't attend on account of being under contract at the time. I wrote to them and told them to put me back near the top of the list, though I'm still waiting for the call to come again.

There was, though, one jolly I was able to attend, when Rupert Lendrum, ultra-smooth former cavalryman, turned public face of the mega champagne house Möet & Chandon, invited us for a grand weekend at the Château de Saran in Epernay.

We were a motley bunch that gathered at Biggin Hill on a Friday morning for the flight over, all friends of the London Möet people. Miriam Francome, ex-wife of the former champion jockey, with Charlie Brooks, former racehorse trainer, now journalist and pub landlord, whose ear I bent, inevitably, with my profound knowledge of nags and taverns; the affable Earl of Westmorland and his wife, Kye; and Roger Taylor, who used to hit the drums behind Freddie Mercury, among others.

I, naturally, in deference to my hosts, tried to put my habitual dislike of champagne on hold, and coped quite well, to the extent that after an amazing dinner I was still motoring and chivvied this eclectic bunch of punters into a session of seriously competitive charades, before spending the rest of the night swapping progressively worse jokes with Charlie. I regretted it a little next day as we were conducted around the *caves*, and the place where they make the stuff, to taste a little more of it – several hairs of several different dogs, you might say. I've even found I can handle a few glasses of the stuff now, although the Möet vintage rosé has probably spoiled me for any lesser varieties.

Not everybody remembers where they were the day John Lennon was killed; he was, after all, a writer of popular music, not a world statesman. I do remember; I was in Queenstown, NZ, with my old friend Jimmy Webb, also a writer of popular music, who'd come to stay and work for a while.

On the other hand, *EVERYBODY* remembers where they were on 11 September 2001.

I was in Canada, at the Toronto Film Festival to publicise *Last Orders*, which had been screened the day before. I was there with Ray Winstone, Fred Schepisi, who directed, Elizabeth Robinson, who produced, and, of course, Lucy. There was a lot of interest in the film and we had a heavy schedule.

On the morning of 11 September, I was being interviewed in an hotel when we were interrupted and the interview immediately terminated as reports came through of the appalling events that were taking place in New York.

While we were shocked and horrified by what had happened, we didn't have the direct personal connection with these events that affected the Americans who were attending the festival. We realised the disaster's effects were far more widespread than the local news reports suggested after Lucy spoke to her daughter, Louisa, who told her that Heathrow had also been shut down for the time being. And for the next couple of days we felt as if we were under siege. Our hotel bookings had run out and the swipe cards to our rooms were disabled, since no one knew who would pay the bill; insurers wouldn't pay up in the face of an act of terrorism.

We managed, though, to hang on to the rooms, and congregated in Ray Winstone's to discuss the situation while he ironed his shirts. Ray and I were due back in London in two days' time to start work on *Lenny Blue*, a two-part TV drama. I got the maps out and tried to plan a route home by road, via Greenland, but there wasn't much enthusiasm for this.

However, as the world slowly struggled from crisis to aftermath, two days after we should have left we were on a flight home – a little nervously, it has to be said. And straight away, Ray and I started on *Lenny Blue*, which was being filmed in London, like *Last Orders*, around Lambeth and Peckham.

Days of working on *Lenny Blue* were interspersed with various screenings at the ICA and BAFTA of *Last Orders*, which was, to my great gratification, very widely and well received. It also had a showing at the London Film Festival, for which Ken Livingstone gave a reception at No. 1 Whitehall, an unexpected event in a splendid location, to which I was able to invite a few of my family and friends.

Thanks to Lucy, the potentially depressing event of my 60th birthday was celebrated in some style with a party at the Mill. There were a few nice surprises thrown in, including a pianist who played songs in which there was much audience participation – a sort of upmarket karaoke, really. A special treat was the appearance of Roy Davenport, at whose family magic shop under the arches at Charing Cross I'd been buying tricks for years. He did some marvellous close-up magic and a full-blown display after dinner with Debs's partner, Mark Kemp, very relaxed by then, acting as his assistant. The party was a great way to mark a man's inexorable decline, and I'd barely recovered when we set off at sparrow's, two days later, to catch a plane to Los Angeles for the opening of *Spy Game* and more publicity for *Last Orders* with Tom Courtenay and Bob Hoskins.

I hadn't been in LA for five years. It still held uncomfortable associations for me and I was a little nervous as we flew in. Things got off to a sticky start when I was asked if I was there to work or for leisure, and I gave the stock answer – 'Good Lord, just for fun, of course!'

'Sorry, sir. Wrong answer. I'm afraid we'll have to take your green card off you.'

I was hauled off to immigration and divested of my US work permit. That didn't matter at all, as I still had no intention of working there again. And I was assured the loss of my green card would not affect Prue's or the boys' green cards.

We went to our hotel, changed and straight on to a screening of *Spy Game*, through the entire duration of which, I'm ashamed to say, I slumbered and snored relentlessly, according to Lucy, who did everything she could to wake me – all to no affect. I suppose I was still recovering from my birthday bash. Over the next couple of days I did more interviews, and on the second night, I was able to introduce Lucy at dinner to my long-time writer friend and golfing partner, Jon Povill, and his wife, Michelle. That was a treat, but after two days I was ready to go home.

On the way to LAX in a limo with Tom and Bob, Tom pulled from a brown paper parcel a squeaky duck he'd bought for his dog, Gus. It wasn't a sitting duck, but a flying one with its neck stretched out.

'David,' he said, looking worried, 'do you think I'll be able to get this duck through airport security? They might think it's a gun. Or do you think I should have got the squeaky octopus?'

Back in England, *Mean Machine* was given its première at the Odeon Kensington a week or two before Christmas. Lucy and I found ourselves in seats with Sting and his wife, Trudi Styler, on one side and, next to them, Guy Ritchie with a funny little woman who turned out, somewhat to my surprise, to be Madonna.

Afterwards there was a party somewhere in Knightsbridge to which all Vinnie Jones's diverse relations turned up, very proud of their boy, upgraded from nose-noshing footie star to polished ac-tor. I bumped into Matthew Vaughn, who had produced the picture, and his mother, Kathy Ceaton, who told me that she'd been at the Bricusses in Los Angeles in the late sixties when an earthquake rumbled beneath us and I'd urged everyone in my usual busy way to shelter under the table. I had absolutely no recollection of the event, but then, that's probably true of about three-quarters of my life.

Last Orders was shown again at the Prague Film Festival, in January 2002, and I was invited over to represent the cast. Lucy and I were put up at the Marriott for three days and wonderfully looked after. After the film had been shown, a party was held at which I became fascinated by the degree of interest in British movies that still remained in post-communist Eastern Europe.

A strange result of *Blow-Up*'s status as an art movie is that, whereas few western films were shown in Czechoslovakia in the sixties, it was, and informed the youth of that time on Western mores and fashion. They held a screening of it the second day we were there, and asked me to take a Q&A session afterwards, which I was happy to do. It was riveting, in a relaxed and informal roomful of people, to hear that some of the original audience, who had come with their student offspring, had seen white jeans as the ultimate fashion statement of the time, and still wore their watches outside their shirt cuffs. They simply didn't see any Western fashion magazines back then, and thus the film had also served as a style guide for them. That the bizarre little picture was still making ripples nearly forty years after it was made, I found extraordinary, though undeniably pleasing.

We returned to Prague in June when I was making *The League of Extraordinary Gentlemen*, with a fairly extraordinary gang of colleagues. Sean Connery led the pack, amid growing tension under Steve Norrington's direction. There was sense of siege among the cast as the director grew more excitable and combative with Sean. Things got so bad, it was even suggested that I should take over directing, which, knowing what was good for me, I promptly declined. It was not the happiest filming experience of my life, but it did give us the chance to see Prague in the sun, which, in my view, rivals Rome for charm and beauty.

On a day off in the old town square, I bought a fur hat for Lucy, as you might in June. I also bought myself a bullwhip, like one I'd had in Australia and with which I'd become quite proficient. I spent a lot of time practising in our room, with Lucy nervously poking a piece of butchered coat hanger from behind a door. On the last night, I felt I was ready, and used the vast empty atrium of the Prague Hilton to demonstrate to Eddie, the stunt man, that it was possible to remove a cigarette from a man's lips with a bullwhip, without touching him. Despite being wrapped in all available protective clothing, Eddie looked nervous. But to his amazement, I managed to pull it off – the skill remained. Not a very useful skill, I admit, but you never know when it mightn't come in useful. Look at Indiana Jones.

In March, I was working for television again, playing a retired, bent policeman in a drama with Trevor Eve called *Waking the Dead*. In the final scene, by the Dome, my character was supposed to be hanged. I was looking forward to doing this bit myself, but they insisted, rather fussily, on using a dummy.

For the purposes of the script, I had also to drive a car – a new maroon Jaguar. I saw Lucy looking at me a little askance as I was handed the keys. Apart from the disastrous episode in Wales with the hire car, I hadn't driven a vehicle since piling Nolan's truck into the back of the people carrier in Ketchum. But I had a licence and I only needed to drive a few yards and pull up in a great empty car park. I could do that. Nevertheless, in order not to make a complete prat of myself, I thought I'd better take the car for a quick spin up the road and round a couple of roundabouts to get the feel of it. No problem at all.

They were set up for the shot. I drove the Jaguar into camera, stopped, turned the engine off and climbed out, as required on the page. As I walked away from the car, it started silently to roll down the slight but definite incline of the ground. I'd forgotten to pull on the handbrake and I'd left the gear in neutral.

I watched in dismay as it gathered speed, pursued by an athletic runner, who managed to leap in and stop it before any damage happened, unlike the last two occasions. Foolish though this may have made me look, it has paid regular repeat fees every time it's run on one of the innumerable out-take bloomer shows.

When I'd finished my bit without further incident, as I was in that part of London I thought I'd take the opportunity to revisit Narrow Street in Limehouse, where I'd lived with Linda Estall Cole while I was making *Blow-Up*.

Of course, I couldn't find it, amid the confusion of one-way streets and my own defective memory. We went to a well-known pub called the Prospect of Whitby to ask for directions, and a non-native Mediterranean type volunteered them.

'You go out of here and you turn left.' He indicated right with his right hand. 'And then you run right.' He indicated left with his left hand.

'Are you sure about this?' I asked. 'That's left?' I pointed right.

'Yes, yes. I amma left-handed, and I getta it always the wronga ways round.'

I was glad we'd cleared that up before we carried on!

In Narrow Street we went into one of my old locals, the Bunch of Grapes, now surrounded by acres of flash new flats, although, thank goodness, the old lightermen's houses where I'd rented Andrew Sinclair's house were still there. I found people in the pub, still there too, who'd been around in those days. It brought on a severe attack of nostalgia, reminding me of the raw energy I'd had then and the absolute determination to extract every morsel of experience, when the future was only a week ahead and life was for living in the moment.

But the past creeps up on you and manifests itself in completely unexpected ways. Shortly after we had been to see Debs in Cornwall, where she now lived, for her 40th birthday – and a daughter's 40th is a distinct reminder of one's own mortality – I got a call that took me even further back into my mottled history.

Jeremy Conway's office rang to tell me that someone called Ann Aspinall, had rung them, wanting to get in touch with me. Ann Aspinall, it turned out, had been Ann Thorn, my great schoolboy crush, with whom I'd wandered the summer pastures around Woking and kissed in the back row of the Swiss Cottage Odeon. She was now married to a British businessman in Manila called John Aspinall. Having failed completely to find her there, I was delighted that she'd suddenly decided to get back in touch with me.

I rang her straight back and we had a wonderful chat, arranging to meet in two days' time, after I'd been filming in London. I went to a flat she and John had in St John's Wood, not a quarter of a mile from her old home in Clifton Terrace. They still lived in Manila, where, I discovered, she had been married to a Filipino for several years and had had five children with him; that relationship had sadly gone wrong, but she was very content with John. She looked, I had to admit, as good as I remembered her; indeed, had worn rather better than I. To my mind her features had hardly changed at all, and her figure was as lovely as ever. Old friends who link you so swiftly to your own past are great to see, and those who are still easy on the eye, even better. She and I sat and talked for hours, until Brian six-one, the driver, began to wonder if I'd been kidnapped. John Aspinall was very charming, and Ann had kept him up to date with my resuscitated career. She was as pleased as anyone that I'd been lucky enough to be granted a good second crack in my less vigorous years.

Naturally, I invited them down to lunch in Calne at the first opportunity, where they met Lucy, who was really touched by Ann's kind present of some Philippine pearls. We had been a little nervous about how the visit would go, but it was a very happy day, and we realised what a great shame it was that we hadn't found them in Manila.

By way of a contrast, Roger Taylor, the Queen drummer we'd met at Möet's château in France, asked us to the opening of the new Queen musical, *We Will Rock You*, which he'd written with Ben Elton. We sat in an audience thick with performers from popular television, a row behind Barbara Windsor with a horde from *EastEnders* behind us. It was, I remarked to my wife in an undertone, rather like being in a washing machine – surrounded by soap.

After the inevitable great first-night bash, we tried to go home. We soon found that every hire car in London was booked, and there wasn't a cab in sight, so we rang Irish John at Atlas Cars, who told us, 'The only bloke I've got up there'll never find you. You'll have to carry on looking for a black cab.'

But it was one of those nights when every taxi in London has fled to the easy fringes; had we been in Wimbledon or Highgate – no problem, but not a single 'For Hire' sign was to be seen in the West End.

There was no alternative, it meant another bus ride, and as luck would have it, along came a No. 19 which would take us the whole way to Battersea. The bus pulled up and we perched ourselves on the inward-facing seats downstairs at the back.

'Hello, Lucy! Hello, David! How lovely to see you on my bus!'

At first, I couldn't identify the conductor under his unfamiliar uniform, until he added, 'It was really nice of you to sign my wife's record of *Camelot*.'

It was one of my former regular co-drinkers from the Eagle Tavern in Battersea Park Road, with whom I'd shared several pints in my early days at Lucy's. At the time, he'd been a council operative with responsibility for waste disposal in Battersea Park, and had proved a very valuable source of additional black plastic bags in the aftermath of excessive jollification at Cupar Road.

We exchanged greetings, and when I tried to pay for our tickets, he drew himself up. 'Put your money away. You're on my bus now, and you're certainly not paying on my bus. I shall pay,' which caused a bit of consternation among the other punters now beginning to fill the other seats.

We felt flattered and very chuffed after an evening spent amid stars in their limos, red carpets, guest badges, snappers and security gorillas with earpieces, to be treated to a bus ride home. It made the evening for us.

My son George came back to see us in the summer with his co-vivant, Sonia, whose brother was an old school friend of his from Ketchum. They were now living in Boise, Idaho, where George was still at college. Sonia had two small children and he felt she needed a holiday; as she'd never been outside the US, he wanted to bring her over and show her England.

I was really glad they decided to come down to the Mill for a while after they'd stayed with Nolan in London for a few days. They had a chance to look around at the prehistoric stones and barrows of ancient Wiltshire, and Sonia caught up on missed sleep while I took George up the lane to one of my local haunts, the Calne Recreation and Sports Club, to see friends of mine whom he'd met on his previous visit and to play a few games of pool.

I'd become a regular visitor to the club, where I was made very welcome and found an inexhaustible supply of opponents at the pool table and the dartboard. It was a good place for me to unwind after a tiring shoot, where I could drone on – no doubt to the deep boredom of many – about what I'd done and whom I'd seen. There was a consistent, down-to-earth normality to the place that was helpful in the readjustment from life on a set to life at home. One of the reasons Lucy and I had wanted to move to a small country town was precisely for the benefits and pleasures of being part of a community, and I was happy to chip in with local activities whenever I could.

As a keen supporter of sport for young people in the area, I found myself on one occasion as starter to four thousand Calne townsfolk, setting out to raise funds for better facilities by breaking a Guinness Record for the largest number of people to pass a single baton (loaned by Olympic gold medallist David Hemmery) in one day.

Wearing a different hat – I have at least thirty – I was asked by our old friend Anna Hall and the organisers to open the Marlborough Jazz Festival. Anna had also invited her friends Carole and John Challis, whom I'd worked with several years before. Standing outside Waitrose on a flatbed cart, drawn by a pair of those heavy horses with shag-pile carpets round their feet, I declared the event open. Soon after, while chatting to John, I heard several of the punters wondering who I was and why I was opening the event, with a lot of 'David Hemmings? Who's he?'

Meanwhile, John was being pestered every few minutes for his autograph (in a way Rex Harrison would have envied).

I looked at him. 'You know, you should have opened this thing, not me.'

In his best Boysie voice, he wrinkled his nose. 'David, the difference is – you're international; and I'm domestic!'

In the same way, I wanted to help where I could with local tourism and media, and when Paul Morrison invited me the following year to do one of his *Startrek* walking programmes for HTV, I was happy to participate, although I had to explain that I didn't do 'trekking'. It was a long time since I'd walked anywhere much, and I suggested instead that we indulge in one of my favourite environs and take a narrowboat along the Kennet and Avon Canal. I was mindful that we could do most of the journey seated, and there were a few very charming pubs en route. Paul agreed and I started boning up on the long and colourful history of the canal.

It was a fine day for it when we boarded Sara and Roger Davis's boat just east of the lock at Bradford-on-Avon and cruised gently to Bathampton in the leaf-dappled sunlight. The plosh of moorhens dipping and the whispering bulrushes took me swiftly back through my sporadic associations with canals since I was a small boy, when I'd hunted up and down the towpath of the Basingstoke Canal near my grandmother's house in Woking. The backdrop may not have been as awe-inspiring as Scorsese's set in Cinecittà, or as dramatic as Ridley

Scott's Rome, but it was as enjoyable two days' filming as I've had in a long time (and without any lines to learn). Another couple of nice local jobs were two radio plays, produced by Sara Davies at the BBC in Bristol, *The Prison Father* – a reading of the letters of a man in prison to his son – and a reflective drama about a minicab operator called *Tommy the Voice*, both of which were subsequently broadcast on Radio Four. I love doing radio plays, partly because they are a bare-arse challenge, consisting, as they do, only of script and voices. There is nowhere to hide and all actors should do them whenever they're offered the chance.

Early September, through Nick Powell, one of the producers on *Last Orders*, I was offered the part of Mickey Rudin in *The Night We Called It a Day*. It was an interesting script, based closely on the real and fairly bizarre story of Frank Sinatra's tour of Australia in 1974, when he indiscriminately insulted the journalists following him around, and the women in particular, whom he referred to as a 'buck-and-a-half hookers'. This caused a great uproar and the trade unions cooperated effectively to seize up the tour and leave Sinatra besieged in his hotel room. It was a dramatic example of union strength and solidarity, led by the future prime minister Bob Hawke, who finally brokered a sort of apology in exchange for calling off the unions.

An old friend, Dennis Hopper, was going to play Frank, Melanie Griffiths was playing Barbara Marx and my character, Mickey Rudin, was Frank's attorney/manager. Filming was due to start in Sydney at the end of October.

This, I thought, would be a wonderful opportunity for a honeymoon.

I'd first asked Lucy to marry me back in 1993 at Henley Regatta, but that was, as it turned out, three years before I was finally divorced from Prue. Now, with the prospect of a honeymoon in Sydney – which I'd only visited fleetingly and where Lucy had never been – I shrewdly thought that with the film company picking up the tab, this might be the moment to keep my word, after a mere nine and half years on approval. Lucy was kind enough to accept my proposal, and an early date was fixed at Chippenham register office. It all had to fit into a tight time frame and the registrar was tremendously kind about accommodating us.

On 18 October 2002, in the beautiful old building that houses the register office, we were married, witnessed only by our close families, plus William and Joybells O'Shei. All advances (and bribes) from glossy magazines having been firmly declined over the years, it was a small, intimate occasion, and very special.

Almost immediately, as a kind of pre-honeymoon, we had to go for a couple of nights to Istanbul, where I had one day's work on a film called *Romantik*, appropriately enough – no dialogue, thank God, because it was being made in Turkish. Filming was done two hours into the country at the house of the director, Sinan Cetin. We were a little startled when, as we left to go back to Istanbul with him, he clambered into the boot of the car, which was lined with a mattress and bedding. Yawning, he announced that he was going to sleep in there as he had another TV show to make that night.

Somewhat unconventionally I'd brought my son along with me on this first leg of the honeymoon. The English producer, Torrie Field, had been nanny for Gayle to Nolan's half-brother, Edward Jenkins, and she'd said she wanted to see Nolan about a possible job, so he'd come out with us.

Back in England for only a couple of days, we heard the very sad news that my old friend and mentor Richard Harris had died. I had to smile when I heard that he was being carried on a stretcher from his permanent billet at the Savoy past a group of onlookers when, although ailing fast, he managed to tell them, 'It was the food, you know.' Pure Harris, right to the end. As usual, he had several jobs in hand at the time, not least as Dumbledore in the third *Harry Potter* film. It must have been a great loss to his millions of young fans, who wouldn't see him in the role again.

The following day, we left for Australia, via Singapore for two nights. In Sydney, which I was visiting properly for the first time, the film company had rented a wonderful penthouse apartment for us overlooking the Cruising Yacht Club in Rushcutter Bay, with a roof garden and, vital accoutrement, a Jacuzzi. It was extraordinary to be back in Australia – my first visit for nearly twenty years – after I'd spent so much time there while the focus of my career shifted from acting to production and directing. I looked back on those times with Tony Ginnane with great fondness, and some of my adventures were pulled back into close-up when we met up with my great Aussie flame, Carmen Duncan. We had a wonderful time seeing her again under the high umbrellas of the yacht club, she as beautiful as ever – truly – and charming and happy for what Lucy and I had found together. Generous-spirited and from strong Catholic-Irish stock, she made no recriminations for my indecisiveness at the time, or the trouble I must have caused her – only fond memories of a powerful affair.

Working with Dennis Hopper, the original *Easy Rider*, recalled even more distant events – like when, in 1968, he and I had planned in minute detail an LA Primer – an art event in which all our guests would be driven round Hollywood while Dennis jumped out and signed one of the walls of the Beverly Wilshire Hotel, and Hollywood Boulevard, even a wave in the sea at Venice Beach, before we returned them to the Ferris Pace Gallery, where the walls were bare and, behind a white, translucent screen, the Mamas and the Papas would endlessly sing 'California Dreaming', while I announced, 'Look at your neighbour. Gaze at each other and see yourself reflected in their eyes. You, the people, all of you are the art of Los Angeles.' What a load of bull – I'm glad we never did it – or did we?

I hadn't forgotten that Dennis had been quite an influence on me then, and first introduced me to modern art, with which I've since lost touch. He gave a wonderful performance as Sinatra, and I hope the picture sees the light of day, or, at least the darkness of a movie theatre in London, before too long.

After a memorable honeymoon, Lucy and I returned to England in December to find an invitation from Cameron Mackintosh to come and talk about my taking over the part of Colonel Pickering in his stage production of *My Fair Lady* at Drury Lane. I was very excited, although Lucy suggested we check out the production first to see how active the Colonel's part was, as she recalled that he had to jump over sofas and things. I talked to Cameron's people afterwards, who seemed keen for me to do it, but I came to the conclusion that, while I might have enjoyed the first week, six evening shows and a matinée would have palled fairly quickly. My boredom threshold was always low and, besides, I didn't think I had the stamina for it. With some regret, I declined the offer.

Shortly after Christmas, in January 2003, *Gangs of New York* was premièred in Leicester Square, and I saw it, in all its goriness, for the first time. The sets were utterly wondrous, and Daniel Day-Lewis's performance was electrifying. Since the inaccurate reports of my minor contretemps with Leonardo DiCaprio over his capricious behaviour in Rome, we hadn't seen each other. On the night, I didn't see him until, while having a pee, a gang of security guards marched into the Gents and cleared the place, except for me, so that the young star himself could pee in peace. We exchanged nods across the urinals, but no more was said.

Straight after the film, there was a party for Martin Scorsese and everyone involved. On our way there, walking through the crowd in the foyer, I heard a woman's voice.

'Hello, David. What are *you* doing here?'

It was Jane Merrow.

When I'd first arrived back in London permanently in 1995, I'd been in touch with Jane and we'd had lunch at the Chelsea Arts Club. Since we'd parted in 1967, she had married a pilot and gone to live in California. She'd carried on working there, appearing in the kind of shows I used to direct – *Magnum, P.I.* and *Airwolf*. I saw her around; she came occasionally to our Sunday brunch parties in Malibu and up at the Pink House.

In 1991, when Prue and I were living in Ketchum, she had rung to tell me that she had left her husband after years of difficult marriage, and she was in Boise, Idaho, with her fifteen-year-old son. I could tell she was feeling catastrophic, and told her just to get on a plane and come over. She arrived and we put her up in our condo in the town for a few days, where she and I talked at length and honestly about the messes we'd both got ourselves into.

But now I hadn't seen her since our lunch at the Chelsea Arts Club. How should I react to, 'What are *you* doing here?'

'Have you just been watching the film?' I asked.

'Yes.'

'Well,' I said, 'you may have spotted me in it – not for very long or very often, but I promise I was there!'

Two days later, we were in Dublin, guests of the splendid John McHugo and his wife, Lily, at an Irish charity première of *Gangs*. In a typically Irish way, this was a very merry occasion with black ties and lavish dinner. Bono sang and the Edge played.

Leo DiCaprio flew in from Germany especially because it was Daniel Day-Lewis who had instigated the charity gig. Leo and Daniel also raised an extra £15,000 by auctioning what the Irish press the next day called a 'snoggio' apiece for the Children's Make a Wish Appeal. It also seemed a good opportunity for me to mend bridges. Leo and I kissed and made up on the stage. I had to concede that his performance was great, and maybe I'd been a bit unfair. And Leo conceded he might have been a bit snotty. All was resolved in a veritable love feast.

For someone like me who has always fancied themselves as a south London snooker hall hustler, my neighbour at dinner was one of the most exciting guests present – Ken Doherty, Irish ace of the green baize. As if sitting next to him weren't privilege enough, the next day he invited me to his private inner sanctum at Jason's Club to play a frame, what an honour! (He won.)

But two nights in Dublin, surrounded by the merciless energy of the Irish, though wonderful, were almost too much for me, I thought, as Lucy and I flew back to England.

The next major excitement in our lives was a family wedding.

I was thrilled when Nolan told us that he and his actress girlfriend, Nicky Grosse, were going to be married. They were pronounced man and wife by the registrar at Burgh House in Hampstead with just the two families and closest friends present, and two days later, on a beautiful May afternoon, Nicky's father, Peter Grosse, conducted a humanist marriage ceremony on the pretty and romantic Temple Island on the Thames near Henley, followed by a wonderful reception there.

Strangely, these were the first two occasions since I'd met him that I found myself alone with Gayle's husband, Simon Jenkins, whom she'd married in 1979. He had for many years been a warm and generous second father to Nolan, and we shared our hopes for his future. We soon found ourselves laughing like drains at the back of the crowd and I was very glad that we'd finally had the opportunity to make a real connection.

By great good chance, my youngest son, William, was also at the wedding. I hadn't seen him since we'd all had lunch in Malibu after the green card visit in 1996. He was in England for a little post-school wandering around Europe with a friend, Caleb, and it was wonderful to see him. Later in the summer he and Caleb called in at Calne on their way back through to the States. They stayed in the cottage next door, which we'd bought, and I converted it into a temporary gambling den, where we played several happy hours of poker, laughing a lot and getting to know each other again.

A little later that summer, William's brother Edward also came to London and I was very glad that he found time for a fleeting visit to Calne on his way to live and work in Barcelona.

For the wedding we had stayed with Lucy's cousin, Charlotte Every, who lived on the river near Temple Island. It was there in 1993 that I'd first proposed to Lucy and, as we drove away next morning from what had been a very happy occasion for both of us, I reflected on the last ten years and the complete turnaround that had taken place in my life.

From a time when I had seemed permanently on the verge of total breakdown, drained of self-esteem and the belief that I could ever achieve anything more, I had found myself again, had been able to work, and give back a little to my family, friends and the community in which I lived.

Whereas my existence in the States had seemed in the midst of perpetual crisis, now it was calm, balanced, and as close as it could ever come to being normal. Although tearing myself away from America had been hard and painful in many ways, I was in no doubt now that it had been the right thing to do. Of course, I was still concerned about the effect of the breakdown of my marriage to Prue on our children, but I could only hope that, in time, the lesions would heal, and they would understand, however irresponsible I may have appeared, that they would always be important to me and paramount in my affections.

Through Lucy's patient tolerance and the deep mutual love and understanding we felt for each other, I'd been able to confront my demons and find peace. I've become aware that this chance is not given to all men; I don't suppose I deserve it, but I am deeply grateful for it. That I should also have been given the opportunity to work in films again, steadily and in a stimulating variety of roles, was, I felt, a bonus which could not have happened without the input of old friends, and Lucy's determination to see me happy again.

As she drove from Henley with her customary quiet efficiency, I lay back in the passenger seat beside her and thought what a very lucky man I was.

Once the wedding and all its ripples had settled, I found that I'd been asked to do two interviews that could scarcely have contrasted more.

The first was with a journalist called Kieran Tyler, who told me, to my utter astonishment, that he was great fan of my first and only album,

David Hemmings Happens, recorded, you may recall, about three hundred pages ago in careless haste back in LA in 1967. He had, which was more than I did, a copy of the record and its original sleeve, the notes on which can only be described as a lengthy apology for what was on the disc. However, Kieran had discovered depths to the music which had hitherto escaped me and he was keen to expand on them, with my help. I did my best, of course.

The second of these interviews was delayed a little as it was going to be filmed. The day before it was due to happen, I was coming out of the back door of our house into the garden, carrying a load of fresh plants which obscured my view, when I tripped and flew like an Exocet missile into a cluster of pots containing hostas and geraniums, carefully tended by my wife. I whacked my eye and was a little slow in applying the beefsteak, with the result that it looked like a sixties psychedelic poster in purples and yellows, and was deemed by Lucy not to be suitable for an onscreen appearance.

However, once it had ceased to throb and the vivid hues had faded, we were visited by John Bridcutt, who was preparing a television programme about Benjamin Britten and the great man's fascination with young teenage boys.

It was not to be a prurient piece, and I was able in any case to tell John that, while I was aware that Ben had been fond of me, he had made absolutely no kind of physical contact with me that could be construed as sexual in intent. In fact, given the rather strange circumstances of my own home life, he had become like a father to me, and a much-loved one at that. I greatly enjoyed the chance to regress in my mind to those times, which had provided, I have to concede, the launch pad of my eccentric career, and which I remembered with great warmth. I haven't seen the programme yet, but I hope very much that Britten is shown in the light in which I saw him.

Besides the interviews, there were a few more jobs lurking on the horizon, one of which I very much wanted to do for my old friend Brian Cook.

We'd seen the Cooks pretty regularly over the years, and indeed, back in February, Lucy, Louisa and I had been to Toby's 21st birthday party at Julie's in Portland Road (and just around the corner from John Cowan's studio, where we had filmed so much of *Blow-Up*).

Now Brian had a strange and wonderful script that he wanted to direct himself. *Colour Me Kubrick* was based on the real activities of a very kooky gay man called Alan Conway, who while Kubrick was making his last film, *Eyes Wide Shut*, liked to go round telling people that he was Stanley Kubrick, capitalising on the eccentricity of the man himself, which meant that he was never seen anywhere in public, never had his photo taken and never gave interviews – by any standards, let alone in the movie world, a serious recluse.

Despite gross inconsistencies in his portrayal of Kubrick and vast lacunae in his knowledge of the director and his works, Conway frequently got away with it, which resulted in several instances of lavish entertainment being extended to him, as well as the opportunity to impress young gay men he fancied.

Of course, Brian's knowledge and regard for Kubrick were substantial, having worked with the great man for many years, and he was determined to see this extraordinary script make it to the screen. He had also managed, and this was a definite coup, to secure the services of John Malkovich to play Conway.

I went to Elstree for a read-through of my part as the lugubrious manager of an old crooner who was going to be played by Jim Davidson. I met Jim, for the first time, as well as James Dreyfus, wonderfully funny star of *Gimme Gimme* and *The Thin Blue Line*, who reminded me he'd met me at Whiteway when he was a little boy – his mother was an old friend of William and Joy O'Shei. To top of the pleasurable anticipation of working with Brian was the knowledge that Robert Powell and Peter Bowles were also in the cast, along with Honor Blackman, Richard E. Grant, Leslie Phillips and, I'm glad to say, Nolan Hemmings. Shooting is due to start next January.

In September, a memorial show for the great Richard Harris had been arranged by his family at the Strand Theatre. It was a fulsome celebration, with film clips of the many fine pictures Richard had made, poems and Celtic music, along with family videos of Richard with his children and grandchildren.

I was thrilled when Jimmy Webb appeared on stage. Jimmy, who had written some of the greatest popular songs of all time – 'By the Time I Get to Phoenix', 'Wichita Lineman', 'Up, Up and Away' – had also written 'MacArthur Park', recorded at the time we were making *Camelot*, which had been a huge, unexpected hit for Richard.

I couldn't wait to see Jimmy after the show, and wasn't going to hang about waiting for the party afterwards before I did. I clambered, with no small effort, to the top of the theatre and a little beyond, it felt, until

David Hemmings

I found his dressing room, where I was able to creep up behind him and cover his eyes with my hands.

Two words I growled before he bellowed, 'David Hemmings!' and spun round for a great bear hug. It was truly wonderful to see Jimmy again, and indulge in a festival of reminiscence.

Snatches of his lyrics in 'MacArthur Park' have never left me:

I will drink the wine while it is warm
And never let you catch me looking at the sun.
I will take my life into my hands and I will use it.
I will win the worship in their eyes and I will lose it.
I will have the things that I desire
And my passion flow like rivers through the sky.

I *have* taken my life into my hands and I have used it and I've won the worship in their eyes; and I've lost it.

It seems to me that now might be the moment when, to all the people in my life, incredibly various, talented, loyal and strange, to some of whom I still cling while others I've passed by (or have passed me by!) or have themselves passed on, we – you and I – should lift a glass and clink, and remind ourselves that today's last orders may just be tomorrow's new beginnings.

Filmography

The Rainbow Jacket [1954], 99 minutes
Director: Basil Dearden
Starring: Robert Morley, Kay Walsh, Edward Underdown, Fella Edmonds, Bill Owen, Charles Victor, Honor Blackman, Sid James. **David Hemmings'** debut role.

Saint Joan [1957], 110 minutes
(based on the play by George Bernard Shaw, adapted by Graham Greene)
Director: Otto Preminger
Starring: Richard Widmark, Richard Todd, Anton Walbrook, John Gielgud, Felix, Aylmer, Jean Seberg.
David Hemmings had an uncredited bit part.

The Heart Within [1957], 61 minutes
Director: David Eady
Starring: James Hayter, Clifford Evans, **David Hemmings** (as Danny Willard), Earl Cameron, Dan Jackson, Jack Stewart, Betty Cooper, Gloria Ann Simpson.

Five Clues to Fortune [1957], 129 minutes
Director: Joe Mendoza
Starring: David Cameron, Peter Godsell, Dafydd Havard, **David Hemmings**, Norman Mitchell, Roberta Paterson, John Rogers, Peter Welch.

No Trees in the Street [1958], 96 minutes
Director: John Lee Thompson
Starring: Sylvia Syms, Herbert Lom, Melvyn Hayes, Ronald Howard,

Stanley Holloway, Joan Miller, Liam Redmond, **David Hemmings** (as Kenny), Victor Brooks, Fred Griffiths.

In the Wake of a Stranger [1958], 69 minutes
Director: David Eady
Starring: Tony Wright, Shirley Eaton, Danny Gree, Willoughby Goddard, Harry H. Corbett, Tom Bowman, Alun Owen, Barbara Archer, **David Hemmings** (as a schoolboy).

Men of Tomorrow [1959], 41 minutes
Director: Alfred Travers
Starring: Vernon Greeves, Penny Morrell, **David Hemmings**.

The Wind of Change [1961], 64 minutes
Director: Vernon Sewell
Starring: Donald Pleasence, Johnny Briggs, Hilda Fenemore, Norman Gunn, **David Hemmings** (as Ginger), Glynn Houston, Ann Lynn, Bunny May.

Some People [1962], 93 minutes
Director: Clive Donner
Starring: Kenneth More, Ray Brooks, Anneke Wills, David Andrews, Angela Douglas, **David Hemmings** (as Bert), Fanny Carby, Harry H. Corbett, Richard Davis, Frankie Dymon, Fred Ferris, Michael Gwynn.

Play It Cool [1962], 82 minutes
Director: Michael Winner
Starring: Billy Fury, Michael Anderson Jr, Dennis Price, Richard Wattis, Anna Palk, Keith Hamshere, Ray Brooks, Jeremy Bulloch, Maurice Kaufmann, Helen Shapiro, Lionel Blair, Shane Fenton, **David Hemmings**.

The Painted Smile (aka: *Murder Can Be Deadly*) [1962], 60 minutes
Director: Lance Comfort
Starring: Liz Fraser, Kenneth Griffith, Peter Reynolds, Tony Wickert, Craig Douglas, Nanette Newman, Ray Smith, **David Hemmings** (as Roy), Harold Berens, Grazina Frame.

Two Left Feet [1962], 93 minutes
Director: Roy Ward Baker
Starring: Michael Crawford, Nyree Dawn Porter, Cyril Chamberlain, Peggy Ann Clifford, Hazel Coppen, Michael Craze, Julie Foster, **David Hemmings** (as Brian), Mike Leigh, David Lodge.

West 11 [1963], 93 minutes
Director: Michael Winner
Starring: Francesca Annis, Kathleen Breck, Ken Colyer, Finlay Currie, Diana Dors, Kathleen Harrison, **David Hemmings**.

Live It Up (aka: *Sing and Swing*) [1963], 75 minutes
Director: Lance Comfort
Starring: David Hemmings (as Dave), Jennifer Moss, John Pike, Heinz Burt, Stephen Marriot, Joan Newell, Ed Devereaux, Veronica Hurst, Penny Lambirth, Peter Glaze, David Bauer, Anthony Ashdown, Douglas Ives, Paul Hansard, Geoffry L'Oise.

The System (USA: *The Girl-Getters*) [1964], 93 minutes
Director: Michael Winner
Starring: Oliver Reed, Jane Merrow, Barbara Ferris, Julia Foster, Harry Andrews, Ann Lynn, Guy Doleman, Andrew Ray, John Porter-Davison, Clive Colin Bowler, Iain Gregory, **David Hemmings** (as David).

Be My Guest [1965], 82 minutes
Director: Lance Comfort
Starring: David Hemmings (as Dave), Stephen Marriott, John Pike, Andrea Monet, Ivor Salter, Anna King, Avril Angers, Joyce Blair, David Healy, Tony Wager, David Lander, Robin Stewart, Monica Evans, Douglas Ives.

Auto-Stop [1965]
Director: Brian Parker
Starring: David Hemmings, Delphi Lawrence, Kevin Stoney.

The Counterfeit Man (GB: *Out of the Unknown: The Counterfeit Man*) [1965], 60 minutes
Director: George Spenton-Foster

Starring: Barry Ashton, Keith Buckley, Alexander Davion, Peter Fraser, **David Hemmings** (as Westcott), Geoffrey Kenion, Lew Luton, Derek Martin, David Munro, David Savile.

Blowup (USA: *Blow-Up*) [1966], 111 minutes
(based on the short story *Las babas del diablo* by Julio Cortázar)
Director: Michelangelo Antonioni
Starring: Vanessa Redgrave, Sarah Miles, **David Hemmings** (as Thomas), John Castle, Jane Birkin, Gillian Hills, Peter Bowles, Veruschka von Lehndorff, Julian Chagrin, Claude Chagrin.

Eye of the Devil (aka: *13*) [1967], 92 minutes
(based on the novel *Day of the Arrow* by Philip Loraine)
Director: J. Lee Thompson
Starring: Deborah Kerr, David Niven, Donald Pleasence, Edward Mulhare, Flora Robson, Emlyn Williams, Sharon Tate, **David Hemmings** (as Christian de Carey), John Le Mesurier, Michael Miller, Donald Bisset, Pauline Letts.

Camelot [1967], 179 minutes
(based on the novel *The Once and Future King* by T. H. White)
Director: Joshua Logan
Starring: Richard Harris, Vanessa Redgrave, Franco Nero, **David Hemmings** (as Mordred), Lionel Jeffries, Laurence Naismith, Pierre Olaf, Estelle Winwood, Gary Marshall, Anthony Rogers, Peter Bromilow, Sue Casey, Gary Marsh, Nicholas Beauvy.

The Charge of the Light Brigade [1968], 139 minutes
Director: Tony Richardson
Starring: Trevor Howard, Vanessa Redgrave, John Gielgud, Harry Andrews, Jill Bennett, **David Hemmings** (as Captain Nolan), Ben Aris, Mickey Baker, Peter Bowles, Leo Britt, Mark Burns, John J. Carney, Helen Cherry, Chris Chittell, Ambrose Coghill.

The Long Day's Dying [1968], 95 minutes
(based on the novel by Alan White)
Director: Peter Collinson
Starring: David Hemmings (as John), Tony Beckley, Tom Bell, Alan Dobie.

Only When I Larf [1968], 104 minutes
(based on the novel by Len Deighton)
Director: Basil Dearden
Starring: Richard Attenborough, **David Hemmings** (as Bob),
Alexandra Stewart, Nicholas Pennell, Melissa Stribling, Terence
Alexander, Edric Connor, Gaston Chikhani, Clifton Jones, Calvin
Lockhart, David Lodge.

Barbarella [1968], 98 minutes
(based on the comic by Jean-Claude Forest)
Director: Roger Vadim
Starring: Jane Fonda, John Philip Law, Anita Pallenberg, Milo O'Shea,
Marcel Marceau, Claude Dauphin, Véronique Vendell, Giancarlo
Cobelli, Serge Marquand, Nino Musco, Franco Gulà, **David
Hemmings** (as Dildano).

Alfred the Great (USA: *A King is Born*) [1969], 122 minutes
Director: Clive Donner
Starring: David Hemmings (as Alfred), Michael York, Prunella
Ransome, Colin Blakely, Ian McKellen, Peter Vaughan, Alan Dobie,
Julian Glover, Vivien Merchant, Julian Chagrin, Jim Norton, John
Norton, Jon Rees, Christopher Timothy, Peter Blythe, Sinéad Cusack.

The Best House in London [1969], 105 minutes
Director: Philip Saville
Starring: David Hemmings (as Benjamin Oakes/Walter Leybourne),
Joanna Pettet, George Sanders, Dany Robin, Warren Mitchell, John
Bird, William Rushton, Bill Fraser, Maurice Denham, Wolfe Morris,
Martita Hunt, Arnold Diamond, Hugh Burden, John DeMarco.

The Walking Stick [1970], 96 minutes
(based on the novel by William Graham)
Director: Eric Till
Starring: David Hemmings (as Leigh Hartley), Samantha Eggar,
Emlyn Williams, Phyllis Calvert, Ferdy Mayne, Francesca Annis,
Bridget Turner, Dudley Sutton, John Woodvine, David Savile, Derek
Cox, Harvey Sambrook.

Fragment of Fear (aka: *Freelance*) [1970], 94 minutes
(based on the novel by John Bingham)
Director: Richard C. Sarafian
Starring: David Hemmings (as Tim Brett), Gayle Hunnicutt, Wilfrid
Hyde-White, Flora Robson, Adolfo Celi, Roland Culver, Daniel
Massey, Mona Washbourne, Arthur Lowe, Yootha Joyce, Derek
Newark, Patricia Hayes, Mary Wimbush, Philip Stone, Glynn
Edwards.

Melody (aka: *SWALK*) [1971], 103 minutes
Director: Waris Hussein
Producer: David Hemmings
Starring: Mark Lester, Tracy Hyde, Jack Wild, Roy Kinnear, Billy
Franks, Ken Jones, Sheila Steafel, Kate Williams.

Unman, Wittering and Zigo [1971], 102 minutes
(based on the play by Giles Cooper)
Director: John Mackenzie
Executive Producer: David Hemmings
Starring: David Hemmings (as John Ebony), Douglas Wilmer, Tony
Haygarth, Carolyn Seymour, Hamilton Dyce, Barbara Lott, Donald
Gee, David Jackson, Hubert Rees, David Auker, Tom Morris, Richard
Gill, Michael Kitchen.

The Love Machine [1971], 108 minutes
(based on the novel by Jacqueline Susann)
Director: Jack Haley Jr
Starring: John Phillip Law, Dyan Cannon, Robert Ryan, Jackie Cooper,
David Hemmings (as Jerry Nelson), Shecky Greene, Jodi Wexler,
William Roerick, Maureen Arthur, Clinton Greyn, Sharon Farrell,
Alexandra Hay.

Running Scared [1972], 98 minutes
(based on the novel by Gregory McDonald)
Director: David Hemmings
Starring: Maxine Audley, Stephanie Bidmead, Georgia Brown, Gayle
Hunnicutt, Barry Morse, Robert Powell, Edward Underdown.

Voices (aka *Nightmare*) [1973], 91 minutes
Director: Kevin Billington
Starring: Adam Bridge, Peggy Ann Clifford, Lynn Farleigh,
Eva Griffiths, **David Hemmings** (as Robert), Gayle Hunnicutt,
Russell Lewis.

The Wild Little Bunch (aka: *The 14, The Fourteen*) [1973], 105 minutes
Director: David Hemmings
Starring: Jack Wild, June Brown, Liz Edminston, John Bailey, Diana
Reevers, Alun Armstrong, Cheryl Hall, Keith Buckley, Anna Wing,
Tony Calvin, Christian Kelly.

No es nada, mama, solo un juego (aka: *Beyond Erotica, It's Nothing,
Only a Game, Lola*) [1974], 85 minutes
Director: José María Forqué
Starring: David Hemmings (as Juan), Alida Valli, Francisco Rabal,
Andrea Rau, Nuria Gimeno, Galeazzo Benti, Aquiles Guerrero, Lucila
Herrera, Gonzalo Fernández de Córdoba hijo, Rudy Hernández.

Juggernaut (USA: *Terror on the Britannic*) [1974], 110 minutes
Director: Richard Lester
Starring: Richard Harris, Omar Sharif, **David Hemmings** (as Charlie
Braddock), Anthony Hopkins, Shirley Knight, Ian Holm, Clifton
James, Roy Kinnear, Caroline Mortimer, Mark Burns, John Stride.

A Dream of Living [1975]; also known as *Private Affairs* (BBC plays).
David Hemmings played F. Scott Fitzgerald.

Profondo rosso (aka: *Deep Red, Deep Red Hatchet Murders, Dripping
Deep Red, The Hatchet Murders, The Sabre Tooth Tiger*) [1975],
126 minutes
Director: Dario Argento
Starring: David Hemmings (as Marcus Daly), Daria Nicolodi,
Gabriele Lavia, Macha Méril, Eros Pagni, Giuliana Calandra, Piero
Mazzinghi, Glauco Mauri, Clara Calamai, Aldo Bonamano, Liana Del
Balzo, Vittorio Fanfoni, Dante Fioretti.

The Old Curiosity Shop (aka *Mr Quilp*) [1975], 119 minutes
(based on the novel by Charles Dickens)
Director: Michael Tuchner
Starring: Anthony Newley, **David Hemmings** (as Richard Swiveller),
Jill Bennett, Sarah-Jane Varley, Michael Hordern, David Warner.

Islands in the Stream [1977], 104 minutes
(based on the story by Ernest Hemingway)
Director: Franklin J. Schaffer
Starring: George C. Scott, **David Hemmings** (as Eddy), Gilbert
Roland, Susan Tyrrell, Richard Evans, Claire Bloom, Julius Harris,
Hart Bochner, Brad Savage.

The Disappearance [1977], 100 minutes
(based on the novel by Derek Marlow)
Director: Stuart Cooper
Producer: David Hemmings
Starring: Donald Sutherland, Francine Racette, **David Hemmings** (as
Edward), John Hurt, David Warner, Peter Bowles, Virginia McKenna,
Christopher Plummer, Michèle Magny, Dan Howard, Robin Sachs.

The Squeeze [1977], 104 minutes
(based on the novel by David Craig)
Director: Michael Apted
Starring: Stacy Keach, **David Hemmings** (as Keith), Edward Fox,
Stephen Boyd, Carol White, Freddie Starr, Hilary Gasson, Rod
Beacham, Stewart Harwood.

La Via della droga (UK: *The Dope Way*, aka: *Drug Street, The Heroin
Busters*) [1977]
Director: Enzo G. Castellari
Starring: Fabio Testi, **David Hemmings** (as Mike Hamilton), Sherry
Buchanan, Joshua Sinclair, Wolfango Soldati, Romano Puppo.

Squadra antitruffa (aka *Swindle*) [1977], 100 minutes
Director: Bruno Corbucci
Starring: Thomas Milian, **David Hemmings**, Leo Gullotta, Bombolo,
Nazzareno Natale, Mimmo Poli, Massimo Vanni, Marcello Verziera.

Les Liens du sang (aka *Blood Relatives*) [1978], 100 minutes
Director: Claude Chabrol
Starring: Donald Sutherland, Aude Landry, Lisa Langlois, Laurent
Malet, Stéphane Audran, Walter Massey, Micheline Lanctôt, Donald
Pleasence, **David Hemmings** (as Armstrong).

Crossed Swords (UK: *The Prince and the Pauper*) [1978], 113 minutes
Director: Richard Flescher
Starring: Oliver Reed, Raquel Welch, Mark Lester, Ernest Borgnine,
George C. Scott, Rex Harrison, **David Hemmings** (as Hugh Hendon),
Harry Andrews, Julian Orchard.

Power Play (Canada: *Coup d'Etat, Le jeu de la puissance*, aka:
Operation Overthrow, State of Shock) [1978], 102 minutes
(based on the novel *Coup d'Etat* by Edward N Luttwak)
Director: Martyn Burke
Producer: David Hemmings
Starring: Harvey Atkin, Dick Cavett, Jon Granik, **David Hemmings**
(as Colonel Anthony Narriman), Peter O'Toole, Donald Pleasence,
Gary Reineke.

Clouds of Glory: The Rime of the Ancient Mariner [1978], 52 minutes
Director: Ken Russell
Starring: Ben Aris, Imogen Claire, Peter Dodd, Barbara Ewing,
Patricia Garwood, **David Hemmings** (as Samuel Taylor Coleridge),
Felicity Kendal, Ronald Letham, Kika Markham.

Murder by Decree (USA: *Sherlock Holmes and Saucy Jack*, aka:
Sherlock Holmes: Murder by Decree) [1979], 124 minutes
Director: Bob Clark
Starring: Christopher Plummer, James Mason, **David Hemmings** (as
Inspector Foxborough), Susan Clark, Anthony Quayle, John Gielgud,
Frank Finlay, Donald Sutherland, Geneviève Bujold, Chris Wiggins.

Thirst [1979], 93 minutes
Director: Rod Hardy
Starring: Chantal Contouri, Shirley Cameron, Max Phipps, Henry
Silva, Rod Mullinar, **David Hemmings** (as Dr Fraser), Rosie Sturgess,
Robert Thompson, Walter Pym, Amanda Muggleton, Lulu Pinkus.

Schöner Gigolo, Armer Gigolo (USA: *Just a Gigolo*) [1979], 147 minutes
Director: David Hemmings
Starring: David Bowie, Sydne Rome, Kim Novak, **David Hemmings** (as Captain Kraft), Maria Schell, Curd Jürgens, Erika Pluhar, Marlene Dietrich.

Charlie Muffin (USA: *A Deadly Game*) [1979], TV
(based on the novel *A Deadly Game* by Brian Freemantle)
Director: Jack Gold
Starring: David Hemmings (as Charlie Muffin), Sam Wanamaker, Jennie Linden, Pinkas Braun, Ian Richardson, Ralph Richardson, Christopher Godwin.

Harlequin (aka: *Dark Forces, Minister's Magician*) [1980], 95 minutes
Director: Simon Wincer
Starring: Robert Powell, **David Hemmings** (as Nick Rast), Carmen Duncan, Broderick Crawford, Gus Mercurio, Alan Cassell, Mark Spain, Alyson Best, Sean Myers, Mary Simpson, Bevan Lee.

Beyond Reasonable Doubt [1980], 129 minutes
Director: John Laing
Starring: David Hemmings (as Inspector Bruce Hutton), John Hargreaves, Tony Barry, Martyn Sanderson, Grant Tilly, Diana Rowan, Ian Watkin, Terence Cooper.

Magnum, P.I. [1980–8], TV, 60 minutes (140 episodes)
David Hemmings was one of 42 directors of the series.
Starring: Tom Selleck, John Hillerman, Roger E. Mosley, Larry Manetti.

Strange Behaviour (USA: *Dead Kids*, reissue title: *Human Experiments*, New Zealand: *Shadowlands*, aka: *Small Town Massacre*) [1981]
Director: Michael Laughlin
Executive producer: David Hemmings
Starring: Michael Murphy, Louise Fletcher, Dan Shor, Fiona Lewis, Arthur Dignam, Dey Young, Marc McClure, Scott Brady, Charles Lane.

Race for the Yankee Zephyr (aka: *Gold Hunt, Treasure of the Yankee Zephyr*) [1981], 108 minutes
Director: David Hemmings
Producer: David Hemmings
Starring: Ken Wahl, Lesley Ann Warren, Donald Pleasence, George Peppard, Bruno Lawrence, Grant Tilly, Harry Rutherford-Jones, Robert Bruce.

The Survivor [1981], 87 minutes
(based on the book by James Herbert)
Director: David Hemmings
Starring: Robert Powell, Jenny Agutter, Joseph Cotten, Angela Punch-McGregor, Peter Sumner, Lorna Lesley, Ralph Cotterill, Adrian Wright, Tyler Coppin.

Turkey Shoot (USA: *Escape 2000*, aka: *Blood Camp Thatcher*) [1981], 93 minutes
Director: Brian Trenchard-Smith
Executive Producer: David Hemmings
Starring: Steve Railsback, Olivia Hussey, Michael Craig, Carmen Duncan, Noel Ferrier, Lynda Stoner, Roger Ward.

Dr Jekyll and Mr Hyde [1981], TV, 115 minutes
Director: Alastair Reid
Starring: Ian Bannen, Diana Dors, Gretchen Franklin, Lisa Harrow, **David Hemmings** (as Dr Henry Jekyll and Mr Edward Hyde), Desmond Llewelyn, Leo Mcken, David Swift, Toyah Willcox.

Prisoners [1981]
Director: Peter Werner
Executive Producer: David Hemmings
Starring: Tatum O'Neal, Colin Friels, Shirley Knight, **David Hemmings** (as Wilkens), Bruno Lawrence, Ralph Cotterill, John Bach, Michel Hurst, Reg Ruka, Rob Jayne, Norman Fairley, Peter Rowley.

Swan Lake [1982]
Director: ANIMATION
Starring: Christopher Atkins, Pam Dawber, Kay Lenz, **David Hemmings** (as Rothbart).

Man, Woman and Child [1983], 99 minutes
(based on the novel by Erich Segal)
Director: Dick Richards
Starring: Martin Sheen, Blythe Danner, Craig T. Nelson, **David Hemmings** (as Gavin Wilson), Nathalie Nell, Maureen Andermann, Sebastian Dungen, Arlene McIntyre, Missy Francis.

The A-Team [1983–7], TV, 60 minutes (98 episodes)
David Hemmings was one of 24 directors of the series.
Starring: George Peppard, Mr T, Tim Dunigan, Dirk Benedict, Dwight Schultz, Melinda Culea, William Lucking, Lance LeGault, Marla Heasley.

Airwolf [1984–6], TV, 60 minutes (58 episodes)
David Hemmings was one of 30 directors of the series.
Starring: Jan-Michael, Alex Cord, Ernest Borgnine, Jean Bruce Scott.

Airwolf [1984] TV, 85 minutes
Director: Donald P Bellisario
Starring: Jan-Michel Vincent, Frank Annese, Ernest Borgnine, Tina Chen, Nick Faltas, **David Hemmings** (as Dr Charles Henry Moffet), Paul La Greca, Helene Philips, Eugene Roche.

Murder, She Wrote [1984–96], TV, 60 minutes (264 episodes)
David Hemmings was one of 34 directors of this series.
Starring: Angela Lansbury, Julie Adams, Tom Bosley, Michael Horton, Ron Masak, Will Nye, Richard Paul, James Sloyan, Ken Swofford, William Windom.

Money Hunt: The Mystery of the Missing Link [1984], TV, 44 minutes
Director: David Hemmings
Starring: John Hillerman, John Ashton, Zane Buzby, Ruth Crawford, Newell Alexander, Lefty Nordino, Lance Bile, Alison Baker.

Calamity Jane [1984], TV, 100 minutes
Director: James Goldstone
Starring: Jane Alexander, Frederic Forrest, Ken Kercheval, Walter Olkewicz, Talia Balsam, Walter Scott, **David Hemmings** (as Captain James O'Neil), Isabell O'Connor, Jack Murdock, Larry Cedar.

Beverly Hills Cowgirl Blues (Australia: *Beverly Hills Connection*) [1985], TV
Director: Corey Allen
Starring: Robin Bach, Brenda Bolte, James Brolin, Wally Dalton, Vince Deadrick Jr, Trent Dolan, Irena Ferris, Michael C. Gwynne, Alexa Hamilton, Lisa Hartman, **David Hemmings** (as Ian Blaize).

The Key to Rebecca [1985] TV, 194 minutes
(based on the book by Ken Follett)
Director: David Hemmings
Starring: Cliff Robertson, David Soul, Season Hubly, Lina Raymond, Anthony Quayle, **David Hemmings** (as Major Smith), Robert Culp, Robert Swales, Charlie Condou.

Stingray [1986–7], TV, 60 minutes (23 episodes)
David Hemmings was one of twelve directors of this series.
Starring: Nick Mancuso.

Harry's Hong Kong (aka *China Hand*) [1987], TV
Director: Jerry London
Starring: Jan Gan Boyd, Mel Harris, **David Hemmings** (as Jack Roarke), James Hong, Julia Nicholson-Soul, Michael Preston, David Soul, Russel Wong.

Three on a Match [1987], TV
Director: Donald P. Bellisario
Starring: Patrick Cassidy, Kendall Conrad, Jim Haynie, **David Hemmings** (as Maxwell 'Newt' Newton), Lance LeGault, Everett McGill, Mitch Pileggi, Deborah Pratt, Reiner Schöne, Dendrie Taylor, Bruce A Young.

Werewolf [1987], TV, 30 minutes (28 episodes)
David Hemmings was one of ten directors of this series.
Starring: John J. York, Lance LeGault, Chuck Connors, Brian Thompson.

Werewolf [1987], TV, 90 minutes
Director: David Hemmings
Starring: John J. York, Lance LeGault, Chuck Connors, Raphael Sbarge, Michelle Johnson, Ethan Philips, Robert Krantz, Stanley Grover, John Quade.

Davy Crockett: Rainbow in the Thunder [1988] TV, 94 minutes
Director: David Hemmings
Starring: Cheryl Arutt, Johnny Cash, Brenda Crishlow, Samantha Eggar, Gary Grubbs, **David Hemmings** (as President Andrew Jackson), Jeff Irvine.

In the Heat of the Night [1988–94], 60 minutes
David Hemmings was one of 30 directors of the series.
Starring: Carroll O'Connor, Howard E. Rollins Jr, Anne-Marie Johnson. Alan Autry, David Hart, Lois Nettleton, Hugh O'Connor, Christian LeBlanc.

Down Delaware Road [1989], TV
Director: David Hemmings
Starring: Adam Carl, Devon Odessa.

The Rainbow [1989], 113 minutes
(based on the novel by D. H. Lawrence)
Director: Ken Russell
Starring: Sammi Davis, Paul McGann, Amanda Donohoe, Christopher Gable, **David Hemmings** (as Uncle Henry), Glenda Jackson, Dudley Sutton, Jim Carter, Judith Paris.

Hardball [1989–90], TV
Directors: Rob Bowman, James Darren, Francis Delia, **David Hemmings**, Bruce Kessler, Guy Magar, Larry Shaw, Virgil W. Vogel
Starring: Jarret Lennon, John Ashton, Richard Tyson.

Nightmare Classics [1989] TV
(based on *The Turn of the Screw* by Henry James and *Carmilla* by Sheridan Le Fanu)
Directors: Gabrielle Beaumont, Graeme Clifford, Michael Lindsay-Hogg

Starring: Laura Dern, John Doolittle, Roy Dotrice, Deholm Elliot, Nicholas Guest, **David Hemmings**, Amy Irvine, Ione Skye, Meg Tilly.

Quantum Leap: Genesis [1989] TV, 89 minutes
David Hemmings directed the pilot episode.

Quantum Leap [1989–93], TV
David Hemmings was one of 33 directors who worked on the series.
Starring: Scott Bakula, Dean Stockwell, Deborah Pratt.

The Turn of the Screw [1990], TV
(based on the novel by Henry James)
Director: Graeme Clifford
Starring: Amy Irving, **David Hemmings** (as Mister Harley), Micole Mercurio, Olaf Pooley, Cameron Milzer, Irina Cashen, Linda Hunt, Bret Culpepper.

Dark Horse [1992], TV, 98 minutes
Director: David Hemmings
Starring: Ed Begley Jr, Mimi Rogers, Ari Meyes, Donovan Leitch, Samantha Eggar, Bojesse Christopher, Natasha Gregson Wagner, Tab Hunter.

Passport to Murder [1993], TV
Director: David Hemmings
Starring: Connie Sellecca, Ed Marinaro, Pavel Douglas, Peter Bowles, Marella Oppenheim, Lynda Baron, Arthur Cox, Mark Burns, Jilli Foot.

Ned Blessing: The Story of My life and Times [1993], TV, 95 minutes
Directors: Jack Bender, **David Hemmings**, Michael Ray Rhodes
Starring: Luis Avalos, Brenda Bakke, Rob Campbell, Gregory Scott Cummins, Brad Johnson, Bill McKinney, Richard Riehle, Tim Scott.

Christmas Reunion [1993], TV
Director: David Hemmings
Starring: James Coburn, Edward Woodward, Meredith Edwards, Myfanwy Talog, Fraser Cains, Geraint Morgan, Melanie Walters.

A Mind to Murder [1995], TV, 120 minutes
(based on the novel by P. D. James)
Director: Gareth Davies
Starring: Roy Marsden, Mairead Carthy, Sean Scanlan, **David Hemmings** (as Godbolt), Robert Pugh, Peter Tuddenham, Donald Douglas, Cal Macaninch, Ann-Gisel Glass, Frank Finlay.

Marker [1995], TV
Directors: Dennis Dugan, **David Hemmings**, Guy Magar, George Mendeluk
Starring: Richard Grieco, Andy Bumatai, Gates McFadden, Nia Peeples, Nick Ramos.

Gladiator [2000], 155 minutes
Director: Ridley Scott
Starring: Russell Crowe, Joaquin Phoenix, Connie Nielson, Oliver Reed, Richard Harris, Derek Jacobi, **David Hemmings** (as Cassius), Tommy Flanagan.

Last Orders [2001], 109 minutes
(based on the novel by Graham Swift)
Director: Fred Schepisi
Starring: Michael Caine, Tom Courtenay, **David Hemmings** (as Lenny 'Len'), Bob Hoskins, Helen Mirren, Ray Winstone, J. J. Field, Cameron Fitch, Nolan Hemmings.

Spy Game [2001], 126 minutes
(based on the story by Michael Frost Beckner)
Director: Tony Scott
Starring: Robert Redford, Brad Pitt, Catherine McCormack, Stephen Dillane, Larry Bryggman, Marianne Jean-Baptisite, Matthew Marsh, **David Hemmings** (as Harry Duncan).

Mean Machine [2001], 98 minutes
Director: Barry Skolnick
Starring: Vinnie Jones, David Kelly, **David Hemmings** (as Governor), Ralph Brown, Vas Blackwood, Robbie Gee.

A Mind to Murder [2001], TV
Director: Gareth Davies (based on P. D. James' novel)
Starring: Roy Marsden, Mairead Carty, Sean Scanlan, **David Hemmings**

Slap Shot 2: Breaking the Ice [2002], Video, 96 minutes
Director: Steve Boyum
Starring: Stephen Baldwin, Jessica Steen, Gary Busey, **David Hemmings** (as Martin Fox), David Paetkau, Callum Keith Rennie.

Equilibrium [2002], 107 minutes
Director: Kurt Wimmer
Starring: Dominic Purcell, Christian Bale, Sean Bean, Christian Kahrmann, Sean Pertwee, Taye Diggs, Emily Watson, **David Hemmings** (as Proctor).

Gangs of New York [2002], 166 minutes
Director: Martin Scorsese
Starring: Leonardo DiCaprio, Daniel Day-Lewis, Cameron Diaz, Jim Broadbent, Henry Thomas, Liam Neeson, Cara Seymour, **David Hemmings** (as Mr Schermerhorn).

Lenny Blue [2002] TV, 141 minutes
Director: Andy Wilson
Starring: Dezzy Baylis, Neil Bell, Kelly Brailsford, **David Hemmings** (as DCI Gillespie), Ivan Kaye, Ray Winstone, Jake Wood.

Waking the Dead [2002], TV
David Hemmings played ex-DCI Malcolm Finlay in the episode entitled 'Deathwatch' (Season Two, Episode Two), broadcast 9 September 2002.

The Night We Called It a Day [2003], 97 minutes
Director: Paul Goldman
Starring: Dennis Hopper, Melanie Griffith, Portia de Rossi, Joel Edgerton, Rose Byrne, **David Hemmings** (as Micky Rudin), David Field, Victoria Thane.

The League of Extraordinary Gentleman [2003], 110 minutes
(based on the comics by Alan Moore)
Director: Stephen Norrington
Starring: Sean Connery, Naseeruddin Shah, Peta Wilson, Tony
Curran, Stuart Townsend, Shane West, **David Hemmings** (as Nigel),
Terry O'Neil, Rudolf Pellar.

Blessed [2004]
Director: Simon Fellows
Starring: Fionnula Flanagam Michele Gentille, Heather Graham,
David Hemmings (as Earl Sidney), William Hootkins, Alan McKenna,
James Purefoy, Andy Serkis, Stella Stevens.

Acknowledgements

Quotations from the work of Dylan Thomas are from *Collected Poems*, published by J. M. Dent and reproduced with kind permission.

Quotations from Dorothy Parker are reproduced with the permission of Pollinger Ltd on behalf of the copyright holders.

Lyrics from *McArthur Park* are reproduced by kind permission of Jimmy Webb.

Lines from the work of T S Eliot are reproduced with the permission of Faber & Faber Ltd.

Index